Joe Joyce is a freelance journalist. He was born in Ballinasloe, County Galway, in 1947 and lives in Dublin. He is a former reporter with the *Irish Times* and *Hibernia* and is now correspondent in Dublin for the *Guardian*. Peter Murtagh works for the *Irish Times*. He was born in Dublin in 1953 and lives in County Wicklow. Both reporters have written extensively on political and security matters in the Republic of Ireland. Their first book, *The Boss*, was published in 1983.

BLIND JUSTICE

JOE JOYCE & PETER MURTAGH

poolbeg press

First published 1984 by
Poolbeg Press Ltd.,
Knocksedan House,
Swords, Co. Dublin, Ireland

ISBN 0 905169 64 6

Photographs courtesy *Irish Times*,
Irish Press and *Irish Independent*

Cover design by Steven Hope
Front cover photograph by Stephen Beckett
Photograph of authors by Matt Kavanagh
Phototypeset by Design & Art Facilities Ltd.,
Herbert Lane, Dublin 2.

To our parents and to Frances and Maev

Acknowledgements

The core of this book is based on the various documents which emerged from the mail train robbery case. The account of the main trial in the Special Criminal Court is taken from the official transcript. In addition, we have relied heavily on the memories of many of those involved. We wish to thank all of them for giving us their time and helping us reconstruct the political events, police investigations and courtroom battles which make up this story. All of our interviews were conducted on the basis that they were confidential.

A number of people gave us special help and to them we are particularly grateful. They include Osgur Breatnach, who gave us access to the various documents he had collected on the case. Thanks once again to the staff of the *Irish Times* library for helping with our research. And a special thanks to those who brought it all together: Philip MacDermott and Hilary O'Donoghue of Poolbeg Press; Ann Quinn and Mike McCartney of Wordplex Word-processing Bureau and, most of all, Ann Kennedy.

Joe Joyce and Peter Murtagh
11 Wicklow Street, Dublin 2

November 1984

Contents

Prologue   1984   11

Part One: A Night In The Bridewell

1   Robbery: March 1976   19
2   Arrests: Monday, April 5th   35
3   Interrogations: Tuesday and Wednesday,
     April 6th and 7th   63
4   Courts: Wednesday, April 7th   79
5   Doctors: Thursday, April 8th   97
6   Awaiting Trial   109

Part Two: Beyond Reasonable Doubt

7   Caught Napping   131
8   The Trial   149
9   Brian McNally   159
10   Osgur Breatnach   193
11   Nicky Kelly: The Prosecution   235
12   Nicky Kelly: The Defence   269
13   Guilty   293

Part Three: Findings and Facts

14   Imprisoned   325
15   Appeals   351
16   Release   375
17   Findings   405

Epilogue   1984   416

Appendices

I   The Events   419
II   The People   426
III   The "Confessions"   432
IV   The Judges Rules   442

Index of Selected Names   445

There must have been a most incredible conspiracy among the Garda Siochana and civilian associates to lie and perjure themselves as well as to behave so disgracefully, as is alleged against them. That is so enormous as to be patently absurd.

Robert Barr, the prosecution

Is the situation that in Ireland in 1978 we have to solemnly sit around and wait for a dead body in a police station before a reasonable doubt is raised?

Patrick MacEntee, the defence

The court...has drawn the inference that the injuries that they suffered...were self inflicted or inflicted by collaboration with persons other than members of the Garda Siochana.

Special Criminal Court

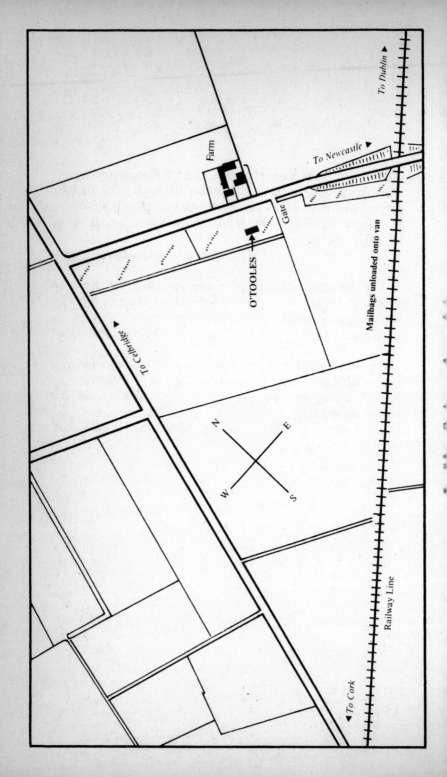

Prologue

1984

In the early autumn the countryside is lush. Some rain after a long dry summer has turned the fields and the foliage a deep green. The hedges are thick, the trees leafy along the quiet back roads of County Kildare.

A narrow road turns at right angles off the road running between the villages of Celbridge and Straffan, a minor road off a secondary road. It runs past three new bungalows on the right and past an older farm cottage on the left, straight down to a hump-backed bridge. High trees line the road as it rises to the brow of the bridge. In spite of the rural calm, it is, as the crow flies, only twelve miles west of the centre of Dublin.

Beneath the road bridge run the twin tracks of the Dublin to Cork railway lines. To the left, back towards Dublin, the line bends gradually into the disused station at Hazelhatch. To the right, towards Cork and Limerick, the lines run straight, pass under another road bridge and climb gradually for maybe a mile. The railway, flanked by bushes, lies on top of a slight embankment that smooths out the contours of the land and eases the gradient down to Hazelhatch.

It was here on a March morning in 1976 that an armed gang held up the Cork to Dublin mail train. They halted it with detonators laid on its track and brought it to a final stop just to the right of this bridge. Mail bags were unloaded, taken through the hedge, down the embankment and tossed into a stolen van that waited in the adjoining field. Throughout the robbery, a family named O'Toole were held at gunpoint in their home, the house nearest the railway.

It was here, too, that Nicky Kelly came at dawn six days after the robbery. He was accompanied by three detectives and he had been in custody for some forty two hours before they arrived at the bridge. They had driven in an unmarked

11

garda car from the Bridewell station in Dublin, travelling down the quays and out the main western road. After Lucan they had turned off towards Celbridge and negotiated four more junctions before arriving at the turn-off at the top of this road. They had driven slowly down to the bridge, stopped, got out and looked at the scene of the robbery.

The detectives said that Kelly gave them all the directions to get them to this spot. They all swore, more than two years later in court, that they had not known how to get here, that they had never been here before. They had followed Kelly's instructions. Since he knew where to go, he must have taken part in the robbery.

Nicky Kelly swore that he did not know how to get here. He said he could not have taken the gardai to the scene of the crime because he had not taken part in it. The detectives had directed him here, he insisted.

The three judges of the Special Criminal Court did not believe him: they accepted the account given by the detectives. The journey was crucial evidence against Kelly. More than anything else, it marked his case out as being different from the cases of his co-accused. It showed the degree to which Kelly allegedly co-operated with the gardai once he decided, as they put it, to tell the truth.

During cross-examination by Kelly's lawyers, one of the detectives was asked how he knew that the house which Kelly pointed out to him was the right house, O'Toole's house. He knew it, he said, because it was the last house in the row. The lawyer, apparently satisfied, passed on to other issues and other questions.

But there was a flaw. The detective's evidence could not have been correct. There was no row of houses on this road in April 1976 when Kelly and the detectives came here. There was just one house on the right hand side, the O'Tooles', and opposite it on the left was the farm cottage.

Unknown to the court and the lawyers there were no other houses on that stretch of road at that time. How was it that the gardai could support their evidence by referring to houses that did not exist at the time?

* * *

The detective is at home in the afternoon, retired. The television is on and he is watching golf. He took part in the investigation into the mail train robbery. He was in the Bridewell garda station the night four people signed alleged confessions but he was not involved in the interrogation of any of them.

Talking about the case, he becomes agitated. Nicky Kelly is so fucking guilty you wouldn't believe it, he says. They were all in it up to their necks, the IRSP. He has not the slightest doubt, they did it. He turns down the competing television commentary.

Were any of them beaten up? Listen, he says, these people are animals. You have to understand that. They spit on you, they're abusive, they're animals. You have to hit them a few belts. But, he adds, but you can't beat a confession out of someone. How could you beat a confession out of someone, he asks. Sure, you give them a few belts but you can't beat a confession out of them. How could you?

He produces a small, buff-coloured notebook, the notebook he had with him that night in the Bridewell. He leafs through it until he finds the pages he wants. It says 4.00 am, April 7th 1976 at the top of the page and he reads out the entry. It describes the train robbery, who was there, what roles they played.

What is it, what is that note? The truth, he retorts. It's all there – he waves the notebook – the whole story. He reads out bits of it again. Yes, but where did the information come from? From one of the lads, he says. He can't remember after all this time – eight years isn't it? – who gave him that information. It was one of his colleagues, he says. Anyway, it's the truth.

Throughout the trial two years after the robbery detectives denied repeatedly that anyone was keeping them informed of developments that night.

*   *   *

The detective is in a hurry: a current investigation is

13

coming to a head. He is having a quick lunch in a pub and he chats generally about the train robbery. He was not involved in that case himself.

People were beaten up during the investigation, he says. The "heavy gang" was certainly in action. He doesn't know whether any of the suspects were guilty or not. He doesn't know who was beaten up either. But he is definite: some people were beaten up.

He wasn't there however: how does he know? He knows, he says. Is it just casual gossip? He hesitates. No, he says, it's more than that. He hesitates again and then he explains how he knows.

It was in 1978 during or shortly after the trial in the Special Criminal Court. He met a member of the Garda Siochana who seemed to be in a bad way. The man had given evidence in the trial and he told the detective he had perjured himself. He had been asked if he had seen or heard anything untoward in the Bridewell. He told the court he had not. But he told the detective that he had.

He had been walking through part of the building when he saw what he thought was a heap of rags on the floor. When he got closer he saw it was a man, huddled on the floor where he had been beaten.

The policeman was very upset about the trial. The detective told him there was nothing he could do to help: it was a matter for his own conscience.

Four and a half years later, when Nicky Kelly was on hunger strike and his health deteriorating, the detective approached his colleague. Would he go to the government now and tell what he knew? the detective asked. The policeman thought about it. He decided to remain silent.

*   *   *

Eight years on, strong passions are still stirred by the events of 1976. The gardai involved remain adamant that they got the right men. The four men who stood trial for robbing the train, all members of the Irish Republican Socialist Party, are equally insistent that neither they nor

14

their party was involved.

Six men were charged with the robbery initially; four went to trial and three were convicted. Two of those subsequently had their convictions overturned by the Court of Criminal Appeal. One – Nicky Kelly – remains convicted of the crime but he has been released finally from prison. He spent almost two years awaiting trial, a year more or less on trial, a year and a half on the run and four years in jail.

The case has remained a live issue mainly because of Kelly's continued imprisonment and the insistence by all of them that they were innocent. It has come to symbolise a particular era of the mid-1970s and the confrontation that followed the crisis in Northern Ireland between the Southern state, its forces and militant republicans. It also tested another institution of the state, the judiciary.

Throughout the long court battles that studded the controversy one issue was central. Everything hinged on what had happened on one night in April 1976 in the Bridewell garda station in Dublin.

Part One

A Night in the Bridewell

1

Robbery: March 1976

The train with the travelling post office was running late. On the last stage of its five and a half hour journey from Cork to Dublin the mail had all been sorted. Registered packets had been gathered into thirteen sacks, each denoted by a red label and the figure "13" painted on the side. More than fifty seven of the packets were addressed to banks in Dublin from their branches in counties Cork and Kerry. They contained banknotes, all used and untraceable.

There were nineteen men travelling on the night mail train – sixteen post office workers including sorters, clerks, a postman and a supervisor, and the train crew of an engine driver and two passenger guards. There was no policeman on board to protect the movement of the cash.

Everyone but the engine driver was relaxing as the train passed the twelve mile mark from Dublin. All the signals were in its favour and it was travelling at sixty miles an hour. Behind the engine there were only three coaches, two of them post office vans and the last the guards' van.

In the first coach, five post office men were reading newspapers and books: two were doing the easy crossword in the previous day's *Evening Press*. A card game was the centre of attention in the second coach: using mail bags as seats, six men were playing while four others watched. The last man was curled up on a mail bag at the end of the van, fast asleep. The two passenger guards were chatting together in the last coach.

Just past the disused station at Straffan in County Kildare, the railway line turned into the mile long straight and sloped down the gentle gradient towards Dublin. The twin tracks were crossed by two road bridges and shielded from surrounding fields by a thick hedge. The line was on top of an embankment, raised several feet above the field. Long abandoned gates were set into the hedges half way down the straight to allow farmers to cross the tracks. They still carried the initials of the Great Southern and Western railway and the warning that anyone who left a gate open was liable to a penalty of forty shillings.

Between the abandoned gates and the second road bridge, the armed gang was waiting for the train. It was close to 3.00 am on a blustery morning on the last day of March 1976.

The robbery plan had been put into action more than four hours earlier. Three men drove up behind Ray Reynolds as he parked his van outside his greengrocery in Manor Road in the Dublin suburb of Palmerstown shortly after 11.00 pm. They blocked his way out with their car and pulled open the two front doors of the van.

The man at the passenger door told him they wanted the van and ordered him out. He refused and they produced handguns. The same man told him to get into the back of the van or they would blow his head off. The man tried to grab the keys from Reynolds' hand but failed. In a brief stalemate, Reynolds suggested that he take his house key off the bunch: they said nothing and he did so.

The gunmen then lost patience. The man at the driver's door swiped at Reynolds' head and hit the roof of the van with his gun. He tried again and hit Reynolds on the forehead. Reynolds slumped sideways and the other man grabbed the keys. Reynolds stumbled out of the van and ran round the back of his shop, broke a window and telephoned the gardai.

He did not see his van being driven away. In the back there were several boxes and bags of fruit and vegetables, including apples, pears, bananas, mushrooms, turnips, rhubarb, and a bale of peat briquettes. Reynolds, a thirty seven year old native of New Zealand, was afterwards detained in hospital for two and a half days and received ten stitches over his left eye.

More than an hour later, at 1.00 am, the O'Toole family was asleep in their modern bungalow at Commons Upper, near Celbridge in County Kildare, a field away from the railway embankment. The telephone rang in O'Tooles' at 1.00 am. Marion O'Toole woke up, turned on a bedside light and lifted the receiver. She said "hello" twice but there was no answer. She replaced the receiver and waited for the caller to try again. Instead, the door bell rang.

She put on her dressing gown, walked down the hall and switched on the outside light. She could see figures through the glass door and she asked who was there. The gardai, a man replied. What was wrong? she inquired. We're the special branch, the man said, we want to come in. She opened the door and one man proffered a pink plastic card. As she reached for it, he walked past her into the house.

Her husband Conal had woken up meanwhile, pulled on some clothes and was coming out of the bedroom. The men were polite and discreet. One held a gun but kept it hanging by his leg. The first man, who appeared to be the leader, showed O'Toole the butt of a gun in his anorak pocket. They did not intend to harm the family or frighten the children, the man said. They were sorry for the inconvenience, he added.

The couple's two daughters, aged eleven and ten, had woken up and looked out of their bedroom: one was beginning to panic. The leader told them all to go into the main bedroom: Marion O'Toole carried their six year old son, still sleeping. The leader followed them in and took the gun from his pocket in order to pull out a pair of red-trimmed black gloves. He put them on, shifted the bedside locker from the wall and bent down to pull the telephone wires from the junction box on the wall.

The gunmen asked for the keys to the three cars parked outside the house: one, a Renault 6, belonged to Marion O'Toole's mother, Rosaleen Rafter, who was staying with the family and slept through the occupation of the house. Her car was driven away and Conal O'Toole's Peugeot 504 was pushed into position for a quick getaway. Petrol was siphoned from Marion O'Toole's car using a plastic hose pulled from the washing machine in the kitchen.

Meanwhile, other members of the gang drove Reynolds' Volkswagen van into the field between O'Tooles' and the railway line and parked it beside the embankment. Down the line towards Cork they laid three detonators on the Dublin bound track. Everything was ready as they waited for the train.

A minute after 3.00 am the first detonator exploded under the wheels of the engine, followed quickly by the other two. Engine driver Tom Roche knew the sound as a warning signal. He shut off the power and put on the brakes, thinking there must be something across his track. Then he saw a man standing on the track and waving a red light. He slammed the brakes on full.

The train shot past the man, its hooter sounding, and carried on for more than a hundred yards before it came to rest. The O'Tooles, still imprisoned in their bedroom by a gunman standing outside the door, heard the explosions, the hooter and the train braking. Inside the coaches, the post office men took little notice of the detonators and the unscheduled stop: such delays were not unusual.

The driver waited in his cab for the man who waved the light to catch up with the train. The man, wearing a railway style jacket with yellow stripes on the shoulders, called up to Roche to open the cab door. Then he tossed a hammer up onto the floor and climbed in. He produced a gun and told Tom Roche to reverse the train back under the road bridge to where a gap had been beaten in the hedge and the Volkswagen van waited.

In the guard's van, passenger guard Joseph Connolly looked out the window as the train reversed. He was about to alight when it stopped again but he noticed a man holding a rifle on the embankment. The gun was pointed at the train. The two guards stayed where they were.

In the second coach, the post office men were still playing cards. One of the watchers, Jimmy McEvoy, stood up and looked out the window as the train moved backwards. A man was hanging from a handrail on the first coach and another was walking alongside the second coach. When the train halted the man pointed a gun up at him.

Open up or I'll blow your fucking head off, the man said.

McEvoy opened the door. The post office men, card game abandoned, watched as two hands appeared at the doorway, one holding a hammer and the other a gun. Is the branch here? the holder of the weapons asked as he climbed in. A second man followed him, brandishing a shotgun, and a third carried a sub-machine gun. All had masks covering their faces.

The first man said they wouldn't get hurt if they did what they were told. He ordered two sorters to toss out mail bags but stopped them after checking the labels. Where's the money, he demanded. Nobody answered and he asked who was the boss. He got no reply but he singled out the supervisor, Joe Cotter, caught him by the lapel and pointed his gun up under his chin. Cotter pointed to the sacks of registered mail.

The gunmen ordered everyone to go through the connecting door into the first coach where post office workers were still reading, oblivious to what was happening. Tom Roche was taken from his cab and put into the first coach as well. The leading gunman warned everybody not to try and get out: hand grenades would be attached to the doors, he said. He left them, saying they would have plenty of "bluebottles" for company shortly.

The gang took twelve sacks of registered mail, leaving the thirteenth behind. By co-incidence or otherwise, the last sack was the only one that did not contain packages of banknotes. The sacks were loaded into the Volkswagen van. Within fifteen minutes of stopping the train, the raiders were finished. The van took off from the field at high speed, its tyres gouging the earth. Several of the raiders ran back to O'Toole's house and drove off in a convoy of cars, including Conal O'Toole's Peugeot.

Nothing happened for another ten minutes or so. The post office men and the train crew stayed where they were. The O'Tooles remained in their bedroom, feeling a draught from the front door which had been left open behind the last man out. The only sound was of the wind and the train idling on the tracks where it had been halted. But the hunt was already on.

A traffic controller at CIE's railway control room in Connolly station in Dublin had noticed that something was wrong. The mail train was overdue on the seven mile stretch from Sallins to Hazelhatch. At 3.15 am, he telephoned the control room at Dublin Castle, the garda headquarters for the city.

Three patrol cars were immediately despatched to the

23

area. The closest, a car from Naas, went to Sallins, more than five miles by rail from where the robbery occurred. Two others from the Dublin suburb of Ballyfermot took separate routes out of the city to converge on the area. One car carried two detectives who had been searching for the greengrocer's hi-jacked van.

Meanwhile,the post office workers and the train driver had emerged from the coach in which they had been put. There was no sign of the raiders and Tom Roche returned to his cab and took the train the mile and a half into Hazelhatch station. There, the train crew found two telephones out of order.

The detectives from Ballyfermot found the train at Hazelhatch at 3.40 am and confirmed to the police control that the mail had been robbed. Five minutes later, at 3.45 am, the hijacked van was parked at an itinerant settlement camp in Finglas, north west of Dublin. A caretaker watched from a distance as the driver got out and walked nonchalantly away. Gardai swarmed to the scene of the robbery, driving at high speed around the maze of narrow roads, in and out of farmyards, knocking on doors. Shortly before 4.00 am they arrived at O'Tooles' and the scene of the crime.

They found the gap in the hedge and a discarded mask, a jacket and a glove. In a ditch the contents of the hijacked van were strewn: fruit, vegetables and a bale of briquettes. There was no sign of the raiders or the money they had cleaned out of the train.

*　　*　　*

As dawn broke on March 31st, 1976 it was clear to the gardai that they had another major crime on their hands. The extent of the haul would not be known for another day or so until all the registered post had been checked and the bank packages accounted for. The amount of money missing would be put officially at £221,000 making it one of the biggest robberies ever carried out in the state. The prime suspects had to be members of a paramilitary group which would have the manpower, intelligence and organisation to carry out such a raid.

The fact that so much money could be transported in such an apparently casual manner was a serious embarrassment to the gardai. Not alone was there no police guard on the train but the chances of recovering the money were slim. Assuming the raid had been carried out by a paramilitary group, arrangements would have been made for its disposal. In any event, there was no way the used banknotes could be traced: nobody had recorded the serial numbers or any other way of identifying the actual cash.

In a wider context the raid was the latest peak on a steadily rising graph of increasing crime, particularly armed crime. The troubles which had broken out in Northern Ireland in 1968 had developed into a full scale guerilla war after the introduction of internment without trial in 1971. The general climate of politically inspired violence had made guns more readily available and their use more likely in the South as well as in the North. The IRA and, more often, its offshoots and freelance groups, had also become more active south of the border.

The events in the North had put enormous pressures on institutions in the South. Their effects were felt on southern politics – most dramatically within the Fianna Fail party – but also on the security and judicial systems. The gardai and the army were totally unprepared for the effects of civil unrest across the border. The army had no permanent post north of Mullingar in County Westmeath and had to be ordered in 1969 to draw up contingency plans for whatever situation might arise. The gardai had neither the equipment, expertise, training nor manpower to deal with an influx of refugees – including gunmen on the run – into border areas and Dublin.

For a time the security situation and the political perception of the Northern conflict became enmeshed. Support for the nationalist community in the North was extremely strong in the South and if there was to be violence then most southerners knew where they stood. In a phrase which aptly described the southern climate, everyone was a Provo. Very often, individual policemen were, because of ambivalent instructions or personal temperament, unsure about what they were to do.

As the immediate crisis at the turn of the decade passed, so too did much of the political and police uncertainty. But the gardai came under increasing pressure as the effects of the violence seeped ever deeper into southern life. Yet the force was little better equipped to deal with the growing lawlessness. Newly renovated border stations swallowed up the growing numbers of recruits while armed crime became more prevalent on city streets. Armed robberies of post offices, banks and company pay rolls every Friday became something of a national joke. The Friday before the mail train raid there were four armed robberies in Dublin alone.

By the spring of 1976, the gardai had had to deal with several major outbreaks of violence, including bombings, kidnappings, and shootings as well as the rash of armed robberies. In Dublin, twenty five people had died in one day in 1974 when loyalist paramilitaries set off three car bombs without warning. Dr. Tiede Herrema, a Dutch industrialist at the Ferenka works near Limerick, had been kidnapped and held for 36 days, 17 of them in a council house beseiged by gardai in Monasterevin, County Kildare. IRA men had escaped from prisons by helicopter and by explosives: the border town of Dundalk was popularly known as "El Paso" in recognition of both its frontier and its wild west atmosphere.

To some people matters seemed close to getting out of hand. The mood was soberly conveyed by an editorial in the Garda Review, the journal of the Garda Representative Body, written in the spring of 1976. "Perhaps for the first time since the present political disturbances in the six counties, there is now real public concern about crime and disorder," it said. The gardai badly needed successes in stemming the growth of crime. Results were very clearly what mattered under Commissioner Edmund Garvey, a Dublin detective who had risen to the top of the force. He put strong emphasis on internal discipline and became closely associated in the public mind with the coalition's stand on law and order.

The administration of the justice system and the judiciary

were also going through significant, although less dramatic, upheavals at the same time. In May 1972 the government had taken cases of politically motivated violence out of the ordinary courts and the hands of juries. It set up the Special Criminal Court after proclaiming that the ordinary courts were inadequate to secure the effective administration of justice and the preservation of public peace and order. Three judges were appointed to sit without a jury.

An amendment to the Offences Against The State Act – under which the special court was established – passed later the same year made it easier to secure convictions. A senior garda officer became entitled to give as evidence his belief that a suspect was a member of an illegal organisation: he did not have to offer any further proof. His belief alone was sufficient to convict.

By April 1976 the single special court was so busy that one of its members, Judge Noel Ryan, called publicly for the establishment of a second tribunal to ease the workload. The government was considering the need for a second court – a crude indicator of the level of Northern related violence in the South. However, a second court was never established.

Changes were also affecting the wider judicial system. The administration of the whole system and the process of taking people to trial was in a mess. An individual garda, no matter how young or inexperienced, could decide without reference to anybody to charge a suspect with murder. There was not necessarily any higher deliberation about the circumstances of the case, the weight of the evidence or the likelihood of a successful prosecution. The case would go ahead on the say-so of one garda and would eventually be prosecuted in court by people from the chief state solicitor's office and the Attorney General's office.

In 1974 the government moved to set up the office of the Director of Public Prosecutions, partly to separate the prosecution of criminal cases from the Attorney General, a political appointee, and partly to try and bring some order into the chaos caused by over-lapping the investigative function of the police and the prosecutorial role of taking the case before a court.

27

The DPP's office began to function from January 1975 with the appointment of the first incumbent, Eamonn Barnes. For the following eighteen months or so, the office was trying to find its feet, establish its procedures and create a system that would ensure that the same set of actions in one part of the country would result in the same charges going before a court as in another part.

The judiciary was also changing. The Supreme Court under Chief Justice Cearbhall O Dalaigh placed a new emphasis and interpretation onto the rights of citizens guaranteed by the constitution. Later in the decade, it and the High Court set out much more clearly the limits on the police powers to detain and to interrogate suspects.

By 1976, the coalition government made up of Fine Gael and the Labour Party was in its third year in office. Law and order and the Northern problem were among its main themes: crime was increasing steadily and its Northern policy had collapsed with the failure of the attempt by the main nationalist and unionist parties to form a regional government in Belfast after the Sunningdale Agreement. The Taoiseach, Liam Cosgrave, had blamed the failure on the Provisional IRA and its continued violence during the lifetime of the power-sharing executive rather than on the general strike by loyalists which directly caused its collapse.

No one doubted the coalition's determination to fight the IRA and government ministers engaged in a continuous propaganda and psychological war against the Provos. The government did not fear the imminent collapse of the state before paramilitary pressure: on the other hand, no one could know for certain how secure the state was and what it would take to topple it. Conor Cruise O'Brien, the Minister for Posts and Telegraphs, led the political battle by constantly challenging and undermining the traditional nationalist and southern beliefs about the Northern crisis on which the IRA depended. Handling the security aspect of the battle was mainly the responsibility of Patrick Cooney, the Minister for Justice.

Cooney looked every bit the small town solicitor that he was by profession. He was first elected to the Dail in his fifth attempt when he won a by-election in Longford-Westmeath constituency. He was thirty nine when he entered Leinster House in 1970 and rose rapidly through Fine Gael to become its front bench spokesman on justice two years later. In 1973 he became Justice Minister.

He had been seen as a member of Fine Gael's new liberal wing when he entered the Dail and was among the leaders of criticism against the Fianna Fail government's extensions to the Offences Against the State Act late in 1972. The changes, he argued, went beyond the limit to the measures a democracy was entitled to take in order to protect itself.

During his four years in government, however, his attitude shifted substantially. One of the events that profoundly affected his thinking was the murder of Senator Billy Fox near the border in County Monaghan in March 1974. Fox, a thirty five year old Protestant and former Dail deputy, had gone to the farmhouse of the Coulson family about a mile and a half from the border to see a girlfriend, Marjorie Coulson. He happened upon some twelve armed men who were ransacking the house. Fox was shot dead.

Cooney is believed to have stayed up all night awaiting news of his fate. His body was found next morning in a field 500 yards from the ruined farmhouse. He had been beaten over the head and shot in the leg: a second bullet in the chest had killed him. When he heard the news Cooney was visibly upset and locked himself in his ministerial office. Fox was not alone a colleague in the Fine Gael parliamentary party but was also a close friend: his death brought home the threat of violence to Fine Gael and deeply affected Cooney personally.

The Provisonal IRA denied any involvement in his murder and extended sympathy to Fox's family. But the gardai and the government ignored their claim as well as a call to a Northern newspaper claiming that the shooting was carried out by the Ulster Freedom Fighters, a loyalist paramilitary group. Four men were later convicted of the murder and joined the group of Provisional IRA prisoners in Portlaoise jail.

The coalition's strategy was to confront the IRA at every

29

turn and in every way. The most dramatic manifestation of this policy came with the funeral of Frank Stagg, an IRA member who died on hunger strike in Wakefield prison in England early in 1976. The government seized the initiative, literally, by taking over his body with the consent of his widow and organising its burial in Ballina. The government was determined to deny the IRA a second opportunity to hold a show funeral from Dublin across the country to Ballina as it had done successfully with the funeral of an earlier hunger striker, Michael Gaughan.

The emphasis by the government and by Cooney on law and order was a constant target of the Opposition in the Dail because of the administration's manifest failure to halt the increase in crime. Gerry Collins, Fianna Fail's spokesman on justice, lost no time in renewing his attacks on the government: on the day of the train robbery he tried to raise a private notice question about what he termed "a scandalous situation". It was ruled out of order but Collins pursued his criticism, accusing the gardai of having taken armed detectives off mail trains because of a cutback in overtime payments. And, he asked rhetorically on a radio programme, what was the point of appeals to Americans to stop sending money to the IRA when the equivalent of a year's collections in the United States could be stolen a few miles from Dublin?

The gardai hastily responded with a statement maintaining that they had provided protection for mail trains. But they admitted that such protection was "not on a routine or permanent basis".

Six days after the raid Cooney did answer Collins' questions in the Dail. He insisted that he could not give details of security arrangements but he denied emphatically that an armed guard had been withdrawn from the particular mail train that was robbed. He disputed Collins' accusation as well that there had been a guard on every mail train until cuts in overtime payments to the gardai had been introduced the previous year. Collins replied that since the overtime curbs, only one garda travelled on one mail train a week.

In a general comment, Cooney noted that security

problems of "quite alarming proportions" were posed by the amounts of money and the frequency with which they were moved around the country. Police numbers could be trebled and they would still be unable to guarantee protection against such raids. He went on to warn that what he termed "stringent laws" would be unavoidable if certain assumptions ceased to be valid. These included the assumption that armed criminals were not in such numbers as to cause a threat to daily life.

Meanwhile, the gardai were making an all-out effort to track down the train robbers. Extra men were drafted into the Hazelhatch area of County Kildare to make house to house enquiries. The O'Tooles were shown scores of photographs of potential suspects in an attempt to identify the men who had taken over their house at gunpoint. Forensic examinations were begun on the bits and pieces left behind by the raiders.

Members of the Special Branch had lost little time in following up the robbery. At dawn that day they had raided several houses to check that the occupants were there. Among those raided was a house in Swords, County Dublin where Brian McNally, a former member of the Irish Republican Socialist Party, lived with his wife Kathleen and four children. Another man, Nicky Kelly, had stayed the night with the family. When they asked the detectives what was up, they were told: "listen to the radio".

Members or sympathisers of the Provisional IRA were also visited and questioned cursorily. The gardai wanted to see if any of their prime suspects had been moving about or acting in an unusual manner.

Little progress was made, however, until Detective Inspector Ned Ryan of the Central Detective Unit in Dublin Castle told his colleagues that he had got the names of three or four people involved in the robbery from a confidential source. Inspector Ryan was one of Dublin's most respected and most feared detectives. A formidable policeman, his physical appearance and his determination had earned him the nickname "The Buffalo". He had been on holiday when the raid was carried out but had returned the following day because of another and unrelated case in which he was involved. He quickly became immersed in the mail train investigation and said he received what he regarded as a reliable tip-off on the night of Friday, April 2nd or the early hours of the following morning.

All of the detectives involved in the inquiry had obviously had their ears open for any snippets of information that were to be had. Reports circulated among them about one man who seemed to know a lot about it – John Lawlor, a small time haulier who operated around the Kingsbridge area of Dublin. The information circulating among the gardai was that members of the Irish Republican Socialist Party or its associated military group, the Irish National Liberation Army, had carried out the robbery. Lawlor was shot dead in a Dublin pub eighteen months later by the IRA which blamed him for the discovery of a shipment of arms and explosives that was about to be smuggled to Britain.

Partly as a result of Inspector Ryan's information the gardai decided on a major round-up of members of the IRSP and of possible members of the INLA. A list of sixteen people was drawn up and plans made to hold all of them in garda stations in Dublin. They were to be detained under Section 30 of the Offences Against the State Act which allowed gardai to detain without charge a person suspected of committing one of the crimes listed in the Act. They could be held for twenty four hours and the period doubled to forty eight hours if a chief superintendent sanctioned it. It was common practice to hold detainees for the full forty eight hours.

On the evening of Sunday, April 4th, four and a half days after the robbery dozens of detectives gathered for a conference and briefing in Dublin Castle. They were under the control of Chief Superintendent John Joy, the highly experienced head of the Central Detective Unit (CDU) and the man in charge of the train robbery investigation. His second in command in both the CDU and the inquiry was Superintendent Patrick Casey.

They had a team of detectives drafted in from several units. Most of the men involved were members of the CDU and the Special Detective Unit (SDU), commonly known as the Special Branch. Both units were based in Dublin Castle and were part of the Dublin Metropolitan Area which retained a separate identity within the force since the days when the Dublin Metropolitan Police was a separate organisation from the Royal Irish Constabulary.

The investigation section from the garda technical bureau had been concerned with the robbery as well since the day it occurred. They worked from the bureau headquarters in Dublin's Saint John's Road but they had no formal expertise or speciality. They were known collectively as "the murder squad" because of their role in investigating major crimes, not necessarily murders. By the mid-1970s much of their time was spent on crimes associated with the Northern troubles. They travelled anywhere in the state – and occasionally into the North – and they were unburdened by local considerations which occasionally made some gardai loath to move against neighbours associated with the IRA. Some of the "murder squad" detectives had come to believe that they were the main bulwark against the takeover of the state by extreme republicans.

A fourth group of detectives was about to be drafted into the inquiry as well. They were people from District Detective Units (DDUs) which were the detective sections attached to local garda stations. Some were drafted in for the round-up, some for interrogations and some for both.

At the Dublin Castle briefing the list of names was circulated. Senior officers tried to arrange that groups of three or four gardai, including an inspector or sergeant, were assigned to arrest each person. Each group was intended to include at least one person who knew the suspect by sight. They were informed of the garda stations to which the suspect was to be taken and they were given search warrants for the houses they were to raid.

The round-up was to be the biggest in the experience of anyone present. It was to begin at dawn the next day, Monday, April 5th.

2

Arrests: Monday, April 5th

Four guards arrived outside Brian McNally's home at Swords in north County Dublin at around 7 am. The man in charge of the party of gardai was Sergeant Francis Campbell, a detective based at Pearse Street garda station. In his pocket, he had a warrant which gave him and his colleagues the legal power to enter the house to search for guns.

Brian McNally was a thirty six year old man from Northern Ireland. He had moved south some years previously and was living with his wife, Kathleen, and their four children at Castle Avenue. He was deeply involved in sports, particularly Gaelic football, and community activities in his area. His friends thought him a bit of a Walter Mitty character: full of great plans and schemes which usually came to little. He was known to some of them as "The Sandman" apparently because of a makeshift security system he had devised while living in the North. Believing himself to be under official surveillance, he spread sand under the windows of his house in the hope of hearing anyone snooping around or of seeing their footprints.

McNally's financial affairs were in something of a mess. Recently he had been brought before Swords District Court because he had failed to pay the rent on his house. He was also being pursued by Allied Irish Finance, which lent him £1,000 to buy a small Renault van. McNally had fallen behind on the repayments. He had been working for a credit hire company as their collection man. Every Friday, Saturday and Tuesday, he would do the rounds for the firm, collecting repayments from their customers.

McNally had also become involved with the Irish Republican Socialist Party and at one stage was the party treasurer in the Dublin area. But he had parted company with his erstwhile comrades because he could not give enough time to the organisation. McNally played the drums in a country and western band and when the IRSP wanted him, he often excused himself by saying that he had to attend a session somewhere. His comrades were not amused but there had been no big falling out, more a parting of the ways.

Sergeant Campbell sent one man around the back of the house before he knocked on the front door. Garda Michael Drew, a member of the Central Detective Unit, took up his position by the kitchen door. The two men who stayed at the front with Campbell were Garda James Grehan, a member of the Special Branch who was also based in Dublin Castle, and Garda Thomas Ibar Dunne, a detective attached to the investigation section of the Technical Bureau.

Kathleen McNally was upstairs in the bedroom with her husband when she heard the knock on the front door. She put on her dressing gown and went over the the window to peer out in the early morning light. There were men outside the house, she told her husband, as she left the room to go downstairs and open the door.

Sergeant Campbell introduced himself and told her that he had a search warrant. He and the other two showed their garda identity cards and walked into the hall. She shouted upstairs to her husband and a few seconds later Brian McNally emerged down the stairs. He told the gardai to search away but they would find nothing.

Garda Grehan told McNally that he was arresting him under Section 30 of the Offences Against the State Act. Twice before he had been arrested under this law: on the first occasion McNally was held for three or four hours. On the second time, he was arrested with two IRSP colleagues, Michael Barrett and John Fitzpatrick, and held for the full forty eight hours. As Garda Grehan told McNally he suspected he had committed an offence, the back door was opened to let Garda Drew into the kitchen.

Garda Drew asked McNally for the keys to his van, took them and went to the garage to search it. He found nothing and he gave the van keys back to McNally. The others were meanwhile searching every room in the house but they found nothing. There were no guns or explosives in the McNally home.

The guards told McNally they would have to take him away to a garda station. He was allowed to get dressed, wash his face and have a quick breakfast, a cup of tea, before leaving. McNally took with him a small carton of tablets which he had been told by a psychiatrist to take three times a day to calm him down and help him relax.

He was driven away and arrived just after 8 am at Fitzgibbon Street garda station, a large north city centre police station near Croke Park football stadium and just off the main road into Dublin from Swords.

Around the same time that the gardai were knocking on the door of the McNally home in Swords, another team of gardai was calling to a flat at Goldsmith Street in Phibsboro which was the home of Nicky Kelly and his girlfriend, Nuala Dillon. The team was led by Inspector Ned Ryan and with him were Garda Kieran Lawlor and Adrian O'Hara, both detectives with the Special Branch, and a colleague from the CDU, Garda Joseph Smyth. Ned Ryan had a warrant to search the flat for guns. They knocked on the door and were let in by Nuala Dillon.

Nicky Kelly's family home was at Arklow in County Wicklow. Christened Eamonn Noel, he was generally known as Nicky after his father, Nicholas. He had lived there for about ten years with his parents and three younger sisters. Kelly was twenty five years old and had spent the first few years of his life at Ferrymountgarret in South Wicklow before his father moved the family to Graiguenamanagh in County Kilkenny. His father worked for the Department of Forestries and, in the mid 1960s, he was transferred to Shelton Abbey, an old estate with a large forest which was in private hands before being taken over by the State as a prison.

The family home in Arklow was at Tyndall's Lane in the old area of the town, down near the harbour which was once a thriving fishing port. The houses were mostly single storey cottages, all higgledy-piggledy on top of each other and in many cases built along narrow streets. Nicky Kelly had gone to the local technical school but left in his late teens to get a job. At the time, Arklow was beginning to experience something of a boom: the State run fertilizer company, Nitrigen Eireann, was about to build a fertilizer factory inland from the town in a valley beside Shelton Abbey. This industry created a number of spin-off companies and for the first time in years, there was a lot of work in Arklow. Kelly got various jobs as a messenger, builders' labourer and even carved a niche for himself locally as a machine installer. He worked for a contractor but was also able to get work on his own.

Politically, Kelly's family were gut republicans. His father was not politically active but he had his views worked out and knew where his heart lay. In the late 1960s there were a number of local issues in which republicans involved themselves and Kelly was drawn in. One such issue was whether or not people should have free access to the beach at Brittas Bay, the finest stretch of beach on the Wicklow coast but separated from the public road by privately owned land.

The landowners had taken to charging people for the right to walk across their land, often nothing more than sand dunes, to get to the beach. Kelly was annoyed that people should have to pay to use what was a natural local amenity and when local Sinn Fein activists started to campaign on the issue, he joined in.

At the time, Sinn Fein was highlighting other issues which appealed to Kelly and he joined the Arklow cumann. When Northern Ireland erupted into violence in the early 1970s and caused upheavals in republican circles leading to various splits, Kelly sided first with Official Sinn Fein against the Provisionals and then with the Irish Republican Socialist Party when there was a further split in 1974.

In that year, Kelly had got steady work at the Clondalkin Paper Mills in Dublin helping to install new machinery. Nuala Dillon, whom he had met first in Arklow, operated the canteen there. She did not share Kelly's politics.

Nicky Kelly was known to his associates as a political lightweight in spite of his passionate interest in politics. He talked politics constantly, was known to be good company, friendly and generous, with little interest in money. His most striking asset, to many of his friends, was his way with women.

Inspector Ryan told Dillon that he had a search warrant to look for guns. The three guards looked around the flat, watched by Dillon, while Ryan spoke to her. He asked about Kelly and his whereabouts. She told him that Kelly had been in Arklow for the weekend and was probably still there. When the search was over and nothing had been found, the gardai brought Dillon to the CDU office in Dublin Castle. The gardai told her they could not let her go until Kelly was arrested: she went with them voluntarily. By that time Garda O'Hara had teamed up with some other gardai and was on his way to Arklow in search of Kelly.

Kelly and Dillon had spent most of the weekend together in Arklow. They went to a number of parties before Dillon caught the train back to Dublin on Sunday to be ready for work on Monday morning. On Sunday night, Kelly dropped around to the home of a friend for a poker session. The game, for small stakes, went on into the early hours and as dawn broke on Monday, it was beginning to disintegrate: some of the players had dropped out and fallen asleep in armchairs, others were making tea.

The garda party on its way to Arklow was led by Inspector Vincent McGrath, a detective with the Special Branch who had a search warrant for the Kelly family home. Apart from Adrian O'Hara, Inspector McGrath had two other men with him: Gardai William Meagher, a detective from the CDU, and Joseph Holland, a detective based at Ballyfermot station in Dublin.

Just before nine o'clock, they arrived at Arklow garda station and got directions to Tyndall's Lane. They reached there around nine, showed their search warrant, asked after Nicky Kelly and were told where he was. They looked around and went back again to Arklow station. They asked how to get to Rockview Terrace and it was decided that the best thing was to bring a local detective, Garda Patrick Looby, with them. Inspector McGrath and Meagher stayed behind in the station as Looby, O'Hara and Holland went off to arrest Kelly.

They arrived at Rockview Terrace around 10 am. Kelly

had got a couple of hours sleep in an armchair but had since woken and made some tea. There was a knock on the door: it was opened and O'Hara came in and told Kelly he was arresting him under Section 30 of the Offences Against the State Act because he suspected he was involved in the train robbery. Kelly was put into a car almost immediately and taken to Arklow garda station. When he arrived there, Garda O'Hara brought him to a room and gave him a copy of Section 52 of the Act to read. The section obliged people arrested under the act to give an account of their movements. Garda O'Hara wanted to know what Kelly was doing on the night of March 30th and the early hours of the following morning when the mail train was held up and robbed.

Kelly said he had gone to McNally's house in Swords and, when McNally wasn't there, he had stayed watching television with McNally's wife. He said that McNally arrived home at around 1 am and they chatted for about an hour, made some tea and went to bed. He said that next morning McNally gave him a lift into town and he went to the IRSP offices in Gardiner Street. He told Garda O'Hara that he spent the day between the office and his and Nuala Dillon's flat. Garda O'Hara took notes of what Kelly said and he left the room to pass on the account to Inspector McGrath. McGrath said they would take Kelly to Dublin and just before 11.00, they put him into the back seat of a car, between Holland and Meagher. O'Hara drove and McGrath sat in the front passenger seat.

The car sped through Wicklow and into Dublin. Kelly knew he wasn't being taken to the Bridewell when the car crossed the Liffey and headed towards the North Circular Road and Fitzgibbon Street garda station. At almost the exact same time, Nuala Dillon was leaving Dublin Castle where she had been taken by Inspector Ryan after the search of the flat. She went immediately to Dame Street to the offices of Pat McCartan, one of the best known of a group of young Dublin solicitors who specialised in the State funded criminal legal aid scheme. She told him that Kelly had been arrested and asked that he look after things. After that, she finally got to work.

Elsewhere that morning, gardai were active at various places around Dublin and outside the city as well – in Cork, Limerick, Monaghan and Carlow. People known to have links with the IRSP were arrested and taken to police stations for questioning. In Dublin, people were taken to a variety of stations: Crumlin, Harcourt Terrace, Fitzgibbon Street, Rathmines and the Bridewell. Most of the party leadership was rounded up, including Seamus Costello, its founder.

Garda Joseph Egan, one of the Special Branch detectives working under Inspector McGrath, wanted to search the IRSP offices and got the keys from Costello. The night before, Superintendent Casey signed a warrant so that Garda Egan and five other gardai could search the building. At around 11 am, Garda Egan and the others arrived at the IRSP headquarters – an impressive red brick Victorian villa style house on Upper Gardiner Street which had seen better days. They opened the door and there was nobody inside. They went into each of the rooms and began searching and reading papers scattered around the place.

Osgur Breatnach, editor of the IRSP newspaper, *The Starry Plough,* arrived around midday as the search was going on. He was brought inside and left in a front room. While he was there watching the gardai, two people telephoned: Maoliossa Costello, wife of Seamus, and the wife of Ronnie Bunting, a Northern Protestant convert to the nationalist cause whose father, Major Ronald Bunting was a disciple of loyalism and the Reverend Ian Paisley. Both women told Breatnach that their husbands had been arrested.

Breatnach was twenty five years old and came from Dun Laoghaire. He had four brothers and one sister, all of whom had been raised to appreciate the Irish language and the nationalist, republican view of Irish history. Breatnach was regarded as aggressive and argumentative and had come to the IRSP after experience in a wide range of political and semi political activities which began in his schooldays. In 1966 at the age of sixteen he was on a march in support of striking teachers and was involved in attempts to set up a secondary school students union. His co-activists included the children of Garret FitzGerald, at that time one of the rising stars of Fine Gael, and Adrian Hardiman, who later joined Fianna Fail. Breatnach was bright. He once entered an essay writing competition in *Inniu,* the Irish language paper, and came first with a piece called "The Day I Joined The Guards". He also won a scholarship to University College Dublin but dropped out of the Arts Faculty shortly after the North began to erupt in civil disorder in 1969. By this time, he had been involved in numerous causes – against the Vietnam War, for better housing, and he was also on the fringes of the "Christian Marxist" group prominent at that time in UCD.

He was in Belfast for the first major riots in August 1969 and the experience affected him deeply. Suddenly he was confronted with the actual stuff of revolution on the streets there having read about it for years. Somebody in Belfast gave him a chain with a bolt screwed onto it and told him to use it for protection if he was attacked. He wrote an eye-witness account for a Dublin newspaper and came home. Not long afterwards in Dun Laoghaire, he spoke at a public meeting about the North. He held up his bolt and chain "weapon" and told the audience that people in Belfast needed guns.

He became involved in the housing issue and was on O'Connell Bridge in 1969 when a sit down protest by the Dublin Housing Action Committee was baton charged by the gardai. He was active in a similar group which operated in Dun Laoghaire and was convicted after the occupation of Frascati House in Blackrock, the stately home of Lord Edward Fitzgerald, one of the leaders of the 18th century United Irishmen. He was bound over to keep the peace for three years and also given a nine month suspended prison sentence. After his experiences in the North, he had joined Sinn Fein and was in a group which occupied the Fianna Fail offices in Dublin in protest at the Forcible Entry Bill, a measure taken by the Government to curb the activities of the Housing Action groups.

Later, he did a journalism course in the Rathmines College of Commerce in Dublin, following in the footsteps of his father, a sub-editor with the *Irish Independent.* But other developments diverted his energies away from a conventional career. When the split came between Official Sinn Fein and the Provisionals, he sided with the Officials. But in 1974, he sided with Costello and helped form the IRSP.

By the time of the train robbery on March 31st, he was well used to dealing with the gardai and to being arrested by the Special Branch. In fact, he was arrested about twelve hours after the robbery by gardai who said they suspected he was involved in the hold-up. He had left the IRSP offices to go around the corner to a chip shop on Dorset Street and was returning when he was arrested by Garda Owen Fitzsimons and three colleagues who were in a patrol car outside the offices.

Breatnach demanded to know who they were as he was put into the car and driven off to the Bridewell. One of the detectives showed him some identification. When they arrived at the garda station Breatnach would not speak to them in English: he demanded to conduct all his business with them in Irish. He gave the desk sergeant his name and address and told Garda Fitzsimons that he wanted to see a solicitor. Which one, asked Fitzsimons. McCartan, said Breatnach.

He was put into a cell in the Bridewell and over the next few hours one or two gardai came and went but he refused to speak to them other than in Irish. They left him alone and he was released just before his forty eight hour period was up in the middle of the afternoon of April 2nd. The solicitor he asked for never came. Unknown to anybody at the time, what happened was that somebody in the station rang the IRSP offices instead of the office of Pat McCartan, the solicitor Breatnach wanted. The garda asked to speak to Mr McCartan. Thomas McCartan, an IRSP member, came to the phone. The garda explained that he was calling from the Bridewell and that Osgur Breatnach wanted him, McCartan, down there. McCartan said okay, hung up and immediately went on the run in the belief that the gardai were after him. No one turned up in the Bridewell.

Now, on Monday, April 5th 1976, Breatnach watched the gardai sift through papers and search the IRSP office

43

and he was not surprised when they arrested him. He was taken away by Garda Joseph Egan and placed once again in a cell in the Bridewell.

One of the other people arrested that morning was John Fitzpatrick, a twenty four year old Dubliner who had lived most of his life in Armagh. When the IRSP was formed in 1974, Fitzpatrick split with Official Sinn Fein and became deeply involved in all aspects of the new organisation. By the time of his arrest in 1976, he was a seasoned para-military. In his late teens and early 20s he was reputed to have been involved in many Official IRA incidents in Armagh. In one, he and some comrades engaged British soldiers in a gun battle. Fitzpatrick was in a Volkswagen car and looking down a street with soldiers positioned on either side: there seemed no way out except straight down the middle through the sights of every British rifle.

He put his foot down and drove at high speed through a hail of bullets. He reached the other end of the street and by the time he rolled out of the car and ran away, there were several bullet holes in his clothes but not, amazingly, in him. Later, it was said that one of the car doors had 57 bullet holes in it. When the Official IRA announced a ceasefire in 1972, Fitzpatrick disagreed. He felt that if they stopped fighting they would be betraying their comrades in prison. But he did not leave until Seamus Costello formed a new organisation and he was disillusioned enough to split. Despite his activities he had a clean record in the Republic although he had been arrested several times under Section 30 because of his known associations. He once had a gun charge against him in Monaghan but the case was dismissed.

The guards knew where to find Fitzpatrick on the morning of Monday, April 5th, when people were being arrested all over the country. He was staying at Killygoan in County Monaghan with two others, Anthony McCluskey and Paddy Loughlin. All three were in a car driven by Fitzpatrick when they were spotted by two gardai in a patrol car as they drove through the village of Drumbear. The men in the patrol car, Gardai Tom Britton and Edward Fitzpatrick from Monaghan garda station, pulled up in front and arrested them all. Fitzpatrick arrived at Monaghan station shortly after 10 am and was put into a cell. Dublin was contacted to say the man they wanted was in custody. Fitzpatrick had asked what he was being arrested for and was told that somebody in Dublin wanted to talk to him. Later that day after a meal in his cell, he was transferred from Monaghan to Ardee in Co. Louth. There, he was met by three detectives – Sergeant Joseph Collins from Ballymun, Thomas Dunne from Kevin Street and Tom Kiely from Dundrum – who drove him to Dublin where he was taken to the Bridewell.

By the time that Fitzpatrick was safely placed in his cell, just about everyone who was anyone in the middle and upper levels of the IRSP was in police custody. Costello was in the Bridewell. The IRSP general secretary, Michael Plunkett, was known to be in Belfast and the guards intended to pick him up once he set foot back in Dublin. Breatnach, editor of the party's paper, had been arrested.

*   *   *

Seamus Costello formed the IRSP in December 1974 after a protracted struggle within the Official IRA and Official Sinn Fein. He and his supporters believed the organisations were beginning to move in directions different to those pursued during the previous decade.

The troubles which blew up in Northern Ireland in 1969 and 1970 and which threatened to boil over into a full scale civil war engulfing the whole island threw the republican movement into a crisis. Throughout the 1960s, Sinn Fein had been involving itself in social issues which tended to highlight class divisions. The North had ceased to be more than the object of ritual sabre rattling since the IRA's border campaign of the late 1950s in which Costello played a part. He was sixteen at the time and earned the nickname the "Boy General": he had great standing among supporters of the organisation in Northern Ireland. Within the army council of the IRA, of which he was a member, he was known as Clancy – it was his *nom de guerre*.

The steady drift of Sinn Fein to more conventional left wing politics caught the organisation on the wrong foot when violence spilt onto the streets of Belfast and Derry. Catholics were burnt out of their homes by loyalist mobs and the North's sectarian police force, the RUC and its ancillary wing, the B Specials, either took no interest or lent a hand to the loyalists. In response, republicans with IRA connections began looking for guns and the support of Dublin headquarters for a campaign of armed resistance.

The IRA was locked in internal debate over the way forward while in the North people, young people in particular, began to turn to anyone who had a gun. Within the Army Council, there was a debate about the relationship between the army and the party and which of them should dominate the other. Two documents were drawn up, one of which, written by Costello and Sean Garland, suggested that the existing structures should be maintained but improved. But events in the North passed them out and those who wanted to use guns didn't wait for permission from the Army Council or anyone in Dublin. They simply did it, thus starting the split which was formalised at the Sinn Fein Ard Fheis in Dublin in early 1970.

The Officials subscribed to Marxist theory and tried to build a movement which crossed the sectarian divide. By doing this they hoped to create a class struggle North and South which, when the working class on either side of the border triumphed, would make partition irrelevant as an issue: there would be no basis for any division between the working class of the North and their brothers and sisters in the South. But when partition itself became the issue, it was the Officials and their theory which lost their immediate relevance. The immediacy of the problem facing the Catholic people of the North ensured a rapid growth for the Provisionals and a corresponding decline for the Officials although in the South, Official Sinn Fein began to lay the basis for eventual electoral success. The Provisionals meanwhile waged a paramilitary war in the North.

In the immediate aftermath of the split, the Officials were much stronger than the Provisionals. In Dublin for instance at the time of the split there were some twenty five units of the Official IRA, each of which in theory had between five and ten members. After internment was introduced in Northern Ireland in 1971, the Provisionals grew by leaps and bounds. The Official IRA was occasionally active even in the South however. In Dun Laoghaire, for example, there was an active unit which tried to link its operations with local issues: the synthesis of revolutionary struggle. A city auctioneer had his offices attacked because of his links with a site in Dun Laoghaire which was to be developed as commercial property at the expense of local housing. The firm which was demolishing the houses also had some machinery damaged.

One of the leading lights in the Dun Laoghaire unit of the Official IRA was Michael Plunkett. He was politically very close to Costello who himself was active a few miles to the south in Bray and north Wicklow. The two became friends and Plunkett, who was also head of the Markievicz cumann of Official Sinn Fein in Dun Laoghaire, organised a number of joint operations including marches to highlight the need for more local authority housing in their areas. Nicky Kelly got to know Costello when he was part of the campaign for better access to the beach at Brittas Bay. In Dun Laoghaire, Plunkett's political associates included Osgur Breatnach and Gerry Roche. For a brief period in the early 1970s, the Dun Laoghaire and north Wicklow areas were something of a hot bed of radical dissent on the republican fringe. Plunkett and the others were impressed by Costello's commitment to local issues and the way in which he involved himself at ground level. He had energy, dynamism and charisma. It also seemed to them that he was the only person high up in the organisation who could understand the Provisionals.

In 1972 Costello campaigned within Official Sinn Fein for a broad front of a wide range of groups on the left – the Labour Party, the Communist Party as well as the two Sinn Feins – to come together and agree a policy on the issue of Northern Ireland. Within the front, the groups could retain their separate identity and remain active on other issues. At the same time he was adjutant-general of the Official IRA and he wanted it to become more active in the war against

47

the British. He believed that Britain would withdraw from Northern Ireland sooner if more bodies were sent back to England.

Early that year, the Official IRA (including Costello and Plunkett) had organised the burning of the British Embassy in Dublin after the British Army paratroop regiment had shot dead 13 people who were on a civil rights march in Derry. At the culmination of three days of demonstrations outside the embassy in Merrion Square, Costello addressed the crowd and gave the signal for the petrol bomb attack. "Eviction notice" was the code phrase and Costello unleashed the attack by telling the crowd they had often come to the embassy with petitions and placards but today they had come with an eviction notice.

In retaliation for the Derry killings, the Official IRA planted a bomb at the Aldershot base of the Paratroop Regiment in February. It exploded, killing five women canteen workers, a Catholic priest and a gardener but no soldiers. There was a backlash against the killings in both parts of Ireland but worse was to come. In May, Ranger William Best, an off duty British soldier based in West Germany, was home in Derry to visit his family in the Creggan. He was murdered by the Officials in retaliation, they said, for the youths of Derry who had been killed by the British Army. There was a powerful wave of popular disgust, particularly among the nationalist people of Derry, against the killing and eight days later, the Officials called a unilateral ceasefire. A statement issued in Dublin said the ceasefire was called because "the overwhelming desire of the great majority of all people of the North is for an end to military actions by all sides". It had been decided that in future, members of the Official IRA would only act in retaliation for direct assaults on them, according to the statement.

The ceasefire was called by the Army Council which was dominated by people who were changing tactics away from a mixture of military action and politics to exclusive involvement in politics. Costello disagreed with the shift but was forced to go along with it. However he and his allies began to campaign against it. In Dun Laoghaire, Plunkett and the entire Markievicz cumann of Sinn Fein resigned in protest but returned to the fold a month later after talks with party headquarters. Despite this, however, they were barred from the ard fheis even though a year previously, they had been stars at the annual gathering because of their work locally and their record of selling about 1,000 copies a month of the party paper, *The United Irishman.*

To Costello and those who supported his approach, it seemed that the combined opposition of the rest of the party leadership and their allies in the Official IRA was being used to stifle discussion. They could find no mechanism which would allow them raise certain issues for general debate. They believed, for instance, Sinn Fein meetings were in effect hijacked by cabals of Official IRA members who met beforehand, discussed contentious matters on the agenda among themselves, decided a line and, having had their practice run, were able to dominate and steer discussion at the main council. The Army Council was dominated by people, notably Cathal Goulding, the chief of staff, who wanted to move the whole organisation into greater involvement in conventional left wing politics without the overt involvement of the Official IRA. Costello, on the other hand, believed that the army was vital to get the British out of Northern Ireland and to wage a guerilla war throughout the whole island in support of the class struggle.

The desire of party headquarters to distance itself from violence was evident in the attitude displayed towards Plunkett when he and some others active in Dun Laoghaire were arrested following incidents inside the town hall. Protesters had managed to get inside the building and in the ensuing melee, a chair flew through the air and smashed a window. Plunkett was arrested and charged. Although he maintained it was an accident, he was ordered to plead guilty and get the whole thing over and done with quickly without fuss. Plunkett wanted to fight the case in court and to use the opportunity to make some points about the system. The party hierarchy was also clearly embarrassed when Plunkett was charged with Breatnach after petrol bombs had been thrown during a housing action demonstration at Frascati House. Plunkett, like Breatnach, got a suspended sentence.

By 1973, Official Sinn Fein was gearing itself up for the local government elections due to be held in the South the following year. Costello was already a successful local politician: he was a member of Wicklow County Council and was chairman of Bray Urban District Council. He did not subscribe to the abstentionist policy which held that people should not take their seats because to do so was *de facto* recognition of a state whose very existence purist republicans were not supposed to accept. By this time, Costello was also director of operations of the Official IRA and was seriously at odds with many of his comrades on the Army Council. He continued to urge greater military action against the British in Northern Ireland but was blocking approval for IRA robberies in the Republic needed to finance the organisation. He wanted things his own way, and if he couldn't get them, he was prepared to use his position to stop others having their way.

Such allegations were contained in what came to be known as the Clancy document: a series of charges against Costello drawn up by his opponents within the Official IRA and circulated to all its units during the winter of 1973–1974. Early in 1974 he was court martialled on foot of these accusations and was dismissed from the IRA. At the same time he was suspended from Official Sinn Fein for six months and ordered not to contest the local elections in May. A car which had been supplied to him by the party was taken away and he lost his income from the party as well. At this point, Costello still hoped that he could fight from within and bring the party and the army around to his way of thinking even though a split looked unavoidable.

In Dun Laoghaire, Plunkett was ordered not to contest the local elections because he had an arms charge pending against him. The Markievicz cumann wanted to run three candidates including him and Breatnach. The party hierarchy wanted to run Tomas MacGiolla, the party president, instead of Plunkett. After an argument a compromise was agreed: Breatnach and another candidate would stand. Breatnach narrowly missed being elected.

Costello defied the party however and stood as an Independent Sinn Fein candidate. After his re-election, he was expelled from Official Sinn Fein in May 1974 because it was deemed he was "generally unsuitable" – a phrase which was being applied to people whom the party hierarchy wanted out.

Information circulated to party members explained that Costello was expelled because he continued to defy directives from the ard comhairle. Specifically, he was accused of standing in the local elections when he was told not to, of continuing to attend county council meetings contrary to orders and of trying to drum up support for a special ard fheis to discuss his disagreements with party and army policy. Once expelled, this avenue was no longer open to him but he hoped to be able to raise things at the ard fheis in November, 1974. In the meantime, his supporters wanted to have matters debated at the army convention, the general meeting of delegates from IRA units all over the country held every two years.

Most of the delegates to the 1974 Convention didn't know where it was held. Some, for instance, were brought to it in a van with blackened out windows. Costello wasn't allowed in but he and his supporters hoped to succeed with a motion allowing him to come in and then, once inside, he would debate the issue of military activity. The attendance motion, however, became the issue. When the meeting began it seemed to Costello's supporters that there was a well planned attempt to short circuit any dissention. There were not enough chairs to go around and many people had to sit on the floor. Costello's supporters noticed that many on his side were missing. Although the meeting began at 7 pm, the question as to whether or not Costello should be allowed in wasn't discussed until 6 am. By this time many of the delegates were too tired to concentrate on the nitty gritty of the debate and willing to agree to proposals which simply got things out of the way. The meeting went on until noon the following day, a marathon fifteen hours.

Costello's supporters lost: well over half the delegates were against his admission to the meeting. Plunkett walked out to the car park where Costello was waiting and told him.

He just shrugged, appeared unflapped and went off to concentrate on the next battle – the November ard fheis.

Costello borrowed his brother's Morris Minor car and drove around the country trying to drum up support among Official Sinn Fein activists for his readmission to the party at the ard fheis and his fight with the leadership. When the time for the ard fheis came, Plunkett was one of a number of people who were barred.

He was told he was "generally unsuitable" and he believed the reason was because he had supported Costello at the Army Convention. A number of Costello supporters – including Nicky Kelly and Ronnie Bunting – tried to provoke a debate on his expulsion and the issues connected to it but were prevented: the hierarchy and the majority of delegates were against them. His supporters walked out in disgust but they didn't waste any time licking their wounds. They started to form a new party of their own.

The Irish Republican Socialist Party was formed at a meeting in the Spa Hotel in Lucan near Dublin the following month. The declared aim of the party was to establish a thirty two county socialist republic "with the working class in control of the means of production, distribution and exchange". The new party accused Official Sinn Fein of betraying the struggle by turning its back on the North during a period of what it called escalating British repression and of being undemocratic in declaring a unilateral ceasefire in 1972.

Secretly and unknown at the time, immediately before the formation of the IRSP, some of those involved met and formed the Irish National Liberation Army with Costello as chief of staff. There was some discussion about the name before the INLA was finally agreed. Someone suggested the National Liberation Army but others were reluctant to forsake the name of the IRA and so it was decided to insert Irish in front of the NLA. The formation of the army was not announced at the time and in fact was denied by Costello himself.

One of the main issues under debate within the organisations was the relationship of the military unit to the political party. Most of those involved wanted to establish a new arrangement. They had seen shortcomings in the traditional arrangement, now operated by the Provisionals, whereby Sinn Fein was subservient to the IRA. They believed that the opposite arrangement had come into existence with the Officials: Sinn Fein was in control of the IRA. They did not like either set-up and set out to create a new one. Initially, as this issue was debated, the INLA and IRSP were set up as quite separate organisations. There was no formal relationship requiring one to support the other. Of course, Seamus Costello was head of both and there were other people whose membership overlapped as well.

At the Spa Hotel, a temporary ard comhairle was formed which would hold office and develop IRSP policy until the first ard fheis of the new party could be arranged. The new party would register itself as a political party in the Republic to indicate that it was not abstentionist.

Costello and Plunkett met Bernadette McAliskey in Monaghan and asked her to join the new party. McAliskey was known world wide for her role during some of the first riots seen in Derry and as an MP for mid Ulster she had been the youngest member of the British House of Commons. She found much to agree with in Costello's brand of nationalism and socialism.

The new party held a public meeting in Dublin in February 1975 which was attended by about 500 people. Costello and McAliskey were the star attractions. Costello said that the struggle for national liberation and the emancipation of the working class was the same struggle but that the major task in the short term was the unity of North and South. McAliskey said that 800 years of struggle against British rule in Ireland had failed because the Left had not concentrated on anti-imperialist issues and class struggle. Plunkett, who was to become general secretary of the new party, said that five branches had already been formed in Dublin.

One of them was the Markievicz cumann of Official Sinn Fein in Dun Laoghaire. Plunkett and Gerry Roche had gone to the Spa Hotel meeting as delegates for the cumann which at the time was in a somewhat ambiguous position. Plunkett and Roche reported back to the cumann and, overnight, the Markievicz cumann of Sinn Fein became the Markievicz cumann of the IRSP. Roche became national organiser of the new party and Breatnach assistant editor of the party's paper, *The Starry Plough*.

It was clear from the beginning that relations between the IRSP and Official Sinn Fein would be strained, to say the least. In Belfast tensions were extremely high between loyal members of the Officials and those who had broken away. There were allegations that some people who had left the Officials were refusing to hand over their guns and were taking from Official IRA arms dumps. The former Officials denied this and believed that some of them were on an Official IRA hit list of people to be punished for defecting. Tensions boiled over into a bloody feud at the end of February 1975 when a member of the new organisation, Hugh Ferguson, was shot allegedly on the orders of Billy McMillan, the Official IRA commander in Belfast. The plan was to kneecap Ferguson but, while struggling with his attackers, he pulled a face mask from one of them and so was shot dead.

His funeral in Belfast was organised by the People's Liberation Army: a group of former Officials who left with Costello but who had not yet been inducted into the INLA because the military wing had not got off the ground. The PLA was formed to protect Belfast IRSP members during the feud with the Officials. Costello gave the funeral oration and denied that the IRSP had any military wing. A day or two after Ferguson was killed, someone in the IRSP/PLA placed a chilling death notice in the *Irish News:* "Kerr", it read, "suddenly. The committee and members of Cyprus Street Social Club wish to express their sympathy to the wife and family of Eamon (Hatchet). All available members please attend the funeral". Hatchet Kerr was a well known member of the Official IRA in Belfast and was very much alive when his death notice appeared.

A few days later, Kerr and an associate in the Officials, Sean Fox, walked into the Divis Flats complex in Belfast. A significant number of the Officials living in the flats had defected to the IRSP and Belfast humourists had renamed the dour slum complex the Planet of the IRPS – a pun on a film current at the time, "Planet of the Apes". Kerr and Fox had gone to Divis Flats to attack some of the IRSP members there but were taken by surprise. On entering the complex, they were greeted by a hail of gun fire. They fired back but Fox was killed and Kerr had to run for his life.

Cathal Goulding gave the oration at the funeral of Fox, a member of the Official IRA's Belfast command. He accused those who killed Fox of being misguided and confused malcontents.

The feud badly damaged the emerging party. McAliskey was elected to the ard comhairle at the first ard fheis which was held in Dublin that April. She and her associates were unhappy with the military activities of people connected to the party and wanted the INLA to be subservient to the IRSP. The problem, identified at the foundation of the organisation, was never properly resolved and McAliskey resigned and left the party late in 1975. She took with her a large number of people at the top of the IRSP but those who remained – the Costello and Plunkett faction – maintained that the bulk of the rank and file members which they put at up to 400 stayed with them.

Right from the beginning the party had the image of a militaristic organisation. The central issue behind the split with the Officials, the subsequent feud and deaths and the departure of McAliskey all served to reinforce this view. Police in the Republic were taking a particular interest in the organisation from the minute it was set up. The investigation section of the Garda Technical Bureau had at least one intelligence report suggesting that the new organisation could grow and prove to be dangerous. Police fears seemed justified when the INLA began to involve itself in armed robberies in the Republic to bankroll its operations in Northern Ireland. A number of successful cash robberies were carried out in 1975 and 1976. Special Branch detectives tailed party members regularly and often lifted them under the Offences Against the State Act in the hope of finding out some useful information.

In June 1975 there was an incident which gave rise to police fears that the IRSP wanted to escalate its feud with the Officials to a new level, although both sides regarded the feud as over by then. A 5 lb bomb on the Dublin to Sallins railway line blew away two feet of the track and damaged a number of sleepers about half an hour after a train load of 300 Officials passed on their way to the annual Wolfe Tone commemoration at Bodenstown. The bomb had been set sometime around 10 that morning and a local man, Christopher Phelan, was unlucky enough to be passing at the time. He stumbled upon whoever was setting it in place and was murdered. His body was dumped in the bushes and found when gardai investigated the unsuccessful attempt to blow up the train. Passengers had included Tomas MacGiolla and Cathal Goulding.

Suspicions were immediately focused on Costello and the IRSP. He was asked by reporters if he knew anything about what had happened and replied that he saw no reason why he, more than anyone else, should be asked such a question. Plunkett condemned the killing of Phelan which he described as a "terrorist act" and MacGiolla said there was a truce between the Officials and the IRSP. He wondered if some Loyalist group in the North was not behind the bombing.

The gardai concentrated on the IRSP. In the days immediately afterwards, six members were arrested and taken to the Bridewell. They included Costello and two of his associates on the ard comhairle, Tommy McCourt and Gerry Jones, as well as Nicky Kelly. They were asked to say what they doing when the bomb went off on the line to Sallins and were also questioned about the existence of an extreme Loyalist group which the gardai suspected existed at the time in Dublin. IRSP supporters picketed the Bridewell and accused the Government and the police of trying to smash their party. The bomb had been planted in fact by a Loyalist group from the North: a fingerprint found at the scene was later identified as that of a Loyalist activist.

Nobody from the IRSP was charged in connection with the Sallins line bombing and murder. But party members bitterly resented what they saw as an attempt to blame them and possibly provoke a new feud with the Officials. They viewed the incident as another example of police attempts to destroy the party before it got off the ground. People were constantly arrested under Section 30 and as often as not just left in a cell for forty eight hours. Sometimes they were questioned about the activities of the party. One or two party members were repeatedly arrested on Friday evenings as they left work and found themselves spending the weekend in a garda station. Anyone who had anything to do with the party had become very familiar with the gardai and so there was no great feeling of surprise when many members, including Costello, were visited or arrested immediately after the mail train robbery and in the succeeding days.

*   *   *

Brian McNally was brought into a large interview room in Fitzgibbon Street garda station by Sergeant Francis Campbell just after 8 am on Monday, April 5th, and left there with Garda James Grehan, the detective who had arrested him, and Garda Drew, another of the guards in the search party which had called to his home.

McNally was told to turn out his pockets and he emptied them onto a table. There was his driving licence and insurance, his glasses, cigarettes and matches, his carton of tablets and a small diary which contained a list of showband managers and dates which had been arranged for the band. The guards told him to sit down. He complained of the cold and Grehan plugged in an electric fire and pushed it over near to him.

They asked him to tell them what he was doing on the night of March 30th and the early hours of the following morning when the train was being robbed. He said that he had been to a film with a girlfriend that evening. They had gone to the Green Cinema and seen "A Date with a Lonely Girl" and had gone back to her house in Ringsend afterwards. He explained that a friend, Brian Donnelly, was dating the girl's sister. McNally said he later met Donnelly near Shelbourne Park greyhound track and gave him a lift to Ballymun where he dropped him off around midnight. He got home around 12.30 to find that Nicky Kelly had called earlier and stayed watching TV with McNally's wife. They made tea and sat around chatting until after 1.00 am when they went to bed. McNally said the next thing that happened was the early morning visit from two Special Branch detectives. They wanted to know who was in the house. McNally said Kelly was there: one of the detectives went upstairs, saw Kelly and then they both left.

Grehan and Drew went over some of the details of what McNally told them. They finished, left the room at 9.45 am and were replaced by Sergeant Campbell and Garda Thomas Ibar Dunne, another member of the party which had searched his house that morning and brought him to Fitzgibbon Street.

Garda Dunne asked McNally about the train robbery. "I know nothing about it," he replied. Dunne said he wanted him to account for his movements at the time of the robbery. "I have already given them to the other officers who have just seen me," he said but Dunne insisted. McNally went through it all again, how he had been in Irishtown, given Donnelly a lift back to Ballymun, gone home himself where he met Kelly and went to bed after 1.30. The gardai told him that they didn't believe his story. Campbell asked him about the IRSP and for a while they spoke about the party, what it stood for, its activities and McNally's role in it. He explained that he was no longer an active member.

Dunne produced a map which he had taken from McNally's house that morning. It was a map of Dublin and he opened it for McNally to look at. He ran his finger along a route and questioned McNally. McNally explained that the map was in the house as part of his work for the credit hire company: he needed it to get about when he was out collecting repayments. Dunne kept questioning him, saying he wasn't telling the truth.

They left at 12 noon and Grehan and Drew came back into the room to replace them immediately. Nicky Kelly had just arrived in the station from Arklow and was put into another room. Campbell and Dunne began to question him straight away after leaving McNally. McNally told Grehan and Drew that he was hungry. Garda Drew promised to try and rustle something up for him and eventually got him a cup of tea and two slices of bread. Both guards asked him again about the train robbery. Grehan said he had plenty of time to leave his home in Swords, go to Kildare, do the robbery and get back home again by the time the two Special Branch men called at 6 am. McNally insisted that he knew nothing about the robbery: he suggested that it was carried out by the Provisional IRA. Grehan said that he should tell the truth: McNally insisted he was, he had nothing to do with it.

They talked to him about the robbery over and over again: where he had been, who was with him, the possibility that he could have had time to do it and interspersed the conversation with chat about Northern Ireland, the IRSP, his work with the band and gaelic football.

Garda Grehan left the room just before half past one and Garda Drew followed him a few minutes later. They were replaced by William Meagher, one of the detectives who had gone to Arklow to arrest Kelly.

Meanwhile, Kelly had been put into a small interview room and joined by Gardai Campbell and Dunne. Campbell wanted to question him because of what McNally had said. They told him they were investigating the mail train robbery. "I can't help you," said Kelly. They pressed him for an account of his movements around the crucial hours of the robbery. Kelly explained that on the evening of March 30th, he left his flat in Goldsmith Street and caught a bus to Swords to get to McNally's house. He said that when he got there, McNally was out but he stayed and watched television with his wife and children. He said he left around 10 pm and telephoned Nuala Dillon to say that he would not be home, that he would stay with the McNallys. Dillon wasn't there but a woman in the house took a message. Kelly said that McNally returned after midnight: they had some tea, talked for a while and then went to bed. He said the Special Branch had called to the house around 6 am when they were all in bed.

Kelly's story was the same as McNally's: there were no discrepancies. Campbell listened and left after about twenty minutes. He had some other business to attend to in Pearse

Street station and also wanted to get some lunch.

He left Kelly alone with Dunne.

The gardai were meanwhile trying to check out some of the information obtained from McNally. Garda Grehan established that what he had said about being in Irishtown with Donnelly and two women friends was true and that he had left sometime just before midnight. Campbell, with help from Dunne, would also be able to confirm details of McNally's version of events relating to when he got to Ballymun and the dropping off of Donnelly. They interviewed Donnelly and took a statement from him. In Fitzgibbon Street, Dunne had left Kelly around 1 pm to be replaced by Garda Michael Finn, a detective based at Store Street station which was part of the same garda district as Fitzgibbon Street. The interrogation continued and Dunne returned around 2.30. Not long after 3 pm Campbell and Grehan came into the room. They asked Kelly a few details about McNally's activities in the IRSP and when he was last active in the party. Then they left.

Meanwhile, Garda William Meagher and McNally were having a relaxed and friendly conversation which lasted some three hours. Meagher was a detective with the Central Detective Unit. McNally told him that he knew nothing about the robbery of the train.

At 4.30 pm Drew came back and Meagher left McNally. Drew again asked McNally about his movements on the night of the train robbery. They were talking – McNally mentioned that he was hungry – when the door opened and a garda whom McNally didn't know walked in. He was Kieran Lawlor, one of the Special Branch detectives who had searched Nuala Dillon's flat. Drew went off to buy some milk and buns and left McNally alone with Lawlor.

Lawlor asked McNally what he had been doing on the evening of the 30th of March. McNally repeated his story about seeing a girlfriend in Irishtown and said he had taken her to the pictures in town before going back to her place and later still returning to Swords via Ballymun where he dropped off Brian Donnelly.

Around 5.30 pm Grehan returned to McNally and stayed alone with him until 8 pm. They talked about the robbery, about McNally's movements and McNally complained about a pain in his stomach. At 8 pm Grehan was replaced by Adrian O'Hara, another of the Special Branch detectives who had raided Dillon's flat that morning and who had gone to Arklow to arrest Kelly. McNally went over his story again for O'Hara: the visit to Irishtown, his girlfriend, back to Ballymun and home to Swords. For an hour and a half they talked, getting nowhere until Drew and Grehan returned. Grehan had heated a tin of Ambrosia creamed rice for McNally's stomach. He ate it all and they remained with him chatting and telling jokes until they put him in a cell just before midnight.

He had been interrogated virtually non stop since eight that morning. He was given some blankets and he lay down to get some sleep.

Nicky Kelly meanwhile had been subject to continuous interrogation during the afternoon. The chief questioner was Thomas Ibar Dunne who was with him from 2.30 pm until 6.15 pm when he was relieved by Garda Joseph Holland. In fact, Holland had paid a brief visit to Kelly during the afternoon to take his fingerprints. While Holland was with him in the evening, he brought him a meal of fish and chips and some cigarettes. For various periods until after midnight he was interrogated intensively by a series of guards including Dunne, Meagher and Michael Finn. Kelly was asked about a telephone call to Nuala Dillon the morning after the robbery: Finn and Dunne insisted that words used by Kelly during the conversation indicated that he had taken part in the robbery. He denied this but they continued to insist – they demanded that he tell the truth.

At one stage late in the evening Finn telephoned Dillon and asked her to meet him in Mountjoy garda station. She went there around 11 pm and was met by Finn and Meagher. They brought her to Fitzgibbon Street and questioned her about Kelly's call to her.

After midnight, Kelly was taken from the interview room, drained and exhausted. He thought he was being taken to his cell for the night. In another cell, McNally was roused from his sleep and both of them were driven off to the Bridewell in separate cars. They were locked in cells there and they tried to get some sleep on wooden beds with wooden pillows. Kelly felt shattered.

Osgur Breatnach had spent the day in the Bridewell after his arrest in the IRSP headquarters. He had a visit from his wife and was given food, drink, chocolate and cigarettes. Nobody had made any serious attempt to question him and he went to sleep that night content in the belief that he would be released in due course, after his forty eight hours were up.

But his and his colleagues' encounter with the gardai had only just begun.

3

Interrogations:
Tuesday and Wednesday,
April 6th and 7th

The Bridewell was the hub of the police system in Dublin. A solid, three storey building with a mock classical facade, it backed up the Four Courts complex and stood alongside the metropolitan district court where most of the city's petty crimes were adjudicated. Inside, the building was divided into two distinct parts and served two separate purposes. The left hand side was a busy garda station, catering for the surrounding district. The right hand side was a prison with two floors of cells, administered and run by gardai. It was used for people on their way to the courts or to jail. It was the holding centre for the capital and for much of the country.

The facade of the building was finished off with a classical quotation which united both wings of the building. *Fiat Justitia Ruat Coelum,* it proclaimed: let justice be done though the heavens should fall.

The day after the round-up of the IRSP members, the Bridewell became the hub of the police enquiries into the train robbery. It began early for some of the suspects.

Brian McNally had woken up from a fitful sleep on his wooden bed and wooden pillow to be told of an order extending his detention for another twenty four hours. It was 6.05 am. Just over two hours later, two gardai took him from his cell to resume his interrogation.

Unlike McNally, who had had to share a cell with two other prisoners, Nicky Kelly was put into a cell of his own. He had lain awake for several hours listening to footsteps and wondering if the gardai were going to come for him again. They did not and he slept but at about 10.00 am he was taken out of the prison section and into a room in the garda station. The questioning began again: detectives told him to tell the truth.

63

Much of the garda activity that morning was concerned with cross checking alibis and accounts of movements given by suspects the previous day. Many of those questioned had said they had been with other members of the IRSP on the night of the robbery. Garda suspicions were naturally aroused but IRSP members insisted that there was nothing sinister in that. Party activists worked together and socialised together to an extent that might seem exceptional to outsiders but was normal for such a small grouping.

Confusion over one of those accounts was one of the first items put to Kelly that morning. Several detectives suggested that his claim that he stayed in Brian McNally's house on the night of the robbery was not true. Another detainee, John Fitzpatrick, had said that he and Michael Barrett had stayed at McNally's that night.

Kelly stuck by his story. He had stayed there and no one else had been there apart from McNally and his family. One of the detectives, Sergeant Joseph Collins, went to another room in the Bridewell where Fitzpatrick was being questioned. He told Fitzpatrick that Kelly denied Fitzpatrick's story about staying in McNally's. Fitzpatrick sorted out the conflict: he had been confused the previous day when he gave the account of his movements.

Fitzpatrick said that he and Michael Barrett had stayed in McNally's on the Monday night. Early on Tuesday they had driven in Fitzpatrick's Volkswagen car to Abbeyfeale in County Limerick where Barrett's family lived. After a meal there, they had driven around Limerick and stayed the night – the night of the robbery – at the home of Tom Hayes in Castleconnell on the outskirts of Limerick. The next morning, Wednesday, they had driven back to Dublin. They read about the robbery in an evening paper when they arrived in the city.

Similar cross-checking was continuing with the accounts of other people but the gardai appeared to be no closer to solving the case. Everyone in custody was still denying any involvement.

Osgur Breatnach had been left virtually alone throughout this, his second period in detention within five days. Whenever anyone asked him to account for his movements, he replied only in Irish and did not tell them. No one pursued the issue.

As well as interrogating those detained, searching homes and looking into alibis, the gardai were still searching for several of the people named on their list of suspects. The previous day's arrests were about to deliver one of them.

*　　*　　*

Michael Plunkett knew there was something up when he arrived in Belfast's Great Victoria Street station to catch the train to Dublin. He noticed that he was being watched by a detective as he boarded the train and several others travelled part of the way with him. Just after 1.30 pm when the train arrived in Dublin's Connolly Station his suspicions were confirmed. He was arrested by a detective, Garda Michael Conroy and two companions as he emerged from the ticket check.

As general secretary of the IRSP, Plunkett occupied a key position in the organisation. In the previous couple of years he had become involved full time in revolutionary politics. He took his politics very seriously and had graduated swiftly from interest in Che Guevara, prompted by his death in 1967, to involvement in the Communist Party, Official Sinn Fein and the IRA and on to the IRSP and the INLA.

Aged twenty four, he was one of ten children and was born and grew up in Dun Laoghaire. After attending the local Christian Brothers School and the technical school, he followed his father into the Dublin Gas Company as an apprentice fitter. He quickly became immersed in trade union politics.

Gas company apprentices were members of the Workers Union of Ireland but had no rights at all within the union. They were not allowed to vote on union decisions or have any say in what was decided. He organised a secret group among the apprentices to agitate for full union rights. When the group finally put a picket on the WUI headquarters, the union capitulated. Plunkett became one of the two

65

representatives of apprentices on the local union committee.

His spare time was taken up partly with a youth club in Dun Laoghaire where his organising talent also came into play. It was run by lay brothers of a religious order and was suffering from vandalism. He suggested that it be run more by a members' committee: the suggestion was adopted and he became chairman.

The fiftieth anniversary celebrations in 1966 of the 1916 rising had influenced him considerably: television documentaries brought alive to him the events of that period. One of his Christian Brother teachers had given him a feeling for the romanticism of the 1916 leaders' sacrifices. He was also a teenager of his time, however, interested in civil rights protests and student rebellions in the United States and Paris. He was 17 when Guevara was killed in Bolivia: he went to Dun Laoghaire library to read all Guevara's books.

The civil rights movement in the North also interested him and he went to some of the marches. But he found the republican movement confusing and concentrated his efforts initially on local issues. He joined the Dun Laoghaire Housing Action group in 1969 because it dealt with an issue with which he was familiar. Housing was a problem for many people locally: the local council was providing little accommodation and the property laws clearly favoured landlords. The committee organised protests to stop evictions and the demolition of houses. When they failed, they organised squats.

The committee was largely made up of members of the Communist Party, Official Sinn Fein and the Labour Party. Plunkett was at different times its secretary, public relations officer and its chairman. But he had come to believe that he had to join a political organisation to have any influence or make any mark on events. He chose the Communist Party.

All of the organisations with whom he had been working had been trying to recruit him. He considered himself to be a communist and was still confused by the mysteries of republicanism. But he quickly became disillusioned with the Communist Party. It had only six members in Dun

Laoghaire at the time, a third of the membership of Sinn Fein. It showed little interest in new members or youth, was stuck in a defeatist rut and put its faith in the Northern civil rights movement.

After nine months or so he left because of all these factors. He had become convinced of the need for armed action in the North and saw the Communist Party as staid and not radical enough for the times. He joined the Markievicz cumann of Official Sinn Fein just after the split with the Provisionals. The split had taken away the element which he saw as obsessed with symbols and metaphysics and had originally confused him about republicanism. At his first Official Sinn Fein cumann meeting, he was elected chairman.

The high level of local activity, primarily over the housing issue, landed him in court on several occasions. With Osgur Breatnach, he was given a suspended sentence by the Special Criminal Court in 1972 for the siege at Frascati House.

On the first weekend in April 1976 he was in Belfast looking after the interests of IRSP men in prison in Long Kesh, the internment camp plus prison run by the Northern authorities. After the split in the Officials the prisoners who had sided with Costello had gone on hunger strike in search of official recognition for their new identity. They won it after a protest that lasted some ten days and Plunkett was appointed their prison welfare officer. That meant that he had unlimited access to the prison and was guaranteed immunity from arrest in the North.

The British were trying to phase out political status for prisoners at the time and had arranged several meetings. They were attended by representatives of all the groups in the prison, the Provisional IRA, Official IRA, IRSP, and the two main Loyalist paramilitary organisations, the Ulster Defence Association (UDA) and the illegal Ulster Volunteer Force (UVF). The main topic was the change-over to the newly built H-Blocks, a purpose built prison with cells which was to replace the huts and compounds in which prisoners were then held. The authorities were offering a reduction of half of their sentences as one of a series of concessions designed to get agreement to the changeover.

But the meetings were also serving a wider purpose. Sectarian assassinations – the murders of Catholics and Protestants by paramilitaries from the other community – had grown into a vicious tit-for-tat battle. It had culminated in the massacre of ten Protestants in January 1976: they were taken out of the bus in which they were travelling from work, lined up beside it and shot dead by masked gunmen. It appeared that the guerilla war in progress was about to expand into a full scale civil war.

The prison talks were a convenient meeting place for the Northern warring factions and the British tried to encourage them to open talks on a ceasefire. Their representatives withdrew from the room where the prison talks were going on, leaving the nationalist and loyalist paramilitaries together. Two sessions were held before the meetings were halted after the Provisional IRA killed the first prison warder to die since the troubles began.

Plunkett was at one of these meetings in Long Kesh when he heard about the widespread arrests of his party members in the South. He decided to cut short his stay in Belfast by two days and return on Tuesday, April 6th to organise a picket on the Bridewell. The placards, complaining about police harassment, were already made. But he never made it to the party headquarters in Gardiner Street.

As he came through the ticket check at Connolly station three detectives arrested him under Section 30 of the Offences Against the State Act, took him the short distance to Store Street garda station and put him into a cell.

Three hours later he was moved across the city to Harcourt Terrace garda station and put in a store room. Two Special Branch men, Garda James Butler and Sergeant Eamonn Carey, asked him to account for his movements on the night of the train robbery. He refused and Garda Butler went out and returned with a copy of the Garda Siochana guide which summarised most laws which the gardai used. He pointed out to Plunkett the resume of Section 52 of the Offences Against the State Act which requires suspects to account for their movements under pain of six months in prison.

Plunkett eventually told them he had gone to Dun Laoghaire by bus with two companions, Gerry Roche and Sean Gallagher, from the IRSP headquarters at about 6.00 pm on Tuesday, March 30th. He had gone home and later got a lift from his sister to Osgur Breatnach's flat in Blackrock where they were designing a poster protesting against repressive legislation. From there he went by bus to the home of Caoilte Breatnach, Osgur's brother, in Deansgrange to do a plumbing job for him. He arrived there about 9.00 pm. As well as Caoilte Breatnach, his wife and a Dutch friend of hers, Els Van Hout, were in the house. Plunkett left about 1.00 am to walk home the two miles or so to Dun Laoghaire. He got there about 1.45 am and had a chat with his brother Philip. He slept there that night.

The detectives went away to check out the alibi, leaving Plunkett with two other detectives.

Ninety minutes or so later Garda Butler and two others arrived at the terraced cottage in Deansgrange occupied by Caoilte Breatnach and his wife. They produced a search warrant and went over most of the house, except the kitchen. They then arrested Breatnach under the Offences Against the State Act and took him off to the local garda station at Kill o'the Grange.

He was kept in a cell for several hours before being taken to a room for questioning. They asked about his movements on the night in question and he told them about Plunkett's visit and who was in his house at the time. He told them about the Dutch visitor and they wanted her name and address. He was allowed to phone his parents to get the address and he talked to his wife who had gone there. They spoke in Dutch and he managed to tell his wife where he was and ask her to call a solicitor before the gardai became suspicious and put an end to the call. Els Van Hout was later questioned by Dutch police and confirmed Plunkett's visit.

Caoilte Breatnach was then taken to the Bridewell and lodged in a large cell upstairs in the prison section.

*   *   *

The questioning of other suspects in the Bridewell had continued throughout the day and into the evening.

After lunch in Cell 19 Brian McNally was taken back to an interview room to be questioned again. Two detectives, Gardai Felix McKenna and Thomas Fitzgerald came in and introduced themselves. It was their first time to question him and they started at the beginning again. McNally denied any knowledge of the robbery.

Nicky Kelly was also taken from his cell to an interview room after lunch. Within the next three hours at least three detectives saw him: Garda William Meagher, Garda Michael Finn and Garda Thomas Ibar Dunne. Kelly denied any involvement in the case.

The persistent questioning of suspects followed several patterns. Relays of detectives made sure that a person was rarely left alone. New detectives arrived all the time, especially during the first half of the detention period. They started all over again, asking for an account of movements, alibis, the truth. As far as they were concerned, "the truth" was not what they were being told but what they wanted to hear. Their strategy was to get the suspect talking and keep him talking. The subject was not necessarily important as long as a conversation was progressing. They would talk about IRSP or republican politics, football, personalities. They would return to the central issue: who was on the robbery? We know you were there; how did you get there? What did you do? What did so-and-so do? Who looked after the money?

Other than the information which Inspector Ned Ryan said he got from his informant and the general suspicion that the IRSP/INLA was trying to raise funds, the gardai still had no definite information to link the detainees with the train robbery. There was no forensic evidence, such as fingerprints, to establish an incontrovertible link. There was a possible identification through a photograph of one of the suspects shown to Conal O'Toole, whose house beside the railway line had been occupied by the raiders, the day of the robbery.

In an attempt to get a visual identification, the gardai arranged to have the two main eye-witnesses view suspects on several different occasions. Conal O'Toole was brought along to garda stations in Rathmines, Crumlin, Ballyfermot and the Bridewell to look surreptitiously at some suspects. He agreed to do so on condition that he did not have to confront anybody. The gardai accepted that proviso and O'Toole was taken at different times to four garda stations and looked at up to twenty men. None of them knew they were being observed; O'Toole saw them through windows with and without venetian blinds and, in the Bridewell, through a peephole built into a cupboard. Some ten men were paraded individually in front of this cupboard. O'Toole thought two of them resembled two people he had seen in his house but he could not make a positive identification.

The second eye-witness was Ray Reynolds, the greengrocer injured when his Volkswagen van was hijacked for the train robbery. He had received ten stitches for the blow he received over his left eye and was left, six days later, with a bandage over the wound. Around 6.30 pm on Tuesday, April 6th, he was brought to the Bridewell to have a look at some people for the gardai.

Nine people were being held and questioned there at that stage. They were Brian McNally, Nicky Kelly, Osgur Breatnach, John Fitzpatrick, Sean Gallagher, Robert Lee, Ronald Bunting, James Doherty and Seamus Costello. They were taken around tea-time to the reception area in the prison section of the Bridewell to be placed against a measure pinned on the wall. They were also seen by Reynolds in the process. He did not identify any of them as being the men who took his van from him.

The interrogations continued as the night wore on. Two detectives, Gardai Felix McKenna and Thomas Fitzgerald, saw Osgur Breatnach in a room and Fitzgerald, a native Irish speaker, asked him in Irish for his name and address. Breatnach, speaking Irish, told him but refused to answer any other questions. He said he would not answer any questions unless he had a solicitor. The two gardai sent him back to his cell and Garda Fitzgerald took Brian McNally from his cell down to an interview room. It was their second session with McNally.

McNally had been put into the cell after he had been paraded before Ray Reynolds and he hoped that he was now locked up for the night. He would have been due for release around 7.00 am the next morning, the end of his forty eight hours in detention. Instead he was taken down to one of three interview rooms in the prison section: it was the largest room of the three and there was a toilet and washbasin through a doorway off it.

McNally would not get to sleep for more than twelve hours.

Nicky Kelly, meanwhile, was being interrogated in the third of the interview rooms. Around 9.00 pm Detective Inspector Ned Ryan dropped into the room for about fifteen minutes and arranged for some tea and biscuits to be sent into him. He left Kelly and Detective Garda John Jordan of the Special Branch who questioned him for the first time for some two hours.

Garda Jordan had just spent an hour or so questioning another of the suspects, Ronnie Bunting. When he emerged from that session he met Inspector Ryan in a hallway. Ryan asked if there had been any developments with Bunting. Jordan said there had not. Ryan told him he had confidential information about Nicky Kelly making a phone call to his girlfriend, Nuala Dillon on the day of the robbery.

Garda Jordan went into the small interview room to question Kelly. For the next fourteen hours, Kelly would be in the presence of gardai almost continuously. He would not get any sleep that night.

Outside the Bridewell other members of the IRSP were parading up and down, carrying pickets in protest at the arrests. Thirteen people manned the picket and the slogans on their placards were noted down by a station sergeant. They said: "End repression now", "IRSP demand the right to organise", "No collaboration with British imperialism", and "No to Special Branch intimidators".

By 11.00 pm on the second night of the round-up, there were still dozens of gardai involved with the investigation in the Bridewell. Many of them had been on duty since early Tuesday morning and would stay on duty until well after daybreak the next morning. The two senior officers in charge of the case, Chief Superintendent Joy and Superintendent Casey, decided to go home about 11.00 pm, leaving instructions that they were to be informed of any major developments. When they left the Bridewell none of the nine interviewees had admitted anything.

All of the suspects still denied that they had taken any part in the robbery of the mail train. In little over nine hours – by 8.15 on the morning of the new day, Wednesday April 17th – the gardai would have four signed confessions.

*   *   *

The departure of the two most senior officers did not slacken the momentum of the interrogations.

Nuala Dillon, Nicky Kelly's girlfriend, had been in their flat about 9.30 that night when two detectives called for her. Nicky wanted to see her, they said. She pointed out that she had been told this the previous night and she had not seen him. They guaranteed that she would see him this time. They suggested that she also bring him some clothes.

She was driven to the Bridewell and taken into a large room where there was a teleprinter. Several gardai dropped in and out and asked her about the telephone conversation she had had with Kelly on the day of the robbery. She could not remember the call although she knew it had taken place.

Some time after 11.00 pm she was taken into a small interview room to see Nicky Kelly. Garda Thomas Ibar Dunne was in the room with him. The meeting lasted only a matter of minutes and she was taken out again. She was brought back to the room with the teleprinter and questioned. She spent most of the night in the room.

Shortly after midnight, John Fitzpatrick was being questioned in a room in the garda station by Sergeant Patrick Culhane, a Special Branch detective, and Garda Michael Drew, a detective with the CDU. They asked him once again to account for his movements on the night of the robbery. He told them about his trip to Limerick with Michael Barrett where he said they were seen by a detective, staying in the home of Tom Hayes and returning

73

to Dublin on Wednesday, March 31st. Garda Drew wrote out a two page statement of his account. Fitzpatrick refused to sign it and was put back in his cell about 1.20 am. He thought he was in the cell for the night.

Brian McNally was still in the largest interview room in the prison section. Garda Grehan, the Special Branch man who had been his most regular questioner, was with him when Inspector Myles Hawkshaw of the Special Branch and Garda John Hegarty from CDU had conversations with him.

By 1.00 am he was alone with Grehan who questioned him about the robbery. McNally mentioned that a Volkswagen van had been used. Garda Grehan wanted to know how he knew it was a Volkswagen van. McNally said he had read about it in the papers.

The interrogations were intensifying. Inspector Ryan was now the senior officer in the Bridewell: years of service gave him seniority over other inspectors present. Detectives were still interviewing suspects in a number of rooms. In addition, there were detectives hanging about, waiting for instructions or waiting for developments. Several of the detectives involved in interrogations found themselves questioning more than one of the detainees, occasionally going from one interview directly to another.

Around 3.00 am Inspector Ryan was told that Nicky Kelly had admitted that he was involved. He was still in the small interview room and was said to have made the verbal confession to three detectives, Garda Michael Finn, Garda Joe Egan and Sergeant Patrick Cleary. Kelly was also offering to show them a spot near Bray where guns might be hidden. There was talk of bringing him to the scene of the robbery and on to Ballymore Eustace on the Wicklow-Kildare border where the mail bags may have been taken after the raid.

Events were moving quickly. Inspector Ryan telephoned Superintendent Patrick Casey at home and told him there had been a break in the case. Superintendent Casey decided to come back to the Bridewell but first telephoned Chief Superintendent John Joy to inform him of developments. Within half an hour Superintendent Casey was back in the

Bridewell and remained in an office in the garda station there until Chief Superintendent Joy arrived about 8.30 am.

Around 4.15 am a written statement began to be drafted on sheets of foolscap paper in the interview room where Kelly was questioned. The statement, which later ran to three typewritten foolscap pages, was written down over an hour. At 5.15 am it was signed by Nicky Kelly and his signature witnessed by Inspector Ryan, Sergeant Patrick Cleary and Sergeant John McGroarty. Arrangements were then made for the three garda officers to drive to the scene of the crime with Kelly.

Meanwhile, Osgur Breatnach had been asleep in his cell. About 5.20 am, however, he was taken out by a uniformed jailer and downstairs to the prison reception area. Two detectives were waiting for him, Garda Thomas Fitzgerald, the Irish-speaking detective from the Central Detective Unit who had interviewed him some eight hours earlier, and Inspector John Murphy, a detective attached to Kevin Street garda station. They brought him down from the first floor cells to the ground floor of the prison section. They turned right at the bottom of the stairs and led him back towards the ground floor cells. But they then directed him towards a stairwell that stood in the middle of the floor.

They took him down the eighteen steep, stone steps and into a tunnel that ran under the building. It continued under the laneway outside and beneath the length of the district court building next door. Large iron gates led off the tunnel into three courtrooms. In the early hours of the morning, however, most of the tunnel was closed off by a steel door. The section from the steps turned slightly and ran for ten yards or so to the locked door. The roof was about twelve feet high and the tunnel was four to five feet wide. A single naked bulb lit the tunnel. At 5.20 am the bulb was on and the steel door was locked.

The two detectives brought Breatnach down the eighteen steps and into the first short stretch of tunnel that was blocked by the gates. They asked him in Irish to account for his movements. Eventually, he said where would anybody be except in bed?

After a while he was taken back upstairs, through the

prison section and out into the garda station. He was taken up some more stairs to a room that doubled as a mess room and locker room for sergeants attached to the station. At least one more detective, Garda Thomas Ibar Dunne, joined them.

By 6.50 am a statement had been written out in Irish by Garda Fitzgerald. Breatnach signed it but not with his usual signature. He also misspelt his first name, writing it in the English fashion "Oscar" rather than in his normal Irish fashion "Osgur". The signature was witnessed by Garda Fitzgerald, Inspector John Murphy and Garda Dunne. All of them signed the Irish versions of their names at the end of it.

The statement inculpated Osgur Breatnach but did not name anyone else.

Brian McNally was still in the large interview room in the prison section. About 5.00 am two gardai that he had not met before came into the room, Inspector John Courtney and Sergeant Michael Canavan, both attached to the garda technical bureau. Two hours later Garda Grehan, back with McNally again, wrote out a statement outlining McNally's part in the robbery. It took until 8.10 am to complete it. McNally signed and it was witnessed by Garda Grehan and Inspector Courtney.

The statement named eight other people as taking part in the robbery as well as himself.

By then, however, McNally had been detained for more than forty eight hours. McNally was told that he was being released and was brought out of the prison section and let out the front door of the building. But Garda Grehan was waiting outside. He arrested McNally again under Section 30 of the Offences Against the State Act, brought him back inside and had him deposited in a cell.

John Fitzpatrick had been back in his cell for a time when he was taken out again. At 5.15 am Garda Frank Madden and Garda Gerard O'Carroll of the CDU took him upstairs in the garda station to a room used by inspectors. Some seventy five minutes later, a statement was being written out by Garda Jordan. It took until 8.15 am to complete it. Fitzpatrick signed and it was witnessed by Gardai John

76

Jordan and Francis Madden.

When typed up later the statement ran to just over two pages. There were no names in it but gaps had been left where names should have been. In the gaps there were the initials JF and JJ. The statement said that Fitzpatrick had been on the robbery.

Meanwhile, Nicky Kelly had left the Bridewell in a car. Before that, however, he had been told he was being released and was let out into Chancery Street, the street running in front of the Bridewell. Inspector Ryan was waiting outside and rearrested him.

Once inside the Bridewell again, arrangements were made for the trip to the area where the robbery had taken place. The three men who had witnessed Kelly's statement went with him. Sergeant McGroarty drove the unmarked garda car and Sergeant Cleary sat in the front passenger seat. Inspector Ryan was in the back with Kelly. On the way down the north quays they stopped at an all night chipper and Inspector Ryan bought some cigarettes and two large bottles of lemonade.

The car drove out the main western road, through Lucan and turned off for Celbridge. It turned sharp left at the village and continued on to the spot where the train had been halted and where the O'Tooles lived in their modern bungalow.

From there they drove to the village of Ballymore Eustace and along several roads, looking for a particular house. They did not find it and went back to Naas garda station. With a local garda they returned to the Ballymore Eustace area but did not find what they were looking for.

The three detectives and Kelly then travelled to Enniskerry and onto the main Dublin to Wexford road. Kelly directed them to a road off the main dual carriageway and through a gateway. There was a hole in the ground and there was nothing in it. It was almost mid morning by then and there were workmen in the area. They drove back to the Bridewell.

Meanwhile, Chief Superintendent Joy had arrived in the Bridewell around 8.30 am to take charge of the investigation again. There had been major developments in the case since he left the station about 11.30 pm the previous night. There were signed confessions from four suspects, Nicky Kelly, Osgur Breatnach, Brian McNally and John Fitzpatrick. Between two of the statements eight others – most of whom had been detained in the round-up – were also named.

The train robbery case appeared to have been broken. How the statements came to be made, however, was about to become the central issue, casting doubt over their veracity and leading to a protracted legal and political battle.

4

Courts: Wednesday, April 7th

Osgur Breatnach was the first of the four who had signed statements to see a solicitor. Efforts to get solicitors to some of the detainees had failed earlier because relatives and friends did not know where they were. Nicky Kelly's girlfriend, Nuala Dillon, had asked a solicitor, Pat McCartan, to see him on Monday evening. McCartan had been unable to find Kelly, however: he was detained in Arklow garda station. Several others were similarly unable to track down the movements between police stations of those arrested.

Garda Philip Bowe had come on duty at 6.00 am on Wednesday, April 7th. He was one of two uniformed gardai on the 6.00 am to 2.00 pm shift as gaolers in the prison section of the Bridewell. About 10.30 am he went around the cells collecting mugs and breakfast utensils. Breatnach asked him to call a solicitor for him and gave him three names, Pat McCartan, Ciaran Mac an Aili and Dudley Potter. Garda Bowe tried to call all three of them about 11.00 am; he could not get through or they were not in their offices. About an hour later, however, he got through to Dudley Potter, the third man on the list.

Potter knew Osgur Breatnach slightly. Several years earlier they had met in a case involving Breatnach and his brother-in-law. He had subsequently seen him when Breatnach worked as a porter in Westland Row railway station in Dublin. They had exchanged some remarks but had not spoken since then. Potter arrived down in the Bridewell about 12.40 pm and was brought into the prison section.

Osgur was brought down from his cell. On the way, his brother Caoilte shouted to him – they were in adjoining cells. Osgur called to him: "prepare yourself for the worst." Caoilte Breatnach was still being questioned about Michael Plunkett's alibi that he had been in Caoilte's house up to about 1.00 am on the morning of the robbery.

Dudley Potter thought Osgur was a changed person when he saw him. Breatnach was pale and shivering and appeared to be irritable and tired. He was not his usual confident self but looked like someone who had been taken down a few pegs. As they talked, Breatnach's attention seemed to wander and Potter had to bring him back to the point.

Breatnach told Potter that he had been beaten up and had signed a statement incriminating himself in order to stop the beating. He told Potter about his arrest and detention for forty eight hours the previous week and of his second arrest in the IRSP office on Monday, April 5th. Then he gave an account, noted in writing by Potter, of what had happened in the early hours of that morning. About 5.00 am or earlier Breatnach had been in his cell and had heard screams from under the cells. He was taken out of his cell and down to the tunnel leading from the Bridewell to the district courts. He was asked by gardai to account for his movements and had said he would when there was a solicitor present. They took off his leather jacket and the sports coat he was wearing under it and began to thump him. Breatnach said that at this stage he agreed to account for his movements and had told them he was in bed with his wife on the night of the robbery.

He said he was then taken into the Bridewell station and upstairs to a room next to the ladies'. There, he was beaten by the gardai, kicked, thumped and kneed. He was threatened and there were screams from a room next to him. The gardai said they had until about ten o'clock that night (Wednesday) to get a statement out of him. They fed him words and added bits as the statement was drafted, he said. The statement was forced out of him: he was beaten for two hours and was told that they would not stop unless he owned up.

Breatnach complained of being very sore on his left arm, near the shoulder. He said he had been slapped and thumped on the head and complained that he was dizzy. Potter asked him to take off his clothes and noted what marks he could see. On Breatnach's right leg there were two bruises, one below the knee cap and the other on the calf of his leg. There was a mark on his left arm and another on his right. There were some blood marks on his chest.

The interview with Potter was interrupted at 1.15 pm when a garda came into the room and said that Breatnach had to have his lunch. Breatnach said he did not want any lunch but the garda insisted that he had to go to his cell anyway during lunchtime. Potter pointed out that Breatnach would have to be released or charged with some offence by 1.30 pm. His forty eight hours in custody would be up by then. Potter then left the Bridewell temporarily.

Shortly afterwards, Osgur Breatnach was brought to the reception area and told that he was being released. He was given back his property that had been taken from him when he was brought into the Bridewell two days earlier. He was asked to sign a form acknowledging the return of the documents but he refused. The form was in English and a search warrant that he had had in his pocket from the IRSP headquarters was missing. Besides, he did not want to sign in case anyone noticed that his signature on the statement earlier was different. One of the gardai wrote in "ainm" and "data" over "name" and "date" on the form but he still refused to sign.

Breatnach was then shown out a back door to the Bridewell and he walked down a corridor. Sergeant Michael Egan of the CDU went down the corridor with him. Outside, Breatnach walked across the yardway to the end of the district court building where he knew there was a phone. It was locked. He walked out onto Chancery Street, turned left and saw a group of gardai on the path. He turned right and there were more detectives there. He thought about crossing the road and going into the back of the Four Courts. Sergeant Egan came over to him and arrested him again under Section 30 of the Offences Against the State Act.

It was the third time within a week that he had been arrested under the same section of the same law in connection with the same offence.

While he was being brought back into the Bridewell and returned to his cell, his solicitor Dudley Potter had been arranging with an Irish speaking barrister to represent him in court. Potter believed that Breatnach would be charged in the Special Criminal Court and the barrister, Andreas O'Keeffe, had gone to the court building in Green Street to await a hearing. He was told there was nothing happening there. Potter arrived back at the Bridewell about 1.40 pm and learned that Breatnach had been re-arrested.

In discussions among lawyers it was decided to go to the High Court and seek an order of *habeas corpus*. The *habeas corpus* procedure was one of the oldest in law, dating back to the *magna carta* of 1215, and was one of the main guarantees against arbitrary arrest and detention. An order required the police literally to produce the body of the person in question and to justify to the courts why he or she was in detention. Patrick MacEntee, a senior counsel and leading criminal lawyer was also involved in the case by then. He telephoned Dublin Castle and spoke to one of the senior officers involved in the train robbery investigation. Unless Osgur Breatnach was charged or released, he told them, he would be seeking a *habeas corpus* order in the High Court.

Breatnach was neither charged nor released. The order was sought from Mr Justice Liam Hamilton in the High Court and granted about 3.30 pm. The judge ordered that Breatnach was to be produced before him at 5.00 pm when the gardai would have to explain his continued detention. The order named two gardai as the defendants in the case, Sergeant William Fennessy of the Bridewell garda station and Superintendent Patrick Casey.

Just before the hearing was due, Breatnach was taken from his Bridewell cell again and handcuffed to Garda Thomas Fitzgerald, one of the detectives who had interviewed him earlier that morning. They walked together across to the Four Courts. The hearing did not go ahead immediately, however. When the High Court sat there were no lawyers present to represent the gardai. Mr Justice Hamilton expressed his annoyance and ordered a brief adjournment to allow them time to contact the chief state solicitor's office.

As the gardai telephoned the offices of the Attorney General and the Director of Public Prosecutions seeking legal help, Breatnach was examined for the first time by a doctor. Doctor Noel Smith was a general practitioner in Dun Laoghaire and had been the family doctor to Breatnach's family for some time. He knew Osgur Breatnach but had stopped being his GP when Osgur got married and moved away from the area.

Dr Smith was in the middle of his surgery about 3.30 that Wednesday afternoon when Osgur's father, Deasun Breatnach, phoned. Would Dr Smith go into the Bridewell and examine Osgur? he asked. Osgur had been beaten up, he added. Dr. Smith said he would do his best to get in as quickly as he could. As he travelled in he was under the impression that Osgur had been beaten up in a street fight and that, perhaps, somebody was being charged with assault. He finally saw Osgur in the Four Courts and examined him in a room there. Two detectives refused to leave him alone with Breatnach.

Dr Smith noticed that Breatnach had walked up the stairs very slowly and with a pronounced limp. He appeared to him to be in severe pain. He began his examination by asking a series of questions. Did Breatnach know where he was? In a police barracks. Did he know what day it was? Monday, no Tuesday, maybe Wednesday he replied. Dr. Smith wrote down the date as 7/4/75 and asked if it was correct. Breatnach said it was. Dr Smith asked him to look at it again: Breatnach said it was correct. The correct date was 1976.

Dr Smith asked him his name and Osgur told him. Dr. Smith wrote it down as "Oscar Breatnach" and asked him if it was his name. He said it was correct. Dr Smith spelled it out for him and asked him again if that was right. Breatnach said it was. Dr Smith knew it was not and he knew from past experience that Breatnach was very particular about using the Irish spelling of his first name, Osgur.

Dr Smith asked what he was complaining of and Breatnach told him he had severe headaches and pains all over his body. The doctor asked what happened. Breatnach whispered: I was beaten up. The doctor asked why was he whispering. Breatnach said they would beat him up again tonight if he said anything. The doctor asked who beat him up. Breatnach pointed to the two detectives who were watching the examination.

Dr Smith then examined him physically. Breatnach's head and scalp were painful to the touch and there was a swelling on the top rear part of his head which seemed to be painful and tender. The top lower third of his left leg had bruises and he had bruises and contusions on the back of his right leg. There were contusions – which Dr Smith defined as preliminary to bruises showing – on the buttocks. Breatnach had pains in his arms, legs, neck and back.

Dr Smith reached the conclusion that Breatnach was severely ill. Breatnach's head injuries and his confusion led him to conclude that he was suffering from concussion. He also concluded that the only way the injuries could have been inflicted was by physical violence, by punching, kicking or knocking around.

When the High Court hearing resumed shortly afterwards, Dudley Potter gave evidence of his first conversation with Breatnach that day and of Breatnach's three arrests under Section 30 of the Offences Against the State Act. Dr Smith also told the court of his findings and concluded: "He apparently has concussion which is a very dangerous medical condition and he should be at least in bed, preferably in hospital with an X-ray of the skull." Asked how the injuries might have occurred, he replied that it was difficult to be dogmatic but he thought that Breatnach had received blows, possibly kicks, on the back of the head.

MacEntee said that he was being kept in custody to make a further statement which would implicate other people. The gardai had no power or right to do that. Breatnach should be brought before a court and charged or he should be released. Mr Justice Hamilton made a conditional order of *habeas corpus* and the gardai undertook to take Breatnach to hospital and that he would not be interrogated overnight.

But the hearing was adjourned again to await a barrister representing the authorities and Breatnach had a discussion with his lawyers in the court. He was shivering and looked shattered and frightened. To Potter his condition seemed to have deteriorated since he had first seen him about five hours earlier. Patrick MacEntee was asking him questions and Breatnach appeared to have difficulty replying. Dermot Walsh, a solicitor from the chief state solicitor's office remarked to MacEntee that he should not ask Breatnach any more questions as it was obvious that he was not well. He should go to hospital as had been arranged, Walsh said.

Breatnach was taken off to the nearby Richmond Hospital in a police car and admitted to the casualty department. He was examined by the casualty officer, Dr. James Leitch, who found him to be pale and anxious but not in acute distress. Breatnach's speech was coherent and lucid. Dr Leitch found that his blood pressure, heart, lungs, abdomen and central nervous system were all normal. Breatnach appeared to be able to move his arms and legs normally although he complained of stiffness in them. Dr Leitch then examined the surface of his body.

He found a small bruise on the left hand side of the chest, a small bruise above the inside of the right ankle and a yellow, blackish bruise on the back of his right leg. There was a tender patch over the triceps tendon of the left arm – the muscle in the top half of the arm. Dr Leitch ordered X-rays of Breatnach's skull and chest, a urine analysis and had him put to bed in the casualty ward. Garda Fitzgerald was still with him but was later relieved by another detective. He was watched all the time he was in the hospital.

Back in the Four Courts, there was another hearing about the case. The gardai had finally got a barrister to represent them. Aidan Browne was a junior barrister who was one of two lawyers on call to act for the Attorney General at that time. He had been involved in the Irish Government's case which accused Britain before the European Court of Human Rights of torturing suspects rounded up for internment in Northern Ireland in 1971.

On behalf of the authorities, Browne made no attempt to defend Breatnach's third arrest. Browne told Mr Justice Hamilton that there was no objection to the *habeas corpus* order being made absolute. But, he added, it was proposed to arrest Breatnach and charge him with an offence. Mr

Justice Hamilton said that the gardai would not arrest him under section 30 of the Offences Against the State Act. Browne said he would be arrested under common law. The judge decided to put off his final judgement on the case until the following Friday on the understanding that Breatnach was left in hospital and would not be questioned further.

Breatnach remained in the Richmond Hospital for a further twenty four hours. He stayed under guard but, in accordance with the assurance given to the court, he was not interrogated again. Elsewhere, however, the interrogations had not been completed.

*   *   *

Michael Plunkett was back in the room in which he had been interrogated in Harcourt Street garda station. He was taken from his cell at 8.30 am, had washed his face and was brought by two detectives back to the room. They wanted him to account for his movements on the night of the train robbery all over again. Sergeant Edward Carey, the Special Branch detective who had heard his account originally and had gone to check it, returned.

He told Plunkett he did not believe his story. Plunkett's mother had told him that he was not at home on the night of the robbery, Sergeant Carey said. Plunkett explained that he had told his mother to tell any callers that he did not live there. He did not want her to be annoyed by the branch, he said.

The interview was interrupted by the arrival of Garda Thomas Ibar Dunne from the garda technical bureau. He was joined shortly afterwards by a colleague, Garda Christopher Godkin, who was also attached to the technical bureau. Plunkett denied any knowledge of the train robbery.

As the afternoon wore on, two detectives arrived with photostat copies of the statements made earlier that day by Nicky Kelly, Brian McNally, Osgur Breatnach and John Fitzpatrick. They were spread out on the table in front of him. Plunkett looked at them and thought to himself, oh shit. He was reassured, however, when he saw Osgur

86

Breatnach's signature: Plunkett knew it was written and spelt wrong. He believed all the documents were forgeries. "I don't care," he told the guards, "I wasn't there".

Meanwhile Nicky Kelly had arrived back in the Bridewell around 11.00 am after his trip with three detectives around the scene of the raid near Celbridge, Ballymore Eustace and Bray. After he was taken back to a cell, he lay down and dozed off. He was woken up again after five hours and taken downstairs. Three detectives, including Garda Michael Finn, were waiting for him. He thought he was being taken to court at first but was then told that he was going to see Michael Plunkett. Kelly did not know where he was taken.

Once in Harcourt Terrace garda station Kelly was brought into a room. There was one detective, Garda Godkin, there and Plunkett was sitting behind a table. Copies of the statements were strewn on the table. The three detectives who had brought Kelly to the station crowded in behind him. Kelly stood, across the table from Plunkett. Kelly was asked if that was his statement and his signature on it. He said nothing. A guard shouted at him to answer the question. Kelly said yes.

Kelly was taken out and put in another room. Later, he and Plunkett were taken out of the station and put into the back seat of a garda car. The doors were closed and they were left together for about twenty minutes. There were numerous gardai around the area. Plunkett was angry that Kelly had signed a statement and told him to pull himself together. Then, Plunkett was taken out and Kelly was driven back to the Bridewell.

At about the same time that Kelly was arriving for the confrontation with Plunkett, Sergeant Michael Canavan from the garda technical bureau was making a telephone call. He rang Conal O'Toole, the man whose house had been used by the train robbers, at his office in the Agricultural Credit Corporation. He asked O'Toole could he call around to Harcourt Terrace garda station: he wanted to ask him some questions. O'Toole agreed and arrived at the station about 6.00 pm.

Since the robbery O'Toole had had several interviews

with the gardai. He had given them descriptions of the men he had seen in his house immediately after they had arrived on the scene. He had spent some time on the day of the raid looking through 180 photographs. Inspector John Courtney and Sergeant Canavan had spread out the pictures on the dining room table, three rows of five pictures a time. Some were put aside for further examination and O'Toole picked out one: a picture of Michael Plunkett.

When he got to Harcourt Terrace now in response to the garda request, Sergeant Canavan told him they wanted him to do a formal identification parade. O'Toole refused and repeated his condition for co-operating: that he would not have to confront anybody. Canavan urged him to think again and argued that it would be very helpful to the gardai if he would do it. Canavan reassured him that there would be no reprisals or anything like that: the guards would look after him. O'Toole was still not convinced and, at one stage, phoned his wife to discuss the situation.

After two hours of discussion, O'Toole changed his mind. The main factor was the garda assertion that they already had confessions from several suspects. O'Toole agreed, in the belief that his testimony would not be the only important evidence against whoever was charged.

The identity parade was arranged and at 8.20 pm O'Toole was taken into the room. There were seven men on the parade, including Michael Plunkett who had chosen to stand near the centre of the line. Two of the men had full beards and moustaches and Plunkett had a moustache and several days growth of beard. They ranged in age from eighteen to twenty four and were of a similar height and build. O'Toole walked up and down in front of the line and paused before Plunkett each time. Then he walked over to the uniformed sergeant who was conducting the parade and told him he could not identify anyone positively.

O'Toole was taken out of the room and a second identity parade was set up. The suspect this time was Gerry Roche, the IRSP's national organiser, and the other person detained and interrogated in Harcourt Terrace garda station. There were ten men in the line-up and Roche decided to stand fourth from the left. All were of similar height and build and four had beards. O'Toole was shown in and he walked down the parade. He stopped in front of the ninth man, put his hand on his shoulder and said: "This is the man alright." The man was a nineteen year old student from County Kerry who was staying at a nearby university residence. He had been asked by the gardai to take part in the parade and had nothing whatever to do with the train robbery.

Roche was released shortly afterwards and O'Toole went back to the room where he had had his discussions with Sergeant Canavan. The gardai made no secret of their disappointment. They gave O'Toole a cup of tea and formal statements about the identification parades were written out, recording what had happened. When that was finished, O'Toole got up to leave and Sergeant Canavan went with him.

Meanwhile, Michael Plunkett had been told that he was being released. Sergeant Michael Egan of the CDU told him he was a free man. Plunkett was suspicious, however; he knew his forty eight hours were not up and the guards seemed in a hurry to hustle him out of the station. As they went out the door of the station Plunkett hung back and asked about the things that had been taken from him when he was arrested. The guards halted and brought him back into the public office.

As Conal O'Toole walked down a corridor with Sergeant Canavan, Plunkett and his escort crossed the corridor. "There is your man," O'Toole told Sergeant Canavan. The sergeant shouted: "Hold him !" Garda Michael Finn went into the public office after Plunkett and asked him to follow him out of the room. Back out in the corridor Garda Finn asked O'Toole if he had ever seen Plunkett before. O'Toole said yes, he could identify him. "That is the man who was in my house," he said. Plunkett said he was making a big mistake.

The guards were jubilant. Plunkett was brought to the door and told to go out. Inspector Ned Ryan was waiting outside and re-arrested him. Plunkett was put into a garda car and driven off to the Bridewell. "You fixed that one nicely," Plunkett complained. But, Sergeant Egan pointed out in delight, he himself had delayed leaving the station. The car drove on across the city.

*   *   *

The Bridewell was still the hub of the gardai activity. Nuala Dillon had been brought back into the station's teleprinter room in the early hours of the morning after seeing Nicky Kelly. She was questioned for a while by different gardai; someone told her at one stage that Nicky was taking them to the money. He asked it she could wait until they came back. She could see him then. She was in the room and the station voluntarily: she was not under arrest.

After a while the building appeared to her to get quiet and she tried but failed to sleep on a wooden bench. She thought she heard a shout or screams and she listened carefully. She heard someone shouting or screaming, obviously in pain. She opened the door to the room and saw a large number of gardai outside. She asked to be let out of there. Shortly afterwards, two detectives came and took her by car to Mountjoy garda station. She asked if she could go home to her flat nearby. They said they had to wait for Inspector Ryan to give them the word. The gardai seemed determined to stop her contacting anybody.

About 8.00 am they said she could go. She walked out of the station and was immediately arrested. A detective and ban garda stopped her on the building's steps and said she was being arrested under Section 30 of the Offences Against the State Act. She was taken back to the Bridewell, put in a cell and photographed.

Eleven hours later, about 7.00 pm, she was released from the Bridewell. Nobody had asked her anything.

Caoilte Breatnach was questioned for two periods during the day, with gardai challenging his statement that Michael Plunkett had been with him on the night of the robbery. During breaks in the questioning he saw Nicky Kelly and Brian McNally being led to cells and shouted to them. They did not respond. His brother, Osgur, had also increased his nervousness by warning him to prepare himself for the worst.

In the early evening he was taken from his cell downstairs to see a solicitor, Dudley Potter. They were in an interview room and there was a large number of gardai outside the door. Potter told him that his brother had been beaten up and suggested that he examine Caoilte. Breatnach took off his clothes to show there were no marks on his body. Potter asked the gardai to close the door and give them privacy. They did not. Potter walked out of the meeting in protest at their refusal.

Shortly afterwards, Caoilte Breatnach was released. He walked outside the Bridewell and joined an IRSP picket that was complaining about the arrests and, a new allegation, that party members had been beaten up. It was after 8.30 pm by then.

The garda officer in overall charge of the investigation, Chief Superintendent Joy, had spent the day evaluating the results of the round-up and deciding what to do. The four signed statements named eight others, some of whom were also in custody, as well as the people who had signed them. Those in custody were coming to the end of their forty eight hour period of detention and decisions had to be made about releasing them. Some were re-arrested again.

In general, the police were required to bring accused persons before a court as soon as practicable. It was obvious from the time that Chief Superintendent Joy arrived in the Bridewell at 8.30 that morning that the four men who had signed statements were going to be charged in connection with the robbery. Next door to the police station, the district courts sat all day until their usual time of 4.00 pm. None of the suspects was brought before a judge.

The gardai obviously hoped to have further breaks in the case. Nicky Kelly's journeys to the area of the robbery, to County Wicklow and to see Michael Plunkett were awaited to see what further information and potential evidence could be unearthed.

In addition, the gardai were anxious to charge everyone named in the statements in connection with the robbery, probably with conspiracy. Once charged, the suspects would be out of police hands and under the control of the court. They would be given bail or sent to prison to await trial.

Their plans were upset somewhat, however, by Osgur Breatnach's *habeas corpus* action in the High Court. After the initial order was presented to Sergeant William Fennessy and Superintendent Patrick Casey and they arrived in court, they were told forcibly by Mr Justice Hamilton that they needed legal assistance. An attempt was made to contact the Attorney General's office but it was after 5.00 pm and there was no one there who could help them.

Superintendent Casey then telephoned the office of the Director of Public Prosecutions and spoke to Michael Liddy, a senior legal assistant there. Liddy conferred with the DPP, Eamonn Barnes. The gardai were looking for advice about the *habeas corpus* proceedings which was not a matter for the DPP's office at all, as Osgur Breatnach had not been charged with anything. As it was still a police matter, it should have been handled by the Attorney General's office. But there was nobody there and the gardai needed help.

Barnes told Liddy to get on to someone from the chief state solicitor's office and Aidan Browne, the barrister who was on call for the Attorney General's office, was contacted. Later Barnes spoke to Superintendent Casey and asked if there had been any breakthrough in the case. The Superintendent told him the gardai had four written confessions, a verbal confession and an identification.

The gardai were eager to charge all of these and everyone else named in the statements. Barnes told them they could not do that. The statements would be admitted as evidence only against those who made them. For a conspiracy charge against the others to stick would require the people who named them to give evidence in court against those they had named. The gardai then framed the charges against five suspects – the four who had made statements and Michael Plunkett – and made arrangements for a special sitting of the district court.

Most others still detained were released. They included

Seamus Costello who had been re-arrested outside the Bridewell earlier in the day and taken to Rathmines garda station. He organised a press conference at the IRSP headquarters in Gardiner Street, bringing along other party members like Gerry Roche who had just been released from Harcourt Terrace garda station after the identification parade. Roche complained to journalists that he had been beaten and kicked and struck across the ears with a truncheon. He displayed a bruise on his ankle which he said was the result of a kick from a garda during interrogation.

Costello said that it was not possible to decide how many IRSP members had been held but seven appeared to be still "missing". Many of them had been beaten up while in custody in the Bridewell and in other garda stations, he said, and the party planned to take legal action over the brutality. The government, he said, was trying to smash his party.

As the press conference ended, six IRSP members emerged from the building, got into a van and drove away. Two of four detectives who were watching from across the road sprinted to their own car and set off in pursuit.

*   *   *

Inside the Bridewell, four of the people to be charged were meeting for the first time since their arrests. Nicky Kelly, Brian McNally and John Fitzpatrick were brought individually to a large room and left there together. The last to arrive was Michael Plunkett.

It was a strange reunion. Plunkett made most of the running. He was annoyed that Kelly and McNally had signed statements. He remarked on this to Fitzpatrick who reminded him that he, too, had signed a statement. Plunkett told the others that he would make a statement about them all being beaten up when they got into court. He intended to take off his clothes and show bruises to the court: he wanted the others to do the same.

They were taken out of the room and put back into cells. About 10.00 pm McNally and Fitzpatrick were ostensibly released: they were immediately re-arrested when they walked outside the building. Shortly afterwards, Inspector Ned Ryan charged all four of them with conspiring to commit armed robbery and with the armed robbery of £221,000, the property of the Minister for Posts and Telegraphs on March 31st 1976 at Kearneystown, County Kildare.

In reply to the formal charges, McNally replied, "that's all right". Kelly, Fitzpatrick and Plunkett said, in turn: "nothing to say." McNally and Kelly signed statements recording their response; the others refused to sign.

Inspector Ryan then took them down the steps to the underground tunnel that linked the Bridewell's prison section to the district courts. District Justice Riobard O hUadaigh had been contacted meanwhile and had agreed to conduct the special hearing. When the four accused emerged up the stairway that led from the tunnel into the court room they immediately changed their minds about making a protest.

As far as they could see there was nobody in the court except gardai, uniformed and in plainclothes. There were no lawyers present, nor were there any journalists. All four agreed immediately to abandon their protest plans: they felt there was no one to hear them.

There was a slight delay before District Justice O hUadaigh came out onto the bench. Inspector Ryan gave evidence on oath of arresting and charging the four men. Then he asked that they be remanded in custody until the following morning. Justice O hUadaigh asked for the names of the gardai in the Bridewell to whom he should remand them in custody. There was a brief delay while someone went out to get the names of two sergeants. The judge then remanded the four in custody to the Bridewell prison until the following morning.

The remand to the Bridewell was an unusual procedure. People charged with offences and kept in custody were normally sent to Mountjoy prison. On arrival in the prison they were normally examined by a doctor shortly after they were checked in. Mountjoy also received prisoners late at night. In this case, however, the four were sent back to the Bridewell for the night. Inspector Ryan later denied that he had asked that they be held in the Bridewell. Justice O hUadaigh could not remember who had initiated the procedure. District justices had power to remand people in the custody of named policemen but it was a procedure used, and expected to be used, in rural areas where it was not practicable to transfer a person to prison at night. It was not normally used in Dublin.

The four prisoners were taken back through the tunnel to the prison section of the Bridewell. Michael Plunkett and Nicky Kelly asked if they could contact lawyers and they were allowed to make phone calls. Plunkett called a solicitor, Garret Sheehan; Kelly called Nuala Dillon and asked her to arrange a solicitor for him.

To their surprise the prisoners were then asked which of them wanted to share cells. Plunkett and Kelly were put together in one cell: McNally and Fitzpatrick were put in another. Most of them spent the night uneasily, apprehensive that there might be more interrogations.

The arrangement to put them in cells together was contrary to the rules of the Bridewell prison which provided that prisoners accused of the same offence should not be accommodated together.

The night passed off quietly, however. The four prisoners were not disturbed. Not far away, in the Richmond Hospital, Osgur Breatnach was not sleeping well.

5

Doctors: Thursday, April 8th

In the Richmond Hospital, Osgur Breatnach woke quite early on that Thursday morning after a less than satisfactory night's sleep. The hospital staff decided that he was fit and well enough to be discharged. One of the nurses telephoned Dudley Potter and told him that Breatnach was fit to be discharged. Inspector Frank Hanlon who was in the hospital came on the line and confirmed what the nurse said. Potter said that an application might have to be made to the High Court and he would get back to him later.

Meanwhile in the Bridewell, the four prisoners there were given breakfast of tea, bread and jam. Brian McNally took another of his tablets and it helped calm him down. He was still feeling tense, however, and his body was stiff and sore. He was careful to move about his cell slowly: he didn't want to aggravate his discomfort. John Fitzpatrick, his cellmate for the night, was also complaining. His ears were giving him a lot of trouble.

In another cell nearby, Nicky Kelly and Michael Plunkett were also being roused and served their breakfast. The two of them had discussed what they might do when they were brought back into court later that morning. Plunkett again wanted them all to strip off their clothes, let everyone see the bruises on their bodies and they could shout accusations about the gardai at the same time. The press would be present this time and there would be people, friends, in the public gallery. When they all met up before going to the court, it was agreed that Plunkett would act for them and that he alone would protest.

Before they went to the court, they had a brief meeting with a barrister, Tony Sammon. Plunkett said they planned to do something in court, show bruises and make allegations.

The guards in the Bridewell told them they could have a wash if they wanted before they were brought down into the

97

tunnel and across once more into the district court. They were led up the stairwell and into the centre of the district court as their names were called aloud by one of the guards in the court. The room was quite full. They could see friends in the public gallery: they acknowledged each other before District Justice Riobard O hUadaigh began the proceedings at 10.30 am.

The charges against the four were read out once more: conspiracy to commit armed robbery and the actual armed robbery of £221,000 from the mail train. Tony Sammon said that some of them needed "urgent medical attention", particularly McNally who he said was taking tablets. Plunkett became impatient and, because he believed that Sammon wasn't making his case strong enough, shouted at the judge that they all needed medical attention. Justice O hUadaigh told him to be quiet and said he could not address the court himself because he was legally represented. Plunkett persisted and eventually ripped open his shirt.

"This is one example of the injuries I have received", he said pointing to a large purple mark on the inside of his left arm. He shouted at O hUadaigh that all four of them had been beaten by the gardai over the past few days and needed medical attention. The Justice said he should make a complaint to the prison when he got there – there was nothing he could do about it now.

Sammon applied for bail but Inspector Ned Ryan opposed him. He said that garda enquiries were not yet complete and he believed that if the four were released, they would interfere with witnesses. He also said that other people were wanted for the crime and that none of the stolen money had been recovered yet. O hUadaigh said his reasons for opposing bail were nebulous. He granted bail but set the bond at £10,000 for each of them. They were taken away to Mountjoy Prison until they could arrange for someone to put up the bail money for them. Before they were removed, however, they spoke to their solicitor, Pat McCartan. He left them to go away and find independent doctors to examine them.

Dudley Potter meanwhile rang Patrick MacEntee, the senior counsel who represented Breatnach in the High

Court the previous day, and told him that the hospital appeared to want to discharge Breatnach. MacEntee advised that technically he was in the custody of the High Court and Mr Justice Hamilton might not take kindly to him being discharged without reference to the court. Potter telephoned Inspector Hanlon at the hospital and passed this on. He then got a message from Breatnach that he wanted to see his solicitor.

Potter got to the Richmond around 10.45 am and told Breatnach to undress in a small room just off the casualty ward: he wanted to examine him and note any marks on his body. There were five yellow marks on his chest and a few blotches of red as well. On his left arm there were two marks of yellow – one about an inch square. On the right arm, there were also some yellow marks. On the right leg there were a number of marks on the front and back. Breatnach also showed Potter his shirt: there were three buttons missing and his jumper also had some rips in it.

A minute or two after Potter had made his examination, he got a call from his office saying that Dermot Walsh had been on from the chief state solicitor's office to say that they had asked Dr Patrick Carey, the senior consultant surgeon at the Richmond, to examine Breatnach. Potter was told that if he wanted someone present he should make arrangements.

He immediately wrote a letter and had it hand delivered to Professor John Paul Lanigan at the Royal College of Surgeons. Both men agreed to examine him early in the afternoon.

Breatnach told the two of them about his period in garda custody and said that he had been forcibly photographed. He said that his arms were held and his head forced up by someone pulling on the back of his hair. He told them what had happened when he was taken into the tunnel between the Bridewell and the courts in the early hours of the previous morning. He said that he was sore all over: he had pains in his leg, arm, his back and head.

Carey and Lanigan examined his head and noticed no bruising around the face, scalp or neck. There was a tenderness however in one particular spot of his head and his left jaw was also sore. One of Breatnach's arms had a bruise at the top of the arm. There were two small bruises around his left shoulder blade and another near his left arm pit. There was further bruising on his back and a skin rash on part of his chest. His right leg had bruising on the calf muscle and on his shin. There was also a small bruise on the left ankle. There was nothing else which the doctors noted.

Carey then checked with the casualty department about Breatnach's condition when he was admitted the previous evening. He later recalled that he was told Breatnach had been acutely distressed, pale and anxious but that his speech was coherent. He was also told that X-rays had been taken of Breatnach's head and chest but there was no evidence of bone injury. Dr Carey concluded that Breatnach was not suffering from concussion, that any injuries he had were superficial and that he was fit to be discharged. Professor Lanigan agreed.

Potter met Dermot Walsh and Aidan Browne, the barrister working for the state solicitor's office, and they agreed it would be a good thing if Breatnach were to remain in hospital until noon the following day, Friday. But later in the afternoon Potter got a message that the hospital was going to discharge him. He immediately rang Professor Lanigan to get the results of his joint examination of Breatnach with Dr Carey. Lanigan said there were bruises on Osgur's body but he doubted if he had concussion. He saw no reason why he should be kept in hospital further and remarked that Mr Justice Hamilton was probably going out of his way to be fair by referring Breatnach to hospital.

Brian McNally, John Fitzpatrick, Nicky Kelly and Michael Plunkett had also spent part of the day undergoing medical examinations. They were admitted to Mountjoy jail shortly after 4.00 pm and were among twenty two prisoners taken to the prison doctor. The examination was a routine check carried out on all new inmates. Dr Paul McVeigh was standing in for the usual doctor, Dr Samuel Davis. McNally, Fitzpatrick, Kelly and Plunkett were taken with the others into a large room and formed a queue in front of a desk. Their names, addresses, ages were taken and their height was measured as well.

Dr McVeigh then examined Brian McNally. He told him to undress and McNally did so with a degree of difficulty: he was still sore and he had difficulty taking off his clothes. He told the doctor that his eye was sore as was the top of his head, his ribs, his hip, legs and one or two other parts of his body. Dr McVeigh made his examination and noted bruising on McNally's left shoulder, left thigh, right arm and wrist, behind both ears and on his lower abdomen. There was also a bruise at his left eye.

The examination of Nicky Kelly showed that he had extensive bruising on both his arms and on his right shoulder. Two thirds of both arms and of the shoulder were covered in bruises. Kelly also complained of a bad headache and of pains in both buttocks. Dr McVeigh gave him a painkiller tablet. Dr McVeigh also examined Fitzpatrick and Plunkett.

Elsewhere, other members of the IRSP who had been detained by the gardai were receiving medical examinations after their release from police custody. Sean Gallagher and Gerry Roche were examined by Dr Sean O'Cleirigh at the request of a party official, Ita Ni Cionnaith. Around the time that the other four were being examined in Mountjoy, Dr O'Cleirigh got a call from Pat McCartan asking if he would go to the prison to do an examination independent of the prison authorities. He agreed and went to Mountjoy. Another doctor, Dr David McGee, also agreed to go to the prison and examine his clients. Both doctors were members of a small panel who had agreed to examine people who had been in garda custody.

They got there around 7.00 pm and examined the four together in a room. Plunkett and Fitzpatrick were looked at first and then Dr O'Cleirigh began his examination of Brian McNally. He told the two doctors that while he was detained by the gardai he was hit with fists, open hands and had his hair pulled. He also said that he was beaten with a black jack, a short, thick leather strap. Dr O'Cleirigh found marks on his left shoulder – bruises and scratches over an area of about two inches by four inches. There were other marks just below his left buttock and on the back of his right thigh and right knee. McNally had some difficulty moving all his fingers and his left wrist was painful. He appeared to be sore and tender all over his body but especially around his lower ribs.

McNally's left eye was swollen and discoloured, the same as a black eye. There was also swelling and inflammation around his left ear. It was not until McNally arrived in Mountjoy that he saw how he looked: peering in a mirror on Friday for the first time since his arrest, he was taken aback by his own appearance. He appeared to Dr O'Cleirigh to be distressed and confused. Dr McGee watched as the examination was carried out. The next prisoner they examined, Nicky Kelly, was by far the most distressed of the four. Kelly struck Dr O'Cleirigh as being particularly stressed: Dr McGee thought he was distraught.

Kelly told them that the gardai had beaten him. He said he had been punched, had his ears slapped, his hair pulled and had been spread-eagled against a wall and knocked from behind. The injuries which Dr O'Cleirigh found were consistent, in his opinion, with Kelly's claim that he was beaten while in custody.

Three quarters of Kelly's left arm, from the tip of the shoulder down, was covered in bruises. He had similar bruising over two thirds of the area of his right arm. There was a large area of bruising, about six inches by six inches, on his back by his left shoulder: it was all bluish black in colour. There was a strip of bruising across the small of his back above both buttocks. It was about two inches wide and very dark blue, like the colour of slate. On the front of his left thigh, there were a couple of minor bruises, over an area about two inches by four inches. There were some similar minor bruises on his chest: one just below his breast bone, another near his left nipple.

Dr O'Cleirigh also found extensive bruising behind his left ear and on the ear itself. Kelly said that he had been slapped on his ears and there were light brown bruises behind his right ear. Dr McGee was struck by Kelly's demeanour: he was tensed up, his eyes moved rapidly about the room, which the doctor thought was a sign of strain, and he was quite giddy.

Meanwhile, in the Richmond Hospital, it had become clear that Osgur Breatnach would be discharged before the day was out: medical staff saw no reason why he should be detained for a second night as he was, in their opinion, fit and well enough to walk out. Dudley Potter telephoned Patrick MacEntee in the Four Courts and told him that Professor Lanigan believed Breatnach was medically fit. MacEntee suggested that a junior barrister, Andreas O'Keeffe, go with Potter to the hospital to speak to Breatnach. They did and advised Breathnach not to leave the hospital until they got back to him.

They returned to the Four Courts and MacEntee telephoned Mr Justice Hamilton. He told him that Breatnach was going to be discharged from the hospital and the sitting of the High Court which had been set for the following day to decide finally the *habeas corpus* action should perhaps be brought forward immediately. The judge agreed and said he would hold a special sitting of the court later that evening. He also got in touch with Aidan Browne, the barrister for the authorities, and told him of the new arrangement.

When the court was ready to sit, Potter telephoned Breatnach in the Richmond and told him to leave and come to the Four Courts. Breatnach by this stage was so anxious about his fate once he left the hospital that he had become slightly paranoid: he wondered for a while if the voice at the other end of the line was in fact Potter's or one of his garda interrogators trying to trick him into leaving. Convinced eventually that his lawyers did indeed want him to come to court, Breatnach walked out of the hospital. There to meet him among the gardai was Inspector Vincent McGrath of the Special Branch.

McGrath and his colleague on the investigation, Inspector Ned Ryan, had discussed what they would do with Breatnach and decided that if the High Court should make his *habeas corpus* order absolute – in effect releasing him from garda custody – they would immediately re-arrest him under common law. McGrath took Breatnach to a car and brought him to the Four Courts. Breatnach was brought into the Four Courts building from the judges' car

103

park off Chancery Street. He was escorted by at least six gardai who walked beside him. On the way down a corridor to the court, they passed Aidan Browne and some of the other lawyers involved in the case. Browne was shocked by Breatnach's appearance: he seemed somehow dehumanised, almost as though he was someone else. It reminded him of some of the people he had seen in Crumlin Road Prison in Belfast after having been interrogated for seven or eight days. Browne, who was working at the time on the Irish government's torture case against Britain, thought that Breatnach was as distressed and frightened as anyone he had ever seen.

Patrick MacEntee spoke with Inspector Ryan before they both went into court. Ryan agreed that if Breatnach was released by the High Court but immediately re-arrested by the gardai and brought before the district court to be charged, he would be remanded in custody to Mountjoy Prison and not back into the Bridewell. Thus he would be removed from the gardai and placed in the hands of the prison authorities.

The High Court appearance at 9.30 pm was little more than a formality. Browne made no attempt to argue against Mr Justice Hamilton making the *habeas corpus* order absolute. Breatnach was released.

He stayed at the back of the court after the judge and the court officials left. He sat there for a while chatting to his wife. Dudley Potter remained but at some distance. Breatnach was trying to explain to her why he was about to be arrested again, this time under a different law but with the same effect: he would not be coming home.

He walked from the court, left the Four Courts building by Chancery Place and was met by Inspectors Ryan and McGrath. Ryan put his hand on his shoulder and said that he was arresting him for conspiracy to commit armed robbery and for the robbery of the mail train on March 31st. They brought him over to the Bridewell but there was a slight delay before they could bring him down into the tunnel again and across to the district court. Breatnach demanded that he be charged in Irish and the written record of the charge had to be drafted in Irish. Andreas O'Keeffe helped them and shortly before midnight, Breatnach was taken before District Justice O hUadhaigh and remanded to Mountjoy Prison.

The one good thing about being in Mountjoy was that everyone was left alone for the night and did not have to face further interrogation by the gardai. The following day, Friday, March 9th, all five – Breatnach, McNally, Kelly, Fitzpatrick and Plunkett – were let out into the exercise yard and decided to put their names down on the list for medical examination by the regular prison doctor, Dr Samuel Davis. Eventually they were seen by him and, with a number of other prisoners, formed a queue to his surgery. As Dr Davis conducted his examination he dictated his findings to a prison officer who was helping him.

Dr Davis told McNally to strip off his clothes. He did and told the doctor about the soreness over his body and how he had sore ribs and a headache. Dr Davis found that he had a black left eye, superficial bruising of his upper left thigh and about four square inches of bruising on his right buttock. McNally's pubic region was tender and there was soreness around his scrotum. There was also bruising on his left shoulder which Dr Davis decided was superficial, as well as some superficial marks on his right calf. McNally also complained of blurring of vision.

Dr Davis gave McNally some tablets and wrapped some bandage around his chest because of his complaint about sore ribs. The examination lasted about fifteen minutes.

Nicky Kelly had more extensive injuries than McNally. Dr Davis found that he had extensive bruising on his left shoulder as well as on his upper left arm. There were a couple of superficial injuries to his chest and Kelly complained of tenderness in the area around his bladder. There was further bruising on both buttocks as well as behind his left ear.

Dr Davis also examined Osgur Breatnach. It was Breatnach's first examination since entering Mountjoy. It was too late when he was admitted to the prison shortly after midnight to have a medical examination. Breatnach had a three by two inch bruise on his left arm and he also complained of soreness on his right arm. There were marks on his right leg. Breatnach also complained of soreness around his spine, and his head and said that he had difficulty breathing. The doctor prescribed some pain killing tablets and told him to take a mild sedative at night before going to sleep. Examinations were also carried out on Fitzpatrick and Plunkett.

Micheal Plunkett once again became spokesman for the four and he went to one of the senior prison officers to discuss their position in the prison. He said that they wanted political status and that they would not do ordinary prison work nor wear prison clothes. These were the traditional demands made by republicans whenever they were sent to prison. He said that all four would set fire to their mattresses unles they were transferred to Portlaoise, the Republic's main security prison where all people convicted of politically motivated crimes were held.

Later that afternoon, all five were transferred to Portlaoise prison where they were subjected to yet another medical examination on admission. This time it was done by the regular doctor attached to the prison, Dr Richard Burke.

McNally told Dr Burke that he had difficulty breathing and that his left eye vision was blurred. Burke noticed a bruise near the left eye. McNally also complained of pains on both sides of his chest and there were bruises around his upper left thigh and left groin. He was given some pain relieving tablets. Nicky Kelly had bruising around his upper left arm and the same area on his right arm. Dr Burke also noticed that there were abrasions, slight breaks on the surface of the skin in both places. Kelly complained of having headaches and pains around his body. He too was given some pain killers. Osgur Breatnach had bruising on his upper left arm and some minor marks on his legs and there was some bruising behind his left ear. He had a bump on his head the size of a ten penny piece, which Dr Burke thought could have been the result of a blow from a blunt instrument. Breatnach complained of a headache, pains all over and of not being able to sleep.

The others, Plunkett and Fitzpatrick, were also examined by Dr Burke and all five went back to him a number of times over the succeeding few days but their bruises and most of the pains they felt cleared up. McNally was taken once to the Eye and Ear Hospital in Dublin for a check on the left eye which he had said was causing him trouble.

On Friday evening as McNally, Kelly, Breatnach, Plunkett and Fitzpatrick were settling into Portlaoise prison, the gardai were closing in on another of their suspects, one who had not been arrested in the initial swoops on Monday. Their target was Michael Barrett from Abbeyfeale in County Limerick who the night before had been with Seamus Costello when he called to the home in Bray of James and Elizabeth Murphy, friends of Seamus and Maoliossa Costello.

The Murphys were planning to go to the pictures when the Costellos and Barrett called. The visit delayed them and soon it was too late to go. When the Costellos had gone home after asking if Barrett could stay the night, the Murphys and Barrett went instead to the Harbour Bar in Bray. They stayed until closing time and, back in the Murphy's flat at Galtrim Park, Elizabeth Murphy made up a place on the couch for Barrett.

The following morning, John and Elizabeth Murphy went to work, leaving Barrett in the flat. Elizabeth worked at the local Quinnsworth supermarket. At midday, she came home to prepare some food for Barrett and again in the evening to get her husband's tea. He drove her back to work shortly after six. The gardai arrived in the flat at 7.30 pm.

The search party was led by Sergeant Edward Carey of the Special Branch. Costello was there when they called: they arrested him and took him away to Bray garda station. Barrett was arrested by Garda Bernard Cullen of the Special Branch and also taken to Bray. Later that evening he was transferred to the Bridewell but Costello was released.

Sometime before 8 pm Elizabeth Murphy's son, Pearse, rushed into the supermarket to say the house was full of gardai who were about to arrest Seamus Costello and Barrett. She immediately went back to the flat but they were both gone.

The gardai were particularly interested in Barrett because he was named in Fitzpatrick's alibi: Fitzpatrick had claimed that he was with him in Castleconnell in Limerick, on the night of the robbery and only heard about it later that day when they both drove to Dublin. The gardai asked Barrett to account for his movements on the night of the robbery to see if his version of events would tie in with Fitzpatrick's. It did but the gardai didn't believe him. He was detained for forty eight hours before he too was charged with robbing the mail train of £221,000. Like the others, Barrett was remanded in custody but was told that if he could get someone to vouch £10,000 bail for him, he would be released.

All six appeared in the district court on a series of occasions throughout April before they finally managed to raise their bail. Eventually the bail was reduced to £5,000 for some of them.They were remanded on bail until October when the case against them would be heard. Inspector Ryan told the district court that he wanted an extension of time to prepare the book of evidence against them.

There was a lot of work to be done.

6

Awaiting Trial

The IRSP was determined to fight the case in every way it could. Politically, Seamus Costello had set the headline within hours of his release when he accused the government of trying to smash his party. Further press conferences, demonstrations and other methods of publicising this accusation were undertaken. On the legal side, the six people accused prepared to fight the charges in the court. But on that front, as well, Costello had promised that civil actions would be taken against the gardai on the grounds of brutality.

Others in the organisation wanted to retaliate in kind. They proposed that members of the gardai should be attacked in a co-ordinated operation that would demonstrate their ability to hit back. They argued that the IRSP and the INLA had to be seen to be able to defend their members. They were overruled, however, and it was decided to concentrate their response on politics and the law.

Action on both political and legal fronts began within two weeks of the first, late night appearances in the district court. The Association for Legal Justice was a group of left wing and republican lawyers formed in Belfast in the late 1960s and had a branch in Dublin under the chairmanship of a barrister, Anthony Walsh. Costello asked the ALJ and a solicitor associated with it, Donal V Carroll, to initiate court proceedings against the gardai on behalf of nine members of the IRSP.

Announcing the action at a press conference on April 20th, 1976, Costello said that IRSP members in all parts of the country had been subjected to harassment since the party's formation. "The most common form of harassment to date has been the raiding and searching of members' homes," he said. He added that twenty six IRSP members had been ill-treated, physically and psychologically, during the arrests over the train robbery. Ill-treatment included lack of sleep and food, continual beatings, threats against prisoners' families, death threats and offers of deals if members became informers. The results of the beatings were people with bruises on their backs, legs, arms, stomachs and heads, partial loss of hearing and, in one case, damaged vision, he said.

The gardai themselves conducted a perfunctory internal inquiry into the allegations of illtreatment made by the IRSP. A questionnaire was given to gardai who had been on duty in the Bridewell when the mail train robbery suspects were being interrogated. It asked individual members if they beat anyone up, saw or heard anything unusual. All replied in the negative.

The Association for Legal Justice took statements from all those who said they were beaten up in police custody in preparation for their court actions. John Fitzpatrick told in his statement of two men being brought to his cell in the Bridewell on the afternoon of his second day in custody, Tuesday April 6th. The detectives who brought them into his cell told him they were members of the crew of the train that was robbed. One of the "crew" asked him where he was from. When Fitzpatrick replied Armagh, the man said "Northern bastard", grabbed him by the throat, pushed him against a wall and threw him across a bed. The "crew" members beat him up with the detectives looking on. Eventually, they all left.

Fitzpatrick maintained that he was severely beaten up in the early hours of the following morning, Wednesday, April 7th. He said he had been put back in his cell after a period of questioning when he heard screaming and a belt or strap hitting a wall. Shortly afterwards his cell door burst open and he was taken to a room in another part of the building.

He said he was grabbed by several men who lifted him up and pulled off his shoes and his jacket. They put him down again in the middle of the room and walked around him. One detective jammed the heel of his shoe into Fitzpatrick's foot. He was kicked, punched and thrown to the ground. One detective held him to the ground with his foot on the side of Fitzpatrick's face. There were shouts of "tell the truth". He lost consciousness.

He said that when he came to he was sitting on a chair. He was slapped on the face and smacked on both ears simultaneously with open hands. A detective lifted him off the ground by his locks and another smacked him over the ears as he was dropped. Blood began to ooze from his right ear. His hands were handcuffed behind his back, he was thrown to the ground and his feet pulled between his manacled hands. He was beaten again.

One detective, he said, had been sitting at the table in the room writing. He, Fitzpatrick, was put sitting up and a statement was put in front of him. He was told to fill in the blank spaces which were left for names and to sign it. The two detectives whom he said had beaten him left and he was with the man who wrote the statement. He refused to sign it and the others came back. He was beaten again.

He could see the dawn coming up through the window at this stage. He felt wrecked and sore, had difficulty hearing and his sense of balance was disturbed. He agreed to sign the statement but he would not fill in the blanks, he said. He signed and the beatings stopped. He asked about the blank spaces that were left in the document: how did he know the gardai would not write in names? He was told to put his initials in the spaces. The final statement produced as evidence by the prosecution showed a statement with gaps. They were filled by the initials of John Fitzpatrick and of the detective who wrote the statement, Garda John Jordan.

Michael Plunkett had a similar story of brutality. On the second day of his detention in Harcourt Terrace garda station, he was being challenged on his alibi by Sergeant Edward Carey. The door burst open, another detective came in and Sergeant Carey left. The detective pulled the chair from under Plunkett, stood him against a wall and slapped him across the face. The detective began hitting him on the upper part of his arms with his fist, slapping him and throwing him to the floor. While he was on the floor on one occasion a uniformed garda walked in with a tray, carrying his breakfast.

The detective put him sitting at the table and told him to eat his breakfast. It was a boiled egg and toast. Plunkett's

111

hands were shaking and he wondered how he would eat the egg without dribbling. He took his time and managed it. After breakfast, the detective moved the table away and started again. He jabbed Plunkett in the stomach with his fingers, and punched him in the upper arms which were by now sore. Plunkett asked how the detective was going to account for the bruises. That provoked more violence: he was thrown to the ground and kicked.

A second detective came into the room. They both demanded that he tell the truth and kept repeating bits of information. Costello was the general and Plunkett led the gang into O'Toole's house. How did he, Plunkett, feel when he was swinging the lamp to stop the train? Plunkett stopped talking and stared at a wall. One detective said: "He's mad". The other asked if he wanted a psychiatrist.

Then they pushed him from one to the other. Several times he fell to the floor and one detective laughed: he must think he was Jesse James, robbing trains all the time. They held his arms and forced his head down to the ground and straightened him up again. That continued until he was out of breath. Then, one grabbed him around the neck and the other lifted up his legs. They held him up and then dropped him to the floor. They did that again and again.

At one stage when he had dropped on the floor, he noticed a ring had fallen off one of the detective's fingers. The detective was unaware of the loss. Plunkett picked it up and handed it to him. The detective muttered, "Oh thanks". Everything stopped for a brief moment as the ring was handed back and the detective put it on his finger. Then they started again. They lifted Plunkett up by the neck and the legs and dropped him to the floor.

The guards told him that prisoners beat themselves up in order to discredit the police. At one stage, Plunkett almost fell against a radiator but was saved from hitting his head off it by one of the detectives. While he was staring at the wall, one detective said to him: "Go on, take a run at the radiator."

The beatings stopped suddenly when two other detectives came in, according to Plunkett's account of what had happened to him.

The garda accounts of the interrogations of both John Fitzpatrick and Michael Plunkett were totally different. They denied that there was any ill-treatment.

In statements prepared for the book of evidence against all the accused, the gardai gave their account. Garda John Jordan of the Special Branch said he saw Fitzpatrick for the first time in a room in the Bridewell at 5.50 am on the morning of Wednesday, April 7th. Fitzpatrick was sitting talking to two other detectives who then left the room. Garda Jordan asked Fitzpatrick if he wanted a cup of tea. He said he did and Garda Jordan got it for him. Garda Jordan had been told that Fitzpatrick had asked for time to think about his position. He asked Fitzpatrick if he had decided to tell the truth. Fitzpatrick made no reply at first but, after some minutes, said: "I am prepared to tell the truth about my part in the train robbery but I will not name anyone in my statements."

According to Garda Jordan, Fitzpatrick then gave him a verbal account of the robbery which named five other men. Garda Jordan said there were more men on the job than he had named. Fitzpatrick then listed twelve names. Another detective came in and Garda Jordan said he began to write down what Fitzpatrick was saying. Fitzpatrick again named the other men he had mentioned but said it would be more than his life was worth to name them in his written statements.

Garda Jordan read over the statement to him and invited him to make any alterations he wanted. Fitzpatrick said it was correct and that was all he could tell the gardai about the case. Fitzpatrick then signed the statement and initialled each page and all alterations.

As the two detectives got up to leave the room, Fitzpatrick said to them: "I have made a right shite of myself, would one of you go out and get a gun and leave me alone for a few minutes." The second detective said it was not the end of the world. Fitzpatrick said his only chance was to fight that statement and say it was made under duress. According to the guards, he added that Costello was a right bastard and if he thought Costello's fingerprints were still on the guns he would take a chance and tell the guards where they were.

Garda Jordan said, in his account, that the two detectives then left the room, leaving Fitzpatrick alone.

In compiling the case against Michael Plunkett, Garda Thomas Ibar Dunne prepared his account of an interview he had with Plunkett on the morning of Wednesday, April 7th. He replaced Sergeant Edward Carey and asked Plunkett to tell the truth. Plunkett said that if he got upset he could injure himself, he would bang his head off the wall or jump through the window. Garda Christopher Godkin, one of Garda Dunne's colleagues from the technical bureau, entered the room. Plunkett told them that some of the lads in the North had obtained thousands from the "Brits" in compensation. They had injured themselves by ramming their heads against walls and using furniture or anything lying around to mark themselves. They then accused the police of assaulting them.

Garda Godkin told him that trick would not work here. Plunkett said he could jump out the window. He then jumped from the armchair he was sitting on and ran towards the wall with his head down. The two gardai held him by the arms and stopped him from injuring himself. Plunkett was very excited and kept shouting: "Let me go, let me go." Garda Godkin gave him a glass of water and asked him if he would like to see a doctor. He declined. Then they had a general conversation with Plunkett and discussed the IRSP's politics.

Overall, the preparation of the prosecution's case was moving very slowly. It would transpire later that the gardai had all the evidence they were going to produce by the end of April. But they were still unhappy that they could not charge all of those named in the statements signed by four of the accused men.

Their enthusiasm for charging all of those named with conspiracy was echoed in the Department of Justice. One of its lawyers, Richard Hayes, believed that charges could be sustained by the DPP and had told Patrick Cooney, the Justice Minister, that they could be charged on the basis of admissible hearsay. Hayes suggested that statements made which were part of a conspiracy to commit a crime could be used against people who were named by their colleagues. The gardai were pressing to have everyone charged who was in the confessions which they had from McNally and Kelly: they were venting their frustration with the DPP on the Department.

Cooney sought guidance from the Attorney General, Declan Costello, but he was out of the country. The query was dealt with by one of Costello's senior advisors, Declan Quigley, who got onto the DPP's office. He and Eamonn Barnes discussed the relevant laws and Quigley accepted that the DPP's interpretation was correct. Admissible hearsay applied only to conversations in which a crime was being planned and did not cover statements after the crime had been committed.

Statements could only be used as evidence against those who made them, not those named in them. For their contents to be used against someone else, the person who made them would have to go into the witness box and repeat the accusations. The accused persons in this case would have to become witnesses for the prosecution.

Individual gardai at the lower levels of the force believed Barnes was running scared of the IRSP. They thought that a golden opportunity to put away people whom they believed to be guilty of crimes was being missed. Barnes stood his ground, however. Four people were charged on the basis of the statements, one on an identification and a sixth because of his connections with one of the four.

The preparations for the case moved very slowly on the prosecution side, however. The garda file on the case – which would include statements of all the evidence – did not arrive in the DPP's office for months after the charges. The reason was simple. The gardai had to prove the money was stolen. Because the accused were charged under a particular section of the Larceny Act, they felt they had to indicate from whom it was stolen.

The sacks of registered mail were made up of scores of packets sent through dozens of post offices in Counties Cork and Kerry. To prove that all the money was stolen would require evidence about every single packet that was on the train. That would mean, in turn, calling as witnesses dozens of post mistresses and post office clerks, the people who collected the packages and the people who put them on the train. The end result promised to be a huge book of evidence – the copies of all the evidence served on an accused person – and a trial that spent weeks just hearing this formal evidence.

By October 1976, when the long summer adjournment of the case was over, the prosecution's preparations were little further advanced. District Justice O hUadaigh granted a further remand until December 9th at the request of the prosecution. But he made it clear that his patience was wearing thin.

The delay was not caused solely by the enormous task of proving the movement of all the money that was stolen. Eamonn Barnes was somewhat uneasy about the case: there appeared to be some holes in the evidence and there was the question of John Fitzpatrick's and Michael Barrett's alibis. In addition, there were the claims of ill-treatment by the IRSP and their political campaign against the prosecutions. Brutality by the police was becoming a matter of growing concern in the autumn of 1976. Barnes was not a hundred per cent convinced that the prosecution should go ahead at all.

After the October hearing of the district court, Justice O hUadaigh telephoned Barnes and told him about his concern at the delays in proceeding. Barnes replied that the problem was not just with the book of evidence: he was undecided about pressing the charges.

When the case came up again on December 9th 1976, the solicitor acting for the DPP asked for another adjournment. He requested a remand for at least six weeks. Justice O hUadaigh indicated that he expected the book of evidence to be served by that day. It was in the interests of justice that a definite date be given, he said. He then adjourned the hearing until the afternoon to allow the solicitor to consult with the DPP's office.

When the hearing resumed, the prosecuting solicitor said that his instructions now were to apply for a remand of a couple of months. Tony Sammon, the barrister for the six accused, replied that he was asking the court for a

116

discharge. Justice O hUadaigh said he was surprised that the DPP could not answer a reasonable question from the court. In the interests of justice and of the accused, Justice O hUadaigh said he would discharge the defendants.

There was a burst of applause from the public benches in the court. Justice O hUadaigh cut it short by snapping: "cut that out". The jubilation would be short-lived, however.

Some of the defence lawyers thought that that was the end of the case. Eight months after the widespread arrests and the first court hearing, they still did not know the full extent of the evidence against their clients. They knew, of course, that statements made in custody were the main evidence but they did not know, for instance, what forensic material was available to the gardai. Until they received the book of evidence they could not know for certain the extent of the prosecution case. When the DPP failed again to produce the book it appeared that this was one way of dropping the prosecution simply by default.

As they walked from the court, at least one of the accused believed their reprieve would not last long. John Fitzpatrick decided that he was not going to wait around to be arrested again: he was going on the run immediately. Nicky Kelly was talking to him as they walked out through the gates of the Bridewell yard and of the court. Fitzpatrick cut him short and said he didn't want to see him again. Kelly looked surprised and Fitzpatrick explained. Kelly turned away and walked off but came running back a moment later. He needed to borrow the bus fare from Fitzpatrick.

Fitzpatrick's instinct was correct. The DPP was still considering the case and called a conference of all the senior gardai involved in it. Led by Chief Superintendent John Joy, more than twelve of them gathered in Barnes' top floor office in St Stephen's Green. Barnes brought them over all the evidence again, the signed statements, the identifications, the alibis. The gardai denied that there had been any oppression in getting the statements signed. There were no doubts among the group of gardai that these men were guilty.

In the end, Barnes was left with making the decision. One

117

of his main concerns was the case of John Fitzpatrick who appeared to have a reasonably solid alibi for the night of the robbery. He claimed to have been in Limerick with Michael Barrett and staying in the home of a friend, Tom Hayes. His story was confirmed by Hayes and other members of his family. In addition, Fitzpatrick and Barrett were seen in Limerick by a local detective on the evening before the robbery.

The gardai believed, however, that Barrett and Fitzpatrick could still have committed the robbery. They had enough time to pretend to go to bed in Hayes' house in St Patrick's Villas in Castleconnell about 11.30 pm and still drive to Hazelhatch in County Kildare and rob the train at 3.00 am. Fitzpatrick and Barrett could then have returned to Limerick, slept for a few hours and driven back to Dublin on the afternoon of the next day.

The gardai carried out their own tests to prove that it was possible. A car was timed travelling from Castleconnell on the Dublin side of Limerick, to the scene of the robbery and back to Castleconnell. It was possible for someone to pretend to go to bed at 11.30 pm, to rob a train in County Kildare at 3.00 am and be back in Limerick by breakfast time.

The DPP, however, was not absolutely persuaded that that was what had happened. The alibi was central not alone to Fitzpatrick's case but to the other accused men as well. Nicky Kelly and Brian McNally both named Fitzpatrick as being present at the robbery in the statements they signed. If his alibi was proven to be correct, then the statements signed by Kelly and McNally could not be correct. The case against Osgur Breatnach and Michael Plunkett would also be undermined. Breatnach had not named any other person, and Plunkett had not made any statement. But both were named as being present in McNally's and Kelly's statements. If their statements were proven to be wrong about one individual, how could they be accepted as being right about another individual?

What was at issue was the facts of the case – particularly of Fitzpatrick's alibi – and the DPP decided to let all the evidence go to court. The courts would have to decide whether or not they would accept Fitzpatrick's alibi. Since there was no substantial evidence against the sixth man in the case, Michael Barrett, the DPP decided that he should not be charged again. He issued instructions that the other five, McNally, Kelly, Breatnach, Plunkett and Fitzpatrick be charged.

Eight days after the discharge by the district court, the gardai swooped. Brian McNally, Nicky Kelly, Osgur Breatnach and Michael Plunkett were arrested once again. The gardai found no trace of John Fitzpatrick.

Later the same day, December 17th 1976, the four arrested were brought before the Special Criminal Court in Dublin's Green Street. They faced new charges which no longer specified the amount stolen from the mail train. Therefore, the prosecution did not have to prove where each individual packet of money had come from. The four faced two charges under Section 12 of the 1916 Larceny Act. Each was accused of stopping the train with intent to rob mail and of stealing mail bags from John Joseph Cotter, the post office supervisor on the train.

When charged before the court's three judges, Nicky Kelly replied that he did not want to say anything. Brian McNally said he was not guilty. Osgur Breatnach and Michael Plunkett said they were innocent. Breatnach wanted the hearing conducted in Irish and an interpreter was introduced to translate.

The court heard evidence of the arrests of the four earlier that day. The prosecution and the defence argued about delays in the production of the book of evidence. Plunkett said from the dock that he was quite happy to face the charges, as he believed there was a state conspiracy against them. He was completely innocent of the charges, he said.

The court eventually fixed a date for the hearing in January and set bail for the four. Each had to produce a £500 bond for himself and a £5,000 bond from someone else. The court promised that the trial would probably be held the following May. Everything appeared to be on course for a reasonably early hearing. As events turned out, however, there would be a full year before the trial in the Special Criminal Court.

*   *   *

119

The twenty one months between the robbery of the mail train on March 31st, 1976 and the opening of the trial on January 19th, 1978 were politically eventful.

The initial defensiveness of the government and of the Justice Minister, Patrick Cooney, at the level of armed crime in March 1976 gave way to some satisfaction with the charging of six people for the mail train robbery. In a debate in the Dail on May 5th, 1976 Cooney shrugged off Opposition concerns about the crime rate. "There was an unfortunate rash of robberies some weeks ago," he noted, "but I am precluded, happily, from commenting on them because the vast majority are *sub judice*. They are *sub judice* because we have an active, intelligent, dedicated, loyal police force whose morale is of the highest."

Cooney maintained that the arrests and charges had more than restored public confidence in the gardai. But allegations of police ill treatment of suspects were beginning to gain currency. They were coming from the IRSP and the fringes of Provisional Sinn Fein. They were also beginning to come from independent lawyers who were dealing with more and more cases in which ill treatment was a factor. The allegations were to grow and grow in the following months.

The morale of the gardai and of the government was severely shaken during those months as well. On July 15th, five men blasted their way out of the Special Criminal Court with two sets of explosives which cleared a way from the cells beneath the building to Green Street outside it. Four were recaptured in chases through adjoining streets but one, Michael O'Rourke, managed to get away to the United States. He was deported from there in 1984 as an illegal immigrant.

Six days later, the newly arrived British Ambassador to the Republic, Christopher Ewart-Biggs, was assassinated by the IRA near his official residence at Sandyford in County Dublin. A bomb was planted in a drain under the road that ran by his house and which he had to travel every day. The vehicle was thrown into the air and came down on its left hand side into a crater made by the blast. Ewart-Biggs and a British civil servant, Judith Cooke, who were

120

on that side of the car, were killed.

Cooney and his cabinet colleagues were shocked and outraged. Ewart-Biggs had been scheduled to meet Cooney on the day of his death as part of the normal round of courtesy calls that new ambassadors paid to ministers. Next to the murder of his friend Billy Fox, the assassination affected him most during his term of office.

The murder of an official representative of a friendly government was seen by the cabinet as a major escalation in the IRA's campaign. The coalition was determined not to let it pass without a response. It recalled the Dail to put to it a motion declaring that a state of emergency existed which affected the vital interests of the state. It arose out of the conflict taking place in Northern Ireland. The motion was necessary to implement part of the government's response – an Emergency Powers Bill which would give the police the power to detain suspects without charge for up to seven days. Once an emergency was formally declared, the constitution could not be used to prevent the passage of the Bill.

The Taoiseach, Liam Cosgrave, based the need for the new measures on two events: the murder of the Ambassador and the explosions at the Special Criminal Court.

"The murder of the British Ambassador struck at the conduct of our international relations while the explosions at Green Street struck firmly at the administration of justice," he told the Dail. "The challenge thus posed called for an unequivocal response."

Giving the gardai the power to detain people for up to seven days was by far the most significant single measure taken by the government and the one which required the formal declaration of an emergency.The gardai had been seeking something like that for some time. They argued that longer detention periods would give them greater time to check alibis and prevent suspects from hindering their inquiries with other people. Although the gardai had the power to hold people for up to forty eight hours without charging them, they believed they needed more time to question them before deciding to release or charge them.

Opponents of the new measure maintained that that was precisely what worried them. Interrogations were becoming an increasingly important part of the police response to the activities of the IRA and other paramilitary groups. It was often difficult to find other evidence and confessions were often the simplest and most water-tight methods of solving crimes. Forensic assistance available to the gardai, apart from finger printing and ballistics, was not as fully developed at that stage as it might have been.

The Emergency Powers Bill was also seen by some gardai as an endorsement for more vigorous methods of interrogation. It gave them an extremely valuable psychological tool in carrying out questioning. Anyone held under the Bill's provision knew that he or she could be held for a week, more or less at the mercy of their interrogators. That, in itself, could be a considerable pressure. In a growing number of cases there was evidence of physical pressures as well.

Bringing the new powers into force generated its own controversy. The declaration of emergency was passed by the Dail on September 1st, 1976 and was followed on September 16th by the passage of the Emergency Powers Bill. On September 24th, President Cearbhall O Dalaigh intervened and decided to send it to the Supreme Court before he signed it into law. Using one of the presidency's few independent powers, he asked the Supreme Court to decide if the Bill was contrary to any part of the Constitution.

But the emergency powers came into force after the Supreme Court had ruled that the Bill was constitutional. Shortly afterwards, another event appeared to be a possible escalation of paramilitary activity in the South. Garda Michael Clerkin was one of a group of gardai who went to investigate a house near Portlaoise after an anonymous telephone caller reported suspicious activity. A booby trap bomb exploded as he opened a door: Garda Clerkin was killed and a detective was blinded.

The gardai thought that the bomb was directly connected to the passage into law of the Emergency Powers Act. They believed the Provisionals set the bomb off as an act of

122

defiance against the new measure.

The President's action brought strong criticism from the Minister for Defence, Patrick Donegan, who told an audience of soldiers in Mullingar military barracks that he was a "thundering disgrace". The story broke in the next morning's newspapers and President O Dalaigh, whose office held supreme command over the defence forces, took a very serious view. He decided that the presidency was being compromised and, in October, he resigned. There was no formal apology from the government and Liam Cosgrave rejected calls to dismiss Donegan. However, he later re-shuffled his cabinet and moved him from Defence. Patrick Donegan's cabinet colleagues thought that his outburst just after Garda Clerkin's murder was provoked by knowledge of the garda reports.

Extreme republican sympathisers living in the surrounding area were questioned in the manhunt that followed Clerkin's death. Several people were hauled into garda stations under the new seven day detention law. The arrests produced a new series of accusations against gardai of ill treating people in custody.

It was not until February 1977, however, that the issue of ill treatment was brought into the open when the *Irish Times* revealed the existence of an impromptu "heavy gang" within the gardai that specialised in interrogations. It backed up its disclosures with interviews and information from victims, lawyers, doctors and some members of the gardai. The "gang" had a floating membership around a nucleus of detectives attached to the garda technical bureau's special investigations unit.

As well as beatings they used crude psychological measures similar to highly publicised techniques that had been used in Northern Ireland in the early 1970s. They had been formally described by the European Commission of Human Rights as torture after Ireland initiated a case against the United Kingdom. The techniques included apparently simple devices like depriving people of sleep and food and disorientating them through the use of hoods over their heads and high-pitched "white noise". Suspects were also forced to stand spread eagled against walls for long periods. The European Court later ruled that the use of the five techniques did not amount to "torture" but to "ill-treatment" because those responsible did not take pleasure in their use.

Although most of the techniques were far from the popular image of "torture," psychologists knew that their scientific application would break a suspect's resistance more effectively than direct physical actions. Unlike the RUC which had members trained in the use of such techniques, the garda "heavy gang" had no training or official sanction. Nevertheless they used some of the same five techniques, depriving suspects of sleep and food and making them stand for long periods by walls. These were intermingled with more traditional methods like beatings and the alternation of "nice guy" questioners with "nasty" interrogators.

In response to the *Irish Times* revelations, Patrick Cooney said that many of the allegations were *sub judice* because they were still to be decided by the courts. Any brutality allegations already tested by the courts had been proved to be unfounded, he told the Dail.

He made it clear, however, that neither he nor the garda authorities condoned brutality against any prisoner: if it was shown to have happened strong action would be taken against those responsible. He also pointed out that the prosecution was required by law to prove in court that any confession was made voluntarily. If there was any doubt about that, the law did not allow the statement to be used.

Partly as a result of this controversy the world-wide human rights organisation, Amnesty International, sent an investigation team to Ireland in June 1977. The team came at the request of individual members of the Irish section of Amnesty. The team had two members: Angela Wright from Amnesty's international secretariat and Douwe Korff, a Dutch lawyer. Some members of the Government were not impressed with their calibre. They thought the two were insufficiently qualified to investigate the police force of an independent state. Members of the Special Branch followed Wright and Korff as they met and interviewed people who maintained the gardai had ill treated them in custody.

Before leaving Ireland at the end of their investigation, they asked to speak to Patrick Cooney. He refused to meet them because of the people with whom they had associated during their visit.

Amnesty compiled a report that was sent to the newly elected Fianna Fail government the following August. Amnesty found that maltreatment appeared to have been carried out systematically by detectives who appeared to specialise in the use of oppressive methods of extracting statements. It based its findings on an examination of twenty eight cases in which allegations were apparently supported by medical and other evidence. Those involved were not named: they included several of the IRSP men charged with the mail train robbery.

Amnesty also directed its attention at the activities of the Special Criminal Court. Its findings confirmed what many lawyers specialising in defence work had experienced. The court, Amnesty said, had seemingly failed or refused to scrutinise allegations of maltreatment according to the principles of law which governed the burden of proof with regard to the admissibility of statements. The onus of proof had shifted: the court effectively required the defence to prove beyond all reasonable doubt that maltreatment had occurred. The prosecution did not appear to have to prove that it did not occur – as the law required the prosecution to do.

With the change of government after the June 1977 general election there was a change in the political climate as well. The Emergency Powers Act, which had to be renewed annually, was allowed to lapse by Jack Lynch's administration. The new government also published Amnesty's report but deleted the section dealing with the Special Criminal Court from the text it released. The government turned down Amnesty's request for an impartial inquiry into the allegations.

Instead, the government set up a three man committee chaired by a judge, Barra O Briain, to recommend safeguards for people in custody and to safeguard the gardai from untrue allegations. The committee was excluded by its terms of reference from looking into the allegations of ill-treatment. Practically all of its recommendations, published a year later, were rejected by the government.

In 1976, however, the judiciary had taken action to stem the whittling away of the rights of suspects. The most important benchmark was laid down by the Supreme Court in its ruling about the constitutionality of the Emergency Powers Act on October 15th, 1976. It pointed out specifically that the new powers must be restricted to exactly what the law said because it made "such inroads upon the liberty of the person". Police actions must conform strictly with Section 2 which gave power to detain for seven days: the police could not try to expand those powers by claiming anything else was covered by it.

The court went further and spelled out in precise detail that the new measure did not change the rights of suspects to lawyers and doctors and to the courts. If the Emergency Powers Act was used in breach of such rights, the High Court might release the person concerned under the *habeas corpus* provisions contained in the constitution.

Within a month, the Supreme Court's admonitions had a practical effect. Eamon Hoey was arrested on October 19th and held for seven days in connection with the murder of Garda Clerkin. He was released on October 26th and was re-arrested again on November 5th on suspicion that he was involved in the murder. His lawyers went to the High Court six days later for an order of *habeas corpus*. The court's president, Justice Finlay, decided that the gardai did not have power to arrest someone twice under the Act in connection with the same crime even if new information was available. He said that the Supreme Court decision left him no alternative but to order Hoey's release.

A second man named Harrington was arrested in connection with Garda Clerkin's murder and he also took court action, claiming that he was beaten by gardai and denied access to his solicitor. Mr Justice Finlay dismissed the ill treatment accusation and found that Harrington had not been deprived of his solicitor's assistance mainly because of the persistence of his lawyer in seeing him. But the judge noted that a suspect must be allowed access to his solicitor in private and out of the hearing of gardai.

A third court decision in November 1976 would have direct consequences for three of the IRSP men still awaiting trial at the time.It involved an appeal by four men who were sentenced to penal servitude for life for the murder of Larry White, a member of Official Sinn Fein, who was killed by a burst of machine gun fire in Cork in June 1975. The case was known to lawyers as the Madden case after one of the four, Bartholomew Madden, and it established several important legal precedents.

The Court of Criminal Appeal decided in the Madden case that the court itself should usually accept as fact anything that had been decided by the Special Criminal Court to be fact. The appeal court could still draw its own inferences from those facts. In effect, however, it meant that the court would not look again at all the evidence heard by the Special Criminal Court so long as that court's decision was not clearly unjustified.

That finding would have a particularly significant bearing on Nicky Kelly's case four years later.

The Madden case also established that there was no obligation on the police to provide a lawyer for people in custody unless the suspect requested a lawyer. It ruled that a written statement from an accused person could not be used as evidence if it was taken outside of the forty eight hours he could be detained under the Offences Against the State Act. Suspects could not be charged or face a penalty if they failed to give an account of their movements a second time: as long as they did it once, that was adequate to satisfy the law.

Many of these precedents had direct bearings on the mail train robbery case for which four people awaited trial before the Special Criminal Court throughout 1977. For instance, Osgur Breatnach had been arrested three times under the Offences Against the State Act in connection with the same matter. Brian McNally had signed a statement about forty minutes after his detention should have ended. The defence lawyers were aware of all of these avenues they could explore once the trial started.

Nobody anticipated that events would take the precise course that they did.

Part Two

Beyond Reasonable Doubt

7

Caught Napping

The inside of the Special Criminal Court in Dublin's Green Street was like an amphitheatre with the proportions of a doll's house. Its style was everything anyone would expect of a court room: tiered, traditional, high ceilinged and lined with dark stained wood panelling.

The long-awaited mail train robbery trial opened there on Thursday, January 19th, 1978. It was like business left over from another era: a ghost from the past threatening to recall things which many people, gardai and lawyers alike, would rather were left alone. The days of the "heavy gang" appeared to be finished. January also saw the replacement of Edmund Garvey as Garda Commissioner: the new Fianna Fail government said it did not have confidence in him but he later challenged successfully their attempt to sack him. While there was never any evidence directly linking Garvey with any of the alleged abuses of power by the gardai, he was associated in the public mind with a period of extremely tough law and order measures.

McNally, Kelly, Breatnach and Plunkett had been on bail since December 1976 and the long delay in bringing their case to trial was due partly to the fact that they were not in prison. Other cases involving people in custody took precedence. Each time their case rose up the waiting list, it dropped down again, to be supplanted by cases involving people held in prison. In one respect, the long delay benefited the defendents: it allowed them time to argue out their differences with their lawyers.

Their solicitors were Pat McCartan and Michael White, partners in the firm Michael D. White and Company. The barristers hired for the case were Patrick MacEntee (representing Breatnach and Plunkett) and Seamus Sorahan (representing McNally and Kelly).

Sorahan was the better known of the two. He cut a dash in court and was particularly effective in front of a jury. His use of language and exaggerated gestures increased the theatricality of many trials, often swinging juries towards his clients. MacEntee relied more on his legal expertise than on courtroom style: he had a brilliant legal mind which could marshal precedent and case history in support of arguments on behalf of his clients. He also had near total recall and was able to pounce on witnesses if they gave conflicting evidence. MacEntee relied on the force of his argument to win his case and was therefore more effective in the Special Criminal Court where three judges were less likely to be swayed by flamboyance than twelve jury members.

From early on in the preparation of the case there were differences of opinion between the four defendants and their lawyers. The IRSP had taken the decision to fight the case politically: they wanted a campaign on the streets, posters everywhere and public meetings to highlight what they regarded as a state conspiracy against their party. They produced posters with pictures of the four accused and slogans like: "Frame Up Through Special Courts" and "Free the IRSP Four". They wanted to turn their trial on its head, place the government in the dock and turn the proceedings into the farce they thought they were.

The lawyers took a completely different approach, wanting to fight the case through the court system. Technically, they were in an awkward position. They were officers of the court, appointed by it under the criminal legal aid scheme to represent the interests of the accused. They could not acquiesce in turning something into a political show trial. Early in their consultations, Pat McCartan took a stand over the conduct of the case. At a meeting with Seamus Costello, an argument developed: it ended with McCartan telling Costello to run his political party while he, McCartan, ran the court case. Costello conceded the point.

The defence lawyers had won the argument and set about preparing for the trial. Once they received the book of evidence in mid 1977, the barristers were hired and discussions began in earnest. The evidence contained no surprises: the only evidence against McNally, Breatnach

132

and Kelly was the statements they signed. Indeed, the main surprise as far as some of the lawyers were concerned, was that there was no further evidence. Neither was there any indication of how the prosecution intended to explain the injuries which these three had when they arrived in Mountjoy prison. The defence strategy was obvious: they had to undermine the garda case that all these "confessions" were made voluntarily. They believed that the medical evidence would then substantiate the accounts given by the accused, at least to the extent of raising doubts about the prosecution. All they needed to do was to show that there was a reasonable doubt about the prosecution case: that was the law.

The team believed the case against Plunkett was the weakest. The only evidence against him was an identification which the defence thought was dubious and a small amount of forensic evidence which the prosecution maintained linked him to the scene of the robbery. Plunkett had not signed any incriminating statement while in police custody. Next to him, the defence team thought the case against Breatnach and McNally was also weak. There were ample grounds for arguing in court that their custody had been oppressive and that various rules and regulations had been flouted by the investigation team. The lawyers thought their toughest case would be Kelly's. His incriminating statement was made within the legal forty eight hour limit and there was also his drive with detectives to the place where the robbery happened and on to Ballymore Eustace and Bray.

The defence team thought the trial was important in another way as well. The prosecution case relied solely on confessions, except in relation to Plunkett. The gardai had produced no corroborating evidence.

The trial opened amid predictions that it could be the longest in the brief history of the Special Criminal Court. The four were arraigned – formally charged before the court – and all pleaded not guilty. The presiding judge was Mr Justice James McMahon of the High Court and he was accompanied by Judge John O'Connor of the Circuit Court and Justice John Garavan, a provincial district justice based in Castlebar, County Mayo. The prosecuting barristers were Noel McDonald and Robert Barr. Both were known as tough lawyers who would leave no stone unturned in presenting the case against the four accused.

The case against them was presented in outline and the crime described in detail. Immediately after this, the prosecution called a series of civilian witnesses: the train driver described being stopped and confronted by a man with a gun; Marion and Conal O'Toole described how their home was taken over by masked and armed men before the robbery.

But the trial quickly became bogged down in a mass of detail. Witnesses were questioned at great length by the defence lawyers, about seemingly minor details. A garda who, for instance, said he gave one of the accused a meal at some particular time might be questioned again and again about the time of the serving of the food. Many of those involved in the trial, defence lawyers included, thought that the proceedings were so bogged down that the crucial points on which the case hinged were being lost. The effect on the garda witnesses of the relentless questioning about minor points was to cause them to stand firmly behind each other: none of the gardai was prepared to give an inch to the defence lawyers.

A notable presence in the court was the bulky figure of Inspector Ned Ryan. He sat throughout most of the hearing in the well of the court, his elbow on his knee and his head resting in his hand, listening intently. The defence believed he had masterminded the garda case. Defence lawyers observed that he often seemed to consult with other gardai when new points were raised in cross-examination. They believed Inspector Ryan was thinking ahead to close off any loopholes in the garda case.

However, the prosecution case was not running smoothly. On the first day of the trial, Marion O'Toole admitted to Patrick MacEntee that the statement from her in the book of evidence was not accurate. She said she had not written the statement which recorded how she had identified a man from a photograph. The statement had been prepared by a garda and handed to her for her

134

signature eighteen months after the robbery. Her recollection now was different from what was contained in the statement.

Later in the trial, Seamus Sorahan scored a telling point while cross-examining one of the detectives in the case, Garda Kieran Lawlor, about his meetings with Nicky Kelly. Garda Lawlor told Sorahan that he had not needed to refresh his memory of events for the trial by looking up the statement he had made some two years earlier. Sorahan noticed that the garda kept tapping one of his pockets. Would you empty out your pockets, asked Sorahan with a flash of inspiration. Garda Lawlor obliged. Among the contents was a copy of his original statement. Garda Lawlor denied that he had read it before he gave evidence.

If the trial itself became laden with irrelevancies to the point of tedium, something else soon caught the attention of some of those in the court room: the pose of Judge O'Connor.

The defence lawyers knew Judge O'Connor well. He had begun sitting in the Special Criminal Court the previous July. He was well liked and there was general agreement that he had a sharp legal mind. But he had a deceptive appearance: he often tilted forward and held his head to one side in such a way that his wig fell slightly forward, down over the top of his forehead. What began to concentrate some minds in the mail train trial was that Judge O'Connor appeared to be falling asleep.

Over the next few days of the trial, it gradually dawned on the defence lawyers that Judge O'Connor was nodding off occasionally in the late morning and early to mid afternoons. The question facing them was what should they do about it? Justice could not be done and could not be seen to be done if one of those supposed to be listening carefully to the evidence and observing the demeanour of witnesses was in fact asleep. There was the added problem with the Special Criminal Court where, without a jury, the three judges were supposed to act as judge *and* jury.

The problem was also noticed by someone in the courtroom who was not among the defence lawyers. Niall Kiely, a reporter with *Hibernia* weekly review, was in the court on Wednesday, February 1st. He saw O'Connor's head slip down until it was almost touching the bench in front of him. It was the tenth day of the trial and Inspector Ned Ryan was giving evidence about events in the Bridewell. After a few minutes, Judge O'Connor sat up again and began to take notes. Shortly after three o'clock, his head dropped again and seemed to be actually resting on the bench. A couple of minutes later, he sat up again and took some more notes.

Kiely left the court and returned to the *Hibernia* offices where he wrote an article entitled "High Drama in Green Street". It was a general piece about the trial, the unusual number of gardai in the courthouse, the armed soldiers outside and the atmosphere in the court itself. In the middle of the report, Kiely recorded his observations about Judge O'Connor appearing to be asleep. The report was written especially carefully: there was no suggestion that Judge O'Connor was incompetent or not listening, merely that he seemed to be asleep. Even with such care, there was a possibility of the Special Criminal Court reacting and calling Kiely and *Hibernia's* editor before it on a contempt of court charge. But nothing happened when the report appeared on February 3rd.

The defence lawyers had hoped that Mr Justice McMahon, the presiding judge, would react in some way. At the least, they wanted him to speak with Judge O'Connor to find out if he was ill. If the trial had to be stopped, the best time was early in the proceedings. The whole business was extremely awkward for the lawyers: there was no known precedent for them to stand up in court and claim that one of the judges was asleep. There was a certain amount of social intercourse between senior barristers and members of the judiciary and such an action would have been very embarrassing for all concerned. Another visitor to the courthouse however was also about to notice the unusual demeanour of Judge O'Connor.

Martin Reynolds was a Dublin architect who specialised in designing small, rather exclusive buildings. He lived with his wife and family in Leeson Street in Dublin and devoted much of his spare time to his hobbies of collecting antiques, paintings and first edition books signed by the authors. He had impeccable social connections and was also active in Fine Gael. In fact, he was the epitome of the sort of person joining the party in increasing numbers: successful and middle class, well educated, conservative but also interested in social issues and civil liberties. He had little in common with the four men standing trial in the Special Criminal Court but his interest in civil liberties and prisoners' rights was about to bring him in contact with them.

On Monday, February 6th, Reynolds left his office for an appointment with his dentist. When he got there, he realised he had come on the wrong day. With time on his hands, he decided to drop down to the Special Criminal Court. He had been reading trial reports in the newspapers but he had never been in the court before. He was surprised when, on entering the building, he was stopped and asked his name, his address, his occupation and why he was there. Gardai searched his briefcase and then frisked his clothes. This was not Reynolds' first experience with the gardai however: some Special Branch officers had called to his home not long after McNally, Breatnach, Kelly and Plunkett were released on bail in 1976.

At that time, capital punishment became an issue when the Special Criminal Court found Noel and Marie Murray guilty of the capital murder of Garda Michael Reynolds, an off-duty garda who was shot dead when he tackled them as they fled through Saint Anne's Park in Raheny, Dublin after a bank robbery. The court passed the death sentence and there was an immediate outcry from a number of quarters.

Martin Reynolds was against capital punishment and went to a public meeting on the subject outside the GPO in O'Connell Street. He felt strongly enough to get onto the platform and make a speech. He told the crowd that he was an officer of the central branch in Dublin of Fine Gael and that he and his party were against capital punishment. It was a barbaric act which no Christian society could tolerate, he said.

Not long after his speech, two members of the Special

Branch called to his home and spoke to his elderly mother. They asked her where he worked, what his beliefs were and with whom he associated. A day or two later, they called again and this time spoke with his wife. Finally, they called a third time and spoke to Reynolds himself. They asked him all the same questions and he in turn asked what possible interest they could have in him. He said he was active in Fine Gael, knew Garret FitzGerald and showed them a picture of himself and Charles Haughey of Fianna Fail as proof that he was a responsible person.

"We regard someone like you as a real subversive," said one of the Special Branch men. He added that if a prominent republican or left wing activist expressed the sort of views which Reynolds had at the GPO, nobody would listen. But when someone of his standing came out against capital punishment and such like, then people might take him seriously. Eventually, the two gardai left but the experience so amazed Reynolds that he drafted a letter to Garret FitzGerald, then Foreign Minister in Liam Cosgrave's government. He had a habit of writing letters to politicians, expressing his views on current problems and suggesting solutions. His experience at the mail train robbery trial would prompt him to write again to Fitzgerald.

When he had been checked on arrival at the building, a garda led him to the public gallery and sat him in the back row, behind a large number of gardai. The courtroom was filled with gardai, some in uniform, others in plain clothes. The four accused could be seen below him in the dock and in front of them, facing the judges, were the two legal teams, defence and prosecution. In front of them, raised and looking down at the court, were the three judges. On either side of the room to the right and left of the judges, there were two jury boxes, perched above the room a bit like boxes in a Victorian theatre. Both were empty.

Martin Reynolds leant forward to hear better: a garda told him to sit up straight. Medical evidence was being given by a prosecution witness of injuries to one of the defendants. Reynolds was startled at the apparent extent of the injuries which were alleged to have been inflicted by members of the Garda Siochana. But he was also disturbed

138

by what he felt was a shoddy presentation of the evidence; his anxiety was not allayed when a succession of gardai gave what he regarded as unconvincing evidence that no violence had been done to the four accused while in custody.

As Reynolds looked around the court, something else disturbed him even more. He noticed Judge O'Connor sitting back in his seat, his head drooping forward and his eyes closed. He was convinced that the judge was asleep: occasionally Judge O'Connor would jerk his head up, apparently roused by the handing up to the bench of some legal documents, but then his head would slowly tilt forward again. He watched this happening from 11 am until around 1 pm when the court adjourned for lunch.

He left the courthouse in a rage and, in his letter to Garret FitzGerald, said that what was happening in the Special Criminal Court was an example of why the Cosgrave government had lost power. He was confident that people did not accept "the blatant denials of Patrick Cooney that there was no ill treatment" of suspects by the gardai. He asked FitzGerald to take a personal interest in the case and wondered if the condition of Judge O'Connor might not be a reason to have the trial stopped. He said he was horrified that people should be tried in the circumstances he had seen in court.

He contacted Pat McCartan, one of the defence solicitors, and spoke along similar lines. The lawyers were becoming increasingly apprehensive about Judge O'Connor's condition and they were also being pressed by the four accused to do something to highlight the situation. The problem was by now a talking point in legal circles and the subject of much conversation in the bar library, one of the best repositories of gossip in Dublin. For a long time, the defence lawyers tried to draw attention to the problem by dropping weighty legal books, coughing, seeking brief adjournments on the pretext of visiting the lavatory and the like. Some of the officers of the court were brought into the plan: a door near Judge O'Connor would be banged or someone would try to nudge him. The defence lawyers also tried on occasion to catch the eye of Mr Justice McMahon to indicate when Judge O'Connor seemed to nod off. None of this worked however and Judge O'Connor's condition deteriorated. The lawyers heard that he was taking pills for a heart condition and some became seriously worried that he was very ill and, for his own good, should not be working.

On Wednesday, April 5th, over two months after the trial began, Niall Kiely paid another of his visits to the trial. Around half past eleven, he noticed Judge O'Connor's head slumped forward to the extent that he was again almost resting on the bench in front of him. At the time, crucial evidence was being given by Sergeant John McGroarty, one of the detectives who had taken a statement from Nicky Kelly. When McGroarty was being questioned and again half an hour later, Judge O'Connor appeared to Kiely to be having difficulty staying awake. Around midday, the judge fell back in his chair, his head rested on his chest and he seemed to be soundly asleep.

The midday angelus bells rang out from a nearby church but the sound failed to have any noticeable effect on the judge. Judge McMahon coughed immediately after the bells stopped and a court official slapped shut a legal book but it made no difference: Judge O'Connor still appeared oblivious to the proceedings. Mr Justice McMahon adjourned the court at five past twelve for ten minutes.

The situation deteriorated to such an extent during April that the defence lawyers could no longer ignore the demands of the four accused that something be done in open court to try to resolve the problem. MacEntee and Sorahan knew that to raise it in open court would be an irrevocable step: it would open such a gulf between the defence and everyone else involved in the case that there would be no going back. If the three judges denied there was any problem, the decision would have to be appealed to the High Court and maybe even the Supreme Court. It would be necessary also to have evidence not just from the four accused and their solicitors as to what had been observed about Judge O'Connor's condition: there would have to be an independent element to their argument.

Martin Reynolds and Niall Kiely agreed at the request of

140

the defence lawyers to swear and sign affidavits. Other reporters who had been in the court for almost all of the trial refused. One said he didn't want to jeopardise his standing with garda contacts.

In one final attempt before bringing the problem up in open court, MacEntee and Sorahan took the unusual step of approaching the three judges in their room behind the court. The lawyers told the judges of the instructions they had received from their clients. They hoped that this discreet approach might persuade the judges to take some action themselves. But there was no change.

On April 26th Sorahan stood up in front of the three judges in open court and announced that it was his unpleasant duty to make an application to the court which caused him profound professional and personal embarrassment.

"From time to time it has appeared that one member of the court was apparently asleep in the sense that he had his eyes closed and at times his head down," he said. "When it comes to the credibility of the witness, it is a difficult thing to expect a member of the court to take a note, to watch demeanour all the time, but something vital may happen in a short time, like five or ten seconds, a bead of sweat on the forehead, shiftiness in the box".

Sorahan said that he wanted the court to discharge itself and a new trial to be held. He mentioned the reference to the problem in *Hibernia* early in February, the dropping of books, and the various occasions when he or MacEntee had asked for short adjournments on the pretext that someone needed to go to the toilet. In reality, it was to allow Judge O'Connor to wake up. Sorahan said the three judges could perhaps retire and consider their position; Judge O'Connor need not necessarily participate in the consideration of the application. Alternately, the court could refer the matter to the High Court for resolution.

MacEntee addressed the issue in a more direct manner. Judge O'Connor had appeared to be asleep on a large number of occasions during the course of the trial.

"Not alone must justice be done but it must be seen to be done and not alone must the people of Ireland see that justice is done, but the accused are entitled to be tried in a court in which they can have reasonable confidence," he told the three judges. He said the court should abandon the trial until the High Court considered the issues involved.

Mr Justice McMahon interjected: "The court will rise but it would appear appropriate that the court should decide for itself. The suggestion that the court might also hear evidence is unattractive".

MacEntee agreed that it would be better not to hear evidence but the prosecution lawyers were completely opposed to the suggestion that the court should discharge itself and begin a new trial. Noel McDonald, the senior prosecution barrister, said there was no reasonable grounds to support the application. He said that reference had been made to the mention in *Hibernia* but the trial was now fifty days old.

"If they (the defence lawyers) thought there was any substance in that allegation at that time, they should have moved the court at that time: not left it to the fiftieth day of the trial," said McDonald.

McMahon, O'Connor and the other judge, District Justice Garavan, retired to consider whether or not they should discharge themselves and allow a new trial to begin. They didn't take long to refuse the application, although they conceded that they had not had to consider a similar suggestion before.

"The court is not aware of any precedent to guide it in dealing with this application", said Judge McMahon when the three returned to the bench. "We have therefore discussed the allegations made with Judge O'Connor and have been guided by our knowledge of the proceedings. The court is satisfied that Judge O'Connor has followed this evidence and can discharge his duties in accordance with the solemn declaration he made on his appointment as a judge to uphold the constitution and the laws so the court is satisfied that no grounds exist for suggesting that justice was not seen to be done in the course of this trial and therefore we refuse the application."

There was a brief adjournment. Mr Justice McMahon said the trial would go on but MacEntee asked for a transcript of what had just been said and Sorahan announced that they would be taking the matter further.

The following day and the day after that, a total of eight affidavits were sworn, each one describing in varying degrees how Judge O'Connor had appeared to be asleep on particular occasions. Breatnach, Plunkett, McNally and Kelly all detailed instances when they saw the judge's head fall forward, or his eyes close or the pen slip from his hand as he slumped forward. Each said they did not believe they were getting a fair trial as a result of Judge O'Connor's condition.

Pat McCartan swore an affidavit in which he referred to his notes taken at the trial in January. "Judge O'Connor fast asleep – head on bench", said one. Similar details were contained in an affidavit sworn by his colleague, Michael White. Perhaps the two most important affidavits sworn were those from Martin Reynolds and Niall Kiely, neither of whom had any connection with either prosecution, defence or any of the accused.

All the affidavits were presented to the High Court on Friday, April 28th, when the defence lawyers argued their appeal against the decision of the three Special Criminal Court judges that they were properly carrying out their functions. The defence lawyers asked the High Court for a conditional order prohibiting the Special Criminal Court from continuing with the trial. The application was refused by the president of the High Court, Mr Justice Thomas Finlay.

He based his refusal on three grounds, none of which appeared related to the evidence contained in the eight affidavits placed before him. Firstly, he said that the three judges of the Special Criminal Court had risen and considered the allegation. They had made a decision that each of them was in a position to discharge his duty. Secondly, he said that if he was to agree with the defence lawyers it would mean the end of the trial in the Special Criminal Court. Finally, he said that there was a "wholly unexplained delay" between the time that Judge O'Connor's alleged sleeping was first noticed and the lawyers doing something about it. He said also that if the allegation was true, the lawyers could make it part of any appeal they might lodge following the trial in the Special Criminal Court.

MacEntee and Sorahan immediately applied to have the case heard by the Supreme Court and a sitting was arranged for the week after the High Court rejection of their arguments. The trial continued meanwhile before the Special Criminal Court and, by the time MacEntee stood up to make his case in front of the five judges of the Supreme Court, the basic arguments were well known. The atmosphere in the court was brittle. The Chief Justice, Tom O'Higgins, was flanked on either side by his four colleagues: Justice Seamus Henchy, Justice Frank Griffin, Justice John Kenny and Justice Weldon Parke.

There was a distinct feeling that the defence lawyers were pushing things too far, that they should have accepted the High Court decision and let matters rest there. There was also some tension within the defence teams. The two senior counsel had agreed that Sorahan should open the case as the more senior. As the judges filed onto the bench, however, Sorahan left the courtroom to handle another case elsewhere. MacEntee, to his irritation, found himself opening the pleadings.

He submitted that there were precedents for his application for a conditional order to stop the Special Criminal Court continuing with the trial. He cited cases from the sixteenth and seventeenth centuries in England which were part of a power struggle between the common law courts and the ecclesiastical courts of the Church of England. The church courts still had jurisdiction at that time over certain matrimonial and probate cases and generally sat as tribunals, that is, with more than one judge. The row was part of a church-state struggle in which the common courts were anxious to exercise total control over the administration of all law. As a result of the antipathy which existed between both courts, the common courts had heard a number of cases where lawyers sought the dismissal of a church court on the grounds that one or other of its judges was incapable of hearing a case because of some incapacity. The issue was precisely the same with regard to

144

the Special Criminal Court in 1978.

MacEntee conceded that it was very late in the day to be seeking to have the trial stopped because of Judge O'Connor's condition. He explained the delay by suggesting that he and Sorahan were perhaps over-protective and had tried to balance their duties towards their clients and towards the courts. Now, however, they had received peremptory instructions to try to have the trial stopped. He submitted that the Special Criminal Court had not ruled explicitly that Judge O'Connor was not asleep: it merely indicated that the three man court could act as a body.

The Chief Justice, however, questioned the evidence that Judge O'Connor was asleep. He said the affidavits expressed opinions only of what seemed to be: Judge O'Connor "seemed to be asleep". MacEntee retorted that the affidavits clearly went beyond what had seemed to be and they stated emphatically that Judge O'Connor was actually asleep.

Chief Justice O'Higgins ordered that the affidavits from Pat McCartan and Michael White, the two defence solicitors, be withdrawn immediately. He also denounced the affidavit made by Martin Reynolds. He said it was not properly drafted because it was expressing what Reynolds had said to someone else – to Garret FitzGerald in his letter.

The defence lawyers were surprised at the tone of the comments made by Chief Justice O'Higgins. He appeared to be hostile and there were several of these tetchy exchanges while the precedents and points of law were being argued out.

"Your lordship submits..." said MacEntee in reply to comments by the Chief Justice. But before he could finish the sentence, Justice O'Higgins interrupted: "No, Mr MacEntee, I do not submit. You submit and I decide."

When it came to deciding, the court was unanimously against the application. Chief Justice O'Higgins under-scored the points made by Justice Finlay in the High Court. The length of the delay in making the application was reason enough to deny the order sought by the defence lawyers, he said. But a less technical reason was the fact that the three judges of the Special Criminal Court had themselves considered the matter and decided that they were fit to preside at the trial. Even though they were involved in the arguments against themselves, the Supreme Court was bound by their findings of fact, Chief Justice O'Higgins said. The application was refused, the High Court decision was upheld and the trial would continue in the Special Criminal Court.

The controversy had an effect on Judge O'Connor. For some days afterwards he was alert and attentive in court but it was not long before his condition began to affect him again and he dozed off periodically. On May 4th, he appeared to be particularly bad. Just before 2.30 pm the judge seemed to be unable to remain upright in his chair, his eyes were closing and he was falling forward. About ten minutes later, as O'Connor's head fell to within six or eight inches of the bench, MacEntee applied for a two minute recess to take what he described as legal advice. When the court resumed after the brief break, Michael Plunkett stood up in the dock and said the adjournment had been a ruse to enable the judge to be woken up. Mr Justice McMahon immediately said Plunkett had no right to address the court if he was represented by counsel. Plunkett persisted and shouted that he wanted it put on record that Judge O'Connor appeared to be asleep just before the recess. He sat down, his point made.

Niall Kiely was in court and reported the incident in the next issue of *Hibernia* on May 11th. There was an interesting observation in Kiely's report: he said that before MacEntee asked for the recess, District Justice Garavan appeared to nudge Mr Justice McMahon as Judge O'Connor's head slipped forward. Judge McMahon "seemed to make an unsuccessful effort to rouse O'Connor," reported Kiely.

The *Hibernia* piece was no more than a small insertion in the paper's *Sidelines* column, a weekly selection of tit bits, gossip and anecdotes. It was nonetheless an extraordinary indictment of the Special Criminal Court, the High Court and the Supreme Court for each had decided that nothing untoward was in fact happening at the trial: Judge O'Connor was not asleep and was perfectly capable of discharging his duties and responsibilities. Yet the paper was able to publish something which clearly stated the opposite and implied that his two colleagues – Judge McMahon and Justice Garavan – were conniving in a charade to ensure that the trial continued. Kiely hoped that the court would take some action against *Hibernia*, perhaps call himself and the editor to account for themselves and demand that they purge their contempt. But nothing happened and the trial continued until fate intervened.

On June 6th, the trial entered its sixty-fifth day by which time it had become by far the longest trial in the history of the state. The gardai, legal teams and defendants turned up as usual in the Special Criminal Court. But the day's proceedings had to be delayed because Judge O'Connor was absent. The judge had risen as usual that morning to dress and prepare himself for work. His housekeeper found him later, collapsed dead on the floor, killed by a heart attack.

When word reached the court, it was clear the trial would have to be abandoned and a new trial begun. There were instant tributes paid to the late judge. Noel McDonald for the prosecution said that O'Connor was a greatly loved man, compassionate and good humoured and he would be greatly missed in the west of Ireland. Seamus Sorahan for the defence lawyers said that he wanted to be associated with McDonald's comments. He said that O'Connor's death was very tragic.

The apparent unanimity of the lawyers in their tributes for the late judge disguised the true feelings of some people in legal circles. Those feelings were perhaps best summed up by Judge Diarmuid Sheridan, one of Judge O'Connor's colleagues in the circuit court. Speaking at a sitting of the circuit court in Thurles, County Tipperary, the day after O'Connor's death, Judge Sheridan felt moved to comment:

"The events of more recent times may well have taken their toll on him and it might be prudent to observe that he deserved a little better than he got".

O'Connor's death meant that, as far as the law was

concerned, the case was back to square one. After sixty five days of hearings, a complete new trial was ordered.

8

The Trial

The new trial opened on Monday, October 10th 1978 and produced an early and dramatic breakthrough for the defendants. On the afternoon of the second day, the newly constituted Special Criminal Court ordered that Michael Plunkett be released and the charges against him dropped. Almost two and a half years after being arrested on suspicion of involvement in the mail train robbery, Plunkett was able to walk free from the Green Street courthouse. It was a major morale boost. For the defence lawyers it also appeared to be a victory for their new tactics.

The new trial presented opportunities and difficulties for both legal teams. The fact that the issue had gone to trial meant that both sides knew the other's tactics, the items of evidence on which they were placing special emphasis and the gaps to be filled or exploited. The first trial was, in retrospect, a rehearsal for the second. Almost all the witnesses who were to be called had already given evidence. Both sides knew which questions would be asked; the witnesses had had an opportunity to familiarise themselves again with the salient points of their evidence. And they knew what to expect when it came to cross-examinations. It would be extremely difficult to trip up a witness as he or she knew the pitfalls.

The defence had reviewed their strategy in the light of the first trial. There was general agreement that it had gone off the rails badly and become bogged down in a morass of detail. Essentially, the defence believed that crucial prosecution witnesses were, at least, fudging the truth and the defence had attempted to expose that by intensive questioning about seemingly minor details. The garda witnesses resented this approach which they perceived to be undue niggling. Everything got out of hand and the trial had become somewhat aimless.

The defence decided to restrict themselves to what they

saw as the central issues, the confessions allegedly made by three of the accused, Brian McNally, Osgur Breatnach and Nicky Kelly. Their fate would rest on whether or not the court was satisfied that these alleged admissions were made voluntarily. The defence set out to undermine the prosecution claim that they were. They also knew now how the prosecution intended to deal with the medical evidence showing injuries on each of the accused. They would argue that all injuries were self-inflicted or mutually inflicted. This claim brought to the fore another question that had received little attention initially: the unusual fact that the four were remanded in custody to the Bridewell after their first court appearance and were then put two to a cell there. The prosecution claimed that this gave them the opportunity to injure each other before they were seen by doctors. The prosecution had not produced any evidence to support this claim, however.

The defence lawyers also decided to rearrange the order in which the individual cases were dealt with within the trial. They hoped to deal first with Michael Plunkett's case because the evidence against him was solely of identification.

In their preparations for the trial, the lawyers were also acutely aware of the membership of the new court. Mr Justice Liam Hamilton, a no-nonsense judge, presided and it was expected that he would keep the proceedings moving swiftly and surely. He was seen as a judge who had little time for matters which did not go right to the central point of a case and he was expected to keep the hearings to relevant issues.

In one respect it was unusual that Judge Hamilton should have presided: he was, in one sense, a potential witness in the case against Breatnach. He had seen Breatnach when Breatnach was brought before him during the *habeas corpus* action in the High Court on Wednesday, April 7th 1976, after he had been in the Bridewell for two days. Other people who had seen Breatnach in the court believed that his appearance corroborated his claim that he had been ill-treated by the gardai while in custody. Breatnach's counsel was not worried about losing Justice Hamilton as a potential witness: in fact, it was hoped that his presence on the bench might work to Breatnach's advantage.

Justice Hamilton had two judges sitting with him, Judge Gerard Clarke of the Circuit Court and Justice Cathal O Floinn, president of the District Court. Nobody wanted a repeat of the sixty five day first trial and the defence lawyers expected that Hamilton would want to move speedily. They were banking on this when they applied to have Plunkett discharged.

The trial began with the sort of legal foreplay which might be expected. The defence questioned the jurisdiction of the court to try the four accused: there was a brief skirmish between the defence and the prosecuting barristers as to whether or not the trial was a "re-trial" or a "new trial". Jesuitical points were made along the lines that because there had been no decision in the other trial due to the death of Judge O'Connor, that trial had not really happened. Justice Hamilton eventually ruled that there was precedent for a court to discharge itself and order a new trial. The four were once again formally charged.

"Not guilty," replied Brian McNally. "Framed by the Heavy Gang. Not guilty," said Nicky Kelly. "We have been made the victims of a state conspiracy. Framed. Not guilty," said Breatnach. "Ned Ryan's Heavy Gang are guilty. I'm not guilty," said Plunkett.

The prosecution case against the four had not changed since the first trial. The evidence against McNally, Breatnach and Kelly was statements amounting to confessions which they were alleged to have made freely to the gardai while in custody. The case against Plunkett would rest on an alleged identification of him by Conal O'Toole. The prosecution was also expected to produce some forensic evidence against Plunkett: a hair found on a jacket discovered in a gap in the hedge beside the raiway line. Gardai said the hair matched Plunkett's hair. The great weakness in the case against Plunkett was that the prosecution could produce no self-incriminating evidence, no statement made while in custody.

Patrick MacEntee had come to regard the case as the most important of his career. He saw it as a test for the legal

151

system and the judiciary. The gardai had nailed their colours to the mast, so to speak, with their near total reliance on confessions with no corroborating evidence. The defence lawyer had also come to believe that they were up against a conspiracy within the gardai because of the very unusual similarities between individual garda statements. There were numerous instances where several gardai used almost precisely the same words to describe what had taken place during the questioning of suspects. Yet the gardai had claimed during the first trial that they did not consult each other when writing their statements. It was implausible that such striking similarities could have occurred by chance and therefore the defence lawyers believed there was a conspiracy among the gardai not to admit, for whatever reason, that they co-operated in writing their statements.

It was also clear to the defence lawyers that the gardai had broken the Judges Rules on several occasions. These were guidelines laid down in the courts for the treatment of suspects in custody. They were not laws as such but courts could and did throw out cases where it had emerged that the gardai disregarded the rules.

The new trial would be the same as the previous one in that the bulk of the proceedings would be a trial within a trial. This was because the central issue was whether or not the statements alleged to have been made freely by the accused should be admitted in evidence against them.

*   *   *

The first two witnesses were a garda mapping expert and photographer, both of whom gave technical evidence of the location of the robbery and what was found there after the thieves had made good their escape. Next came Ray Reynolds, the grocer whose van was taken from him at gunpoint and later used in the robbery. He was followed by Conal O'Toole, the most important witness against Michael Plunkett.

O'Toole told prosecution lawyer Robert Barr exactly

what happened a few hours before the robbery when armed men entered his home. He described also how later that day, Inspector Michael Canavan, a sergeant at the time of the robbery, called to the house with a pile of photographs for him to examine. O'Toole said he sat at the dining room table as Canavan spread out the pictures in groups of fifteen at a time, three rows of five.

MacEntee interrupted. He asked whether the prosecution would be in a position to prove that any of the photographs were in fact photographs of any of the four accused. Did the prosecution have negatives to prove that the photographs had not been altered? Could they produce the photographer to give evidence that the person in the picture was the person of whom the photograph was taken?

"To invite your lordships to speculate that the image of a person in a photograph is that of one of the accused is to invite your lordships to become expert witnesses and to circumvent the entire requirements of law in relation to the proof of photographs," said MacEntee.

Barr disagreed. He said that O'Toole would give evidence that he identified a photograph of one of the four accused and he would go on to give further evidence of identifying the same person on another occasion.

Justice Hamilton ruled in favour of MacEntee. He told Barr that the evidence relating to the photograph and any other evidence connected to it could not be admitted. Barr had no choice but to drop his questioning about photographs and continue another line of inquiry with O'Toole. He asked him about a visit to Harcourt Terrace garda station on April 7th 1976, the day after Michael Plunkett had been arrested at Connolly Station when he got off the train from Belfast.

O'Toole described an identification parade in the garda station in which he thought he recognised one person as being one of the men in his house on the night of the robbery but said he could not be sure. He also recalled a second identification parade in which he mistakenly singled out a student as one of the robbers. Then he told the court about identifying a man as he was escorted along a corridor by some plainclothes gardai.

"Do you see that man here in court," asked Barr.

"Yes," replied O'Toole pointing towards the dock and Michael Plunkett.

MacEntee began his cross examination by bringing O'Toole through his story once again from the beginning – from the time he was woken in the early hours of the morning by the men entering his house, to his two to three minute encounter with the gang leader in his bedroom, to his tour of various garda stations where he took part in surreptitious identity parades and finally his visit to Harcourt Terrace garda station where he took part in two formal identity parades which culminated in his positive identification of Plunkett.

He admitted to MacEntee that his identification of Plunkett was based only on a sense of movement which he gathered from a fleeting glance of him in a corridor which lasted a matter of seconds.

MacEntee: In the end of the day, I take it that you are telling their lordships that the initial identification, in any event purported identification, of Mr. Plunkett in Harcourt Terrace was based on a sense that you have apparently of movement?

O'Toole: Yes.

MacEntee: And of general shape?

O'Toole: General shape.

MacEntee: How long had you watched him move?

O'Toole: In my house or in the....

MacEntee: No, no. We have had that. In Harcourt Terrace until the point where you shouted "That is your man"?

O'Toole: A matter of just a very fleeting glimpse.

The cross examination ended on one of the many niggling inconsistencies between what witnesses said at the first and second trials. O'Toole described Plunkett's accent as being that of a working man. MacEntee quickly picked him up on this and said that at the previous trial he had described the accent as middle class Dublin.

Marion O'Toole was called next and described in similar

154

terms as her husband what had happened in their home on the night of the robbery when the man entered. There was a brief cross examination by MacEntee but Mrs O'Toole's contribution to the trial was very limited: nothing hinged on her evidence.

The trial resumed the following morning, the second day, with evidence from a variety of witnesses who were on the periphery of the case. Joe Cotter and Joseph Connolly, a Post Office supervisor and train guard respectively, described what happened to them and what they heard when the train was stopped and robbed. Gardai John Murphy, James Heffernan, Thomas Connolly and Pierce Freaney described how they had variously been called to the scene of the robbery shortly after it took place, searched the area and called to the O'Tooles' house. Noel Dempsey and Henry Kirwan, the caretakers of the itinerant site in Finglas, told how a greenish blue Volkswagen van (stolen from Ray Reynolds) was dumped in the site at 3.45 am on the morning of the robbery. Herbert Connett, a security guard at Irish Meat Packers in Leixlip, and Detective Garda Gabriel McCarthy of Terenure station described how Peugeot and Renault cars, both stolen from the O'Tooles', were found abandoned in Leixlip and Rathgar after the robbery. Superintendent Hubert Reynolds of the garda technical bureau told how he was given certain items found at the scene of the robbery – a black jacket with yellow patches on the elbows and shoulder and a piece of paper.

The evidence from all of these witnesses was not directly related to the case against the four accused. It merely proved that a robbery had taken place, that mail bags were stolen, that some things were found at the scene of the robbery and that cars stolen on the same night and apparently used in the robbery were later found abandoned.

The next witness, Garda James Grehan, was one of the key detectives in the case against Brian McNally. He was one of the Special Branch men who arrested McNally at his home on Monday April 5th, and subsequently questioned him in Fitzgibbon Street garda station and the Bridewell. Garda Grehan was not long in the witness box before the court adjourned for lunch.

During the break, MacEntee confirmed with Noel McDonald, the main prosecution barrister, that there would be no further evidence against Plunkett. McDonald had decided that the forensic evidence which the gardai said they had on Plunkett was too weak to stand up in court. MacEntee also believed that Hamilton would treat the evidence with a great deal of suspicion.

The gardai believed they could link Plunkett directly to the scene of the robbery via the jacket which was found beside the railway line. There was a hair on the jacket and, when Plunkett was in custody, gardai took a sample hair from his head. Both hairs were sent for examination to the forensic science laboratory. However, lawyers experienced in criminal cases were aware that the most which could be said about hairs was that they were similar, not identical. A one for one match could only be made if the hairs had been dyed and the chemical in them analysed. In the case of Plunkett, it had not been possible to conclude more than that the hair in the jacket was similar to his own. MacEntee would have had an easy fight in court arguing that many people had hair similar to that found on the jacket and so there was nothing proven about Plunkett.

MacEntee told McDonald that immediately after lunch he wanted to make an application to the court concerning the case against Plunkett. McDonald agreed that it would be convenient to deal with it now rather than later in the trial. When the court resumed at 2 pm, McDonald told Judge Hamilton that he had no further evidence to offer against Plunkett. MacEntee said he wanted the court to examine the evidence against Plunkett and, on the basis that he could not be convicted beyond a reasonable doubt, find him not guilty.

MacEntee said that the only evidence against Plunkett was the identification made by Conal O'Toole who initially failed to recognise him during an identity parade in a well lit room in Harcourt Terrace garda station.

"It was only in a corridor, when he saw Mr Plunkett in the custody of two police officers and being escorted by them, that he made an identification apparently based on a

156

silhouette and movement. Even at that stage, whilst he purported to recognise the person in the corridor in Harcourt Terrace as the person he had seen in his house, he did not even then relate that person to the person he had some minutes since seen in the (identification) room," said MacEntee.

There were other significant aspects about the evidence which MacEntee said the court should take into consideration. He said that the O'Tooles saw the man who entered their home in distressing circumstances and Conal O'Toole admitted that he had only concentrated on the man he believed to be Plunkett for two or three minutes. MacEntee said it was important to note that both Mr and Mrs O'Toole gave the same description of the man they thought was Plunkett. They said he had dark wavy hair, a heavy dark moustache and that he was tall. Plunkett was thick set, rather squat and definitely not tall. His hair was also dark brown not black. MacEntee mentioned one or two relevant precedents but let his argument rest essentially on the point that, without questioning the sincerity or good intentions of Conal O'Toole, there had to be a doubt about the identification of Plunkett.

"Your lordships are well aware the most appalling miscarriages of justice have resulted from misidentification of prisoners when the circumstances of the identification were considerably better than they were in this particular case," he said.

Noel McDonald argued that the evidence against Plunkett was given by a person "who was obviously extremely cautious." He said that Conal O'Toole had initially been reluctant to become involved because he feared for the safety of his family. McDonald said that when O'Toole had examined the first identity parade, he had stopped in front of Plunkett and paused for a moment. Although the room was well lit, it was not until he saw him in the corridor in poorer lighting and observed his movements that he recognised him as the man who had been in his bedroom on the night of the robbery.

"That is the only evidence, I agree," said McDonald, "but in my submission it is very clear evidence by a person

157

who is being very careful about giving his evidence and who is very careful in his examination of the accused at the times he saw him: both identification parades where he was left in some doubt and is unable to positively identify him. Subsequently, when he sees him one hour or so later, in movement, listening to the sound of his voice, he tells you he has no doubt but that that was the person."

It was, said McDonald, a very positive identification and one which the court could act upon.

The court adjourned to consider MacEntee's application that Plunkett should be found not guilty on the basis of the evidence against him. When the three judges returned a short time later, Judge Hamilton said they had decided to discharge Plunkett. He said there was no question but that Conal O'Toole was an honest and credit worthy witness but identification evidence had to be examined cautiously and critically. Because of this, it would be unsafe to continue with the prosecution against Plunkett and he was therefore discharged.

Plunkett left the dock and was free to leave the court. McNally, Breatnach and Kelly remained where they were.

Plunkett's delight at being a free man again was tinged with one slight feeling of regret. He had hoped to be called to give evidence in his own defence. He looked forward to sitting in the witness box and, one hand gesturing towards his three co-accused in the dock, asking the judges did they honestly think that if he wanted to rob a train he would do it with them.

9

Brian McNally

"You are on the wrong track," Brian McNally said to the gardai when they called to his house on the morning of Monday, April 5th 1976 to arrest him on suspicion of taking part in the mail train robbery. Right track or not, McNally was now standing trial (for the second time) for the robbery. The gardai had begun to give their evidence against him.

The prosecution case opened with a series of gardai telling the court of his interrogation on the Monday of his arrest and the following Tuesday. They outlined the account that McNally had given of his movements on the day of the robbery and they confirmed that details had been checked out. They agreed that McNally continued to deny any involvement in the train raid until the early hours of Wednesday, April 7th. They all denied that any violence was done to him in custody.

Garda James Grehan, the detective who spent most time with McNally during his detention, was the first police witness against McNally. "I know nothing about the robbery," McNally had told them. "It looked like a Provo job."

McNally's story was that he had been out in town and returned home after midnight on the morning of the robbery. His wife and Nicky Kelly were there when he arrived and they sat up for some time drinking tea and chatting before retiring to bed. Garda Grehan told prosecuting barrister Robert Barr that he discussed McNally's relationship with the IRSP and his work with the band of which he was a member. He described how he gave him a tin of Ambrosia creamed rice late in the evening before putting him in a cell where he went to bed just after midnight.

The next day Garda Grehan continued his questioning, this time in the Bridewell. He told McNally that he did not believe his story and said he urged him to tell the truth. McNally insisted that he was not lying. Around 1 am on Wednesday he found himself alone with McNally. Garda Grehan said that at this stage he asked McNally about the removal of the mail bags from the train and the transporting of them in a Transit van which was later abandoned in Finglas.

"He said it was a Volkswagen van that was used. I asked him how he knew it was a Volkswagen. I said it was a Transit van, how did he know it was a Volkswagen van that was used?" said Garda Grehan. He asked the question a few times but McNally gave no reply. Garda Grehan said that at around 3.30 am McNally asked to see the officer in charge of the investigation and about ten minutes later, Inspector Ned Ryan came into the interview room.

Barr: Did he say anything to the accused in your presence?
Grehan: He asked Mr McNally what he wanted to see him for.
Barr: Did the accused reply?
Grehan: He did.
Barr: What did he say?
Grehan: He said "I was on the job. I did not know it was going to be done until after I got there."

Garda Grehan said that he then cautioned McNally that he was not obliged to say anything but that if he did, it would be taken down and might be given in evidence. Neither he nor Inspector Ryan wrote down what McNally had said, however. Garda Grehan said that McNally then said he did not know what to do and asked for time to think. He and Inspector Ryan left and McNally was on his own for about an hour until Garda Grehan said he returned. He said that McNally said nothing until about five to five when two detectives, Sergeant Michael Canavan and Inspector John Courtney, entered the room to take a written statement from him.

Garda Grehan said that he was in and out of the room on a couple of occasions until the taking of McNally's

160

statement was finished at ten minutes past eight. McNally signed the statement and it was witnessed by Inspector Courtney and Garda Grehan. McNally was released twenty minutes later and immediately arrested again under Section 30 of the Offences Against the State Act for allegedly taking part in the mail train robbery. Garda Grehan said he put him back into a cell in the Bridewell at 8.30 am.

Seamus Sorahan, McNally's defence barrister, began his cross examination. Garda Grehan told him that a container of tablets was left with McNally when the rest of his property was removed. Sorahan said that McNally would swear that the tablets were taken from him.

Sorahan: The idea did not strike you that if you were to take tablets out of the possession of some person that it could cause unease at least, if not something worse, in his mind?

Grehan: I didn't think about that because they were not taken from him in the sense that they were not removed from where he was sitting.

Garda Grehan denied under further questioning that McNally had ever asked for a solicitor.

He recalled an encounter late on the Tuesday evening between McNally and Inspector Myles Hawkshaw, a detective with the Special Branch. It was around 10.30 pm and Garda Grehan said that Inspector Hawkshaw, although not one of the team investigating the robbery, came into a room where he was interviewing McNally and told McNally to tell the truth. Sorahan mentioned a second meeting between McNally and Inspector Hawkshaw and he asked Garda Grehan if on that occasion the detective offered money to McNally in exchange for information. Garda Grehan said that nothing like that had happened.

Sorahan then began questioning Garda Grehan about McNally's reference to a Volkswagen van as opposed to a Transit van being involved in the robbery. Sorahan put it to Garda Grehan that McNally had said he knew a Volkswagen van was used because he had read it in the

161

papers. Grehan said this was not so, McNally had not replied. Sorahan maintained that Garda Grehan mentioned a Transit van as a deliberate ploy to trap McNally but the garda denied this.

Sorahan mentioned the incident early on the Wednesday morning when Garda Grehan said McNally asked to be left alone after his alleged admission of having been "on the job". He asked Garda Grehan if he recalled returning to McNally to find him on the floor and two other detectives there who had been beating him. Sorahan said that one was Garda Michael Finn but the other was unidentified by McNally. This garda had hit him with a blackjack. Garda Grehan said that this had not happened.

Sorahan: I have to put it that you assisted him up from the floor gently and slowly from the floor to his seat?

Grehan: He was never on the floor.

Sorahan: And he was in great pain from bruises on his testicles?

Judge Hamilton: This witness said this incident never happened.

Sorahan dropped his line of questioning and moved on to the period later on the Wednesday morning when Inspector Courtney and Sergeant Canavan took a statement from McNally.

Garda Grehan denied that McNally was ill treated at any stage during the time his statement was being written down on Wednesday morning. He rejected suggestions by Sorahan that he had been shoved back and forth between Inspector Courtney and Sergeant Canavan or that some other detective stood beside him when he was seated and tapped on his head with the top of a pen.

"I wrote out a statement, read it over, he made a correction and he signed it and I signed it after him," said Garda Grehan. Nobody forced McNally's hand to write his signature.

Next to enter the witness box on behalf of the prosecution was Inspector Francis Campbell, the detective who was a sergeant at the time that he led the search party to McNally's home in Swords. He said he had questioned McNally in Fitzgibbon Street garda station with another detective, Garda Thomas Ibar Dunne. Inspector Campbell said he asked McNally to account for his movements on the night of the robbery. In a momentary slip not noticed by the court, he said McNally recalled arriving home to find his wife with a visitor, a Mr Ned Kelly. Seamus Sorahan asked about Garda Dunne's conduct during the interview.

Sorahan: I put it to you that Detective Garda Dunne shouted at Mr McNally and Mr McNally will so swear – "We want an account, you thieving bastard"?
Campbell: No my lord, that did not happen.
Sorahan: And at the same time during or a little before that remark, Detective Garda Dunne slapped my client on the side of the face with open hand, not with any great force?
Campbell: No.
Sorahan: It did not happen?
Campbell: No my lords.

The next witness was Garda Michael Drew, who had questioned McNally with Garda Grehan in Fitzgibbon Street station immediately after his arrest. Garda Drew described McNally's arrest, initial questioning and how he, Garda Drew, had taken food and drink to him at various stages during the day. He said that the following day, Tuesday, he had seen McNally in the Bridewell and had fetched one of McNally's tablets for him when McNally complained of a pain in his stomach.

Seamus Sorahan concentrated his cross examination on whether McNally had asked for a solicitor. He maintained that McNally asked for one shortly after his arrest, again around midday when he was in Fitzgibbon Street station, again later that afternoon and also later that evening. Garda Drew said that at no time did McNally make any such request.

Garda Drew also denied that a colleague, Garda Kieran Lawlor, hit McNally when they were questioning him together on the Monday afternoon.

Garda Thomas Ibar Dunne was called and briefly recounted McNally's arrest and questioning him about the IRSP.

During cross examination, Seamus Sorahan began almost immediately to concentrate on the period when Garda Dunne questioned McNally with Inspector Campbell. Garda Dunne said he spoke to McNally calmly.

Sorahan: Did you say to him "We want an account now you thieving bastard" or words to that effect?
Dunne: No, my lords, I did not.
Sorahan: With that, did you give him a slap on the side, not with any great violence?
Dunne: I didn't slap that man at any time, my lords.

Garda Dunne also said that at no time did McNally make a request to see a solicitor.

The next witness, Garda William Meagher, told of interviewing McNally in Fitzgibbon Street station for three hours on the Monday during which time McNally said he had nothing to do with the robbery. He was followed into the witness box by Garda Kieran Lawlor who had questioned McNally for about half an hour on Monday evening. Garda Lawlor said that McNally explained his movements on the night of the robbery.

Lawlor denied that he was carrying a newspaper when he entered the room to speak with McNally.

Sorahan: I have to put it to you that he wrote his name on your newspaper with Detective Garda Drew's pen and that he turned the newspaper around to you and looked at you – I'll hazard a guess at the word – cynically?
Lawlor: That is incorrect, my lords.
Sorahan: And that you then, what shall I say lest my client berates me for it, understandably lost your temper because of his provocative, perhaps sneering, attitude?
Lawlor: While I was in the room, my lords, McNally was friendly at all times.
Sorahan: It didn't happen? You never slapped or hit my client in any way?

164

Lawlor: No, my lords, I didn't interfere with McNally in any way, my lords.

Garda Felix McKenna, a detective with the Central Detective Unit, then gave evidence. He had interviewed McNally in the Bridewell on the Tuesday afternoon and evening with a colleague, Garda Thomas Fitzgerald, also a member of the CDU.

Cross examined by Seamus Sorahan, Garda McKenna agreed that during the first interview with McNally he and Garda Fitzgerald "behaved in a very mannerly and courteous way". Sorahan then described what McNally said happened in the second interview. He said that McNally sat on what seemed to be a two-seater sofa with Garda McKenna beside him and Garda Fitzgerald sitting on a nearby table with his legs dangling over the side. He said that McNally lit a cigarette but before he could take more than a few pulls from it, Garda Fitzgerald snapped it from his mouth. He said McNally would also swear that Garda McKenna suddenly stood up, making the sofa lop-sided and causing McNally to tumble onto the ground.

To each of the allegations, Garda McKenna replied: "Never happened."

Sorahan: Mr McNally was then caught by the shoulders by you and you looked down at him standing erect and said "What are you doing down there," in a very sarcastic tone?
McKenna: Never happened, my lords.
Sorahan: He was then pulled to his feet by you and he was shoved from one to the other of you, between Guard Fitzgerald and yourself – my instructions are without any great force – and shoved from one to the other several times and repeatedly?
McKenna: Never happened, my lords.

Sorahan continued to ask Garda McKenna if he had slapped McNally and hit him on the torso, in the kidneys and under his arms but the detective denied that any such events took place. Garda Fitzgerald then entered the witness box and was asked by Robert Barr for the prosecution if he had snatched a cigarette from McNally and pushed him about the interview room. He said he had not.

Seamus Sorahan asked Garda Fitzgerald if he had told McNally that his wife had been arrested and might be charged with conspiracy. Garda Fitzgerald replied that he had said no such thing and agreed that it would be a cruel thing to do.

The next man to give evidence against McNally was Garda John Hegarty, a detective with the Special Branch, who told prosecuting barrister Noel McDonald that he was with McNally briefly around midnight on the Tuesday. He said that when he went into the interview room in the Bridewell, Inspector Hawkshaw and Garda Grehan left.

Cross examined by Seamus Sorahan, Garda Hegarty denied that while he was in the room, a group of his colleagues burst in the door, motioned for him to leave and then set upon McNally. He denied also that when he went back into the room he found McNally on the floor, soaking wet as though someone had thrown water over him and that he helped him back into a chair.

"Nothing like that happened," said Garda Hegarty.

Inspector Hawkshaw gave evidence that he told McNally he should tell Garda Grehan the truth. He said he had a "general conversation" with him before leaving.

Inspector Hawkshaw told Seamus Sorahan that although he was not a member of the investigating team, he had been making some inquiries and called to the Bridewell on Tuesday night "to see what progress had been made". Sorahan asked him if he was aware that McNally was in debt and Inspector Hawkshaw said he was not.

Sorahan: Are you one of a number of officers who have, as part of their duties, liaising with, getting information from and paying police informers or touts?
Hawkshaw: I wish to claim privilege on that, my lords.
Sorahan: You claim privilege?
Judge Hamilton: On what basis do you claim privilege Inspector?

166

McDonald: Public interest, in the public interest I would have thought, my lord.

Judge Hamilton: Yes but I asked the question of the Inspector. He is the person who is claiming privilege, Mr McDonald.

McDonald: I beg your pardon, my lord.

Hawkshaw: An internal garda matter, my lords, and a matter really of public interest.

Sorahan said he had to suggest to Inspector Hawkshaw that he gave McNally a glass of water and gained his confidence. Having done that, he offered McNally a lump sum of £1,000 to clear his debts and a weekly payment of £25 for information on the IRSP. "If you don't do this, I can't save you," Inspector Hawkshaw had said, according to Sorahan. The Inspector denied that the incident happened. He said he would not be in a position to make such an offer.

The next witness was Superintendent John Courtney, the head of the murder squad but who at the time of the robbery investigation had been an inspector. He told the court that he interviewed McNally around 5 am on Wednesday morning with Sergeant Michael Canavan. According to Superintendent Courtney, McNally said that he was not involved in the robbery and explained his movements on the night in question.

"Then, after a while," said Superintendent Courtney, "he said he was not involved in the robbery but he knew the names of persons involved. Then, after a while, he said that he was involved himself but he said that he didn't know what was happening until he arrived there".

He said McNally went on to describe how he arrived home and Nicky Kelly told him to drive to see some friends. They went in McNally's car to Sallins via St Margarets, Dunboyne and Maynooth. They parked the car a bit outside Sallins in a lane, said Superintendent Courtney. He began to read from his notes.

"They then went through a hole in a hedge and across the fields to the railway line," the Superintendent continued. "He said he saw a Volkswagen van in the field and about

167

three cars. He said Seamus Costello, IRSP, was on the railway line. Costello, IRSP, and Thomas McCartan were on the railway line. He said Osgur Breatnach wore a mask and Michael Plunkett wore a donkey jacket and he was carrying a lamp and a flag. He said Kelly – he said Nicky Kelly and Roche were dallying around and Fitzpatrick was directing things on the line. He heard three bangs, the train braked and stopped and reversed back and he said that then Fitzpatrick and Osgur Breatnach got into the carriage and then, after they got into the carriage, Osgur Breatnach threw out the mail bags and McCartan, Roche and Fitzpatrick took the mail bags. He and Kelly threw them to Barrett. After the van was loaded, Barrett closed it. I think he, Barrett, drove the van and he was accompanied, he thinks he was accompanied by Roche and Fitzpatrick and he said that Seamus Costello told him to get out of the place. Then he said that Costello was standing over the driver, I'm sorry the engineer, Costello was standing over him with a gun."

Superintendent Courtney said that he and Sergeant Canavan left the room at 6.50 am and he returned a few minutes later. He said that he and Garda Grehan then took a written statement from McNally. Superintendent Courtney said they finished taking the statement at ten past eight.

McNally was by then illegally in custody because his forty eight hour detention expired at ten past seven and he should have been released at that time.

During a lengthy cross examination by Seamus Sorahan, Superintendent Courtney said that when he and Sergeant Canavan went to see McNally at 5 am they had not been told that at 3.30 am he had made an admission that he was "on the job." He said that they repeatedly asked McNally to tell the truth and that "sometime later" he admitted that he took part in the robbery and gave details of what happened. Sorahan asked why this alleged admission was not written down at once, as required by the Judges Rules. Superintendent Courtney said there was no reason.

168

Sorahan: You are well aware of the Judges Rules, I take it?

Courtney: Yes.

Sorahan: More aware as any member of the Garda Siochana?

Courtney: Yes.

Sorahan: You have been cross examined about them dozens, if not hundreds of times in court?

Courtney: Yes.

Sorahan: The caution reads: "he wasn't obliged to say anything, unless he wished to do so, but what ever he might say would be taken down in writing and might be given in evidence"?

Courtney: Yes.

Sorahan: Why did you not write down what he was saying, he was being willing, speaking slowly, being co-operative and all the rest of it. Why did you not observe the Judges Rules and write down what he was saying?

Courtney: I did what I had done on a number of occasions and what I have given evidence here of verbal admissions, without taking them down in writing.

Superintendent Courtney said that it was not until 9.30 am (an hour and a half after he had finished taking McNally's written statement with Garda Grehan) that he and Sergeant Canavan sat down together to recall what McNally had said earlier. They made notes of what they remembered he said of the robbery: his initial admission about taking part and then after being cautioned, his description of what had happened.

The case against McNally was to hinge on these notes of what the two gardai remembered McNally saying shortly after 5 am plus his alleged verbal admission earlier in the morning that he had been "on the job" but was unaware of what was to happen until he got to the railway line. The written statement he made afterwards was not presented as evidence against him at the trial because the prosecution suspected that it would be rejected by the court on the grounds that part of it was taken when McNally was detained illegally.

The next witness was Inspector Canavan, a sergeant at the time of the train robbery investigation. He confirmed Superintendent Courtney's account of their interview with McNally: the initial admission of involvement followed by a more detailed explanation of what had happened. He told the court that he left the interview room before Superintendent Courtney and Garda Grehan took a written statement from McNally.

Cross-examined by Tony Sammon, another of the defence lawyers, Inspector Canavan explained that when he met Superintendent Courtney at 9.30 am they went to the inspector's office in the technical bureau. He said they sat down at two desks and wrote notes from their memory of what McNally had said to them. He denied this was "sloppy police practice". He said he didn't see much point writing down what McNally said because Garda Grehan was about to take a written statement.

Superintendent Ned Ryan entered the witness box to give evidence next. Since the robbery and the first trial, he had been promoted from inspector. He repeated Garda Grehan's account of how McNally said around 3.30 am that he had been "on the job" but didn't know that a train was about to be held up. He then gave evidence to the effect that McNally said he was a paid agent of the police.

"In a low voice he says, 'you can't charge me, I'm a paid agent.' It is recorded here," said Superintendent Ryan looking at his note book. At the first trial he had claimed privilege on this information in his note book but defence lawyers wanted him to reveal the contents.

Cross examined by Seamus Sorahan, Superintendent Ryan said that he had been on holidays at the time of the train robbery but was forced to return to Dublin because he was needed unexpectedly in a court case. It was while he was in Dublin that he got a tip off which he said involved the names of three or four people. He agreed with Sorahan that as a result of this information, the gardai arrested between twelve and fifteen people.

Superintendent Ryan said that on the night of Tuesday, April 6th, he was the senior Inspector in the Bridewell but he would not accept a suggestion from Sorahan that he was co-ordinating the interrogation of the various people detained in connection with the robbery investigation. He was involved in arranging a number of things – search parties looking for the stolen money and guns used in the hold up, for instance. He said he was not aware that McNally had been questioned by various gardai for virtually the entire day and most of the night when he went to see him around 3.30 am on Wednesday. He said McNally appeared physically fresh and not under any duress and he didn't consider there was anything unfair about him being questioned from midnight until dawn.

Seamus Sorahan also questioned Superintendent Ryan about the circumstances in which the district court took the unusual step late on Wednesday night, April 7th of remanding the four people accused at that stage – McNally, Kelly, Plunkett and Fitzpatrick – to the Bridewell rather than, as normal, to Mountjoy Prison. Superintendent Ryan denied that he asked District Justice O hUadaigh for a remand to the Bridewell.

> Sorahan: Did you in any way intimate to the Justice that you were wanting, or would welcome, a remand in custody to the Bridewell for the night?
> Ryan: No way, my lord.
> Sorahan: Absolutely not, are you sure of that?
> Ryan: Yes.

Superintendent Ryan said that he was aware of allegations of garda ill treatment by the time that the four were taken back to the Bridewell after the brief hearing in the district court. He said he found nothing unusual or extraordinary about putting the prisoners into cells together: McNally with Fitzpatrick and Kelly with Plunkett. It was done often, he said. Sorahan asked him if he accepted that this practice was against the regulations and Superintendent Ryan said he did. (Later in the trial, he would indicate the opposite.)

Superintendent Ryan said that after the four were in court again the next day and Michael Plunkett shouted that he had been assaulted by the gardai, he made enquiries from his colleagues. He was satisfied that nobody had been assaulted by the gardai.

A number of garda witnesses followed Superintendent Ryan to give largely technical evidence. Sergeant Patrick Bohan, station sergeant at the Bridewell in April 1976, explained some of the administrative duties of his position and how in the evenings, the prison section of the building came under the control of the station sergeant. During the day, there was a special prison sergeant responsible for the cells.

Another guard, Sergeant William Ryan, told the court that he was on duty at 5.45 am on Tuesday, April 6th, when he told McNally that he was being detained for a second period of twenty four hours. The order authorising a second twenty four hours in custody was made by Chief Superintendent John Fleming who, since the mail train robbery investigation, had been appointed an Assistant Commissioner of the Garda Siochana.

*   *   *

Brian McNally entered the witness box to give evidence in his own defence. He told Seamus Sorahan about his arrest and how, when leaving his home with the gardai to be taken for questioning, he took with him some tablets prescribed by a psychiatrist to help him relax. He was supposed to take them three times a day, he said. He said that he had been arrested before under Section 30 of the Offences Against the State Act and when he got to Fitzgibbon Street station he asked for a solicitor. His request was ignored.

He described his first period of questioning on Monday morning, April 5th by Garda Grehan and Garda Drew. They were polite and courteous but they were nonetheless strict. He gave them an account of his movements on the night in question and then the two gardai were replaced by two others – Sergeant Campbell and Garda Thomas Ibar Dunne. Garda Dunne demanded an account of his movements.

"I said I had given a full account of my movements to the

172

last two gentlemen," said McNally. "He turned around and, sorry when I say turned around I mean he says to me 'I want a fucking complete' – now he split the word complete to put the four letter word inside it – 'a fucking complete account of your movements' and he struck me on the cheek. Now I was completely shattered because this was the first time that had ever happened to me in custody."

McNally said he asked the two gardai where he was. Garda Dunne replied: "You don't need to know, you thieving bastard you." He described Sergeant Campbell as a "very profound, nice man," but said that Garda Dunne was pretty high and shouted at him. Garda Grehan and Garda Drew came back around noon and McNally said that he again asked for a solicitor and also for one of his tablets. He maintained that both requests were ignored: the gardai merely steered the conversation away in another direction. They questioned him over and over again about the robbery until around half past one, said McNally.

The next man to question him was Garda William Meagher, said McNally, and he was "very nice" but later he was visited by Garda Kieran Lawlor who was "pretty nice when he came in". He said that Garda Lawlor had a newspaper in his hand when he came into the interview room. He asked McNally his name and McNally got up-tight, having been already asked the same question about twenty times. He wrote his name on the newspaper and slapped it down on the table saying nothing.

"It seemed to spark off something within his complex...the next thing I knew I got a wallop across the side of the face", said McNally. Garda Lawlor then abruptly sat down on a chair directly in front of him and demanded a full and detailed account of his movements. McNally said he gave an account. When Garda Lawlor left, there was a trickle of blood coming from McNally's nose but Garda Drew said he had brought it upon himself, McNally told the court.

He described how for the rest of that Monday in Fitzgibbon Street station he was repeatedly questioned about his movements, his relationship with the IRSP and various other aspects of his life. A number of gardai got him things to eat. He said that around midnight he was put in a cell and was just about to settle down to sleep when he was roused and taken to the Bridewell. There, he lay down on a wooden bed with a wooden "pillow" and had a night's sleep disrupted by noises around him and a sergeant waking him to read him the order extending his detention for another twenty four hours.

In the morning he was given tea and two bread and jam sandwiches but he said that he gave the bread to another prisoner. Then Garda Grehan and Garda Drew took him from his cell for more questioning.

"I felt tired," McNally told the court. "I had a very uncomfortable night because I had been lying on a wooden form, or a wooden bench, and I was tired and fatigued. I had very little to eat other than a drink of tea. My stomach was at me."

Garda Drew got him one of his tablets and both gardai then resumed their interrogation. McNally told them he had once been a treasurer of the IRSP but that he had left the party, been expelled, because he was not devoting enough of his time to it. He said that by this stage in his interrogation, he had given up asking for a solicitor and the questioning went on until lunch – "spuds and corned beef" – which he said he did not eat. In the afternoon he was taken from his cell by Garda Thomas Fitzgerald and Garda Felix McKenna for an interview which ended when Garda Grehan came and took him out, past the station sergeant's desk where he was left standing in a sort of a hallway, just in front of a small room.

"There was just men looking out at me. They were in the same kind of clothes I was in, casually dressed, but none of them said nothing to me," McNally explained to the court. "I wasn't brought into that room nor none of them came out of it, but I was then taken from the desk, turned around and headed towards the iron gate...(leading) into the garda barracks."

McNally said he was then brought into another small room where he was confronted by a man standing with one foot on a chair and with a patch over one eye. He was told to remove his jacket, place it on the back of a chair and walk, slightly bent forward. After he did this, he was taken back to his cell again. The man with the patch over his eye was Ray Reynolds, the greengrocer. McNally was left in his cell from around 6 pm until around 8.30 pm when Gardai McKenna and Fitzgerald came for him again and brought him to a very large interview room where there was a table but no chairs. McNally said there was a large seat which he would call a bus seat.

He said that he sat down on the seat with Garda McKenna beside him. McNally took out a cigarette and lit it.

"Mr Fitzgerald suddenly removed it and he said, putting it on the ground, 'We'll tell you when to smoke'...Mr McKenna stood up and as he did, I fell," said McNally. "I didn't know then why I had fallen but there's only one leg on the bus seat and when he stood up the side that I was sitting in had no leg so naturally my weight, such as it is...I landed with my arse on the ground....Mr McKenna came round – seemed to come round to the back – and asked me what I was doing down there and suddenly and quickly he was getting me by the shoulders and bringing me up and as he brought me up, I seemed to go forward, I seemed to go forward in the direction of Mr Fitzgerald and he seemed to push me backwards and I seemed to be getting slapped and pushed. I couldn't figure out why."

McNally said the whole atmosphere had changed since his first encounter with Garda McKenna and Fitzgerald. He said they told him that his wife had been arrested and would be charged with conspiracy and they wondered out loud if she would stand up to interrogation with her heart condition. What would happen to his children if both he and his wife were charged?

Garda Grehan returned and the other two left. "I have no recollection of time now," said McNally and went on to describe the arrival in the room of Inspector Myles Hawkshaw. He spoke in a soft voice, said McNally, and fetched him a glass of water. He said that Inspector Hawkshaw seemed to know that he was in financial difficulties over his house rent and the repayments on his car.

"He said that if I had £1,000 it would help my debts and if I had £25 a week it would help to subsidise my dole and all I would have to do would be to pass on information to a contact. He didn't give me any particular name or any contact – as a matter of fact, at that particular time I was hurt," said McNally.

Inspector Hawkshaw went to the door and opened it: McNally said he saw around ten men standing outside, just looking in at him. Inspector Hawkshaw said that he could not help McNally unless he told him the truth, implying that he would let the men at him.

"I said that I can't make a deal with you because I am in nothing. How would I make a deal with anybody – I am in nothing. He said to me, you are afraid of your leader and I says I have no leader: I just have no leader, I am in nothing," said McNally.

McNally told the court that Inspector Hawkshaw then left the room and Garda Grehan returned again and told him that he should have listened to the Inspector. It came near to midnight when Garda Grehan was replaced by Garda John Hegarty.

"As Mr Hegarty is talking to me in a soft voice – he is asking me questions and I am answering them to the best of my ability – when suddenly the door bursts open, bursts wide open...and men just pile in," McNally told the court.

"Someone shouted at me: 'Stand up you Northern bastard' and I stood up and men seemed to gather all around me in all directions. I got a slap across the face. I got a backhander across the ear. Mr Egan (Garda Joseph Egan) didn't come to the front really to hit me. He seemed to do it around the side of someone else, you know, what I would call sneaky."

McNally said that he was pushed around the room from garda to garda to the stage where his clothes were beginning to come off him and he seemed to lose consciousness.

"The next thing I remember is I could see someone standing. My head seemed to be wet as if someone had either squeezed a sponge on it to put water on it...I was on the ground lying," said McNally. He told the court that he could not remember whether Garda Grehan or Garda

176

Hegarty helped him to his feet but they were the only gardai in the room when he came to. He told Seamus Sorahan that at that point he felt pathetic: his shirt was torn and buttons were missing and his spectacles were broken.

It was by now the early hours of the morning on Wednesday, April 7th. McNally said that Garda Grehan or Garda Hegarty (he could not remember which) seemed to be expressing concern for him and almost pleading that if he knew anything, he should tell.

"I could hear screams as if down the hallway, not so far distant, not so far away," said McNally. "And someone was screaming IRSP or something – it seemed to be a Northern accent – screaming with a high pitch voice: 'I know nothing about it, I didn't do it.' There seemed to be an awful lot of noise." McNally said he asked who was screaming and he was told "some of your friends."

Not long after this, two other gardai came into the room: one of them was Garda Michael Finn. McNally said that Garda Finn shouted at him to stand up and the garda who was with him brought his knee sharply upwards between his legs and hard into his stomach, missing his crotch. He was then struck on the top of his head and got "an enormous blow over the left eye." He was hit with a blackjack on the back, ribs, shoulders, legs and he was punched.

"I know I was screaming and crying. Somebody was shouting: 'We know you done it, we know you were involved.' This runs through my head. Every time I think about this, you could always picture – at least I can get it – what happened. I know I was screaming and the pain that was coming through me was severe. I think I cuddled my testicles and I seemed to roll off the table coming on to the ground. Having struck the ground – I don't even remember striking the ground – but I remember being on the ground. I know I must have rolled off the table: being on the ground my first sense again...I seemed to creep in under the table, possibly for protection."

McNally said he remembered that the door opened then and the garda with the blackjack quickly put it in his pocket. Two other gardai came into the room and one bent down, called him by his first name and asked if he was all right.

177

The two gardai who he said had beaten him left the room. He told Seamus Sorahan that he could not be sure if the garda who asked if he was all right was Garda Grehan but in any event he recalled trying in vain to go to the toilet and then being interviewed again by Garda Grehan.

He and Garda Grehan spoke again about the robbery and the van used to remove the cash. McNally said he told Garda Grehan he knew it was a Volkswagen because he had read it in the newspapers. He said the next thing to happen was the arrival of Inspector Courtney and Sergeant Canavan.

"You have been messing this man about all night," Inspector Courtney said, according to McNally. "I have only twenty minutes to spend with you."

McNally said that another garda came into the room and stood by him tapping a tender spot on his head. There was much shouting and then suddenly it stopped and a piece of paper was put in front of him. "A signature was wanted on that particular piece of paper," said McNally. The man tapping his head asked if he wanted to get the blackjack again. McNally said that he refused to sign again and again but he eventually did so.

"I could take no more. I couldn't stand any more. I wanted to get away out or somewhere. It all became too much. I could bear no more pressure: it is inexplicable – I would have written all over the Bridewell."

He described meeting the others before they were all taken into the District Court late on Wednesday night and again the following morning. The others had various injuries: Fitzpatrick had dried blood about his ears, Plunkett complained of sore arms and Kelly looked pale and whitish, said McNally.

His direct evidence to the court included details of his medical examination when he was finally taken to Mountjoy Prison. Sorahan finished by asking had he any hand, act or part in the robbery.

"I am innocent of the charges," said McNally.

Prosecuting barrister Noel McDonald then began his cross examination, concentrating on McNally's allegations that he was assaulted by various gardai from shortly after

178

he was taken to Fitzgibbon Street station on Monday morning, April 5th. McNally repeated much of what he had already told the court but McDonald kept asking him why he did not complain to the gardai. "It seemed pointless," said McNally.

McDonald: I must put it to you that you were not ill treated at all by any garda while in the custody of the guards?

McNally: That is not correct. I have given my direct evidence.

McDonald: And I suggest there was a pre-arranged plan by the IRSP, of which you were the treasurer, to allege garda brutality in the event of arrest?

McNally: There was no plan. You are correct in saying I was at one time a member but at the time of my arrest I wasn't a member of the IRSP and I know of no pre-arranged plan of any sort.

The following thirty or so witnesses fell into two main categories: those who gave medical evidence detailing the various injuries found on McNally after his period in garda custody and various gardai who were called by the prosecution to rebut his allegations of ill treatment.

Dr Sean O'Cleirigh, the doctor asked to visit McNally, Kelly, Plunkett and Fitzpatrick to provide independent medical evidence of their condition after they had been taken to Mountjoy Prison on Thursday morning, April 8th, told the court about his examination of McNally. He described in detail the shape, size and colour of the various bruises on his buttocks, his legs, shoulder, arms and ears. He also mentioned the various scratches he found and said that his general state was one of distress. During cross examination, he told Robert Barr that he thought the injuries could have been inflicted in the manner alleged by McNally – ie during beating by the gardai.

He agreed that some of the scratches could have been self inflicted – by a "metal top taken from a Fanta tin," suggested Barr. He accepted that all the injuries on McNally were minor ones which were "not the product of great force." Barr sought to cast doubt on the extent and

179

seriousness of McNally's injuries but Dr O'Cleirigh said that he believed McNally's distress was genuine.

> Barr: I have to suggest to you that, in reality, his sense of stress as you have described it, was no greater than would be that of most people finding themselves in the predicament in which he was, being accused of a very serious crime?
> O'Cleirigh: Well, I thought this man's stress was different to that of the other men that I examined at that particular time. I noted a difference in his case compared with the others.

The next medical witness was Dr David McGee who had assisted Dr O'Cleirigh. He told Seamus Sorahan that when he examined McNally, he had a "dark red crimson coloured bruising" injury to his left eye as well as the sort of other bruising and scratching described by Dr O'Cleirigh.

Robert Barr asked early in his cross examination if Dr McGee had previously given evidence on behalf of people making allegations against the gardai. He said that he had, on one occasion, following a request by Pat McCartan, the solicitor.

McNally's wife Kathleen was called next and she told Seamus Sorahan in detail what had happened the morning the gardai called to their home and arrested her husband. She maintained the gardai said they were taking Brian to the Bridewell. As a result of this, she had difficulty finding out where he was in fact being held. She said she knew nothing of what was to happen to her husband until mid morning on Wednesday, April 7th, when a garda came to the house to say he was going to be charged with the robbery.

"I just couldn't believe it. I lost my temper – it just couldn't be true. Something you read about in a book or something," she told the court.

She said that when she went to see him in the Bridewell later that day she was astonished at his condition: his hair was unkempt, his shirt was torn, his hands were black and dirty, he was white and had a black eye. She said he complained of sore ribs but mainly asked if she and the children were all right. She left the station angry and in a rage and tried to get a doctor in Swords to visit her husband. He refused because he said it was not his area.

Robert Barr cross examined Mrs McNally and accused her of not reacting speedily after her husband's arrest because she was aware of a plan to claim garda brutality, claimed that she did not make a very serious effort to get a doctor after seeing her husband and that she brought her children with her to the Bridewell in the hope of getting publicity in the media. Mrs McNally denied all Barr's suggestions and said that her husband was innocent.

The medical officer at Mountjoy, Dr Samuel Davis, gave evidence on behalf of the prosecution concerning his examination of McNally the day after he was admitted to the prison. He told prosecuting barrister Noel McDonald that McNally had bruising of his buttocks, legs, shoulder and complained of blurred vision. He also had a black left eye and complained of tenderness around his crotch. Dr Davis said the bruising was superficial although in one place, the left buttock, it was extensive. He agreed with Seamus Sorahan that the injuries he found on McNally could have been caused by an assault on him.

Further medical evidence was given by Dr Richard Burke, the doctor who examined McNally after he was transferred on April 9th to Portlaoise Prison. He told prosecuting barrister Robert Barr that McNally had bruises on his thigh, groin, above his left eye and was also complaining of blurred vision. He explained how in succeeding days, McNally came to see him on a number of occasions and was once taken to the Eye and Ear Hospital in Dublin for tests.

Cross examined by Seamus Sorahan, Dr Burke agreed that the injuries on McNally were consistent with an assault.

Before the trial proceeded further with more defence witnesses on behalf of McNally, Justice Hamilton made a ruling on a procedural matter raised by Patrick MacEntee. He pointed out to the three judges that some of the defence witnesses about to give evidence concerning what they heard in the Bridewell when McNally was detained there would be giving the same evidence in relation to Breatnach and Kelly.

The issue still being fought out was whether or not the court should admit the alleged confessions in evidence: the trial within the trial.

Judge Hamilton ruled that this issue would have to be dealt with separately for each of the three accused. This meant in effect that some witnesses who would give their evidence in relation to McNally, would have to be called back into the witness box to repeat their evidence twice: for Breatnach and again for Kelly. Judge Hamilton said that the verdict on the admissibility issue would be given after the court had heard the case against all three accused. Legal submissions could be made after the case against each of the three had been heard but there would be no ruling until the end of the trial within the trial.

George Royale was the first of the other witnesses to be called who had been locked up in the Bridewell on one of the nights that McNally, Breatnach and Kelly were there as well. Royale had a lengthy record. He was in the Bridewell because he had been re-arrested after the district court had struck out some charges against him. He was placed in a cell in the Bridewell along with two others arrested with him – his brother William and an associate, Peter Harrington.

George Royale told the court that around 11pm on Tuesday, April 6th, he began to hear shouts. People were coming and going along the passage outside the cell where he, his brother and Harrington were held. During the night the noise got louder.

"Later on we heard screams and shouts coming from the tunnel under the court. It went on for a very long time, I can remember I was very tired, couldn't go to sleep and later on in the night, going into the early hours of the next morning, there was an awful lot of screams and shouting from the tunnel. At the earlier stage, the first fifteen minutes, the only thing I could hear was 'You were driving, you bastard' and a few minutes after that, roars of 'Who was driving?' Later on in the morning, in the early hours, there was more screaming, shouting, and words similar to what I had heard earlier on. I went to sleep about 3 am."

Royale said that he had been in the Bridewell many times but he never heard anything like this on previous occasions. He said that he, his brother and Peter Harrington began shouting and kicking their cell door in protest at what they heard. A guard came, he told the court, and said they would be better off keeping their mouths shut.

When prosecuting barrister Noel McDonald took over questioning Royale, he immediately concentrated on his criminal record. Royale admitted that he had seven previous convictions in Ireland for housebreaking, assault, possession of guns and such like. McDonald attacked the credibility of his evidence.

McDonald: I must put it to you that this is pure invention?
Royale: There was shouting and screaming in the Bridewell – I know what I heard. I had never heard it before. It's absolutely true what I have said.

The next defence witness was a man called James Lawlor who was, at the time of the trial, serving a sentence in Mountjoy Prison but who, like the Royale brothers and Peter Harrington, had been in the Bridewell on the night of Tuesday, April 6th.

"I heard screaming and roaring and shouting in the Bridewell that night. I started banging the door to tell him to shut up screaming and another guard came over and told me to shut up," he said.

He told Noel McDonald under cross examination that he was in prison for pick-pocketing and was serving a twelve month sentence. He said that it was the first time that he had heard screaming in the Bridewell.

Peter Harrington who was also serving a sentence in Mountjoy at the time of the trial told Seamus Sorahan that he had been in the Bridewell "at least thirty times" before he was taken there with the Royale brothers on April 6th 1976. He repeated more or less the same evidence as George Royale: he heard the sound of screaming and someone being beaten.

Noel McDonald began his cross examination by listing Harrington's previous convictions: April 1976, Cavan district court, three months for stealing and receiving stolen property; December 1972, Kilmainham District Court, three months for driving without insurance; October 1972, Dublin district court, two sentences of twelve months for robbery with violence, breaking and entering and theft; also in 1972 at Dublin district court, two sentences of three months for loitering with intent. The list continued for some time before McDonald asked a question about events in the Bridewell.

"I could hear someone saying 'You did it, you did it' and someone getting thumps, you know, someone getting thumps and the bloke was saying 'I didn't do it, I didn't do it,' things like that. He wasn't saying these things but screaming these things because you could hear the words that were uttered," said Harrington.

He rejected the suggestion from McDonald that his account of what he heard was "an invention and it never happened".

"I am not in the habit of telling a cock and bull story," said Harrington.

William Royale told almost the exact same story as his brother George and once again, Noel McDonald began his cross examination with an attempt to discredit him by listing his criminal record. It began in 1964 in the Dublin Juvenile Court and continued with convictions virtually every year into the 1970s. He then queried him about what he said he heard in the Bridewell and Royale stood by his story.

Another prisoner in the Bridewell on the night of Tuesday, April 6th, supported what the other witnesses were saying. Alan Martin told the court how he had been arrested and held in Crumlin garda station until being transferred to the Bridewell around midnight. He said he heard someone shouting "You were there, you were there."

"The answer to that was 'Leave me alone, please leave me alone. Leave me alone' As I said, during the time he was screaming and crying and it seemed like to me as though somebody was being banged viciously against a door, the door of a cell, and there was reference made to 'under a bridge' but I couldn't go any further than that," said Martin.

Robert Barr asked Martin if he had been arrested in connection with the robbery investigation and had subsequently been convicted of house breaking in Bray. Martin said this was correct and he confirmed also that he was a member of the IRSP at the time of his arrest. Barr questioned him at length about his allegations and concluded with the suggestion that his evidence was "an entire fabrication."

"Definitely not," replied Martin.

The trial then heard one final piece of medical evidence from Dr Paul McVeigh, the doctor who stood in at Mountjoy Prison for Dr Samuel Davis, the regular prison doctor who was unavailable on the afternoon of April 8th when McNally, Kelly, Plunkett and Fitzpatrick were admitted to the prison. Dr McVeigh told prosecuting barrister Robert Barr that he found bruising on McNallys' body: on his left shoulder, left thigh, right wrist and around his right arm. There were also marks around both his ears and bruising near his left eye.

*   *   *

The following two days in the trial were taken up almost exclusively with gardai going into the witness box to deny and refute the allegations from McNally that he had been beaten and from other prisoners in the Bridewell that they heard screaming and people being hit. A total of eighteen officers ranging from detective gardai right up to the most senior man in the investigation, Chief Superintendent John Joy, all denied that anything incorrect had happened in relation to McNally's detention and interrogation. Some of the gardai who gave evidence were among those directly involved in the questioning of McNally, including Garda Grehan and Garda Finn. Others included station sergeants from the Bridewell – men whose responsibility it was to know what was happening while people were held there.

The denials were powerful evidence for the prosecution:

185

guard after guard said that they neither heard nor did anything wrong in relation to McNally while he was in custody. Despite often intense cross examination, the defence achieved very little: the gardai stuck rigidly to their version of events. The only non police witnesses (apart from one retired officer) were three women. One provided food for the prisoners in the Bridewell, the other two were called Matrons: they supervised the section normally reserved for female prisoners.

Mary Surdival and Ann Fitzpatrick were both on duty at various times during the period that McNally alleged he was being assaulted by gardai and when other witnesses at the trial had said they heard screaming. Both women said they heard nothing unusual while they were on duty and both, when cross examined by Seamus Sorahan, confirmed they were widows of gardai.

"I don't see what that's got to do with you or me," said Mrs Fitzpatrick.

Anne Bride lived in Church Street just around the corner from the Bridewell and she told the court that during April 1976 she was caterer to the prison section where she delivered breakfasts every morning. Sorahan asked her no questions.

There were no further witnesses after the gardai had given their evidence rebutting the allegations and the lawyers began to make their submissions to the judges. The process lasted for a day and a half.

The defence argued that McNally was illegally detained because his arrest was not carried out properly, that he was denied his constitutional rights by not being allowed to see a solicitor, that the gardai broke the Judges Rules, that he was detained illegally after the forty eight hour limit had expired and there were, of course, the allegations of garda brutality.

The prosecution case was that there was no ill treatment of McNally while in custody and that the statements made by him were voluntary. Any breach of the Judges Rules was merely a technical breach, not serious at all.

"It is the submission of the prosecution," said Noel McDonald, "that the statements made here by the accused were entirely voluntary statements and that they should be admitted in evidence; that they were not obtained in breach of any of the Judges Rules or in denial of any of the constitutional rights of the prisoner."

However it was not long before he was forced to concede that the Judges Rules had in fact been broken and McDonald also told the court that the prosecution was not submitting McNally's written statement because it was completed during a period when he was illegally detained.

Mr Justice Hamilton queried McDonald closely about the length of time that McNally was questioned. McDonald quickly pointed out that the Offences Against the State Act used the word interrogate and he said that McNally was not interrogated continuously for a full forty eight hours. There were only three breaks, said Hamilton.

McDonald argued that the judges should exercise their discretion and allow McNally's alleged verbal admissions of taking part in the robbery to be admitted in evidence against him. He said the breach of the Judges Rules was only a technicality. The last of the nine rules stated that any statement made by an accused person in custody should where possible "be taken down in writing and signed by the person making it after it has been read to him and he has been invited to make any correction he may wish."

McDonald suggested that the reason McNally's verbal admissions were not written down was because his account of events was going to be recorded fully in the written statement he was clearly about to make following his verbal admissions. The prosecution could not submit the written statement however because part of it was taken when McNally was illegally in custody. He argued in these circumstances that the verbal admission should be allowed in evidence.

"Any statement that you seek to have admitted must comply with the Judges Rules," said Justice Hamilton.

"I am putting it forward," said McDonald, "in this case that the court should exercise its discretion in favour of admitting the statement in evidence, that the breach of the Judges Rules was in the nature of a technicality."

With regard to the allegations that McNally was beaten while in garda custody, McDonald said there was nothing

187

oppressive in either the questioning or the length of time it lasted but he nonetheless had to answer the claim of brutality.

"My answer to it is that it does necessitate the court believing that there was this massive conspiracy between the gardai right up to coming into court here a second time and just perjuring themselves from the highest officer to the ordinary humble member of the Garda Siochana involved in this investigation," he said.

Seamus Sorahan addressed the court for several hours over two days and spent a great deal of his time going over what had been said in evidence by various witnesses. He argued first that McNally was in unlawful custody by reason of the "inadequacy of the words used in the arresting formula." The defence argued that suspicion of robbing a train was not an offence listed in the schedule of the Offences Against the State Act.

Sorahan also suggested there was a "deliberate and conscious" violation of McNally's constitutional rights by the failure of the gardai to get him a solicitor after he made several requests for one. The gardai denied that McNally asked for a solicitor but Sorahan argued that it was improbable that a man who had been arrested before under Section 30 of the Act would not seek a solicitor when taken into custody.

He said there were clear breaches of the Judges Rules due to the manner in which McNally had been questioned. He said also that McNally contested making any admissions of involvement but, in any event, the alleged verbal admissions should be excluded.

"I would ask you to exclude the verbal admissions on the grounds of oppression, and not oppression merely, but generally the course of the interrogation, the lack of rest, lack of refreshment..." said Sorahan.

Later in his submission, Sorahan mentioned the allegations of ill treatment. He conceded there was an "absolute chasm" between McNally's and the garda version of events but there was medical evidence from Dr O'Cleirigh concerning injuries to McNally.

" I ask the court to regard him as an absolutely honest,

candid and decent honourable witness whose evidence the court can accept," Sorahan said. "It is backed up to a great extent by Dr McVeigh, Dr Davis and by Dr McGee. So there is the position, my lord. The onus is on my friend (Noel McDonald) to prove beyond a reasonable doubt my client wasn't ill treated, he wasn't pressurised, that he wasn't shouted at, he wasn't thrown around like a shuttle-cock, that he wasn't felled to the ground, that there wasn't this wonky seat, that a cigarette wasn't drawn from his mouth, that Mr Fitzgerald (Garda Thomas Fitzgerald) never said these shocking things that he did say, shocking, reprehensible, dastardly things, lies about my friend's wife, the blackjack, the drumming on the head – all the rest of it. The onus is on the prosecution to prove beyond a reasonable doubt."

Sorahan's assistant barrister, Tony Sammon, addressed the court briefly on the Madden case. He said that in it, the Court of Criminal Appeal said the Judges Rules should not be departed from without adequate explanation. The Court of Criminal Appeal had quashed Madden's conviction because it decided that the gardai knew he was illegally detained when they overran the forty eight hour limit as they took a written confession from him. Sammon said that the same had happened with McNally: his written statement was not being submitted in evidence against him because it was taken in part when he was illegally held by the gardai. The two gardai who claimed that McNally gave them a verbal admission, Inspector Courtney and Sergeant Canavan, said they did not write it down because McNally was about to repeat it all again for his written statement. Sammon said this was not an adequate explanation for not complying with the Judges Rules.

Noel McDonald replied to Sorahan and Sammon by reiterating much of what he had already said in his initial submission. The underlying theme of the prosecution approach to the trial was perhaps best summed up by his colleague Robert Barr when he made a brief submission at the end of the case against McNally.

The gardai, he said, had a very vital role to perform in apprehending criminals and bringing them to justice.

189

Nothing should be done by the courts which would put "unreasonable stumbling blocks in the way of the gardai carrying out their duties..."

*   *   *

When it was time, twenty two trial days later, for the three judges to give their ruling on the admissibility of McNally's statements, it was clear that the Special Criminal Court was not about to place any obstacles in the way of the police. Announcing the ruling, Judge Hamilton said there were three statements being put forward by the prosecution and all should be allowed to stand against McNally.

The first alleged admisson that he was "on the job" was said around 3.40 am on Wednesday, April 7th, when McNally was being interviewed by Inspector Ned Ryan and Garda James Grehan. McNally had made the admission before he was cautioned that anything he said would be written down and could be used in evidence against him. Rule 6 of the Judges Rules said that statements made before prisoners were cautioned were not necessarily inadmissible but the caution should be said as soon as possible afterwards. On this basis, Mr Justice Hamilton said, the statement should be allowed in evidence.

The two other statements allegedly made by McNally were said to Inspector John Courtney and Sergeant Michael Canavan: the initial one was said without a caution and it was followed by another which neither officer wrote down, contrary to Rule 9.

"The verbal statement made by the accused to Detective Superintendent Courtney and Detective Inspector Canavan after caution was not taken down by them or either of them, was not read over to him and he was not invited to make any alterations as required by the Judges Rules. The court is however satisfied that the statement was made, was a voluntary statement and that the Judges Rules would have been complied with if the accused had not agreed to make a statement in writing, and should in the exercise of its

190

discretion hold it to be admissible unless helped by and being obtained by means of or as a result of a deliberate and conscious violation of the accused's constitutional rights," said Judge Hamilton.

The ruling declared that the gardai were telling the truth about what they said happened when McNally was held in Fitzgibbon Street garda station and the Bridewell. It rejected all evidence given on behalf of McNally except the evidence from Dr O'Cleirigh and Dr McVeigh, the two doctors who examined him immediately after he was released from garda custody and found bruises consistent with a beating.

The medical evidence demanded an explanation, however and, at the end of the ruling on all three defendants, the three judges made it clear that they accepted the theory that the three beat themselves up. They did this even though there was no evidence put before the court to support such a proposition.

"The court accepts that inherent in its findings with regard to each of the accused it has drawn the inference that the injuries that they suffered at the time of their respective medical examinations were self inflicted or inflicted by collaboration with persons other than members of the Garda Siochana."

10

Osgur Breatnach

The domestic problems of the Breatnach family upset proceedings in the Special Criminal Court. Osgur Breatnach's defence barrister, Patrick MacEntee, asked the court for an adjournment for the day because of certain exceptional circumstances. The decision of Judge Hamilton to grant his request was recorded by court officials in the sort of language that appears comical amid the often turgid legalese of the rest of the trial.

The court was adjourned "consequent on ceiling of Mr Breatnach's flat falling in on family and child taken to doctor...", said the official record. It added that the State offered no objection.

The day's respite from the trial provided all those involved with a welcome break. The opening remarks and the hearing of evidence for and against Michael Plunkett and Brian McNally plus the legal submissions on both had taken eleven days: about as long as many other criminal trials took from start to finish.

The trial resumed on October 26th 1978 with eight garda witnesses giving evidence of Breatnach's arrest on March 31st 1976, some hours after the mail train robbery and his detention in the Bridewell for forty eight hours. The evidence of the gardai in this section of the trial was crucial for the defence although all the witnesses were for the prosecution. Their evidence established two things: firstly, the fact that Breatnach had been arrested under Section 30 of the Offences Against the State Act as a suspect in the robbery investigation and, secondly, his conduct in custody. When he was arrested, Breatnach immediately asked for a solicitor and demanded the right to speak (and be spoken to) in Irish.

Breatnach was arrested again on Monday, April 5th 1976, in connection with the robbery investigation and under Section 30 of the same Act. However, in November 1976, the president of the High Court, Mr Justice Thomas

Finlay, had ruled in the Hoey case that the gardai did not have the power to arrest a person twice in connection with the same crime. Although the Hoey precedent was set in November 1976, well after the train robbery investigation, the court was bound by it in 1978.The defence team intended to use it in their argument that the gardai acted illegally by arresting Breatnach again on April 5th. The prosecution set out to show, however, that the multiple arrests were not deliberate violations of Breatnach's constitutional rights.

Sergeant Owen Fitzsimons of the Special Branch, a detective garda at the time of the investigation, gave evidence of arresting Breatnach on March 31st 1976 and taking him to the Bridewell. Other gardai – Sergeant Michael Egan, Sergeant Bernard Cullen, Garda James Grehan and Garda John Hegarty – gave evidence on questioning Breatnach and of taking his fingerprints. There was agreement between them that Breatnach had strongly insisted on conducting his business through Irish and that he persistently asked for a solicitor, naming Patrick McCartan as the one he wanted contacted on his behalf.

A string of garda witnesses would later swear on oath that Breatnach never asked for a solicitor when he was re-arrested on Monday, April 5th. The defence questioned the credibility of this assertion, given his agreed conduct when arrested on March 31st. The man in overall charge of the investigation, Chief Superintendent John Joy, was called and told prosecution barrister Robert Barr that he held a conference in Dublin Castle on Sunday, April 4th, at which a list of suspects was drawn up for a series of arrests the following morning. The list included Breatnach, and Chief Superintendent Joy swore that he was unaware Breatnach had already been arrested in connection with the investigation.

The Chief Superintendent told Patrick MacEntee that when he ordered the series of arrests he took no steps to find out if anyone on the list had already been arrested. The second arrest of Breatnach posed a very serious threat to the prosecution case against him and produced some exchanges of semantic conversation between Noel

McDonald and Justice Hamilton after lunch on the first day of the hearing of evidence against Breatnach.

McDonald said the state of mind of the gardai carrying out the second arrest was important. The question arose "as to whether that second arrest was carried out in conscious, which is a matter of mind, and deliberate, which is a matter of mind, breach of constitutional rights of the individual involved..."

Hamilton: How do you differentiate between a matter of mind and a matter of intention, Mr McDonald?
McDonald: I don't think anyone could have an intention if they didn't have a mind.
Hamilton: I accept that.

McDonald said he wanted to recall Chief Superintendent Joy to establish when he became aware that Breatnach had been arrested twice for the same alleged offence. The officer told the court that it was not until about 5.15 pm on April 7th during the *habeas corpus* action by Breatnach in the High Court that he became aware of the double arrest. Justice Hamilton asked him if Sergeants Fitzsimons, Egan, Cullen and Garda Grehan (each of whom had been involved in the first arrest and detention of Breatnach) had been present in the Dublin Castle conference which drew up the list of people to be arrested, including, for the second time, Breatnach. The Chief Superintendent said he could not remember, he could not be absolutely sure if they had. The defence lawyers felt certain that some of the gardai who dealt with Breatnach during his first arrest must have been at the conference which decided his second, illegal, arrest because some were key people in the whole investigation: Garda Grehan who arrested McNally on Monday, April 5th, the day after the conference and who helped interrogate Nicky Kelly; Sergeant Egan who helped interrogate John Fitzpatrick, Michael Plunkett and Michael Barrett; and Sergeant Cullen who helped question Plunkett and Barrett.

Confirmation that at least one of the gardai involved in Breatnach's first arrest was indeed at the conference which decided his second illegal arrest was not long coming. Superintendent Patrick Casey told the trial that he issued a search warrant for the IRSP officers in Dublin which was executed on Monday morning, April 5th. Among the gardai who carried out the search was Garda Joseph Egan, a detective based at Dublin Castle, who said that during the search he arrested Breatnach and brought him later to the Bridewell.

Cross-examined by Patrick MacEntee, Garda Egan said that his namesake, Sergeant Michael Egan, who had questioned Breatnach after his first arrest, was at the conference. He also confirmed that Sergeant Egan took part in the search of the IRSP offices where Breatnach was arrested. MacEntee continued to undermine the credibility of garda insistence that when Breatnach was arrested on the Monday nobody was aware that he had already been arrested once before. He asked Garda Egan if he recalled hearing any of his colleagues making a remark to Breatnach when he brought him into the Bridewell. Egan said he didn't hear anything.

MacEntee: I have to suggest to you that clearly and audibly in your presence the guard who received him said words to the effect: 'You weren't out long, Osgur,' or 'Back again already, Osgur,' or words to that general effect.

Egan: No, my lords, that didn't happen in my presence.

Garda Egan also said that he did not hear a request for a solicitor when he arrested him but he confirmed that he insisted on speaking Irish. "He always asserts that," he said.

Robert Barr asked Garda Egan a few brief questions before he left the witness box. "Had you any reason to believe that you were not lawfully entitled to arrest?" he asked him. The detective said he had not. "I got my instructions and I carried them out," he replied.

Sergeant Michael Egan told Barr that the search for guns at the IRSP offices produced no results. Cross-examined by MacEntee he said he was aware that Breatnach had been arrested once – he had carried out that arrest himself. But he insisted that he was not actually present in the IRSP offices at the moment that Breatnach was arrested the second time. He said he had left to deliver some footwear to the forensic laboratory for examination.

> MacEntee: I have to put it to you, Sergeant Egan, that indeed you were present at the IRSP headquarters when Mr Breatnach was arrested?
> Egan: No, I was not.
> MacEntee: And that this account of having gone away with the boots is a device to avoid what are believed to be the implications of constitutional infirmities of a double arrest under Section 30?
> Egan: No, not at all. No.

The next witness was Garda Felix McKenna, one of the Central Detective Unit members involved in the interrogation of a number of the mail train robbery suspects held in the Bridewell. He said that with a CDU colleague, Garda Thomas Fitzgerald, he had questioned Breatnach for about twenty minutes around 8 pm on Tuesday, April 6th. He told MacEntee that he believed he and Garda Fitzgerald were asked to see Breatnach because Breatnach insisted on speaking Irish and Garda Fitzgerald could speak Irish. He denied that Breatnach asked for a solicitor and described the interview as a total non event.

Garda Fitzgerald told prosecuting barrister Noel McDonald that when he and Garda McKenna went to Breatnach, Breatnach said in Irish that he didn't have to answer any more questions until his solicitor was present. Under cross-examination from MacEntee, he agreed that Breatnach spoke good Irish. He said he took no steps to get a solicitor.

His evidence over, Garda Fitzgerald left the witness box and Justice Hamilton asked Noel McDonald if the court was going to be told what had happened to Breatnach between 1.30 pm on the Monday when he arrived in the Bridewell and 8 pm on the Tuesday when Gardai McKenna and Fitzgerald questioned him. McDonald said that

Breatnach was not interrogated during that period. There were, however, a number of gardai who gave largely technical evidence confirming the fact that Breatnach was in custody during the period mentioned. Assistant Commissioner John Fleming was also called because, as a Chief Superintendent, he signed an order permitting Breatnach's detention for a second period of twenty four hours – that is, the full forty eight hours allowed under the Offences Against the State Act.

Assistant Commissioner Fleming told Robert Barr that he believed Breatnach was in lawful custody when he signed the order extending his detention. Patrick MacEntee asked what reasons were given to him when he was asked to sign the extension order but Assistant Commissioner Fleming said he could not remember.

The extension order was read to Breatnach not long after midday on Tuesday, April 6th, by Garda Peter Canavan. The gardai did not question Breatnach for the rest of Tuesday, apart from the twenty minute unproductive session with Gardai McKenna and Fitzgerald. It was not until around 5.20 am on Wednesday – the middle of the night when other suspects in the Bridewell were being subjected to intense interrogation – that some officers took him from his cell. The first of those to give evidence was Inspector John Murphy, a detective normally based at Kevin Street garda station, who said he spoke to Breatnach first in what he described as a "passageway" downstairs from his cell and later in a room upstairs.

He said he questioned him with Garda Fitzgerald who spoke Irish and that in the "passageway" Breatnach was asked to account for his movements on the night of the robbery. Inspector Murphy said that Breatnach replied: "Ce'n ait a beadh aon duine ag an am sin ach sa leaba agus ta fhois ag mo bhean cheile ar sin." (Where else would anyone be at that time but in bed and my wife knows that.) Inspector Murphy told prosecuting barrister Noel McDonald that neither he nor Garda Fitzgerald believed Breatnach and they told him so.

They then spoke to Breatnach about his family, his schooling, his old job as a porter with CIE and his work as

198

editor of the IRSP paper, the *Starry Plough*. By the time that Inspector Murphy and Garda Fitzgerald spoke to Breatnach in the "passageway" from 5.20 am until 5.40 am, Nicky Kelly had already made a statement, according to the gardai, and was embarking on his car trip with Inspector Ned Ryan and others to Ballymore Eustace and Bray. Breatnach was among the people named in Kelly's alleged confession. Brian McNally had also allegedly said to the gardai that he was "on the job". As Inspector Murphy and Garda Fitzgerald entered the upstairs room with Breatnach around 5.40 am they were joined by Garda Thomas Ibar Dunne who had been involved in the arrest of McNally and his subsequent interrogation as well as the interrogation of Kelly.

"I again asked him to tell the truth about it," Inspector Murphy told the court, "and Detective Garda Fitzgerald then said to him that other people had made statements in which he was involved. At that stage, Breatnach says 'Dearfaidh me mo phairt fein.'" (I will tell you my own part.) According to Inspector Murphy, Garda Dunne then got some paper and Breatnach made a statement which was written out by Garda Fitzgerald. He said the statement was finished at 6.50 am and signed by Breatnach.

Inspector Murphy was then cross-examined by Patrick MacEntee who asked him if he was being frank and honest when he spoke of a "passageway." MacEntee put it to him that the so-called passageway was in fact a tunnel which led from the Bridewell to the district courts, with a stairway of eighteen steps down into it, that it had a single light bulb hanging from the ceiling and one end blocked off by a steel door. He got Inspector Murphy to agree that the place had no table or chairs. The Inspector said that he interviewed Breatnach there because the Bridewell jailer said there were no rooms available.

MacEntee: Did it strike you as a curious place, to say the least, to conduct an interview?
Murphy: Well, I had intimated to the jailer that I required a room and my understanding was that it would be only a few minutes duration in wherever we would be.

MacEntee: You agree with me that it would be a very, very frightening few minutes to find yourself being conducted, in the early hours of the morning, by a number of policemen into a tunnel, an underground tunnel?

Murphy: I don't agree, my lords, it was part of the Bridewell – it was part of the prison section.

MacEntee: Have you ever interviewed anyone in that tunnel before?

Murphy: No, my lords.

Inspector Murphy told the court that it was only intended to interview Breatnach in the tunnel temporarily but he admitted that the gardai had not told Breatnach this when they took him there. MacEntee put it to Inspector Murphy that Breatnach had been taken into the tunnel – "the bowels of the earth at twenty past five in the morning" – to terrorise and beat him. Inspector Murphy said this was not so but he agreed that while he and his colleagues were in the tunnel with Breatnach, other gardai from the Special Branch were standing around the mouth of the tunnel watching. He denied that the instant Breatnach was in the tunnel he asked for a solicitor and he said that Breatnach appeared to him to be "natural, normal" while in the tunnel.

MacEntee suggested that the gardai then took Breatnach upstairs to what was a locker room to continue their "devilish brutality in peace": Inspector Murphy said this was not correct. Shortly after this, MacEntee became exasperated and asked the three judges if there was any point in his putting detailed allegations to garda witnesses in view of their blanket denials. Mr Justice Hamilton said it would be better if he detailed things.

MacEntee painted a different picture from that given by Inspector Murphy. He said that Breatnach would say he was slapped, punched in the arms, chest and stomach while Garda Fitzgerald shouted at him: "You were there." He said that Breatnach would claim a garda was acting like a character in a dumb show and saying in a sing song voice that Breatnach was seen throwing mail bags onto the track and that Plunkett was waving the lamp to stop the train.

Inspector Murphy said this version of events was not correct.

Inspector Murphy also denied that Breatnach was "frogmarched" out of the tunnel and up to the locker room. He said that in the locker room Breatnach indicated he would make a statement.

"Are you telling us that that just came out of the blue?" asked MacEntee. "Downstairs lying like a trooper – upstairs in the locker room total change of heart?" Inspector Murphy replied there was no change of heart, that Breatnach had spoken freely downstairs when he said he was at home in bed with his wife. "To what do you attribute his astounding change of heart in the locker room?" asked MacEntee. Inspector Murphy said he didn't know. MacEntee said that as far as Breatnach was concerned, there was a repetition in the locker room of the garda conduct in the tunnel.

He asked Inspector Murphy why Garda Dunne joined them in the locker room so that three gardai were interviewing Breatnach. The Inspector said he didn't know.

MacEntee: Detective Garda Dunne – Thomas Ibar Dunne – is a member of a group of detectives encountered frequently in these courts in relation to interrogation. Isn't that so?
Murphy: He is a member of the Technical Bureau, my lords.
MacEntee: He is one of this group which includes Detective Sergeant Canavan, Detective Inspector Courtney, Detective Garda Christopher Godkin, who are expert interrogators, isn't that so?
Murphy: Yes, they are all in the Bureau, my lords.
MacEntee: As interrogators, I suggest.
Murphy: I don't know what their function is, my lords.
MacEntee: I suggest, Inspector, that you know perfectly well, as does everyone in this room.

MacEntee put it to Inspector Murphy that when taken to the locker room, Breatnach was slapped in the face, punched on the arms, kicked on the legs and hit on the back of his head, on his chest and on his back, as well as being banged against furniture and walls. "That never happened, my lords," said Inspector Murphy.

"Mr. Breatnach will say that eventually he was so frightened that he said he would sign anything," said MacEntee. "Breatnach will say that Detective Fitzgerald was writing and he, Breatnach, said 'I was there. Write it down and I'll sign it.' He will say that somebody then roared at him 'That's not good enough,' pushed the table aside and began to beat him again."

Inspector Murphy said this did not happen. MacEntee asked him towards the end of his cross-examination if he had taken any steps between the time of the interrogation and his evidence in court to check if Breatnach's alibi of being at home was true.

"No, my lords," said the inspector.

Garda Fitzgerald repeated virtually the same evidence as Murphy when questioned by prosecuting barrister Robert Barr. Under cross-examination by MacEntee, he said that he did nothing to see if Breatnach had got a solicitor following his conversation with him on Tuesday evening, April 6th 1976. He said also that he told nobody of Breatnach's refusal to speak until he had seen his solicitor. MacEntee then questioned him about his period in the tunnel with Breatnach in the early hours of Wednesday morning.

"Are you telling your lordships to this very day you see nothing wrong with conducting an interview in a tunnel down eighteen steps?" asked MacEntee. No, replied Garda Fitzgerald, he saw nothing unusual about it in a garda station. He rejected the suggestion that the only reason Breatnach was taken to the tunnel was so that he could be beaten. MacEntee pointed out that there was a room available in the Bridewell: the room where Nicky Kelly had been questioned and which became available at almost precisely the same time that Breatnach was taken from his cell to the tunnel.

MacEntee concentrated the bulk of his questioning of Garda Fitzgerald on an examination of the statement written by him as Breatnach allegedly confessed to the gardai in the locker room. The typed up version of the statement was barely more than one side of a foolscap sheet of paper and just thirty two lines long. The original written by Garda Fitzgerald was full of scratchings and changes: twenty three changes, just two of which were initialled by Breatnach instead of all of them. Breatnach's christian name in the statement was given as Oscar. "Would it surprise you to know that it is a form of his christian name that Mr Breatnach never uses and never did use?" MacEntee asked. Garda Fitzgerald said he didn't know: there was a statement and Breatnach had signed it.

There were certain grammatical errors in the Irish used in the statement and the language appeared at times to be crude, basic and rather primitive: not of a standard which might have been expected from a person well versed in the language, MacEntee suggested. In the first line, the final letter h in "haon-deagh" (eleven) had been interfered with so as to remove it. Garda Fitzgerald said he was sure this was done as the statement was being written down. He accepted that the h should not be there and said it was a mistake. MacEntee asked him if he inserted another h in the word "clog" to make it "chlog" (clock). Garda Fitzgerald said he did it when he was writing the statement. MacEntee pointed out that two different phrases were used to describe a railway. In one sentence of the statement, the phrase used was "iarann roid"; in another, the phrase was "bothar iarainn".

There was a sentence which used an unlikely word for a good Irish speaker. "Bhi se ag tiomaint gluaistean dubh," (He was driving a black car) followed by "nil fhios agam an deanamh a bhi ar an ngluaistean" (I don't know the make of the car). The word "deanamh" in English means "make" as in "make a cake" rather than a model or type.

MacEntee continued to analyse and question Garda Fitzgerald in this fashion about the statement. Eventually he said he had to put it to him that the "choppings and changings" in the statement indicated it was made by "a very very angry man doing a very stormy interview and not a document made by a man who was relaxed, at his own pace, writing down what somebody was saying to him."

"I have to put it to you that the statement is your creation based on what you believed you knew about the crime and what you imaginatively believed had been Mr Breatnach's part in it," said MacEntee. "It is not my creation," replied Garda Fitzgerald.

The next witness, Garda Thomas Ibar Dunne, told Noel McDonald that he cautioned Breatnach in Irish when he met him in the sergeants' mess which he said was commonly known as the locker room. He said that he got some sheets of paper on which Garda Fitzgerald took down the statement and that at one stage he fetched a glass of water for Breatnach. He was then cross-examined by MacEntee.

He said he had gone off duty at midnight but got a phone call later asking him to return to the Bridewell at 5 am. He said that when he got there, he learned that Nicky Kelly was accompanying some gardai to places where it was believed guns and money were hidden. He then learned that Breatnach was being questioned about the robbery and offered to assist Inspector Murphy and Garda Fitzgerald. He described how he arranged for the interviewing of Breatnach to be switched from the tunnel to the locker room.

> MacEntee: I suggest that during the course of that interview that Breatnach was beaten in your presence?
> Dunne: At no stage was Breatnach beaten in my presence by me or by anyone present. In no way was he abused or ill treated. He made one request for a drink. I got him a drink of water. That was the only request he made to me.

Garda Dunne rejected the suggestions put to him by MacEntee that the statement alleged to have been made by Breatnach was in fact made up by Garda Fitzgerald.

The prosecution maintained that Breatnach made further verbal confessions after signing his written statement about 6.50 am. Three other gardai took over then and the first of them to be called in evidence was Garda William Meagher, the detective who had been involved in the arrest of Nicky Kelly and the interrogation of Brian McNally. Garda

Meagher said one of his colleagues remarked to Breatnach: "It's all over, Osgur," and that Breatnach replied: "I know." He said that Breatnach told them first in Irish of his involvement in the train robbery, then in English.

Meagher: Mr Breatnach said to us in English, "Two days before the train robbery a man came in to our office and he said you do not know who I am and that is the way I want it to be. I am a member of your party and I know Costello and others of the men throughout the country. I want your assistance for a money job. I will collect you at the bus terminus at 11.20. He told me to establish an alibi. He said I was in no danger: everything was well planned. He collected me at the bus terminus at the time we agreed on in a big black car like a Cortina. We drove off and on the way down he said we were going to rob the Cork to Dublin mail train. When we arrived we parked beside the railway line and waited. I heard the train stopping and reversing back the track. This man then gave me a mask and I put on a nylon stocking mask. He asked me if I wanted a gun. He had a gun himself. I declined. This man, another man and myself then boarded the train. The other man pointed out certain sacks which I threw to another man outside the train. In all, I threw out six to eight sacks. I then travelled back with this man and I arrived at my home at around 5 am." During the interview Detective Garda (Gerard) O'Carroll and Breatnach spoke both in Irish and English. Breatnach said "If I knew who squealed on us I would shoot him dead." I asked Breatnach how he was feeling.
Judge: Did you take this down in writing?
Meagher: I didn't take it down.
Judge: Did you hear the caution being administered – anything he would say would be taken down in writing?
Meagher: Detective Garda O'Carroll took it down in writing. I didn't take it down.

Patrick MacEntee asked Garda Meagher what he thought Breatnach meant when he said he knew that it was all over. Garda Meagher said he didn't take any meaning from it.

Garda Dunne had asked him to go in and stay with Breatnach for a while. He agreed that it would be normal for a prisoner to be returned to his cell after making a statement and he did not know why that hadn't happened with Breatnach.

MacEntee: Tell me, did somebody in your group have a truncheon or a strap or some device like that?

Meagher: No, my lords.

MacEntee: I wonder could I have the sawn off truncheon that was here the last time? Was there some talk about "filling in the gaps" in the statement?

Meagher: No, my lords.

MacEntee: Mr Breatnach recalls somebody speaking about, some of the police present mentioning this phrase "filling in the gaps?"

Meagher: No, my lords.

The sawn off truncheon was given to MacEntee by a court official and he showed it to Garda Meagher. The detective said he did not recognise it and MacEntee said that Breatnach would allege that during the interview with the three gardai, someone used it to bang the table and hit him once on the knee. "Definitely not," said Garda Meagher.

MacEntee suggested that the three gardai tried to get names out of Breatnach and told him what an awful place Portlaoise was – how one of their colleagues could earn £100 a week in overtime there but gave it up because the place was so unpleasant to work in. Garda Meagher said this was not true. He eventually took it upon himself to return Breatnach to his cell.

MacEntee: Was this because you had enough of him?

Meagher: No.

MacEntee: Before doing that did anybody bother to read the notes over to him and ask him in fact was that what he wanted to say?

Meagher: No.

MacEntee: Did anybody proffer their notes for signature?

Meagher: No, my lords.

MacEntee: Was there any reason why you decided to ignore the Judges Rules?

Meagher: (no answer to question)

MacEntee: You accept you did decide to ignore the Judges Rules?

Meagher: I didn't decide to ignore them.

MacEntee: Well you ignored them, isn't that right?

Meagher: I didn't feel at the time I was ignoring the Judges Rules.

MacEntee: Why not? Don't you know the Judges Rules require you to read over the statement that has been made by an accused and reduced to writing, it requires you to ask him if he wants to make any amendments and proffer it for signature?

Meagher: It wasn't done at the time, my lords.

MacEntee: We know it wasn't done but I am asking you if there is any reason why it wasn't?

Meagher: No, my lords.

MacEntee: Will you accept that the proffering of notes for signature and the reading over is an important protection for an accused person against things being fathered on him which he didn't say or having them recorded in a way that alters their emphasis or might alter their emphasis. Do you accept that?

Meagher: I accept it is an added protection.

Garda Meagher said that he did not tell his superior officers what Breatnach said about the robbery. MacEntee asked him to explain "without insulting our intelligence" why he did not do so given that he had what amounted to a confession. He said he may have told Inspector Ned Ryan later that morning.

Garda Gerard O'Carroll, the detective who said he asked Breatnach to tell the whole story, explained to prosecution barrister Noel McDonald that his Irish was poor and he could not remember at what stage Breatnach began to speak in English. He said that the interview ended around 8 am and that there was no ill treatment of Breatnach.

Cross-examined by Patrick MacEntee, Garda O'Carroll said that he had been home in bed when a patrol car fetched

207

him at four in the morning and brought him to the Bridewell for what was to be his first experience of a major interrogation.

MacEntee: And I think you are the owner of this sawn off truncheon here?

O'Carroll: That is my baton.

MacEntee: It is sawn off, it is an adapted one. Isn't it?

O'Carroll: I cut it when I was attached to the Detective Unit. It was the custom before to have special detective staves for plain clothes men but it had been discontinued and when I was in uniform, I had that old Dublin Metropolitan Police baton you see there, my lords.

MacEntee: And you got it sawn off to fit in your pocket?

O'Carroll: That is right.

MacEntee: And I think you told us you carry this around with you from time to time?

O'Carroll: I don't normally carry it. I should carry it more often, my lords. I should say I find that I have often gone when I should have carried it and not taken it but I do take it if I was on an important job or in danger to myself.

MacEntee: You see, I have to suggest to you that you had it with you in your room in which you interviewed Mr Breatnach on the night of the 7th of April.

O'Carroll: That is not true, my lords. I did not have it with me.

MacEntee: And I have to suggest that you tapped it on the table menacingly and once struck him lightly on the knee with it?

O'Carroll: That is not true, my lords. I did not have that baton and I did not use it.

The court was not told how the existence of the truncheon was known to the defence. MacEntee questioned Garda O'Carroll about the notes he said he made at the time that Breatnach was speaking. He asked him why in that case the notes were in the past tense: "Breatnach spoke in Irish," for example. Garda O'Carroll said it just happened like that and he explained that as Breatnach spoke in Irish, he translated what was being said into English for his colleagues while at the same time taking notes in Irish.

At one stage MacEntee accused O'Carroll of having what he called "monstrous" Irish. "Is it your evidence that an Irish speaker, a person competent in Irish said to you 'D'fheach an fear go raibh se a ra an fior' which is no language known to man," asked MacEntee. Garda O'Carroll said this was the nearest he could come to what Breatnach was saying. "Why not translate it into Urdu – what is the sense of translating it into a private language?" MacEntee spent about half an hour questioning Garda O'Carroll in great detail about the Irish he said Breatnach used.

Garda O'Carroll told the court that it was not until around 1 pm (some five hours after his interview with Breatnach) that he passed on to a senior officer what had been said to him. He also said that he had not read his notes over to Breatnach and asked him to sign them, as required by the Judges Rules. He said he was not aware of this obligation.

The third guard to have interviewed Breatnach with Gardai Meagher and O'Carroll was Garda James Butler, a detective with the Special Branch, who said he had known Breatnach for perhaps thirteen years. He gave almost precisely the same evidence as his two colleagues and added little to either the prosecution or defence arguments. He was questioned in detail by Patrick MacEntee as to how his notes of the interview were virtually word for word the same as Garda O'Carroll's even though he insisted that he never saw Garda O'Carroll's notebook nor his statement prepared for the trial.

Following Garda Butler, there was a series of witnesses who gave medical evidence and details of what happened to Breatnach during the period of his *habeas corpus* action in the High Court and while he was in the Richmond Hospital. The first was Dr James Leitch, the casualty officer on duty in the hospital in 1976 when Breatnach was taken there on the orders of the High Court on the evening of Wednesday, April 7th – just over twelve hours after the start of his interview with Inspector Murphy.

Dr Leitch told prosecuting barrister Noel McDonald that when Breatnach arrived he complained of having been assaulted. He said he had pains in his arms, head, legs and was also complaining of having difficulty breathing. He said that when he examined Breatnach he found him to be in distress but his blood pressure and pulse were normal. His central nervous system was also normal, said Dr Leitch but he found a number of bruises on his body.

There was a small bruise on the left side of his chest, above the heart, on the inside of his right ankle and elsewhere on his right leg, said the doctor. He ordered that Breatnach be X-rayed, noted his findings and checked on him from time to time during the night.

Patrick MacEntee asked Dr Leitch how long was the time lag between being hit and a bruise actually showing. The doctor said his opinion on that would not be expert enough but he agreed with MacEntee that the injuries that were visible on Breatnach were consistent with an assault – a minor assault, said the doctor.

Dr John Reidy had been asked by the gardai to examine Breatnach as a result of the *habeas corpus* proceedings in the High Court and he gave evidence after Dr Leitch. He recalled visiting the Richmond around 8.45 pm on the Wednesday and seeing Breatnach sitting up in bed. He said that Breatnach told him he would not allow him make an examination without first speaking to his solicitor.

Barr: Did he show any signs of anxiety?
Reidy: Not that I noticed.

Cross-examined by MacEntee, Dr Reidy said that he saw Breatnach for about eight minutes. The court heard next from Dr Samuel Davis, the prison doctor in Mountjoy prison who examined Breatnach on Friday, April 9th 1976, the day after he was admitted to the prison. He said that Breatnach had bruising on his left arm, complained of soreness around his right arm, had a bruise on the left side of his chest, others on both legs and complained of tenderness around the back of his head. He said that Breatnach also complained of pains when he breathed.

Dr Davis told MacEntee that he thought if a person was hit or beaten with fists or the palm of a hand an impression would be left where the blow struck. He said that he gave Breatnach some pain killing tablets. He said he was satisfied that Breatnach had no fractured ribs because, if he had, it would have been "very painful."

In the middle of this medical evidence, the prosecution called Garda Philip Bowe, one of the gardai acting as jailers in the Bridewell in April 1976 when Breatnach was held there. He was on duty at 1.20 pm on April 7th when Breatnach was released because his forty eight hours under the Offences Against the State Act was over. It was Breatnach's immediate re-arrest which prompted his solicitor at the time, Dudley Potter, to initiate *habeas corpus* proceedings in the High Court. In order to formally release Breatnach, he had to be given back his property which was returned to him by Garda Bowe. He told the court there was a long list of items including diaries, papers, social welfare cards, an IRSP membership card, a nail file and three bunches of keys. He said that when Breatnach signed for the items he was very alert. "Just the same as he had been on the other days when I was on duty in the jail," said Garda Bowe.

MacEntee suggested that Breatnach's conduct was odd when Garda Bowe was giving him back his property: counting everything. Garda Bowe said that he found Breatnach "to be a particularly sour person....generally speaking."

The trial then turned back to the medical evidence with Brendan Breen, a prison officer at Portlaoise Prison, explaining that he examined Breatnach on April 9th after he was transferred there from Mountjoy in Dublin. He told the court that he found bruising on Breatnach's left upper arm, both his legs and a lump on the top of his head.

The medical officer at Portlaoise, Dr Richard Burke, described his examination of Breatnach on the same day. He said that Breatnach complained of pains all over his body, of a headache and insomnia. Like Breen, Dr Burke found bruising on his left upper arm and bruising on both legs which he described as minor. Dr Burke also saw a lump, about the size of a ten penny piece, on the crown of Breatnach's head.

"I think ... you are of the opinion that it could not or it is most unlikely to have been self-inflicted," asked Patrick MacEntee. "I think it is improbable," said the doctor.

He agreed also that the length of time that it took for bruising to appear after a blow was struck depended on the quality of muscular structure of the blood vessels under the skin and the capacity of the individual concerned to recover. "I would expect the major signs to be evident within three days," he said.

Sergeant Michael Egan of the Special Branch got into the witness box once again, this time to tell Robert Barr how he re-arrested Breatnach just after he was released, mid way through his consultation with Dudley Potter.

"He came out from the court section of the Bridewell yard, the courtyard section, out onto the street and I was standing across the road," said Sergeant Egan. He said that he told Breatnach that he was arresting him for a scheduled offence – the robbery of mail from a train on March 31st.

"You knew that this was the third time that Mr Breatnach had been arrested under Section 30 in connection with this offence," asked MacEntee. "It was, my lord," agreed Sergeant Egan. The detective claimed that he was not aware until the first trial began that the arrest of Breatnach on March 31st 1976 had also been carried out under Section 30. He accepted however that the third arrest meant that two in a row had been carried out under Section 30 – something which had since been declared illegal in the judgement of the Hoey case of November 1976.

The question of the double and triple arresting of Breatnach came up yet again with the next witness – Inspector Vincent McGrath of the Special Branch. He told Robert Barr that he went to the Richmond Hospital on Thursday night, April 8th 1976, and brought Breatnach to the High Court for the final decision of his *habeas corpus* action.

Cross-examined by Patrick MacEntee, Inspector McGrath said he was not aware that Breatnach had been arrested on March 31st and neither was he aware that he had been arrested for a second time at the IRSP headquarters by gardai carrying out a search there. He said he was aware, however, of the third arrest – the one carried out by Sergeant Egan. MacEntee questioned Inspector McGrath about the co-ordination of garda activities in the Bridewell.

MacEntee: Was there any one person whose duty it was to supervise the constitutional rights of persons in custody?

McGrath: No, my lords.

MacEntee: Was there any co-ordination or any device, structure, established to see to it that arrests conformed, arrests and re-arrests and custody and detention, conformed with the law and constitution?

McGrath: No, my lords, other than the normal procedure that is followed under Section 30 arrests.

MacEntee: What do you mean by normal procedure?

McGrath: That the arresting member bring to the notice of the Chief Superintendent in Dublin Castle, if it is necessary to secure an extension to a detention order and the subsequent issue of an extension order and dispatching it to the Sergeant in Charge of the Bridewell, so that it can be read over to the prisoner.

"Was there any structure of responsibility specifically directed towards vindicating the legal and constitutional rights of persons in custody," asked MacEntee. "There were no instructions, my lords," said Inspector McGrath.

Superintendent Ned Ryan told the court that he arrested Breatnach immediately he left the Four Courts after the High Court had ordered his release under common law and at the instructions of the Director of Public Prosecutions.

Dr Patrick Carey, a surgeon and senior consultant at the Richmond and a man whose evidence was rated highly by the prosecution, took the witness stand. He was the doctor who examined Breatnach at the request of the Chief State Solicitor's office. When Dudley Potter heard of Carey's imminent arrival at the Richmond, he contacted Professor John Paul Lanigan of the Royal College of Surgeons and asked him to do an examination as well on behalf of Breatnach. Professor Lanigan agreed with Carey's findings and the defence did not call him to give evidence at the trial.

Dr Carey told prosecuting barrister Robert Barr that he found no evidence of loss of consciousness when he examined Breatnach but there was bruising on his left arm, the left side of his chest and on his right leg. "I thought the bruising on the arm was consistent with a thump or pinch. The bruising on the right leg could be consistent with a kick – all the bruising was of a superficial type," said Carey. He added that he didn't find the lump on Breatnach's head which other witnesses had said was there. He told Patrick MacEntee that Breatnach's various injuries would be consistent with "minor thumping and shoving and being generally abused but not to any great extent."

Barr told Justice Hamilton that the prosecution had no more evidence against Breatnach and MacEntee wondered if the court would at this stage entertain a submission from him. He said the court should hold that there was a conscious and knowing breach of Breatnach's constitutional rights and that his questioning in the tunnel and locker room was oppressive. Justice Hamilton said that the court would prefer to hear all the evidence before making any ruling.

"I thought you might," said MacEntee as he called Breatnach into the witness box. His direct evidence in his own defence would paint a different picture to the garda account of what happened to him.

He described his first arrest on March 31st as he walked around a corner on his way back to the IRSP offices, having bought chips for his lunch. He stressed that he did not tell the gardai he wouldn't co-operate with them, only that he wanted his solicitor present.

"When I got to the Bridewell, the sergeant asked for my name and address," said Breatnach. "I told him I wanted to conduct my business in Irish – I gave my name and address in Irish, I asked why I was arrested. I was told I was arrested under Section 30 of the Offences Against the State Act. I asked for a copy of the Act." He said the gardai told him it was on suspicion of involvement in the train robbery

214

which he regarded as ridiculous. He was released after forty eight hours and there had been no serious questioning by the gardai. He said that at one stage, a garda asked if his solicitor had come and when Breatnach said no, the garda laughed and said that he must not have paid him last time.

He went on to describe his second arrest on Monday, April 5th 1976, which occurred when gardai were searching the IRSP offices. Breatnach said he called to the offices and, as soon as the hall door was opened, he was pulled inside by a detective. He said that he sat in one of the rooms watching detectives sift through documents before he was taken to the Bridewell.

MacEntee: When you got to the Bridewell, what happened?
Breatnach: I cannot remember whether at the desk...I asked for a solicitor so many times it is difficult to remember the times and places I asked...I am sure I asked either in the sergeant's office or the desk in the prison section, or both. I was brought to the prison section and asked to empty my pockets after coming into the prison section. The jailer ... was there and he had been there during my first arrest.
MacEntee: Did you speak to him during your first arrest?
Breatnach: Numerous occasions, either asking for a drink of water or to wash my face and we were talking Irish. He said "Osgur aris." (Osgur again).

He described how, during his detention on the Monday, he was given food and minerals, newspapers and also had a visit from his wife. He said that he gave her a list of the people in custody and instructions to contact the IRSP offices and Seamus Costello's wife. He said that during the visit, a detective entered the room and said he wanted to take his photograph. Breatnach said he asked the detective (he thought it was Thomas Ibar Dunne) what law allowed him to take his photograph. The hatch through which he was speaking to his wife was slammed down and he was pulled away.

"Both my arms were held under my side, my chin was

215

held firmly in somebody's hand around the back of the head, I was pulled back by the head and the photograph taken, a couple of flashes."

Breatnach said that later in the day, he was questioned by Garda Thomas Fitzgerald who was a native Irish speaker. He asked him for a solicitor. After he had gone to bed that night, he was woken and taken downstairs to the tunnel beneath the Bridewell. There he met Garda Fitzgerald once again along with other gardai. "I knew they were going to beat me," he told the court. "I put up my hands, I said stop, I will give an account of my movements." He said that one garda pulled his coat off and he was told that the money and guns had been found.

"They just laid into me...slapped me, punched me," said Breatnach. "I got kneed back against the wall a few times – my arms were pulled back."

> MacEntee: What was your mental condition at this stage?
> Breatnach: Well my throat was dry and beginning to get sore. I was crying. I was annoyed, I was angry, I was scared and I felt, what is the word, I felt degraded.
> MacEntee: Can you describe the third person you say was there, or fourth person?
> Breatnach: I remember his cheek bones were very prominent. I am fairly certain it was Detective (John) Jordan – I could not swear a hundred per cent, I am not sure.
> MacEntee: How long did the treatment continue?
> Breatnach: I had no watch, I wasn't timing it.
> MacEntee: How long did it appear to continue?
> Breatnach: A hell of a long time, at a guess maybe three quarters of an hour but it is possible it was only twenty minutes.
> MacEntee: How did it terminate?
> Breatnach: What I remember is being shoved aside in disgust...I thought they were finished with me at that stage. They said come on, they said get your coat. I picked up my coat, I cannot remember whether I put it on, I was a bit sore. I definitely brought it with me. I was taken up the steps to the Bridewell.

Breatnach then described what he said happened to him in the locker room although he mentioned that his memory was hazy about events there.

MacEntee: Do the best you can to reconstruct.
Breatnach: I remember the coat on the back of the chair at some stage. I was sitting on a chair. I remember being pulled off a chair or the chair being pulled from under me. I remember being thrown from detective to detective.
MacEntee: Do you know any of the detectives who were pushing you?
Breatnach: Fitzgerald was there, the others I cannot say.
MacEntee: Do the best you can. What impression do you have of the number of people?
Breatnach: At some stage definitely more than one: two, it might have been as high as seven – numerous detectives. I cannot tie myself. Four, five, numerous – a hell of a lot more than in the tunnel.
MacEntee: What did they do?
Breatnach: I was thrown from detective to detective. Thrown against the locker, table and chairs. I was kneed, punched, slapped, kicked. I tried to get myself into a corner to get them in front of me to defend myself by putting up my hands. I could not get into position but was backed off.

He maintained that while this was happening, detectives were screaming at him to confess and that eventually he said in Irish: "Write this: 'I was there.' " He said that Garda Fitzgerald took a pen from his hand because he was shaking so much.

MacEntee asked him what happened next and Breatnach said that the gardai would tell him to say something, he would say it and they would then write it down. "I would say 'what can I say?' and they would say 'you got there, didn't you?' and I would say 'yes, I got there.' They would say 'well, how did you get there, you got a bus' and I would say 'yes, I got a bus into Dublin.' That kind of way." He said that he didn't use his proper signature when signing the statement. "It was my last means of defence to prove to somebody that the statement was not voluntary," he said.

The next thing he said he could remember about his interrogation was being questioned by Garda Butler and Garda O'Carroll.

> Breatnach: Detective Garda Butler sat on my left, slightly forward, Garda O'Carroll on my right. I am not sure whether he was sitting down...I cannot remember what he said. I said to him the only reason I had signed the statement was I was being beaten and signed to stop the beatings. He said 'now Osgur, you don't expect me to believe that', or something like that, words to that effect.
> MacEntee: Was there some mention made at some stage about filling in the gaps?
> Breatnach: At the tail end of the other interview there was something said about gaps, or filling in gaps – I am not sure was it to me or somebody else – and I heard it.
> MacEntee: To your knowledge were there any gaps to be filled in?
> Breatnach: A hell of a lot in the statement – it didn't really say anything. It implicated me but did not implicate anybody else which they wanted it to. There were lots of gaps. I was hoping they would not cop on about the signature.

He described how Garda O'Carroll sat leaning forward with his jacket slightly open and something visible sticking out of the top pocket. He said that Garda O'Carroll used this to hit the table and once hit him on the knee – not hard but hard enough to sting him. Breatnach said that anything he told the gardai was derived from his knowledge of the robbery as a result of reading newspaper reports. He said that when he was brought back to his cell, he saw Garda Bowe, the jailer whom he told of his treatment. "It can't be that bad," Garda Bowe said according to Breatnach. "There's no blood showing."

> Breatnach: I lay down in the bed and I remember considering hanging myself in the cell.
> MacEntee: Why?

Breatnach: I had visions of being pulled out again to fill the gaps, as it were, and name other people.

MacEntee: Did you in fact do yourself any injury in the cell?

Breatnach: No, I remember staring up at the ceiling and trying to figure out how I could hang myself; I was thinking with the – there was a kind of a bar leading to the lamp flex and trying to figure out how I could hang myself from that, turning the bed on its side and using it as a ladder and using my jumper as a rope and I remember wondering were they watching me through the spy hole and what they would do if they caught me half way and the next thing I remember then is the keys in the cell again and Garda Bowe saying my solicitor was downstairs.

Breatnach said that when he saw Dudley Potter he was mentally and physically exhausted. He told Potter what had happened to him and Potter immediately asked him to strip and started to note his injuries. But before he and Potter could finish their business, Garda Bowe said his dinner was ready and he would have to return to his cell. The next thing, however, he was returned his property but he refused to sign for it because a copy of the warrant to search the IRSP offices which he had kept was missing. He said that he was released into the courtyard between the Bridewell and the district court building, to be met by Sergeant Michael Egan who re-arrested him.

He said he was brought back to his cell and the next thing he could remember was being brought to the High Court for the *habeas corpus* hearing which resulted in his transfer to the Richmond Hospital. He described his period there, his various examinations by doctors and visits from his family. He maintained the place was swarming with gardai who never let him out of sight and he said that he refused to leave the hospital until Potter gave him instructions. He described his eventual release by the High Court, his immediate re-arrest, being charged in the District Court and then removed to Mountjoy where he was examined again.

"Did you inflict any injury on yourself?" asked

219

MacEntee. "No" said Breatnach.

During a lengthy cross-examination by Robert Barr, Breatnach made it clear he totally rejected what the gardai said in evidence about him. "I am not accepting anything the prosecution is saying," he stated.

Barr brought him through all his evidence again. He suggested that members of the IRSP who were picketing the Bridewell on Monday night after many people had been arrested were chanting slogans about garda brutality several hours before any of the alleged assaults on the three people being tried. Breatnach said this was not true: they were only shouting about police harassment.

> Barr: Would it be fair to say to you, Mr Breatnach, that your story of police brutality pales into insignificance compared with that retailed by Mr McNally and that which has been retailed to a previous court here by Mr Kelly (we'll no doubt be hearing in due course)?
>
> Breatnach: I accept that, yes, and the others.
>
> Barr: You had no blackjack on the testicles?
>
> Breatnach: That's correct.
>
> Barr: You didn't have your head thrust into a toilet bowl?
>
> Breatnach: That's correct.

Barr went on to suggest that the reason why Breatnach had not given "a similar colourful account of alleged garda brutality" was because he only had the opportunity of inflicting a few slight signs of injury and, unlike McNally and Kelly, hadn't the benefit of others in custody to help him. "That's rubbish," said Breatnach and MacEntee immediately objected to the manner of Barr's cross-examination. He said it was "irresponsible and incorrect" for Barr to ask a witness something that he had absolutely no evidence to support. Barr said that his information from the gardai was that they never laid a hand on Breatnach and thus there was no other way he could have sustained injuries because he wasn't in the company of anyone else during his custody. Justice Hamilton said he would allow Barr to continue.

Barr: What you are saying is you deny having caused any of these injuries to yourself?

Breatnach: Absolutely.

Barr: Or any injury while in garda custody?

Breatnach: Absolutely.

Barr: Or while in the Richmond Hospital?

Breatnach: Absolutely. I think I would be capable of – if I wanted to injure myself – of doing more damage than that.

Barr: What you are contending then to the court is that you were compelled to admit participation in the train robbery by reason of intensive violence done to you by various members of the gardai?

Breatnach: The use of physical and mental torture.

"What happened to me is not a figment of my imagination: it'll be with me for the rest of my life," said Breatnach, refuting any suggestion that his confession was made without the gardai beating him. Barr questioned him about his injuries: he asked him precisely where he was hit and kicked. Breatnach said that the terror of his experience had not worn off months later and caused him to have a nervous breakdown.

Barr quizzed him about his wife's visit: why hadn't she got a solicitor for him when he asked her on Monday? "Because she phoned the IRSP office which was in the custody of the gardai at the time, who answered pretending they were IRSP members and said they'd take care of it." The cross-examination continued in this way: Barr questioned Breatnach in detail about what he claimed had happened and, at each turn, tried to find holes in his account so that he could knock it down.

There was one curious detail in Breatnach's alleged confession. The statement said that the man who gave him a lift to the robbery had met him at the 7A bus terminus at Burgh Quay. Michael Green, a CIE inspector called by the defence, confirmed for the trial judges that the 7A terminus was not at Burgh Quay, it was at Eden Quay. The defence maintained this was an example of how Breatnach had deliberately put an error into his statement to back up his assertion that it was not a true account of something he had done.

Dudley Potter gave evidence on behalf of Breatnach and described in detail his visit to the Bridewell at lunchtime on Wednesday, April 7th 1976; how it was interrupted; the subsequent *habeas corpus* action in the High Court and Breatnach's transfer to the Richmond. He also recalled making a detailed examination and note of Breatnach's injuries and described his condition and appearance. He said that Breatnach seemed to deteriorate during the day.

"I saw him after the *habeas corpus* and he seemed to be shivering and then when he came into the court, he seemed to be...at around 5 o'clock...he seemed to be confused and upset and I recall that counsel was speaking to him and somebody from the chief state solicitor's office remarked that he should not be speaking to him. It was obvious the boy was not well and he seemed to be confused and upset then. He was asked a question and he said, 'No, no, I want to answer that question.' He was very confused at that stage. That was the low ebb of his condition at that time," said Potter.

The next witness for the defence, Dr Noel Smith, told MacEntee that he was the Breatnach family doctor and was asked by Osgur's father to visit his son in the Bridewell. He said that he managed to carry out an examination in the Four Courts during the *habeas corpus* proceedings. He described the injuries he saw on Breatnach and the various pains which Breatnach said he had in various places. Smith said he reached the conclusion that Breatnach was severely ill and he feared that he might have concussion.

Robert Barr brought Dr Smith through his evidence once again, questioning him in detail about most of what he said. He suggested finally that while Smith might have honestly and sincerely believed Breatnach to be seriously ill, he was in fact taken in by the sight of Breatnach taking off his clothes as if in pain and limping. Smith said he had thirty five years' experience as a doctor and did not "rush into any hasty conclusions".

Then Barr made a suggestion which appeared to startle Justice Hamilton.

Barr: Dr Smith, there is another aspect to your feelings, I suggest, that it might be more difficult to divorce. I would appreciate that you are not a member of the Irish Republican Socialist Party or associated with it but are you associated with the Provisional Sinn Fein?

Smith: No. No, sir. No.

Hamilton: Is that question in accordance with your instructions?

Barr: I asked the question.

Hamilton: Yes, but I am asking you is that question in accordance with your instructions?

Barr: My instructions are that Dr Smith's surgery is used as a regular meeting place for the Provisional Sinn Fein.

Smith: That is absolutely untrue and unfounded.

Barr: And I can call evidence to that effect, my lord.

Hamilton: I expect you to.

Sorahan: I hope he will be cross-examined on it.

Hamilton: All right, Mr Sorahan, it doesn't concern you.

Smith: That is completely untrue, my surgery is only used for the treatment of patients solely and nothing else.

Barr: Perhaps I should specify, as you might have more than one surgery. This is your surgery in Monkstown, at or near the ring in Monkstown?

Smith: Yes.

Barr: You have a surgery there?

Smith: I have, yes.

Barr: And I suggest to you that that surgery has been used repeatedly as a meeting place for members of Provisional Sinn Fein.

Smith: Not to my knowledge and my surgery...

Hamilton: It is all right, you have said no and Mr Barr is bound by your answer.

Smith: But he also said that he was going to bring evidence to show that it was.

Hamilton: That is a question that goes to your credibility and Mr Barr is bound by your answer.

Smith: Yes.

Barr: You are still retaining the view as to Mr Breatnach's injuries that he was in fact suffering from concussion at the time you examined him in the Four

Courts?
Smith: Yes.

Although the cross-examination ended there, Dr Smith was
clearly upset at Barr's conduct and he found an ally in
Judge Hamilton. Before he left the witness box, he asked
the judge was the allegation just going to be left "hanging
over me". Justice Hamilton said it was unfortunate the
suggestion was ever made. He said the court accepted the
doctor's assurances and he hoped that Barr did as well. Barr
never produced the evidence he claimed to have to support
his allegation.

Smith was followed into the witness box by Aidan
Browne, the barrister who had appeared for the gardai when
Breatnach applied for the *habeas corpus* in the High Court.
Browne had turned defence witness because of what he saw
that day and he was also to undergo strenuous cross-
examination by the prosecution. He was first examined
however by MacEntee and told him that when he watched
Breatnach walk through the Four Courts on the day of his
habeas corpus action, he appeared dehumanised and as
distressed as anyone he had ever seen. He said he had an
impression of what Breatnach looked like because it had
made such an impact on him at the time.

"It was an overall impression of somebody who had been
to a sense dehumanised, that the attributes of the human
animal that distingushes him from the non human animal
were missing," he said. Browne had seen Breatnach as he
was escorted by gardai into the Four Courts and along a
corridor towards the court room where the High Court
would sit.

Cross-examined by Noel McDonald, he said he had
never before spoken to Breatnach but he knew who he was
because Breatnach had stood in local elections in his area.
He said that he thought a lot about what he should do: he
decided it would be inappropriate to raise it with the gardai
or the Department of Justice and he said he didn't see
"much point" raising it with the Director of Public
Prosecutions. He did speak about it however at the Fianna
Fail ard fheis the following February but didn't mention

224

Inside view of the post office carriage of the robbed train in a garda photograph produced as an exhibit during the trial.

Members of the IRSP late in 1976. From left: John Fitzpatrick, Michael Barrett, Seamus Costello, Nicky Kelly, Gerry Roche, Sean Gallagher.

Michael Plunkett on his way to court in Paris after his arrest there in September 1982.

Seamus Costello, IRSP founder and chief of staff of the INLA, who was shot dead in Dublin in October 1977.

Brian McNally (left) with his wife Kathleen and Osgur Breatnach and his wife Irene, after the Court of Criminal Appeal had quashed their convictions and sentences in May 1980. *(Photo: Dermot O'Shea/ Irish Times.)*

Nicky Kelly with his mother Stella at their home in Arklow, Co Wicklow, after his release in July 1984. *(Photo: Peter Thursfield/Irish Times.)*

Superintendent Ned Ryan at a garda press conference in November 1983.

Superintendent John Courtney in 1982. *(Photo: Jack McManus/Irish Times.)*

The Release Nicky Kelly Campaign: one of the many press conferences attended by (from left) Caoilte Breatnach, Mary Reid and Osgur Breatnach. *(Photo: Dermot O'Shea/Irish Times.)*

Patrick MacEntee, SC.

Robert Barr, SC.

Seamus Sorahan, SC.

Noel McDonald, SC.

Mr Justice Liam Hamilton (left), presiding judge in the Special Criminal Court during the second trial, and Chief Justice Thomas O'Higgins, the head of the judiciary. *(Photo: Pat Langan/Irish Times.)*

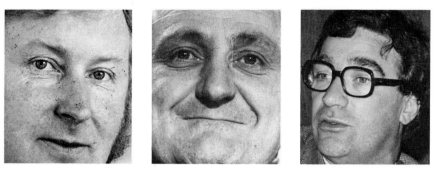

Justice Ministers (from left): Sean Doherty (1982), Gerry Collins (1977-'81), Jim Mitchell (1981-'82).

Patrick Cooney speaking at the 1977 Fine Gael Ard Fheis as Justice Minister. *(Photo: Paddy Whelan/Irish Times.)*

Justice Minister Michael Noonan, who ordered Nicky Kelly's release from prison in July 1984. *(Photo: Peter Thursfield/Irish Times.)*

Breatnach by name. Shortly afterwards, he was contacted by the gardai and confirmed that he was referring to Breatnach. McDonald tried to get him to elaborate on exactly what he had seen.

McDonald: Now this had meant a great deal to you and do you solemnly tell this court that you cannot recount one fact that justified this view that this man was in distress – just distress, we will come to the dehumanised in a moment?

Browne: What I said, Mr McDonald, what I perceived through my senses as you say, was an overall vivid impact of extreme distress and whether it be as a result of that impact or not I don't know but what I can recall is I can recall clearly and vividly the overall impact on me and I cannot recall what I described as the constituent parts or constituent impressions that would have made up the overall impression.

Later the prosecuting barrister tried again.

McDonald: Would you accept that dehumanised suggests something very much more than mild distress?

Browne: Clearly yes.

McDonald: What does dehumanised in the circumstances which you have used it mean to you in relation to Mr Breatnach? What did you see that led you to believe he was a dehumanised being?

Browne: What it meant to me and what I meant by the use of the word was that the overall impression of distress that I saw and the overall conditions of Mr Breatnach that I saw seemed to suggest to me that this was not a person who was distressed in a mild form but he had been distressed to the extent that he didn't appear to know what or where or who he was and that is what I meant by dehumanised. I think I qualify....

McDonald: Didn't appear to know what?

Browne: Who or what or where he was. I think I qualified this when I gave my direct evidence (evidence for the defence). I think I said that I used the word in the

225

sense that he seemed to be somebody not having the use of his human faculties.

The prosecution was unable to obtain any further details from Browne and the remaining witnesses in Breatnach's case were mainly prisoners who had been in the Bridewell when he was there and who reiterated their earlier evidence of hearing screaming, or gardai who said that nothing unusual happened in the Bridewell when they were there.

Sergeant Michael Egan was re-called by the prosecution because one of his garda colleagues had given evidence which agreed with Breatnach's version of events and contradicted his. Sergeant Egan had stated on oath that when Breatnach was released, mid way through his consultation with Dudley Potter, he (Egan) left the Bridewell through a front door and went across the street. Egan stated that Breatnach was released through a side door and walked out onto the street via some gates where he was arrested again. But Garda Philip Bowe, one of the jailers in the Bridewell, said that Egan walked with Breatnach out through the side door and stayed close to him. In other words, Breatnach's contention that he was never really released from custody appeared to be confirmed by a garda. The prosecution hoped that by recalling Sergeant Egan they could clear the matter up.

When he was re-called, Sergeant Egan said that he went out a back door of the prison section into a corridor. At the end of the corridor were two doors – one to the right which led into the yard between the Bridewell and the district courts and another to the left. Sergeant Egan said that Breatnach went out the right-hand door while he went through the left-hand door. He said this door brought him back into the Bridewell.

Another garda witness was to provide valuable information for the defence. Sergeant Patrick Bohan was on duty in the Bridewell on Monday and Tuesday evenings when the various IRSP members were detained inside. The prosecution had claimed that people on an IRSP picket outside were shouting slogans alleging garda brutality long before the three accused said they were beaten. Patrick MacEntee

226

asked Sergeant Bohan what he had written in one of the station record books on Tuesday evening about the picket. The sergeant listed a series of slogans from placards carried by the picketers: *End repression now*; *IRSP demand the right to organise*; *No collaboration with British imperialism*; and *No to Special Branch intimidators.* There was nothing about garda brutality.

The prosecution also re-called Dr Patrick Carey because of the evidence from Dr Noel Smith concerning Breatnach's condition and his conclusion that he may have had head injuries. Dr Carey agreed that the apparent disorientation of Breatnach when examined by Dr Smith would be an indication of head injuries. During the course of a detailed examination by Robert Barr and cross-examination by Patrick MacEntee, Dr Carey said that he examined Breatnach's head and X-rays of it and found no lump. Dr Smith said in his evidence that he found a lump on Breatnach's head and Dr Burke, who examined him in Portlaoise Prison, also said there was a lump on his head. The conflict between the three doctors was never resolved.

For the next day and a half, legal arguments were made by both defence and prosecuting lawyers as to why Breatnach's alleged confession should or should not be allowed to be used as evidence against him. Noel McDonald said that it should because it was a voluntary statement, not induced by any threat or promise. There had been no refusal by the gardai to get Breatnach a solicitor and there was no conscious or deliberate violation of his rights by virtue of his second arrest under Section 30 of the Offences Against the State Act.

It wasn't long before Justice Hamilton interrupted him to ask if he accepted that Breatnach was in fact unlawfully arrested on Monday, April 5th 1976, when he was detained in the Bridewell a second time under Section 30 on suspicion of involvement in the same offence.

"We start off with an accused, illegally arrested, in unlawful detention and a statement obtained as a result of this unlawful detention," said Hamilton to McDonald. "So then," he continued shortly afterwards, "in effect you are asking us to exercise our discretion to admit in evidence

227

evidence that was obtained by unlawful means."

McDonald replied by referring to the O'Brien case which concerned gardai who entered a premises to search it, unaware that the wrong address had been written on the search warrant. Although they were in fact searching the place they wanted to search and recovered stolen property in the process, the search was nonetheless technically illegal, although the gardai had not been aware of any illegality. He said it was his contention with regard to Breatnach's double arrest under Section 30 that although the gardai acted illegally, they did not do so consciously. There was no deliberate violation of his consitutional rights. He argued that although the statement had been obtained unlawfully, the court should allow it to be used because "the public interest so requires".

McDonald suggested that the gardai had not failed to get Breatnach a solicitor because in fact Breatnach had not asked for one. He said that Breatnach had a constitutional right of access to a solicitor but had told the gardai that he was not prepared to answer any questions in the absence of his solicitor. This was not a request for a solicitor, said McDonald. Justice Hamilton said there was an obligation to have the personal and constitutional rights of all citizens vindicated. McDonald said that Breatnach had only requested a solicitor twice: after he had been arrested on March 31st and Garda Owen Fitzsimons attempted to question him and on Wednesday, April 7th, when Dudley Potter was summoned for him. He said it was clear from the evidence that on other occasions Breatnach did not request a solicitor and therefore the gardai did not refuse him one.

On the question of garda brutality, McDonald repeated the proposition put forward during the summing up in McNally's case. To believe Breatnach suggested a conspiracy and cover up on the part of the gardai.

"You have got to accept the proposition that this was a massive conspiracy by all persons connected with the Garda Siochana, including the matrons, the jailers, the prison officers, the interviewing gardai and so on, to cover up and to come here and solemnly take oaths and swear falsely that nothing of the sort that is alleged by the accused occurred," he said.

He described Breatnach as "a bit of an actor" and said the questioning in the tunnel was not oppressive. "He knows the ropes, he knows the procedure, he knows all about it," said McDonald.

"*Ignorantia juris haud excuseat*," MacEntee said as he opened his submission. It was a long established legal maxim that ignorance of the law was no excuse for illegal activity, he said. He added that where rights were at hazard and no steps were taken to ensure that those rights were vindicated, ignorance of the law was no excuse even if no structures existed to ensure that individuals were protected. He said that Sergeant Michael Egan knew about Breatnach's first arrest and very quickly became aware of his second period of detention.

"It would appear to me," said MacEntee, "and I submit to your lordships, it is barely conceivable that human liberty would be held in such low regard in Ireland in 1976 that a person could be held for forty eight hours in prison and that nobody would bother referring to that arrest at the conference which assembled for the purpose of directing and organising re-arrests and at which it is very probable that some of the members of the first arresting party were present.

"It's not a question of this being an accidental lapse based on the fact that the second arresting party were ignorant that they were doing anything wrong but they didn't even know that factually he had been arrested before. That, in my respectful submission, is an intolerable position in a society governed by the rule of the law: where people are so disregardful of human liberty that they don't even factually know that a person has been detained once, twice, in this event three times illegally in this case, three times – two of them apparently illegally."

He said that this illegal deprivation of liberty in the investigation of a crime was more subversive than the particular crime under investigation.

On the question of access to a solicitor, MacEntee said the gardai did not discharge their duty and vindicate that right merely by making a phone call and not checking to see if in fact a solicitor arrived. He said the onus was on the prosecution to establish why Breatnach had not gained access to his solicitor – it was not enough merely to state that the gardai did not refuse to get him one.

The prosecution was alleging there had to be a massive garda conspiracy if the court was to accept what Breatnach was saying about his treatment in custody. So be it, said MacEntee.

"Your lordships are not asked to adjudicate upon any massive conspiracy: your lordships are asked to decide, bound by law, a single, simple issue on the law of Ireland as it presently is – is the statement, the statements, allegedly made by Mr Breatnach admissible in law in this court? The onus of establishing that they are lies on my friend (McDonald) beyond a reasonable doubt and if there is any intrepretation of the facts consistent with the absence of untrammelled will then, as a proposition of law your lordships are bound to give the benefit of doubt to the accused and exclude the statements made by him."

Regarding the written statement, MacEntee said there was no explanation if, as the prosecution maintained, Breatnach was telling the truth why there should be "at least one serious error of fact in it" – namely, the reference to the location of the bus terminus. How could it be explained that the statement, made by a person supposedly proficient in Irish, turned out to be "the most appalling gobbledygook." He said the prosecution offered no explanation for the marks on Breatnach's body after his period with the gardai. "But they brazenly invite your lordships to do the very one thing that neither your lordships nor I am entitled to do and that is bring in a finding based on speculation... that the injuries were self-inflicted."

He said that Garda Bowe had given evidence that the picket outside the Bridewell on the Monday evening did not include allegations of garda brutality. The injuries found on Breatnach were seen by the solicitor Dudley Potter and a number of doctors: Dr Smith, Dr Leitch, Dr Carey and Dr Burke. He said that all doctors in the case accepted that Breatnach's injuries were consistent with a roughing up or beating.

A certain tetchiness which appeared to exist between the defence lawyers and the prosecuting barrister Robert Barr surfaced when MacEntee referred to the attack on the credibility of Dr Smith. It was not the first attempt at character assassination, said MacEntee.

Noel McDonald repeated his contention that the gardai did not refuse to get a solicitor for Breatnach. "There has to be a seeking before you can have a refusal. There has to be a positive refusal before there is a breach of his consititutional rights. The only requests he made were complied with," he said. Robert Barr said that Breatnach was not solely dependent on the gardai to get him a solicitor: he could have got word to the picket outside the Bridewell and he could have asked his wife when she visited him. He did not want particularly to see a solicitor, said Barr, rather he wanted to prevent questioning unless one was present.

There had been garda evidence that the picket outside the Bridewell included a person shouting through a megaphone and alleging garda brutality, said Barr. He said that MacEntee had overlooked this when recalling the slogans on the placards. He repeated the assertion that to believe the allegations of ill-treatment suggested a large-scale conspiracy on the part of the gardai.

With Justice Hamilton, he became somewhat bogged down in a discussion on the issue of conscious and deliberate violations of a person's rights. Occasionally, comments became almost incomprehensible as when Judge Hamilton asked: "Does the conscious and deliberate refer to the act which constitutes the violation of the constitutional rights or to conscious and deliberate violation of the constitutional rights."

Barr urged the three judges to bear in mind the balance which had to be maintained between the rights of the individual and the "common good". He went on to suggest that if rigid constraints were placed on the gardai then the rights of the individual would outweigh the rights of the common populace. He said the prosecution regarded Breatnach as a person guilty of a very serious crime and he should not be allowed to go free "on a very flimsy technicality".

He stood over his contentious remarks about the use of Dr Smith's surgery by Provisional Sinn Fein. He said that MacEntee's reference to him over this was a "disgraceful misconduct" which he bitterly resented. He would make no apology for what he had said and only dropped the subject after he was repeatedly asked to do so by Justice Hamilton. With regard to the medical evidence, Barr took up an image of Breatnach first mentioned by McDonald who referred to him as "a bit of an actor." Barr said that he had performed for the doctors which had given rise to the "absurd contentions" by Dr Smith.

In a brief summing up, Patrick MacEntee concluded by referring to one of the great principles behind the administration of law in Ireland. He said that Barr had put forward an "extraordinary proposition".

"Mr Barr... maintains that in establishing the balance that he wishes your lordships should take between the rights, constitutional rights of the citizen, and the constitutional rights of the citizenry to have the criminal law implemented, which I don't doubt there are conflicts and that they must be kept in balance, he asks your lordships to regard Mr Breatnach as a man whom the prosecution maintains is guilty of a serious crime. For a lawyer appearing for the Director of Public Prosecutions to put that proposition before your lordships is, in my respectful view, nothing short of an outrage. This court and every person practising in this court must regard Mr Breatnach as a man in respect of whom the presumption of innocence applies."

The lofty principles of law and of justice which were mentioned by MacEntee did not, however, affect the outcome of the case for Breatnach. Justice Hamilton said that the court accepted that he was unlawfully arrested and illegally detained but the gardai had not deliberately or consciously violated his constitutional rights. The statements obtained in such circumstances by the gardai should be admitted as evidence against Breatnach because, he said, it was in the "public interest".

                        *   *   *

The court read out its decision on whether it would
accept the evidence against Osgur Breatnach fourteen days
later when the three judges gave their ruling as to whether or
not the statements by McNally, Breatnach and Kelly
should be admitted in evidence against them. Justice
Hamilton said that Breatnach's arrest on Monday, April
5th 1976, was not in accordance with the law and was a
breach of his constitutional right to liberty because of his
first arrest on March 31st. He said the court arrived at this
view having considered the judgement of the president of
the High Court in the Hoey case of November 1976.

"The court is satisfied beyond all reasonable doubt that
the second arrest and detention of Mr Breatnach was not a
deliberate and conscious violation of his constitutional
rights by any of the persons involved in it, and his
statements are not therefore rendered inadmissible," the
court declared. "The detention of the accused in the
Bridewell station between the 5th and the 7th day of April
1976 was undoubtedly unlawful and the statements made by
Mr Breatnach were obtained by means of and as a result of
such unlawful detention. The statements so obtained are
only admissible if, having considered all the circumstances
of the case, the court is satisfied that the public interest is
best served by the admission rather than the exclusion of
the said statements. The court has considered all the
circumstances in this case and in particular the fact that it
was not realised by the garda authorities until the decision
of the president of the High Court in Hoey's case that the
power of arrest under Section 30 did not extend to a second
arrest in connection with the same crime and is satisfied
that the public interest is best served by the admission of the
said statements. The court is satisfied also, having
considered all the evidence that at no stage prior to the
making of the said statements did the accused Mr
Breatnach during his second period of detention ask
members of the Garda Siochana or any of them to contact a
solicitor on his behalf. He did say that he would not answer
any questions unless his solicitor was present but at no

stage asked for or was refused a solicitor. Consequently the court is satisfied in this regard there was no violation of the accused's constitutional rights. Consequently, the court is satisfied that the statements tendered on behalf of the prosecution are admissible in law."

The fact that Breatnach had injuries, found by several doctors, after his period in garda custody did not affect his fate either. The court decided that he was not beaten by the gardai and his statement not made as a result of any ill treatment.

The judgement concluded with the paragraph applied to all the accused.

"The court accepts that inherent in its findings with regard to each of the accused it has drawn the inference that the injuries that they suffered at the time of their respective medical examinations were self-inflicted or inflicted by collaboration with persons other than members of the Garda Siochana."

11

Nicky Kelly: The Prosecution

On the twenty second day of the second trial, November
10th, 1978, the court began to hear the prosecution case
against Nicky Kelly.

The first four witnesses gave evidence about his arrest in
Arklow at 9.55 am on Monday, April 5th 1976 and his
transfer to Fitzgibbon Street garda station in Dublin. All
denied that Kelly had asked for a solicitor in Arklow or on
his arrival in the Dublin station.

Garda Adrian O'Hara of the Special Branch, who
actually arrested him, said he had told Kelly that he
suspected him of committing a scheduled offence under the
Offences Against the State Act, the armed robbery of a
CIE mail train near Sallins on March 31st. Before being
taken to Dublin, Kelly gave an account of his movements
on the night of March 30th/31st: he said he had gone to
Brian McNally's house and stayed there overnight.

Garda O'Hara told the court that he had interviewed
Kelly later that evening with Garda Thomas Ibar Dunne,
who asked Kelly if he had telephoned his girlfriend, Nuala
Dillon, on March 31st and told her that the job went okay
and they got plenty of money. Kelly said that was not true.
Later, O'Hara transferred Kelly to the Bridewell.

Cross-examined by Seamus Sorahan, Garda O'Hara
said Kelly did not look in the least distressed when he
interviewed him at 9.30 that evening. He, Kelly, had just
finished a meal of chips. He denied that Garda Dunne had
shouted at Kelly, banged the table or slapped him. Garda
O'Hara said he had left Garda Dunne with Kelly about
10.15 pm.

Garda Joseph Holland, a detective attached to
Ballyfermot station who had also been in Arklow, said he
bought fish and chips for Kelly about 7 pm on that Monday.
Later, he bought cigarettes with two pound notes that Kelly
gave him. After he was given the money, he inquired of

colleagues if there was any way of identifying the money taken in the robbery but was told there was not. Under cross-examination, he denied that Kelly had ever been ill-treated in his presence.

Garda William Meagher said he and Garda Michael Finn had questioned Kelly on the Monday evening. He denied that Garda Finn pushed Kelly against lockers, banged his head off a locker door and shook him. They both sat at a table and had a friendly chat with Kelly, he told Sorahan. Garda Finn never leaned the legs of a chair on Kelly's outstretched palms as he lay on the floor.

Garda Meagher said that he and Garda Finn again questioned Kelly the following day, Tuesday April 6th in the Bridewell. Kelly continued to deny involvement in the robbery. Mr Justice Hamilton asked if the detective was aware that the Judges Rules required that a person be cautioned before he was questioned. Why was Kelly not cautioned? Garda Meagher said Kelly had not said anything that incriminated himself.

That was not the point, the judge added: why did he question a person in custody without cautioning him first? "Now I cannot gave a reason," Garda Meagher replied, "but that particular time we did question him."

He went on to deny that Garda Finn had stood behind Kelly and slapped him over the ears or hit him on the shoulders. Kelly did not look pale or distressed when he saw him at that time, 3.00 pm on Tuesday, he said. Both his interviews with Kelly on Monday and Tuesday were friendly and relaxed, he told prosecuting barrister Robert Barr.

The first of the witnesses to give evidence about the crucial period beginning late on Tuesday night was Inspector Vincent McGrath of the Special Branch. He was the second most senior officer in the Bridewell that night after Chief Superintendent John Joy and Superintendent Patrick Casey had left the station.

About 11.30 that Tuesday night, Garda John Jordan asked himself and Inspector Ned Ryan, the senior officer on the spot, to go to the room where he had been questioning Kelly. Inspector Ryan said to Kelly: "I

236

understand you have made certain disclosures to Detective Garda John Jordan." Inspector Ryan then cautioned him with the formal warning: he was not obliged to say anything unless he wished to do so and that anything he did say would be taken down in writing and might be given in evidence.

Inspector McGrath told the court that Garda Jordan then read out notes he had taken to Kelly. When the prosecution asked the inspector what was in the notes, the presiding judge interrupted him. The witness could not be asked the contents of the statement until the court had decided whether or not to admit it as evidence, Justice Hamilton said.

His ruling appeared to differ from the practice that had been adopted in McNally's and Breatnach's case over the previous eighteen days of hearings. During the trial within a trial about the evidence against McNally, garda witnesses had been allowed to give the contents of statements whose admission the court was considering. The same had happened with regard to Breatnach.

Inspector McGrath said that after the notes were read to Kelly, Inspector Ryan asked him if Nuala Dillon knew about the raid. (Seamus Sorahan objected to the answer to that question. The judges first agreed with him – pointing out that this was a trial within a trial – but subsequently agreed to allow it.) Inspector McGrath said Kelly had replied: "She knew about the planning of it."

Under cross-examination he agreed that the alleged statement to Garda Jordan was the first break in the case since the arrests the previous morning. He denied there was any directive to keep suspects awake and agreed that Kelly was in one small interview room in the Bridewell continuously from 9.00 pm on Tuesday, April 6th to after 5.00 am on Wednesday, April 7th.

He said he did not hear any screams in the Bridewell that night: neither did he hear any noises or scuffling. He had not heard any protests from Section 30 prisoners nor had anyone come to him with such information. Nicky Kelly did not look tired or distressed or unusual in any way.

Inspector Francis Campbell from Pearse Street garda

station told the court about interviewing Kelly with Garda Thomas Ibar Dunne shortly after his arrival in Fitzgibbon Street on Monday and in the Bridewell the following morning. Under cross-examination, he said he did not see Kelly being ill-treated.

On the next day of the trial Garda Dunne from the technical bureau gave evidence. When he and Inspector Campbell first met Kelly in Fitzgibbon Street Kelly told them: "I can't help you." He gave an account of his movements, of staying in McNally's house on the night of the robbery. After forty minutes, about 12.45 pm, Inspector Campbell left the room and Garda Dunne said he had a general conversation with Kelly about himself, his politics and the IRSP. At 1.00 pm he was relieved by Garda Michael Finn and he returned at 2.30 pm.

Garda Dunne said from 2.30 pm until 6.15 pm he asked Kelly to tell the truth about the train robbery and had a general conversation with him. He did not admit involvement. At 9.45 pm he saw Kelly again with Garda O'Hara and put it to him that he had telephoned Nuala Dillon and had a conversation with her about the robbery. Kelly said this did not happen.

Garda Dunne said that Garda O'Hara left the room at 10.15 pm and he himself had a further conversation with Kelly. He added that Kelly admitted that he rang Dillon that day but said he had no conversation with her in relation to the robbery. At midnight, Garda Dunne said he asked Kelly to tell the truth and Kelly asked for time to think. At 12.55 am Gardai Finn and Meagher took him from Fitzgibbon Street station.

Next morning Garda Dunne saw Kelly in the Bridewell and asked him was he prepared to tell the truth about the robbery. Kelly replied: "I have nothing to tell you." He saw Kelly again between 3.30 and 6.30 that afternoon. "I again asked him about the train robbery and had a general conversation with him," Garda Dunne said. At 6.30 Kelly was given his tea and put in his cell.

At 11.50 pm that night, Garda Dunne saw Kelly again. He was with Inspector Ryan, Inspector McGrath and Garda Jordan.

Cross-examined, Garda Dunne said he had been involved in the train robbery investigation since the day of the crime and had interviewed the people on the train. He knew the details of the robbery but he had never met Kelly before April 5th 1976. The first he had heard about Nicky Kelly was in the course of interviewing Brian McNally earlier that day. He admitted that he never cautioned Kelly in any of his interviews with him: that, he said, was the responsibility of the arresting garda. In the eleven to twelve hours he was with Kelly he never cautioned him, he told Seamus Sorahan.

Sorahan: Nor did anyone ever caution him in your presence, isn't that right?

Dunne: That's correct, my lords, yes.

Sorahan: In fairness, the whole eleven and three quarter hours were not taken up by questioning, but wasn't a great proportion of that aggregate of eleven and three quarter hours taken up with questioning by you as distinct from general conversation or lulls or periods of silence?

Dunne: No, my lords. There was a lot of it general conversation. He was a very nice fellow to talk to. He was friendly. He wasn't rude or ill-mannered in any way. He was a fellow that was easy to speak to.

Sorahan: Was the position then as far as you were concerned, Mr Dunne, that you more or less – he was a likeable fellow?

Dunne: He was a likeable fellow, my lords and I believed that he was the fellow that was going to tell the truth in relation to the train robbery.

Garda Dunne said that at all times the atmosphere was friendly. He had brought Kelly back cigarettes after lunch on the Monday in Fitzgibbon Street. He agreed that he had not made a note of that or included it in his statement in the book of evidence.

Sorahan: I put it to you, and my client will so swear, that you never gave him cigarettes?

Dunne: My recollection, my lords, is that I brought back cigarettes to him on that occasion.

Sorahan: And that, indeed, the relations between you – I won't say war to the knife – but they were such that there would appear to be no likelihood or reason why you should give him cigarettes.

Dunne: No, my lords.

Sorahan: I have to put it to you that, all through, your attitude to Mr Kelly was one of hectoring and threatening him?

Dunne: No, my lords.

Sorahan: First of all, that on several occasions you slapped him?

Dunne: I never touched Mr Kelly, my lords.

Sorahan: That on several occasions, not one or two, but many more than one or two, you punched him?

Dunne: No, my lords. I did not.

Sorahan: Particularly on the arms?

Dunne: No, my lords.

Sorahan: And threw him around the room, generally.

Dunne: No, my lords.

Sorahan: Both in Fitzgibbon Street and subsequently the next day in the Bridewell?

Dunne: No, my lords, I did not.

Garda Dunne agreed that he did not believe Kelly's protestations of innocence. As an experienced policeman he believed that Kelly was going to tell the truth after he had asked for time to think at midnight on Monday. He denied that Kelly may have said that to gain a respite.

He added: "He was a nice fellow, my lords, as I have stated. He was not the normal villain, if I should use the phrase, and I believed he would tell the whole truth in relation to the story. How much he was involved at that stage I didn't know."

Seamus Sorahan asked if there was any conversation with a religious motif. Garda Dunne said he did not remember anything about religion being discussed.

Sorahan: My client instructs me that at some stage – he can't pinpoint it – that you shook some liquid on him ...

Dunne: No.

Sorahan: ...intimating that it was holy water and you were shaking it on him because he was some kind of an atheist or communist or something like that?

Dunne: No, my lords, that never happened.

Sorahan: That would be a very strange thing to do, wouldn't it?

Dunne: It would, my lords, very improper.

Sorahan: But haven't there been other cases, Mr Dunne, where evidence came out – indeed, that you admitted – that you had produced a crucifix to a prisoner or prisoners in the past?

Dunne: Other cases, no, my lords. One case in the trial of the Billy Fox murder case I admitted having my rosary beads and producing it to a prisoner in...

Sorahan: Well, at any rate, this never happened, this thing about the liquid?

Dunne: No, my lords.

Garda Dunne denied that he had ever told Kelly that his mother was in hospital with a heart attack. He said he did not know Kelly had a girlfriend named Nuala Dillon until Kelly told him in general conversation. He denied he ever told Kelly that she had been or was about to be arrested. He said he never gave Kelly to understand that she would not suffer if he co-operated. He did not know that Nuala Dillon was in Fitzgibbon Street station on the Monday night but he knew she was in the Bridewell the following night. He denied that he had brought Kelly out the door of a room in Fitzgibbon Street so that he could see Nuala Dillon talking to a detective. She did not see him, Sorahan said.

Garda Dunne said that around midnight on Tuesday, April 6th, Kelly was visited by Nuala Dillon in the Bridewell. He said he allowed them to speak to each other but did not listen to every word they said. He agreed it was a small room but said he was only there for security reasons. "I wasn't listening," he said. "They were allowed a visit, my lords. As such, I didn't interfere." Garda Dunne said he was with Kelly for thirty-five minutes surrounding the Dillon visit. That was the last time he saw Kelly during the investigation.

After most of a morning in the witness box, Garda Dunne was replaced by Garda Michael Finn, a detective in Store Street garda station in Dublin. He would spend the afternoon and some of the following morning giving evidence.

Garda Finn said he replaced Garda Dunne with Kelly at lunchtime in Fitzgibbon Street on Monday, April 5th. He also met Kelly in the same place that evening when he asked Kelly about his phone call to Nuala Dillon on the day of the robbery. Kelly said he had phoned her but had said to her, "everything is all right." He said he meant that he knew the police had been looking for him and that he was all right. Later, Garda Finn said he had taken Kelly to the Bridewell. He saw Kelly in the Bridewell on Tuesday afternoon and at 1.40 am on Wednesday, April 7th.

Garda Finn said that when he entered the room at 1.40 am, Kelly was speaking to two other detectives, Sergeant Patrick Cleary and Garda Joseph Egan. He appeared to be calmly telling them about the robbery: he showed no signs of distress or agitation. Sergeant Cleary was writing. Garda Finn said that he and Sergeant Cleary left the room for fifteen minutes and returned at 3.00 am. The judge said that the Garda was not to say at this stage what he heard.

Later that Wednesday, Garda Finn said, he went with Kelly to Harcourt Terrace garda station where they saw Michael Plunkett. Asked about Kelly's demeanour, he replied: "He appeared to wish to assist as far as possible and he didn't contradict anything he had said earlier. He was quite relaxed on the journey in the car and in Harcourt Terrace."

Kelly's appearance then, according to Garda Finn, was the same as when he had seen him first, more than forty eight hours earlier. He denied that he had ever struck Kelly or done him any injury. He had been courteous at all times, he told the court. Neither did he see or hear anyone else ill-treating Kelly.

Cross-examined by Seamus Sorahan, Garda Finn said he had received confidential information about the telephone call Kelly made to Nuala Dillon on the day of the robbery. He could not remember the name of the Special Branch officer from whom he received the information.

He denied ill-treating Kelly in any way. Specifically, he denied that he had taken up a chair and either hit or pretended to hit Kelly with it. He was asked if, when Kelly was on the floor, he told Kelly to put his hands out above his head. Garda Finn said that did not happen.

> Sorahan: My instructions are, you then got one of the chairs, sat on it and put the legs, the two front legs of that chair down on Mr Kelly's upturned palms?
> Finn: No, my lords.
> Sorahan: And that you sat looking down into Mr Kelly's face with his chin nearer your eyes than his forehead, you looking down into his eyes?
> Finn: Mr Kelly was never on the floor. For the duration of the interview he was seated at the table.
> Sorahan: You shouting insults at him, among other things?
> Finn: No, my lords.
> Sorahan: Perhaps asking him to confess?
> Finn: That was never an expression of mine.
> Sorahan: After some seconds, you took the chair off Mr Kelly's hands and he eventually got up?
> Finn: No, my lords, he wasn't on the ground.

Garda Finn denied that Kelly was so distressed that night in Fitzgibbon Street station that he was crying actual tears. He said he did not bring Kelly up to a cell in Fitzgibbon Street after the interrogations. He did not shove his head down towards a toilet bowl several times, take him around the corner and put him up against a wall and hit him with his knee in the thigh. He denied as well that he had told Kelly he was adopting him. Garda Finn said he only saw Kelly in the cell when he went up to take him out to bring him to the Bridewell. Garda O'Hara was there as well.

He said he had asked Nuala Dillon to meet him in Mountjoy garda station and had taken her from there to Fitzgibbon Street because Mountjoy station was being reconstructed and there was dust everywhere. He denied that the real reason was a ploy to show Kelly that she was in the station and make him believe she was in custody.

Garda Finn denied asking what Kelly thought of him at that stage during the car journey to the Bridewell. He also denied saying something like: "If you had a gun would you shoot me?" Garda Finn said he asked Kelly if he had enough cigarettes.

Garda Finn denied that Kelly was being shouted at when he saw him in a small interview room in the Bridewell at 1.40 am on Wednesday morning. He also denied that names were being suggested to him, that leading questions were being put to him, and that the atmosphere in the room was tense and menacing. He denied that he and Sergeant Cleary had ill-treated Kelly or that they ever interviewed him together.

Garda Finn denied that he beat Kelly with a blackjack on one occasion and that Sergeant Cleary beat him with it on two occasions.

The prosecution produced a chair in court which Garda Finn said was similar to those used in Fitzgibbon Street and in all garda stations. There were rubber tips screwed into the legs.

Superintendent Ned Ryan took the witness stand around mid-morning on the twenty fourth day of the trial. He had gone to Nicky Kelly's flat to arrest him on the morning of April 5th but did not meet him for the first time until 11.30 am on Tuesday, April 6th in the Bridewell. Kelly told him he was not involved in the robbery. Superintendent Ryan said he saw Kelly again at 9.00 pm that evening, had a conversation with him and got him tea and biscuits. On both occasions Kelly appeared normal and relaxed.

The Superintendent said he and Inspector Vincent McGrath went back into the room in which Kelly was interviewed about 11.30 pm after Garda Jordan called him. Kelly was sitting on a chair. "I said to him 'I believe you have told Detective Officer Jordan certain things' and I cautioned the accused, Kelly, that he was not obliged to say anything unless he wished to do so but that anything he would say would be taken down in writing and may be given in evidence," Superintendent Ryan said.

"Kelly replied 'I have' and, on my instructions, Detective Garda Jordan read over the notes that he had written down. When the notes had been read by Detective Garda Jordan, I said, 'Nicky, are they correct?' and Kelly replied, 'it is.' I then said 'did Nuala know about the plans for the job?' and Kelly replied, 'yes, she knew about the planning of it.'' Inspector McGrath left at this stage. I remained with Kelly. Detective Officer Jordan asked Kelly if he would sign the notes that he had written down and Kelly declined to sign those. There was ...we had a general conversation and I offered him a cup of tea and he accepted it and tea was brought to the room to him. We had a general conversation, my lords, and I said to him, 'Just tell the truth and nothing more'."

Superintendent Ryan said there was no difference in the atmosphere between this interview and his first session with Kelly. He went back to the same room about three hours later, about 3.00 am, with Garda Finn and Sergeant Cleary. "I said to Kelly, 'I believe you have told about your involvement in the train robbery on the 31st of March last.' I cautioned him that he was not obliged to say anything unless he wished to do so but that anything he would say would be taken down in writing and may be given in evidence... He replied, 'I have told everything I know' and then he made a verbal statement without any questions put to him by me or Detective Sergeant Cleary or Finn."

Superintendent Ryan then read out from notes he said he had taken at the time the account of the robbery that Kelly gave him.

"The job was planned a couple of weeks ago. Mick Barrett asked me to go on it with him. On the night of the robbery I went to McNally's house as I have said and when he came home I left with him at about 1 or 1.30 and the two of us travelled in his car by the back roads into town. He drove to Celbridge and outside Celbridge, we met Mick Barrett, Gerry Roche, Michael Plunkett, Seamus Costello, Sean Gallagher, John Fitzpatrick, Osgur Breatnach, Thomas McCartan, Ronald Bunting. McNally parked his car in a laneway over the bridge on the right hand side near the railway line.

245

"We went into a field through an open gate near a house. We all went down the field which was beside the railway track. Spoke to Michael Barrett and John Fitzpatrick in the field. They said everything was alright and that some of the lads were in the house. I got a revolver and my job was to help McNally to throw mail bags from the railway line up on to the field where we had a van to take them away. We waited around. Detonators were put on the track to stop the train. When the train stopped Seamus Costello took the driver from the train and took him to another carriage. Mail bags were thrown from the train onto the track. McNally and myself and maybe some of the others lifted the bags up on to the field. They were then put into the van.

"When it was finished Costello told me to get to hell out of the place. We walked back to McNally's car and the van drove out the gate of the field and turned right. McNally and myself then drove back the way we came to Swords."

Superintendent Ryan said he then asked Kelly if that account was the truth. Kelly replied: "It is. I will show you the place where the robbery happened." Kelly added that he would show them where the guns were hidden in Bray and that the mail bags might have been taken to Ballymore Eustace. Kelly described the place in Bray where the guns were and Superintendent Ryan said he himself drew a sketch map there and then.

Kelly also said he would make a written statement, the Superintendent told the court. He added that he left the room at 3.20 am to try and pinpoint the places near Bray and Ballymore Eustace that Kelly had described.

Superintendent Ryan said he returned to the interview room at 4.25 am. Sergeant Cleary was taking down a statement in writing and Sergeant John McGroarty was there as well. Kelly was dictating the statement; Superintendent Ryan said he took no part in what was going on but remained there until the statement was completed. The statement was read over to Nicky Kelly and he agreed it was correct and he signed it. It was 5.15 am then.

He then said to Kelly:"Nicky, would you not go and have a sleep first and show us the places later?" Kelly replied: "I'm okay, I would rather go with you now." He showed no signs of distress or anxiety.

Nicky Kelly was then released under Section 30 of the Offences Against the State Act. He was allowed to leave the Bridewell and walk out into Chancery Street where Superintendent Ryan said he arrested him under common law. He told Kelly he was arresting him on a charge of conspiracy to commit an armed robbery. He cautioned him again and Kelly replied: "I understand. I have told the truth anyway." They went for a short walk up Chancery Street to get some air, he told the court.

Kelly said he was still anxious to go on the journey and was cautioned again, Superintendent Ryan said. Kelly replied: "I only hope I can help you to find the money." Kelly was offered tea but asked for a mineral. About 6.00 am they set off on the journey: Sergeant McGroarty drove and Sergeant Cleary was in the front passenger seat while Nicky Kelly and Superintendent Ryan were in the back. They stopped at a late night cafe on the quays and he bought two large bottles of lemonade and cigarettes.

"We travelled out to Celbridge. At Celbridge we turned left and drove along the roadway and we passed a house and Kelly pointed to the house," he said. Kelly gave the directions on the journey. "I hadn't a clue where the robbery had taken place," Superintendent Ryan told the court. Kelly pointed out a bungalow type house. "I subsequently learned there and then it was O'Toole's house."

Superintendent Ryan said that Kelly pointed out the field beside the railway line where the robbery took place. All four of them got out of the car and Kelly pointed from the gate to where the van was parked in the field as well as a car. None of the policemen present had been to the scene before, he said. Then they drove a short distance to a railway bridge and Kelly pointed down the tracks to where the train was stopped and to a gap in the hedge where the mail bags were put up over the ditch. They stood around for a while having a chat and Kelly then said there was a laneway up at the next canal bridge where McNally parked the car.

They then drove to Ballymore Eustace and Kelly said he

247

could direct them once they got to the square in the town. They got there about 7.00 am and Kelly directed them along different roads but they failed to locate the house. They drove to Naas garda station to get someone with local knowledge to go with them. Kelly was given tea and something to eat in the car and they set off for Ballymore Eustace again with a uniformed garda, Garda Noonan. They failed to locate the house they were looking for and then they went on to Bray: Kelly directed them to a laneway off the main road and pointed out a hole in the ground near a tree root. It was empty.

Other gardai arrived in the area and Superintendent Ryan said that he took Kelly back to the Bridewell. They arrived there about 11.00 am.

On the journey from Ballymore Eustace to Bray, Kelly had said without any questioning: "I did not tell you all about the house at the railway line. We were all in that house. I was one of the fellows in the bedroom."

Superintendent Ryan said he next saw Kelly at 10.30 that night, Wednesday, April 7th when he was charged with the robbery and brought to a special sitting of the district court.

The cross-examination of Superintendent Ryan was to take more than a day and began after lunch on the 24th day of the trial, November 14th 1978. He said that he was the person directing the interviewing of Nicky Kelly on Tuesday, April 6th and saw him for the first time at 11.30 that morning. Seamus Sorahan said it was his instructions that Superintendent Ryan never ill-treated Kelly in any way: the Superintendent said that was correct and nobody in his presence had ill-treated the accused either.

Superintendent Ryan said he had ordered the transfer of Brian McNally and Nicky Kelly from Fitzgibbon Street to the Bridewell because there were no facilities for feeding them in Fitzgibbon street. There was no ulterior motive to cause an uncomfortable night's sleep.

He told Sorahan he had confidential information that Nicky Kelly, Brian McNally and Osgur Breatnach and their associates in the IRSP did the mail train job and the guns were kept in Kelly's flat.

Sorahan: Accepting for the moment that you got such information, it might well be absolutely true, isn't that right?

Ryan: Well, I mean you have to listen to thunder. I'll put it that way.

Sorahan: On the other hand, isn't it fair to say it might, in fact, be false, isn't that right?

Ryan: Oh, certainly.

Sorahan: Wasn't your state of mind then with regard to Nicky Kelly that he was guilty – is there any doubt about that?

Ryan: I wouldn't go that far.

Sorahan: How far would you go?

Ryan: I had my suspicions.

Superintendent Ryan denied that it was ever decided not to allow Kelly to go to bed that night, that he was to be kept up until he made an admission. "I am sure if Mr Kelly had made no admissions that he would have been put to bed at around three or four o'clock, maybe," he told the court. Nicky Kelly looked normal to him when he saw him at 11.30 that night, Tuesday, April 6th. He did not look distressed, nor particularly tired. Superintendent Ryan agreed that he told Garda Jordan at that stage that Kelly could see Nuala Dillon if she was still in the Bridewell. But he denied that Kelly said he would do certain things if he was allowed to see her. He sanctioned the meeting for humanitarian motives. He said he was not in the room for the meeting between Kelly and Dillon.

He said he did not know why Nuala Dillon was in the Bridewell, who had brought her there and that she remained in the Bridewell after her meeting with Kelly. Asked why he had not recorded her visit in his notebook or statement, Superintendent Ryan said it was not important: this visit did not seem to him to be important.

Superintendent Ryan said he first heard that Kelly had confessed about 2.45 am on Wednesday, April 7th. Up to then, he agreed, Kelly had maintained his innocence to relays of detectives.

Sorahan: Can you say or point to any factors that manifested themselves that may have caused him to change his mind, from any discussion you had with him or anything you heard or anything you saw?

Ryan: No. In my experience that is human nature. It is human nature for a person to deny his guilt and they come to a stage where they sort of put...

Sorahan: For many reasons, conscience – get it off their chest?

Ryan: They come to that point. This is what happened in this case.

Sorahan: I have to put it to you that he was not making these submissions at all?

Ryan: He was.

Sorahan: Leading questions were being asked of him?

Ryan: No.

Sorahan: I put it to you that he was under great pressure at the time you went into the room when you saw him and heard him reeling off these matters and that he looked like a man under pressure?

Ryan: No.

Sorahan: That there was an atmosphere of tension, menace, uneasiness in the room itself?

Ryan: That is not true.

.....

Sorahan: And the atmosphere, you say, was friendly and easy?

Ryan: At all times.

Sorahan: And he was co-operating and getting the thing off his chest?

Ryan: That is correct.

Sorahan put it to him that his main priority would have been to recover the money if Kelly had really told him that it might be in a house near Ballymore Eustace. Superintendent Ryan said he made phone calls to Naas to try and pinpoint the spot and he made arrangements to send some men to Bray to try and locate the weapons. He said he felt that they should go to these areas first but it was decided to take down Kelly's written statement first. He admitted that he did not know to whom he had spoken in Naas when he telephoned the garda station there.

He denied that he had left the room in which Kelly was making his written statement because he knew Kelly was going to be beaten after he had turned recalcitrant and gone back on whatever admissions he had made. He said he did not contact the gardai in Naas after Kelly made his written statement which appeared to give further details of the house in the Ballymore Eustace area. That did not occur to him, he said.

Kelly looked a young, fit fresh man after he signed the statement, Superintendent Ryan said. He agreed that he had taken no special security precautions when Kelly was released into Chancery Street about 5.30 am to be re-arrested by Ryan. There were other gardai on the street, he added. Sorahan said that at the first trial Superintendent Ryan could not remember if there were other members there: now he said he recollected some others, guards coming on duty and so on. He suggested to Kelly after he re-arrested him that they walk a short bit, get a bit of fresh air.

Sorahan: Did you see anything wrong with his (Kelly's) walk?
Ryan: No.
Sorahan: Did he limp?
Ryan: No.
Sorahan: Did he walk in any way stiff-legged, bent, crouched?
Ryan: No.
Sorahan: Didn't look pale; didn't show any signs of coming very slowly out of the Bridewell negotiating a step or two, having any physical difficulties?
Ryan: Nothing at all like that.
Sorahan: If that be so, you being fatigued, you giving away twenty years of a handicap, he being a reasonably strong young fellow – were you not afraid he would break away from you and make good his escape, a thing that you might be ragged about for the rest of your life?
Ryan: There were members outside and they were

known .... definitely Nicky Kelly was not going to escape. There was nothing wrong with him. He was quite normal but he was not going to escape.

Sorahan: Wouldn't it have been an elementary precaution...? When did you decide to take the walk? Was that while you were out on the path?

Ryan: Yes, there would have to be members around there when I walked down the street with Kelly. I do not want to give the court the impression the street was vacant.

Sorahan: I put it to you it was vacant. My client will so swear there was nobody else around.

Ryan: There was.

Sorahan: No pedestrians, no sign of any garda personnel, uniformed or plain clothes, as far as he can remember.

Ryan: He is wrong.

Sorahan: The position I want to put to you: wasn't Mr Kelly in such a physical condition... that you knew damned well that he would not be able to run if he attempted to run: even you, forty six years of age, big fellow that you are, fatigued as you were, giving him away twenty years, would be easily able to catch him?

Ryan: There was nothing wrong with Kelly. He was as I saw him that morning.

Sorahan: Did you hear my question?

Ryan: Yes.

Sorahan: Answer it.

Judge: He doesn't agree with you.

Sorahan: You don't agree with that?

Ryan: No.

Superintendent Ryan said that none of the gardai who travelled with Kelly to the scene of the crime, Ballymore Eustace and Bray were armed. They did not have ropes to restrain Kelly: he could not remember if they had handcuffs but they were not used. He denied that Kelly was in such a physical condition that the gardai knew he could not escape. He made no attempt to escape because he was co-operative, Superintendent Ryan said.

He told Sorahan that it was his deliberate decision that none of the gardai accompanying Kelly had ever been to the scene of the crime so that it would not be alleged that Kelly was guided there. He said he had not seen any maps or aerial photographs of the area. He denied that the gardai in the car had given all the directions on the journey.

Superintendent Ryan denied that Kelly asked for a solicitor before he was taken into the district court late that Wednesday night. He asked the court to remand the accused in custody and may have asked that they be remanded overnight. He did not prompt the decision to remand all the accused to the Bridewell. "It was not what I wanted," he said. "If I was asked what frame of mind I was in I would expect to see them going to Mountjoy that night." He said there was nothing sinister in the fact that Kelly was put into a cell with Michael Plunkett: it was the normal procedure.

He told Seamus Sorahan he had a broad idea of the rules of the Bridewell prison. Was he aware of a rule that required prisoners who were charged with the same offence to be kept segregated? "I am not aware of it. I think if that is there it is a new one. If I and a friend are in for a crime and if we have made our admissions and the two of us ask to be left in a cell together, I don't think we should be kept apart."

Sorahan made no comment on the fact that Superintendent Ryan had said earlier in the trial that he accepted it was against the regulations to put such prisoners together.

After Michael Plunkett complained about ill-treatment in court the following morning, Superintendent Ryan made his own inquiries, he said. The results were negative: everybody concerned denied ill-treatment and he knew from his own knowledge that nobody was assaulted or abused in his presence in the Bridewell. His lengthy cross-examination ended on the issue of ill-treatment:

Sorahan: As far as you know, as far as your inquiries have gone, you never saw or heard directly or indirectly anything that would leave you to believe that anyone was ill-treated?
Ryan: That is correct.
Sorahan: And that includes the Breatnach *habeas corpus* proceedings, the picket and the agitation since?

Ryan: That is correct.
Sorahan: The civil actions taken by the four accused and other suspects who were arrested for the train robbery?
Ryan: That is correct.

Sergeant John Jordan of the Special Branch, the next witness, a detective garda at the time of the robbery, told the court of a conversation he had with Kelly on the night of Tuesday, April 6th, after Superintendent Ryan had left the room. He got Kelly two cups of tea and Kelly asked him would Nuala Dillon get into trouble if he told what he knew. Garda Jordan said he replied, "Not unless she was involved in the robbery." Kelly then said the following, which Garda Jordan said he wrote in his notebook at the time.

"About two weeks ago I went into the County Bar, Parliament Street for a drink on my own. When I went into the bar Michael Barrett and John Fitzpatrick, being old friends of mine, were sitting at a table near the counter. There was a third man with them whom I did not know. I was going to join them but the impression I got from Barrett when he looked at me, was that he did not want me to join them. So I sat on a stool at the counter near them and I had a drink on my own and I could hear Barrett and Fitzpatrick and the other man talking between themselves. I knew they were talking about a stroke that was coming off but I could not hear everything they said and I knew it was a big job they were planning. I knew it was an IRSP job. After finishing my drink I left. That night I told Nuala Dillon about what I overheard Barrett and Fitzpatrick talking about."

Garda Jordan said he interrupted Kelly at that point to ask him for a description of the third man. Kelly told him he was twenty three years old, five feet eight inches tall, clean shaven and about twelve stone. He then asked Kelly if Inspector Ryan had mentioned a telephone call to Nuala Dillon. Kelly replied: "I phoned Nuala Dillon at her work at twelve noon the day of the robbery and said to her the job went off all right."

Garda Jordan said he asked Kelly what he was referring to. Kelly answered: "I was referring to the train robbery and I took this to be the stroke Fitzpatrick had arranged. On the day of the robbery (I) went to the IRSP offices, 34 Gardiner Street, at about 12 noon. When I went (in) Michael Plunkett and Osgur Breatnach were reading newspapers. I did not join them but I heard them say 'the big money'." Garda Jordan said he interrupted again to ask what they were referring to. "The train robbery, of course," Kelly replied.

Garda Jordan said he timed this note, signed his name at the bottom of it and left the room. He returned with Inspector Ryan and Inspector McGrath and read out the note he had taken to Kelly. Kelly told Inspector Ryan that the note was correct. Inspector Ryan asked if Nuala Dillon knew about the robbery and Kelly replied: "She knew all about the planning of it." Garda Jordan said he asked Kelly to sign his note but Kelly declined. He and Inspector Ryan left the room around midnight and Garda Thomas Ibar Dunne entered.

Under cross-examination, Garda Jordan said that Kelly was pleasant, calm, collected, a normal person in every sense of the word when he saw him. He did not raise his voice to Kelly, shout, bang the table or lay a hand on him. Sorahan said that Kelly would swear he never said anything about going into the County Bar and the account Garda Jordan had read out. "That is what he said to me," Garda Jordan replied. He denied that he had left the room several times and that each time a number of gardai would enter and give Kelly a quick beating and leave before he, Garda Jordan, returned.

Sorahan asked if he had shouted at Kelly: "Repeat after me, one, two, three." Garda Jordan replied: "My lords, again at the last court this was put to me and I said it was ridiculous. Nothing like that ever occurred, nothing like that." He denied that he kept shouting at Kelly: "You did say the job went all right." He denied that Kelly eventually shouted back: "Everything went all right."

Garda Jordan said he had nothing further to do with Nicky Kelly after the visit of Nuala Dillon to him. Kelly did not go back on anything he had said to him, Garda Jordan, he said.

Sergeant Patrick Cleary from the Central Detective Unit said that he and Garda Joseph Egan saw Kelly just after the previous witness left him, about 12.30 am on Wednesday, April 7th 1976. He cautioned him and Kelly said: "I have told the man gone out everything I know." Kelly then repeated what he had said about overhearing Barrett and Fitzpatrick talking about a stroke in the County Bar. Asked about his phone call to Nuala Dillon, Kelly said he had told her: "I am okay, everything was a success."

Sergeant John McGroarty replaced Garda Egan. Sergeant Cleary said he asked Kelly to repeat his story again and he did. "I then told Mr Kelly that I did not believe his story and that I felt that he was holding something back. Detective Sergeant McGroarty then told him he should tell the truth and if he was involved himself he should say so. Kelly then said, 'suppose I was involved, only suppose, would Nuala be involved in anything over the phone call?' I told him I didn't think so. I again asked him to tell the truth and he replied, 'it is not easy, we have been told in the organisation about speaking to the police.' Detective Sergeant McGroarty then asked him what organisation and he replied the IRSP. He then asked if he could be left on his own for a while. I asked him why did he want to be left on his own and he said he wanted to see what he was going to do. It was now 1.20 am and Detective Sergeant McGroarty and myself left the room." Kelly was left on his own.

Fifteen minutes later, Kelly opened the door of the room and called him and Garda Joseph Egan in, Sergeant Cleary said. He went on: "As I walked into the room he sat down and he said, 'the job was planned a couple of weeks ago. Barrett asked me to go on it. I went with McNally in his car from outside his house in Swords to outside Celbridge where we met the rest there. They were there before us.'"

Sergeant Cleary said he was writing it down as Kelly spoke and he asked him who was there. Kelly listed nine names. While he was doing so, Garda Michael Finn came into the room. Kelly continued with an account of the robbery. "When McNally and myself got there we met Michael Barrett and John Fitzpatrick in a field near the railway line where we held up the train. They said everything was okay and that Plunkett, Roche and Gallagher were in a house beside this field which was part of the plan. The train was to pass at 2.50 am. Detonators were on the track to stop the train. We had a Volkswagen van for the mail bags. Some of the lads were beside the track and the rest were hiding about. Michael Plunkett went onto the line. He was like a linesman with a donkey jacket. When the train stopped we grabbed the bags we wanted."

Sergeant Cleary said that Garda Egan asked at that stage how they knew the bags they wanted. Kelly replied: "Costello and Breatnach knew which ones to take. We were all armed. Bunting and somebody else had rifles. We had revolvers. Joe Heaney and Thomas McCartan were keeping guard. When the van was loaded it was driven away to Ballymore Eustace." Sergeant Cleary said he asked why Ballymore Eustace and Kelly replied: "Barrett has a friend there and I think the mail bags were going there."

Kelly subsequently offered to take the gardai out and show them the place, Sergeant Cleary said. Then he added that Seamus Costello and Michael Barrett had planned the job. Costello had told them to have alibis ready and Barrett had asked him to go on the job: "He (Barrett) said only sound men were going on this," Kelly said.

Sergeant Cleary said Kelly then asked him how Nuala was. "I was going to get married to Nuala but this has ruined everything," Kelly said. "I will try and show you where the money is or was in Ballymore Eustace. If we could find the money it might make a difference to my sentence. Will I get ten years for this?" Sergeant Cleary said he did not know.

Sergeant Cleary said that Kelly had tea during the interview but had refused sandwiches. He then left the room for about five minutes and returned about 2.55 am. Then Inspector Ryan came in and Kelly told him the account that the Inspector had already given the court. Before and after Inspector Ryan came in, Kelly asked several times if they could go on the journey. At 4.15 am, while waiting for Inspector Ryan, he asked Kelly if he would make a written statement and Kelly said all right.

On the journey to the scene of the robbery they were travelling at all times on Kelly's instructions, Sergeant Cleary said. "When we went into Celbridge we went over a small bridge there and Mr Kelly said something like, 'just a minute, hold it,' and he looked out the rear window and he said that we should have taken a left turn there. Detective Sergeant McGroarty then turned the car around and it went back up the road which was indicated by Mr Kelly."

Under cross-examination, Sergeant Cleary said he had been involved in the train robbery investigation from a day or two after it occurred. He was trying to check out a tag on a sheet found at the scene of the robbery.

He denied that his attitude to Kelly was one of bullying mixed with persuasion. He never shouted at him, laid a hand on him or slapped him: no one else laid a hand on Kelly in his presence. He denied that he had concocted all the alleged verbal admissions that Kelly had made to him. He said he had not asked Kelly to sign his note of admission. It did not occur to him and was not his practice at that time, he said.

Sergeant Cleary denied that he had taken out a blackjack during his first session with Kelly. He denied that during a second interview either he or Garda Finn threatened Kelly's face with the blackjack while the other jerked his head back. "I saw no blackjack," he said.

He also denied that he had sat down with some documents and was writing for a long time, during which Kelly said nothing. Sorahan went on: "At the end of half an hour, three quarters of an hour, you writing fast, consulting the document before you, faced him with a document, a number of pages. You said, 'now sign that' and that Mr Kelly said, 'no, I won't sign that'." Sergeant Cleary replied: "That is not correct, my lords. I had no document whatever and I had no knowledge about how the train robbery had been committed."

Sorahan: That, having refused to sign after your great

258

industry, you then started to beat him with the blackjack for the third and last time?

Cleary: That never happened, my lords.

Sorahan: Having beaten him with the blackjack, shoved him around, he said, "very well, I'll sign it"?

Cleary: Nothing like that ever happened, my lords.

Sorahan: That you did then put the paper over to him, that he signed his name on it, that you then signed, Mr McGroarty then signed and, finally, he doesn't remember, Mr Ryan signed?

Cleary: That never happened.

Sorahan: My instructions are that from the moment he signed the atmosphere was transformed and profoundly transmuted from one of tension to quite the opposite. He was asked would he have something to drink, he was given some kind of sweet drink and a cup of tea. Can you recollect that?

Cleary: None whatever. The only drink I saw was tea.

Sergeant Cleary denied that words had been crossed out in the statement and changes marked with the initials NK in order to lend authenticity to it.

The next two witnesses, Garda Joseph Egan and Sergeant McGroarty, gave evidence about the verbal statements allegedly made by Kelly to the previous witness and denied that he was ill-treated by them or in their presence.

Sergeant McGroarty told Sorahan in cross-examination that he had been wearing an anorak, suit and tie when he first saw Kelly in the early hours of that morning. He denied that he was in a shirt, carrying a belt, out of breath and sweating a little. He never said anything like: "What a way to earn a living."

Dealing with the journey to the scene of the crime when Sergeant McGroarty drove the garda car, Sorahan picked him up on one phrase contained in his statement of evidence. It said: "... we came to a bungalow on the right, occupied by Conal O'Toole and which I was aware was a bungalow entered by the gang of men who had robbed the Cork-Dublin mail train..." Sorahan asked what he meant by the phrase, "which I was aware was the bungalow," if he was not, as he had said, aware of the scene of the crime.

Sorahan: How did that phrase get into your statement?
McGroarty: I was aware it was the last house in a row of houses was the house taken over by the men who held up the train.
Sorahan: That's all it amounts to?
McGroarty: Yes.

On the drive Kelly gave the first instructions to drive to Lucan as they were travelling down the quays, Sergeant McGroarty said. After Lucan, Kelly directed him to take a second left turn. He agreed that these directions were not in his notebook but they were in his statement which, he said, he had made a few days after the journey.

The next morning, the twenty seventh day of the trial, November 17th 1978, the prosecution called two doctors who had examined Nicky Kelly in prison. Dr Paul McVeigh told the court he examined Kelly when he was admitted to Mountjoy Prison on Thursday, April 8th 1976. He said he found "extensive bruising on both arms and right shoulder and both buttocks." Kelly complained of headaches and was prescribed Panadol.

Noel McDonald: What was the nature of these injuries? Were they superficial or otherwise?
McVeigh: Superficial.
McDonald: And what would they be consistent with?
McVeigh: Consistent with a number of things.
McDonald: A number of possible causes?
McVeigh: Possibly.

The prosecution asked the doctor nothing more and Sorahan cross-examined him. McVeigh said he remembered one of the prisoners he examined that day complaining of being beaten by the police. It might have been Nicky Kelly but he could not remember.

Mr Justice Hamilton: Doctor, what exactly do you mean by extensive bruising of both arms?

260

McVeigh: Covering two-thirds of the arms.

Judge: On each arm?

McVeigh: On each arm.

Judge: And what about the right shoulder?

McVeigh: Bruising of two thirds of the right shoulder.

Judge: You have described the bruising as superficial. What do you mean by superficial? There are two types of bruises, one that appears on the surface and the other an internal bruising. Those bruises which appeared on the surface, would you describe as superficial bruising?

McVeigh: Yes. Another doctor might describe it in a different fashion.

Judge: When you use the word superficial you are using it to show that the bruises appeared externally?

McVeigh: Correct.

Judge: And not just that they were light bruises. What kind of bruises were they?

McVeigh: They had mobility of the arms and shoulders and that is how I came to the conclusion they were superficial.

The judge went on to ask with what the bruises were consistent. McVeigh said that Kelly could have been hit or fallen. They could be consistent with being hit by a cosh or blackjack.

Dr Samuel Davis told the court that he was acting as medical officer in Mountjoy on Friday, April 9th 1976 when he examined a number of people, including Nicky Kelly. He dictated the results of his examination to Joseph Deignan, a member of the prison staff, who noted them down. He told Seamus Sorahan he adopted this practice in relation to five train robbery prisoners because of the number of injuries and things he had to call out.

Dr Davis said that the prisoners told him they were beaten by the police: Kelly might have been one of those who said that. "The injuries were consistent with a person having come into contact with some object," he said. Such as? Sorahan inquired. "It could be anything," Davis replied. "There is nothing to indicate that there was anything specifically given."

Re-examined by the prosecution, he said that the bruising was not severe. It could possibly have been caused by banging against a wall or falling on the floor.

Dr Richard Burke, the medical officer at Portlaoise Prison, gave evidence of seeing Kelly when he was admitted to the prison on the same day, Friday April 9th 1976. Kelly complained of headaches and pains in his body and arms and behind his left ear.

He found bruising and some superficial abrasions on both his upper arms. They could have been inflicted anything from one to three days before he saw them, he said.

Cross-examined by Sorahan, he agreed that he could have missed some things. He said he was not aware that Dr Davis had recorded numerous other injuries earlier the same day in Mountjoy. He had no recollection of the examination other than what was recorded in the prison medical book.

The court then went back over the evidence of two witnesses it had already heard in relation to Kelly, Garda Michael Finn and Inspector Vincent McGrath. In their earlier evidence, they had been stopped from giving details of Kelly's alleged admissions on the grounds that the court had yet to decide if they were admissible. They were re-called now to give evidence that they had not given earlier. Justice Hamilton asked if it was necessary to hear Garda Finn's evidence about what Kelly had said to Sergeant Cleary. The prosecution said it was at the foundation of the case.

Garda Finn said that after Kelly made a verbal admission to Sergeant Cleary, repeated it to Inspector Ryan, he asked Kelly to repeat it again. He took notes, he said. He agreed that he had not cautioned Kelly. He said that Kelly told him Plunkett had the lamp; that Gerry Roche had been watching the Volkswagen van for about a week; that Roche, Plunkett and Seán Gallagher hijacked it; that John Fitzpatrick "knocked" a Cortina; that six of them left in two cars on Tuesday night.

"They were to stay near the railway until the time of the job at 3 am on Wednesday, 31st March, 1976. McNally had done a dry run before; Brian McNally and I left

McNally's house in Swords at about 1.35 am and went down in his car which is a Renault, white colour. We got down to the road beside the railway track. We got there at about 2.30 am. We met Michael Barrett and he gave me a .45 gun. It was loaded with six rounds. He gave me a scarf. He gave McNally another handgun. Roche, Gallagher and Plunkett were in the house beside the railway track. They went in at about 1 am as far as I know. There were detonators on the track.

"The train came along and the detonators went off and frightened me. The train stopped. Bunting, McCartan and myself were on the far side of the track from the road. Bunting and Fitzpatrick had a rifle each. Osgur Breatnach and Barrett got on the train. They took out a man in uniform and put him into another carriage. They then threw out about one dozen mail bags, on to the bank. Roche, McNally and me carried the bags from the bank and threw them into the Volkswagen van. We had seven handguns and two rifles. The fellows in the wagon threw out the bags and they were checked by Seamus Costello and Breatnach. There was one bag left behind when the job was over. We gave the guns back to Barrett. I left with McNally and we went back to McNally's house." Garda Finn said that Kelly then listed twelve names, including his own, as being involved. Kelly told him that some of the mail bags were about five feet by three feet wide. Some were smaller.

> Justice Hamilton: How did it come about he gave that information. Surely it was the result of questions you asked?
> Finn: I cannot say, my lords, but he had mentioned mail bags earlier and I may have asked him to describe them.
> Judge: Would I be right in thinking nearly every statement of fact there was in answer to a routine suggestion or an answer he gave to a question asked by you?
> Finn: No, my lords.

Garda Finn said he had read over his notes to Kelly who

agreed that they were correct. Sergeant Cleary was present during this account, he added.

Garda Finn said that Kelly agreed later that day, Wednesday, April 7th, to go to Harcourt Terrace garda station to see Michael Plunkett. Kelly identified the statement he had made to the gardai in Plunkett's presence. Plunkett asked: "Did you mention me in it?" and Kelly told him: "I did."

He told Sorahan in cross-examination that he did not ask Kelly to sign his note: he did not think of asking him at all.

Inspector Richard Murphy, who was a detective sergeant at the time of the robbery, said Kelly told him he had no objection to going to Harcourt Terrace to see Plunkett. He showed Plunkett a photostat copy of Kelly's alleged statement and Kelly said the statement and the signature on it were his. Inspector Murphy said he later saw Kelly in a room in Harcourt Terrace and asked him how he was. Kelly replied: "I'm fed up with the whole thing. I'm sorry I ever joined them." After a few minutes, Kelly added: "I was to be married but that's all over now. I had to do what I was told. My job was to throw the mail bags over the hedge to where the van was parked up against a ditch. I got nothing out of it: I am finished with them now, anyway. I told the truth."

In cross-examination, Inspector Murphy said it was his idea to bring Kelly to Harcourt Terrace in the hope that he would get the truth out of Plunkett. He would not have brought Kelly unless he agreed to go, he said. He only asked Kelly about the statement once and did not raise his voice. Kelly could not be taken back to the Bridewell immediately after the confrontation with Plunkett because there was a picket on the station, the Inspector said. He knew nothing about Kelly and Plunkett being put into a garda car and left alone.

Garda Michael Mullen of the Special Branch said that he had also gone with Kelly to Harcourt Terrace. After the meeting with Plunkett, Kelly had said to him: "I was going to get married soon... I will still be of marrying age when I get out." A few minutes later Kelly said he hoped Plunkett would tell the gardai where the money was as it would help reduce his, Kelly's, sentence. Kelly went on: "The money was to buy guns and probably for the new offices in Gardiner Street. If Plunkett does not know where it is Costello certainly does as it is always somebody close to Costello who buys the guns."

He took him back to the Bridewell later. At all times, Kelly appeared to him to be quite relaxed, quite normal, Garda Mullen said.

Under cross-examination, Garda Mullen said that he stayed with Kelly for three quarters of an hour for security reasons. He did not speak to Kelly at all: "Any conversation that was made, it was he who made it," he said. He denied that he was truculent with Kelly or questioned him about crimes in country areas.

The prosecution then went back, in terms of the evidence, to produce Garda Michael Noonan from Hollywood, County Wicklow, the local garda who was summoned to help during Nicky Kelly's journey to Ballymore Eustace. He was called upon to try and locate a bungalow farmhouse occupied by a man called John who lived with an old man and a woman. Inspector Ryan sat in the front of the car and Garda Noonan sat in beside Kelly in the back.

Asked by Robert Barr for the prosecution who had told him what they were looking for, Garda Noonan said Inspector Ryan and Kelly.

Barr: How did you come to take the road you had taken out of Ballymore Eustace? Who selected the road, do you remember?
Noonan: Well, it would be I selected the road.
Barr: Why did you do that?
Noonan: Well, it was Mr Kelly had said and Detective Inspector Ryan that this house would be about half a mile from the village...
Barr: Yes?
Noonan: And that it would have been on this road or... by directions they gave when you would be in the centre of the village, turn right and over the bridge about a half a mile from the centre of the town.
Barr: Yes. What I want to know is, who gave you that

265

direction and who was supplying the information about the house and the people in it?

Noonan: Mr Kelly was supplying the information.

Garda Noonan said that either he or Kelly asked the driver to stop outside houses but they did not find the house they were looking for. Kelly was nice and quiet and seemed to be very friendly with the detectives.

Garda Noonan said in cross-examination that he had been telephoned at home and told to meet the detectives at Ballymore Eustace station at 8.00 am. He was not told what case they were concerned with. He did not make notes about it at the time. On January 15th 1977 – some nine months later – Sergeant Cleary called down to see him in Ballymore Eustace station. They discussed the incident and he, Garda Noonan, dictated a statement to Sergeant Cleary and signed it.

Sorahan: Can you say was the whole statement entirely stemming from your mind and, ergo, from your memory or was it prompted or unprompted – any parts of it – by anything Mr Cleary had said to you in the preliminary discussion before you made the statement or, for that matter, while you were making the statement? Forgive the long, involved question.

Noonan: Well, I suppose, when you discuss a thing it...

Sorahan: Comes back to you?

Noonan: Comes back to you, yes.

Sorahan: When people mention the details, the details...

Noonan: Yes, yes.

Sorahan: ....come back to your mind?

Noonan: I may not have remembered myself but on my being reminded when we discussed it...

Sorahan: You had to be reminded?

Noonan: Well, that the...

Sorahan: That's the exact point I wanted.

Barr: All right let him finish. He's trying to say something.

There was a pause but Garda Noonan said nothing.

Sorahan continued his cross-examination. Garda Noonan said that no one was taking notes in the car during the journey. Kelly did not look distressed, shaken, weak or like a man who was under great strain and had been beaten. Asked if Sergeant Cleary had remained silent before the car moved off, Garda Noonan replied; "It was Inspector Ryan, as far as I can gather now, it was Inspector Ryan who did all the talking."

Sorahan: All the talking? And may Inspector Ryan have mentioned these matters, John forty years, five foot eight, living with his father and his wife, the father being an old man, is that reasonably possible?
Noonan: Oh, he may have mentioned it as well.
Sorahan: Yes. But you are quite certain Mr Kelly also mentioned it?
Noonan: Yes.
Sorahan: That it wasn't that the details were put to him in your presence and Mr Kelly assented, either by saying yes or nodding his head or assenting by gesture?
Noonan: No.
Sorahan: Are you sure about that?
Noonan: Yes.

Garda Noonan said that there had been searches in the Ballymore Eustace area in relation to the train robbery before this incident. He said that there was not any house in the area to his knowledge which was occupied by people fitting the descriptions given to him.

Sergeant Martin Dowling gave evidence of being the station sergeant at Fitzgibbon Street station on Monday, April 5th when Nicky Kelly was brought in there. He said he saw Kelly twice while he was being interviewed: he knocked on the door and looked in without waiting for an answer. The first occasion was about 12.30 pm and Kelly was with Garda Adrian O'Hara and two other detectives. About 1.30 pm he went back again and there were a number of detectives there whom he did not know, possibly including Garda O'Hara whom he knew. There could have been more than three detectives there the second time.

Kelly was seated at the table on both occasions and seemed relaxed and in good spirits. The prosecution then produced a chair which Sergeant Dowling said he had taken from the same room in Fitzgibbon Street a week earlier. He said it was representative of the type of chairs used in the station in 1976 and still used. He said that the sergeant's locker room in which Kelly was sitting was very very narrow: it was eighteen point five feet long and six feet wide and its windows looked out on Fitzgibbon Street.

Sergeant Dowling said he did not hear any screams or shouts from that room.

The prosecution then called several gardai, simply to make them available for cross-examination by the defence. They were all people whom Kelly would swear in his evidence had played varying roles in his interrogation. All denied in advance the accusations that he would make. The prosecution pointed out that one of its main witnesses was in hospital but agreed with a court suggestion that they could wait to hear him until after the defence made its case.

The prosecution case against Nicky Kelly had taken six and a half days to hear. Thirty five witnesses had given evidence about the circumstances and terms of his alleged confessions. Two of the witnesses were prison doctors and a third a prison officer: all the rest were gardai.

12

Nicky Kelly: The Defence

Nicky Kelly walked down the steps from the dock in the Special Criminal Court, crossed the floor of the court and stepped up into the witness box. He took a bible in his right hand and repeated the words of the oath after the court registrar. He was asked to give his name and sat down to begin more than two full days of evidence. It was the afternoon of November 28th 1978, the twenty ninth day of the trial.

In his defence, Kelly would give evidence himself. His girlfriend at the time of the arrests, Nuala Dillon, would give evidence about her experiences. And two more doctors who examined Nicky Kelly in Mountjoy Prison would also give evidence.

Kelly said that on the night before his arrest he had been in a friend's house in Arklow, chatting, drinking and playing poker. He slept for a couple of hours in an armchair and was awake when the gardai arrived and took him to Arklow garda station and later to Fitzgibbon Street in Dublin. He asked for a solicitor in both stations. He was questioned by Sergeant Campbell and Garda Thomas Ibar Dunne who asked for an account of his movements. Then Sergeant Campbell left after a short time.

He said that Garda Dunne slapped him on the face and ears and shouted at him. Garda Dunne told him Nuala Dillon would be arrested and charged with conspiracy and that his mother was in Elm Park Hospital in Dublin with a heart attack. Garda Dunne said he had been speaking to Kelly's school teacher who said he was an odd ball. Garda Dunne said he was a psychopath, a fucking atheist and a communist and he sprinkled water over him.

Then Garda Michael Finn came in and Garda Dunne left, Kelly said. Garda Finn told him to sit down, stand up, sit down, and at one stage pulled the chair from under him. In the afternoon, Garda Dunne returned and was one of a number of gardai who questioned him then. They included Garda Kieran Lawlor, whom he knew, and who said at one stage that he was going off to arrest Nuala Dillon as she got off her normal bus from work. Garda Dunne kept punching him on the upper arms.

That evening, he said, Garda Finn grabbed him by the hair and by the bottom of the ski-jacket he was wearing and rammed his head against the lockers in the room. He was told to stand spread-eagled against the wall; the gardai kicked his legs apart so that he would fall, jabbed him in the side with their fingers. At one stage the gardai turned off the light when he was spread-eagled against the wall.

"I didn't know what to do. The light was out and obviously they were outside, you know, and just then the door came in and it knocked me down. The door made contact with my body and knocked me down and they ran in and they blamed me for falling."

Then he was spread out on the floor on his back with his hands above his head. "A chair was placed on my hands, in the palms of my hands and Garda Finn, he sat on it and what I can remember...about Garda Finn – continuously, the whole time, with all the dealings I had with him he always seemed to have a grin or a leer on his face."

Sorahan: Garda Finn is sitting on the chair?
Kelly: He sat on the chair, that's correct.
Sorahan: Where is his face, is he looking down at you or looking across the room?
Kelly: He is looking directly down into my face and he is saying that I won't help my mother or my girlfriend. Sprays of spit came out onto my face...sprays of spit as if he is spitting in my face.
Sorahan: Can you say how long did that last for, was it several minutes, was it some seconds or can you really say?
Kelly: It didn't last very long but it was the worst thing that happened to me.
Sorahan: In what sense?
Kelly: Well, it frightened me completely.
Sorahan: For what reason?

270

Kelly: Well I thought the whole thing was gone crazy at this stage. I didn't know exactly what was going to happen.

Sorahan: At this stage, can you say, did you say anything or can you say whether or not you made any remark by way of protest or not?

Kelly: Well, immediately they got up they just left. This was the first thing they done to me I think, you know. Like one thing I'll never forget is the composite grin on Garda Finn's face...

Sorahan: Did you say "composite"?

Judge: He said composite grin. Whether that's what he intended to say or not is another thing.

Kelly: Well, it was the main thing I remembered about him, the whole time I think, you know. Eventually when Garda Finn finished with me some time – I put it some time Wednesday morning – he seemed to be a lot bigger in physical size than he actually was at the start.

With that, the court adjourned for the day and Kelly resumed his evidence next morning. He said that Garda Dunne told him in Fitzgibbon Street station that Monday night that Nuala Dillon was crying in a cell and wanted to see him. Garda Dunne left the room, came back a few minutes later and dragged him to the door to look out. Kelly said that Garda Dunne said to him: "Look you fucking cunt, you thought we were joking." Kelly said he saw Nuala Dillon at the end of a corridor with a man: she did not see him. Up to then, Kelly said he did not believe the garda stories about Nuala Dillon or his mother.

Garda Finn returned later and took him up to a cell where Garda Finn grabbed his hair and pushed his head up and down towards the toilet bowl. His head never hit the water. Garda Finn was saying that tomorrow would be another long day. Garda Finn then took him out of the cell and put him up against a wall. He said he was adopting Kelly. Garda Finn spat in his face and said that Kelly would sign a statement when he was finished with him. Garda Finn then kneed him in the thigh. Then, Kelly said, he was brought by car to the Bridewell.

271

On Tuesday morning, April 6th, he was taken to a large room in the Bridewell garda station, Kelly said. He stood against a wall himself. Garda Kieran Lawlor and Garda Thomas Boland pushed him from one to the other; Garda Lawlor, whom he knew from raiding his flat, made insulting remarks about his mother and Nuala Dillon. "At one stage, I fell on the floor and Guard Boland picked up a chair and hit me with it. That was the second period I was hit with a chair... they were shouting at me to get up off the ground, I was refusing to get up off the ground." Kelly said he had a pain in his left buttock for several weeks afterwards.

Inspector Ned Ryan came in then and Kelly said he gave the Inspector an account of his movements. As Inspector Ryan left, he said he would have to send in these men again: Garda Lawlor and Garda Boland were looking through the glass window of the door at the time, he said. They returned as the Inspector left and punched and slapped him.

After lunch he was brought to the big interview room in the prison section of the Bridewell where there was a seat like a bus seat for three people. Garda Finn sat on one end of it and Kelly said he sat on the other end: Garda Finn got up and the seat collapsed under Kelly. He said he fell to the ground. Garda Finn laughed and accused him of jumping on the ground. Garda Finn then stood behind him while he sat again and was questioned by other people about events in the Wicklow area. Every time he did not answer or give a satisfactory answer, Garda Finn would slap him over both his ears at the same time.

Gardai kept telling him what part he had played in the mail train robbery. Garda Dunne was shouting all the time and telling him he had been in the house, in O'Toole's house, that he had hijacked the van.

He was put into a cell and given tea. At that stage, he said, he felt shattered, sore all over, his stomach was sick and his head was spinning. Afterwards, he was brought to a small interview room in the prison section where Garda Dunne was waiting for him. He punched him on the upper arms, invited him to fight and told him to "own up".

He said that he was later questioned by Garda John Jordan who concentrated all the time on the telephone call he made to Nuala Dillon. Other detectives came in on three occasions when Garda Jordan left the room. One of them was Garda Dunne and they came in shouting and punched him about, he said. Garda Jordan got him to shout after him, one, two, three, and to shout his answers. "Eventually I agreed with him that I said on the phone 'everything is all right, the job went okay', something like that: whatever he wanted me to say, I said it." Why did you say it? Sorahan asked. "Obviously, at this stage it was to stop the beatings," Kelly replied.

He said that Garda Jordan suggested to him that the raid was planned in the County Bar and the Ormond Hotel and in Grogan's Bar. "I was continually denying, saying it never happened.... they said that everyone who had been on this robbery had met in the Ormond Hotel prior to the day it happened."

Sorahan: Was there any reference to Miss Dillon now around this time?
Kelly: Well, they were continuously mentioning her, saying if I agreed to do this or to do that, that she would be released and eventually, I agreed to say some things in her presence.
Sorahan: What things now, as far as you can remember?
Kelly: Well, if I agreed to say we had been in Grogan's Bar with Michael Barrett and, as they wanted the contents of the telephone call, everything was okay, the job went all right.
Sorahan: Eventually then, what did you say in that regard in the presence of Mr Jordan?
Kelly: It was agreed, they said they would allow me to see Miss Dillon and then she would be released.
.....
Sorahan: What's the next thing you remember?
Kelly: Well, they got a towel and they washed my face.
Sorahan: Who did?
Kelly: Garda Dunne wiped my face and I either combed my hair myself or I was told to comb it.
Sorahan: And what was the next thing you remember, did anyone come into the room?

273

Kelly: Inspector Ryan and Nuala Dillon came into the room.

Kelly said that it was a fairly short meeting. Garda Dunne told him to tell Nuala what he had told the gardai. "I said, 'remember, Nuala, we were in Grogan's with Michael Barrett when the robbery was planned?' and also I said about the phone call, 'everything went okay, the job went all right.' "

Sorahan: Did Nuala say anything?
Kelly: She said absolutely nothing as far as I can recollect now.
Sorahan: How did she look herself?
Kelly: I don't think I was even really conscious of the situation. I knew she was there.

Kelly told the court that he asked Inspector Ryan if Nuala could go then and he indicated that she was being released. Garda Dunne remained in the room and Kelly said he then went back on what he had said in Nuala Dillon's presence. There were several gardai present: "They just started to beat me again; it was at some stage after this that Sergeant Cleary first produced the blackjack." He said he was beaten with a blackjack by Sergeant Cleary and Garda Finn on three occasions.

On the first occasion, Sergeant Cleary beat him on the upper arms and the legs. They were shouting and punching him as well. "It was at this stage I told them there was guns in the Bray area," he said. "I was personally thinking at the time that again we would get out there and discover there was no guns and they would search and it would save me three or four hours' beating." The second time he was beaten with the blackjack it was wielded by Garda Finn, the third time by Sergeant Cleary. The third time was after the statement was written out and he refused to sign it: it was by far the worst, he said.

He said he had agreed earlier to make a statement and Sergeant Cleary wrote it out. "All I was doing was attempting to recover from what happened, I wasn't even

274

taking much interest." After the third beating with the blackjack, he said he signed the statement and put his initials where he was told. He had no recollection of whether or not it was read over to him. He said he knew the statement would implicate him in the robbery "but I was delighted initially after I signed the statement." Why? Sorahan asked. "Well, the beatings had stopped and I got tea and orange immediately." He denied, however, that he had asked for any changes to be made in the statement.

Kelly: That would have been impossible.
Sorahan: Why?
Kelly: Well, for a start, I didn't do the robbery. I didn't know the contents of the statement as such. It would have been impossible for me to make amendments to something I didn't know.

He said he was told he was going on a trip to the scene of the robbery. Ballymore Eustace and three houses – two together and one separated – had been mentioned to him several times during the night by Garda Finn. Kelly said the only place he knew there was a pub called Murphy's that he had been in months earlier with Michael Barrett. On the journey, he said: "I was absolutely delighted to get out of the Bridewell. It was the last place on earth I wanted to see again... The reason I didn't resist physically, it would have suited me to get out of the Bridewell." He said he never gave the gardai in the car any directions at any stage: "I was in no position to tell them anything... they were telling it to me." He agreed, however, that he had pointed out a spot to the gardai near Bray.

Kelly said that when he was taken from the Bridewell to go and see Michael Plunkett his initial impression was that he was being taken to court. It was only in the car that he was told he was going to see Plunkett. Some time after the confrontation with Plunkett, the two of them were put alone into the back of a garda car.

Nicky Kelly's direct evidence took up a day of the court's time: his cross-examination by Robert Barr for the prosecution would take a little longer again. Barr put it to him that all his oral and written confessions had been voluntary, that he was actively co-operating with the gardai and that he was not injured by them. Kelly denied all his assertions.

Barr questioned him about staying at three different houses in Arklow on the weekend before his arrest. Was that pure coincidence or was he going to ground to escape a police dragnet? Kelly denied that he was on the run: "If you visualise the size of Arklow, it would be very futile to be going to ground."

He agreed that he had exonerated a number of gardai from ill-treating him. Why did he not complain to some of them about the way in which he said he was treated? Because, Kelly said, some of them could see the state he was in and the ones who had beaten him were all members of the gardai.

After listing numerous gardai who Kelly agreed did not touch him, Robert Barr turned to what he termed "the list of assailants" – Gardai Dunne, Finn, Boland and Sergeants Cleary and McGroarty.

Barr: When we come to Detective Garda Boland we are talking about actual physical violence done to you by him. Is that right?
Kelly: That is right.
Barr: On about how many occasions?
Kelly: My recollection is that it was only on the Tuesday morning. He was accompanying Garda Lawlor.
Barr: On the Tuesday morning. Garda Lawlor interviewed you on the Tuesday morning, according to the garda timetable, from 10.30 to 1.00 pm. Is that the period you associate with Detective Garda Boland as well?
Kelly: That is correct.

(The presiding judge interrupted to correct Barr: it was from 11.30 to 1.00 pm)

Barr: 11.30 to 1.00 pm.
Kelly: He wasn't with me up to 1.00 pm because I

remember prior to 1.00 pm being taken back to the cell; it was the guard from Letterkenny who was with me.

Barr: Yes, this was Garda Waters whom we have already discussed.

Kelly: Yes.

Barr: Accompanied by Detective Garda Lawlor. I have to put it to you that Garda Boland never interviewed you, never came near you at any time, particularly not during that morning period that you refer to?

Kelly: He was with me, both himself and Garda Lawlor were with me that morning.

Barr: What injury did Garda Boland do to you?

Kelly: The only significant injury he done to me was that he hit me with a chair on one occasion. I was on the ground.

.....

Barr: I have to suggest to you that did not happen and that, in fact, Garda Boland had nothing whatever to do with you during that period and you contest that?

Kelly: Yes.

.....

Barr: Have you any doubt about his identity?

Kelly: I have no doubt about his identity.

Barr: You have seen him in court several times?

Kelly: I have.

Barr: You have no doubt now in the wide world.

Kelly: None whatsoever.

Kelly agreed that everybody who interviewed him would have known that he was being ill-treated. Barr said that the court had heard from almost all of them and they had sworn categorically that they did not see anything wrong with him. "Are you saying to this court that there is a conspiracy of naked perjury involving a very large group of the Garda Siochana from the rank of superintendent, if not even chief superintendent, downwards?" Barr asked. "I am saying to the court what happened to me in the custody of the gardai," Kelly replied. Those who said they had not beaten him or who said that he looked perfectly all right were lying, he agreed.

Barr suggested to him that the incident in which he said Garda Finn had sat on a chair with its legs resting on the palms of his hands must have been excruciatingly painful. Kelly agreed that it was painful.

Barr: The weight of the man coming through the legs into the palms of your hands?

Kelly: It was painful, yes.

Barr: Very painful, excruciatingly painful I suggest to you?

Kelly: It was more weird and frightening than painful.

Barr: Oh no, Mr Kelly, if what you say is true and the weight of this man bearing down into the palms of your hands, it must have been horrifically painful, I would suggest.

Kelly: I suggest to you I was there and I know how I classified one of the events that happened to me that night.

Barr: If it had happened you would have been screaming the house down?

Kelly: I probably did scream, yes. I was crying.

Barr: And screaming?

Kelly: I don't know, I could not say for definite.

Barr: Very probably you were?

Kelly: Very probably was.

Barr: And your hands would have been very sore afterwards?

Kelly: They were sore. I don't know how significantly sore.

Barr: Well, I would suggest to you that when it came to the time to see a doctor it would have been very high up in the list of complaints you would be making?

Kelly: Maybe.

Barr: Did you ever complain to the prison doctors about any injury to the palms of your hands?

Kelly: Well, regarding the prison doctors, it was a very cursory, to say the very least, examination that I got from them.

Barr: Did you complain to Dr O'Cleirigh?

Kelly: There's a lot of things I didn't complain of to Dr

O'Cleirigh which were wrong with me. I cannot say whether I complained about it.

Barr: Do you see, if what you described happened, not only do I suggest to you would you be grievously bruised but there would have been a serious risk that you would damage, perhaps break, the small bones that form a man's hand?

Kelly: Well, all I can say is that I don't know whether it was a priority or not when I reached Dr O'Cleirigh but he asked me, I cannot say whether I even told him about it – if you have the medical evidence there – I don't know exactly whether I did or not but as regards the event with the chair it definitely happened.

Barr: What I have to suggest to you is, the reality is you never complained about it because it never happened and that this is something you thought of as a further lurid refinement to add to your story about lies of ill-treatment by the Garda Siochana?

Kelly: I am suggesting that the lurid refinements were developed by Garda Finn.

Barr wondered why Kelly did not attack Garda Finn when he said they were alone in a cell in Fitzgibbon Street. Kelly agreed that he would have liked to but he was not up to it physically. "I was the very same – to use a country expression – as a sack of spuds," he said. The gardai who terrified him most were Finn and Dunne: "Finn because he always seemed to leer and grin at me and Dunne because he seemed to hover... he seemed to be above me and shouting and roaring the whole time."

Kelly said that he did not complain about ill-treatment to the uniformed garda who was present when he was brought in to the Bridewell. Neither did he ask him for a solicitor, a doctor or a priest. In his cell that night, he sat on the wooden bed, "going half crazy just listening to their footsteps on the tiles because every time they came near my door I thought it was me they were taking out." He went on: "My state of mind at the time was that the door was closed and there was nobody inside, I was okay. It was when anyone came to the door that was my state of mind. I was terrified that another bunch of detectives might come in."

Barr put it to him that he and the gardai ill-treating him must have been heard by other gardai in the Bridewell, even by members of the public going into the fines office, if his account was true. Was he suggesting that there was a vast conspiracy of silence embracing all the Garda Siochana? Kelly replied: "I was beaten constantly over a period of days until I signed a statement for something I didn't do. If you want to put your interpretation on that..."

> Barr: I suggest if there was any tittle of truth you would have screamed at the top of your voice for aid. That was a place where there would be people who would hear you?
> Kelly: I thought of it since. There is a lot of things I would do if it happened now.
> Barr: That would have been a fundamental, obvious course to take if you were in that state?
> Kelly: I don't know. I am saying I would do different things now. A lot of different things to what I done then.

Dealing with the events of Tuesday night and Wednesday morning, April 6th and 7th 1976, Barr suggested to Kelly that he would have made a full statement earlier but for his over-riding fear of the IRSP leadership and of Seamus Costello. That was a totally hypothetical situation, Kelly replied; "I had no involvement whatever with the robbery, therefore I could not have been in that state of mind." Barr asked how Kelly had been able to sign the statement in such a "clear, bold hand" if he had suffered the injuries he said he had received. Justice Hamilton suggested that one did not sign statements with one's arms.

Kelly said that none of the four who had appeared at the late night sitting of the district court had made a protest because of fear. Barr suggested that the real reason was that a protest would be premature at that stage: none of them had any injuries to show? Kelly replied that he had injuries on the Monday and Tuesday nights, before the Wednesday night court sitting. He denied that his bruises were the work of Michael Plunkett with whom he shared a cell after the court sitting. "The bruises that were on me were the trademark of the so-called group called the Heavy Gang and nobody else," he said.

His cross-examination and prolonged session in the witness box ended on that note on the thirty first day of the trial. But the defence had three other witnesses to call: Nuala Dillon and the two doctors who examined Nicky Kelly in Mountjoy prison, Dr Sean O'Cleirigh and Dr David McGee.

Nuala Dillon was first and she gave evidence about garda searches of their flat looking for Kelly on the day of the robbery and again on the morning of the round-up. On the second occasion, she went voluntarily with the detectives to Dublin Castle and stayed there for more than two hours. About 11.00 pm that night she got a phone call asking her to go to Mountjoy garda station: "Nick wants to see you," she was told. Two detectives waited there for her and then took her to Fitzgibbon Street station. She understood that she was being brought to see Kelly.

Garda Thomas Ibar Dunne told her there that Kelly had confessed to the robbery and had phoned her afterwards and told her the job went all right. She said she denied that Kelly had said that to her and she accused the detective of putting words in her mouth. Meanwhile, she was moved around three rooms in the station. Then she was brought out to a corridor. She thought she was waiting to see Kelly but after five minutes or so was told she could not see him. She was brought back to her flat then.

The following night, Tuesday April 6th 1976, two detectives called on her again and said that Nick wanted to see her. They guaranteed that she would see him this time. They told her Kelly wanted some clothes and she brought some. She arrived at the Bridewell about 10.00 pm and was taken into a biggish room which had a teleprinter in a room off it. Various people kept coming in and out, including Inspector Ned Ryan who asked her about the telephone call on the day of the robbery. He went out and returned later to say that Nicky was now saying that he and she had been drinking in Grogan's and had planned the robbery.

She went on: "I said this could not be true and it was not

281

true. He said, 'well, come on and Nick will tell you'."
Inspector Ryan took her into the prison section and into a
smallish room. Inspector Ryan came in with her: Nicky
Kelly and Garda Dunne were there. The room was hot and
she was surprised Kelly was wearing a ski jacket. He
seemed to be upset, was running his hands through his hair
and was sweating slightly. At one stage, his hand was
shaking. She asked him was he all right and he said yes.

Then Garda Dunne told him to tell her what he had told
the gardai, that they were drinking in Grogan's with
Michael Barrett. "Nick turned around and looked at me
and said, 'do you remember, Nuala, and we planned the
robbery?' He added, 'but she was not in the final details'."

She thought he also said that he had phoned her the next
day and said that the job went all right. As she was leaving
the room, Kelly said: "can she go now." She was taken
back to the room beside the teleprinter. She told Inspector
Ryan that she didn't know what Kelly was talking about: it
was not true. She added that she thought she needed a
solicitor. Inspector Ryan replied that she was lucky she was
not in a cell already and if she continued in that vein, she
would be.

She was questioned by several plain clothes gardai. At
some stage Inspector Ryan returned and said that Kelly
was taking them to the money. She was asked to wait until
he came back and she could see him then. She continued:
"The place got very quiet and I was getting tired and I tried
to sleep on the wooden bench and I could not. At some
stage or other I heard a shout or a scream or something like
that. I thought I had imagined it so I listened carefully and I
heard somebody distinctly screaming or shouting in
obvious... I don't know ...it sounded like somebody in pain
saying 'please not there' or something to that effect.... I
went outside and there were a lot of gardai outside the
door.... I said, 'please let me out of here: I can hear
somebody screaming.'"

Shortly afterwards two detectives came into the room
and took her to Mountjoy station. They would not let her go
home: they seemed to be afraid she might contact
somebody. About 8.00 am, they told her she could go. She

walked out the door of the station and was arrested under Section 30 of the Offences Against the State Act. She was brought back to the Bridewell, put in a cell and left there until 7.00 pm when she was released. She was taken out of the cell once to be photographed but she was never questioned.

Cross-examined by Noel McDonald, she said that she went to the office of Pat McCartan, the solicitor, after she left Dublin Castle about noon on Monday, April 5th. She told McCartan that Kelly had been arrested and asked him to get in touch. She subsequently went to work and went back to her flat afterwards. She said she knew that Kelly had phoned her on the day of the robbery because he phoned her every day: she could not remember what he said.

McDonald: Could it have been that everything was all right, the job went okay?
Dillon: No, I could not think of any context he could have said that in.
McDonald: It meant nothing to you?
Dillon: No.
McDonald: You have no recollection of its being said to you?
Dillon: No.

She said she had never overheard nor been involved in any conversations about the robbery. She didn't know what was happening when she saw Kelly in the Bridewell. "At that stage Inspector Ryan had told me that he had done the robbery and I thought he had done the robbery because the gardai had told me and when I went in he was very upset. I knew he was lying. I didn't know what was happening and he was upset. That is why I said nothing. I knew he was lying and I didn't know why: I had no idea."

Pat McCartan had come back to her on the Monday to tell her that Kelly was not in Arklow station, she said. He told her he could not find him anywhere. Next day, she left a message for McCartan to contact her: she heard nothing more from him.

283

Dr Sean O'Cleirigh then gave evidence of examining Nicky Kelly in Mountjoy Prison on Thursday, April 8th 1976. Kelly told him he had been punched on the arms and in the groin, low down in the abdomen, that he had been hit with a strap on the arms and neck, that his hair had been pulled, that he had been slapped, hit over the ear with the open hand and that his ear had been twisted, that he had been spread-eagled against a wall and knocked from behind.

He described the bruising that he found on Kelly's arms, shoulder, back, above the buttocks, thigh, chest and ears. He found Kelly very distressed and in a state of acute anxiety. He said he remembered that, of the four prisoners he saw at the time, Kelly was particularly stressful. All the injuries were consistent with a beating of the type Kelly had described to him, he said.

Kelly had come to him again on April 16th after leaving prison. He was in a state of anxiety and depression. Kelly told him he had had nightmares in which the alleged assault was re-enacted on someone else. He felt like killing himself. Dr O'Cleirigh said that the bruises had cleared very well but the chest was still tender in one place so he arranged for an X-ray to rule out a fracture. The X-ray found no fracture.

Noel McDonald, for the prosecution, produced the chair put before the court as an exhibit from Fitzgibbon Street station and pointed out Garda Michael Finn to the doctor. If somebody of Garda Finn's build was sitting on that chair on top of the palms of somebody's hands, would it not cause excruciating pain? he asked. Dr O'Cleirigh said it should with the full weight of a man on top of it. He suggested that it would be necessary to put a lot of weight suddenly on the hands to cause serious damage to the palms. It would not necessarily cause an abrasion on the palm. One would not see very much on the hand two days later but one would look for pain, he said. Dr O'Cleirigh said his attention was not drawn to it and he did not look at Kelly's hands.

He agreed that such an incident would cause pain for weeks afterwards when the bones in the hands were pressed. Would there be some pain on moving the bones in

284

the hands? That was likely, Dr O'Cleirigh replied. He agreed that taking up a pen and writing one's name might be a painful experience.

Dr David McGee gave evidence of being present during Dr O'Cleirigh's examination but he did not take notes at the time. He described the bruises he remembered seeing and said that Kelly appeared giddy, tense and gave the impression of being under strain. He estimated that most of the bruises were between one and three days old. Cross-examined by Noel McDonald, he said that the injuries that could be caused by a man sitting on the chair could range from no lasting injury to quite extensive injuries.

That concluded the defence case in the trial within a trial about the alleged confessions of Nicky Kelly. The prosecution then produced no less than twenty three witnesses to rebut Kelly's evidence: all of them were gardai and they included uniformed jailers and station sergeants who were present in the Bridewell at the relevant time. The first was Garda Thomas Boland who denied that he had struck Kelly with a chair in the Bridewell on the morning of Tuesday, April 6th 1976. He denied that he was in the Bridewell at the time and that he had had any dealings with Nicky Kelly at all. He said he had never met Kelly at any time anywhere.

Garda Thomas Ibar Dunne denied that he had seen Kelly in Harcourt Terrace station and that he had spoken to Nuala Dillon in Fitzgibbon Street station. "I never had any conversation with her," he said. Superintendent Ned Ryan denied that he had spoken to Nuala Dillon in the Bridewell on Tuesday night, April 6th and that he brought her in to see Kelly. He said he was not in the room during the meeting. He did not see her after the meeting either, he said. He agreed with Seamus Sorahan that Nuala Dillon would have known him because he had visited her flat the previous day. But he denied that he ever had any conversation with her in the Bridewell.

Sergeant Patrick Bohan gave evidence of having counted the number of people passing through the public office in the Bridewell on a normal weekday during 1974. They numbered more than 300 people, excluding those going into the fines office to pay parking fines. The numbers were even higher in 1976, he said. There were fifteen to sixteen uniformed men on each shift at the station and nine detectives attached to it. There were around forty people employed there as office staff.

He said the room in which Kelly was questioned on the morning of Tuesday, April 6th 1976 was on a very busy corridor. It was about fifteen feet from the station sergeant's office.

Superintendent Ned Ryan was recalled to the witness box the afternoon after he had last given evidence. The defence had found a discrepancy between his denial of any knowledge of Nuala Dillon's presence in the Bridewell and the evidence of Garda William Meagher. Fourteen days earlier, Garda Meagher had told the court he had brought Dillon to the Bridewell at Inspector Ryan's request: he said that as far as he knew Inspector Ryan had met her in the Bridewell. Did Superintendent Ryan have any comment to make on that? Seamus Sorahan asked.

"That is not correct, my lords," Superintendent Ryan replied. "But I do recall there was a discussion about property.... There was some discussion with someone about Kelly's property because we hadn't taken any property from Kelly's flat on the Monday morning." He again denied that Dillon had been taken to the Bridewell at his behest.

The prosecution wound up its case with a succession of gardai who had been acting as jailers and station sergeants from the Bridewell. All denied that they had seen or heard anything untoward on the night in question or that they had received any complaints from Nicky Kelly. Noel McDonald then addressed the court for the prosecution, urging the three judges to admit several statements made by Kelly as evidence.

The onus was not on the prosecution to establish precisely how Kelly received his injuries, he said. "The onus is to satisfy you that they were not caused by the gardai and it is a submission of the prosecution that that has been proved, we hope to the satisfaction of the court, by all the guards who are alleged to have been involved, either as

286

witnesses of such things or as perpetrators of them."

He submitted that the evidence showed that Kelly had never asked for a solicitor. At all times, he was treated most humanely; he received all the food and refreshment that he required. But the main issue to be determined was that of ill-treatment. He maintained that the suggestion of ill-treatment was patently preposterous: the chair incident was fantastic and, had it occurred, would have resulted in some form of injury that would have been noticed. This outlandish proposition was in keeping with the rest of Kelly's allegations, he said.

Seamus Sorahan urged the court to reject the alleged oral and written confessions on the grounds that they were not made voluntarily. Firstly, he submitted, they were obtained from Nicky Kelly by force: beating, shouting and the threat that he could be detained for more than forty eight hours. Secondly, the court could exclude the statements on the grounds of oppression, as distinct from physical ill-treatment. Thirdly, the statements could be excluded because they were obtained in breach of the Judges Rules. Fourthly, the court had a general discretion to exclude evidence if it was obtained unfairly. Fifthly, he said that he adopted all the arguments used by Patrick MacEntee in relation to Section 30 of the Offences Against the State Act.

There was also the matter of whether Kelly was denied a solicitor in breach of his constitutional rights. Justice Hamilton remarked that Kelly had never suggested that he made the statement because he had not seen a solicitor. To exclude the statement on that issue required that it be established that it was made as a result of that breach of constitutional rights.

Sorahan dealt in detail with Kelly's account of what had happened to him in custody. On the incident with the chair and Garda Michael Finn, he said there was not merely a conflict of interest but an unbridgeable chasm between the two accounts. It was not capable of being reconciled. The court had to ask itself was it intended to besmirch the reputation of the police or did it really happen as an attempt to degrade and insult a person rather than to torture or

287

inflict pain. "It's a startling thing to think a thing like that could happen or be inflicted on a person in a police station here," he remarked.

The garda evidence showed that this session with Garda Finn ended abruptly at 9.45 pm, just the time when the station shift changed. Sorahan suggested that several things pointed to the accuracy of Kelly's account of events in Fitzgibbon Street: Garda Thomas Ibar Dunne admitted using a rosary beads in a previous case when he was questioned about sprinkling water on Kelly and calling him an atheist. Nuala Dillon confirmed that she was in a corridor in the station which was in line with Kelly's statement that he was shown her briefly.

There was another deep conflict of evidence over Nuala Dillon's visit to Kelly in the Bridewell. Kelly and Dillon told of how he had said to her that they had been in a bar when the robbery was planned. But that admission was not recorded in any garda notebook nor contained in any statement of evidence: "It is strange and mysterious and perplexing in many respects," Sorahan said. Dillon was the only person, other than members of the gardai, to see Kelly. To her, he looked distressed and his hand shook. That contradicted the descriptions of the gardai that Kelly always looked normal and that the atmosphere was easy.

Dealing with the alleged confessions, Sorahan suggested that it was unlikely that someone like Kelly would – as the gardai claimed – actually call detectives into the room after he had been left alone for fifteen minutes to think things over. Why would he do that? "It is something I stress has certain unlikely implications inherent in it," Sorahan replied to his own rhetorical question.

Sorahan argued that even if the garda case was accepted, there were breaches of the Judges Rules. The prolonged questioning of Kelly went on for some thirty hours in all and the gardai admitted that they did not caution the accused every time he was questioned. There was also a question of fact: did the gardai issue the cautions they said they had and which Kelly had denied? As a result, it was open to the court to refuse to admit into evidence the alleged verbal and written statements.

288

The length of the questioning in Fitzgibbon Street station was also oppressive. Kelly was questioned all day in Fitzgibbon Street and all day the following day in the Bridewell. Then there was the question of ill-treatment. On one hand there was the evidence of Kelly, corroborated by the medical evidence and Nuala Dillon's description of his condition. That was consistent with other evidence, he suggested. There were no marks, for instance, on Kelly's face and if somebody took a quick look at him they might not notice anything other than worry consistent with being questioned or charged with a serious crime. None of the jailers appeared to have gone into the room with him. The court should ask itself if Kelly's evidence could reasonably be true.

The onus was on the prosecution to prove beyond reasonable doubt that Kelly was not beaten. If the court were to decide that the prosecution had not discharged that onus, it would not follow at all that the court was saying the gardai had beaten Kelly. It would merely be a finding to the effect that the prosecution had not proved its case beyond reasonable doubt: it would not find that any particular gardai had beaten his client.

Sorahan then argued a legal point about the fact that Kelly had been arrested at 5.30 am on Wednesday, April 7th under common law which required that he be brought to court as soon as possible or as soon as practicable. Instead, he was brought off on a journey to County Kildare, Ballymore Eustace and Bray and was not brought to court until late that night. He contended that everything that occurred from his arrest under common law was therefore illegal and all the things he supposedly pointed out or said were inadmissible in law.

Robert Barr submitted for the prosecution that the idea of oppression had to be considered in the light of several factors, including the age and physical and mental condition of the person involved. In addition, the nature of the crime was a factor: in this case, the public interest required the police to recover the money as well as apprehend the robbers. One had to consider the clear obligations on the police to fulfil both these requirements.

Justice Hamilton remarked that if the court were to consider oppression on that basis their decision would not survive for long.

Barr added that another factor was the amount of rest given to the accused while in custody before making his admissions. The crucial time appeared to be 1.20 am on Wednesday, April 7th when Kelly called Sergeant Cleary into the room and, from there on, admitted to his participation in the robbery. On the previous night, Kelly had nine hours and twenty minutes rest in the cell in the Bridewell. During the Tuesday, he had two periods free of interrogation – from 1.00 to 3.00 pm and from 6.30 pm to 9.00 pm. His interrogation was divided up into three sessions that day: "Looked at, in overall, one sees therefore that he was afforded very reasonable periods of rest to refresh his mind and his body," he maintained.

A fourth factor to be taken into account was Kelly's own desire to help the police to trace the money and the guns. Kelly was taking a realistic view, he suggested: the more he helped the gardai the more it would redound to his benefit at a subsequent trial.

Barr submitted that one of Kelly's allegations gave a clue to all the others – the extraordinary account of the chair being put on his hands. Justice Hamilton asked if Barr had had any tests carried out with the chair. "I would be afraid to carry out a test," Barr replied. "You needn't be afraid," Justice Hamilton said. "You could try it yourself some time, perhaps with Mr Haugh (the third prosecution barrister) sitting on the chair." The judge added that it depended on how one sat on the chair.

The statements made to Sergeant Richard Murphy and to Garda Mullen in Harcourt Terrace should be looked at separately because neither detective had anything to do with the Bridewell. Kelly accepted that neither laid a hand on him. "Why would he voluntarily make admissions of guilt unless the previous submissions were completely voluntarily made?" Barr argued.

The submissions concluded on the thirty third day of the trial, Monday, November 27th 1978. The court had by then spent thirty one days hearing evidence about the statements that the three accused men had allegedly made in garda custody. The judges had decided initially to hear the evidence about the alleged confessions of Brian McNally, Osgur Breatnach and Nicky Kelly in that order. They had also decided to give their ruling on each when all were completed.

The judges now went away to consider their decision, announcing that they would adjourn until the following Thursday afternoon. On Wednesday, however, they returned to say that they would not be in a position to give their decision until Friday, December 1st.

On that Friday, they did give their ruling. They said that all the evidence that the prosecution wanted to tender against Kelly was admissible.

"This court is satisfied beyond all reasonable doubt that the statements alleged to have been made by the accused were made by the accused voluntarily and were not made as a result of any assaults, ill-treatment or improper methods employed by members of the Garda Siochana or any of them, and that the injuries of which he subsequently complained were not inflicted by any member of the Garda Siochana."

The judges said they had taken account of the seriousness of Kelly's allegations and the fact that he was found to be injured, the demeanour of the witnesses and the manner in which they gave their evidence. They were satisfied that the garda witnesses were truthful and had given a truthful account of what transpired during the different interviews in Fitzgibbon Street and the Bridewell and on the journey to the scene of the alleged robbery.

They categorised the questioning of Kelly as protracted and continuous over long periods but they said that it was not oppressive and did not overbear or lessen the will of the accused. They found that Kelly had gone voluntarily on the journey to the robbery scene, Ballymore Eustace and Bray, and to Harcourt Terrace garda station.

The court said that Kelly's account of ill-treatment in Fitzgibbon Street was one "of quite savage brutality, at times of a horrific nature". If it were true, it was inconceivable that ordinary members of the gardai engaged in their ordinary duties at the station would not have been aware of what was happening. Likewise, they said that gardai in the Bridewell could not but have been aware of what was happening if Kelly's allegations were correct. Members of the gardai alleged to have taken part in the ill-treatment had been subjected to intense and rigorous cross-examination by counsel for the defence and denied the accusations.

The judges ruled that Kelly had been cautioned once in Arklow, once in Fitzgibbon Street, four times in the Bridewell on Tuesday and seven times in the Bridewell on Wednesday. The court did not consider that the nature of the questioning was in breach of the judges rules. "If any questioning was in fact in breach of the judges rules, the court is satisfied that any answers given to such questions were voluntary, that such questioning was not unfair and should in the exercise of its discretion admit any answer in evidence," the court said.

The court also said it was fully satisfied that Kelly did not ask for a solicitor either at Arklow or at any relevant time. The judges said they were fully satisfied that the evidence of the prosecution was to be accepted.

The judgement concluded with the paragraph that applied to all three accused.

"The court accepts that inherent in its findings with regard to each of the accused, it has drawn the inference that the injuries that they suffered at the time of their respective medical examinations were self-inflicted or inflicted by collaboration with persons other than members of the Garda Siochana."

13

Guilty

Everyone knew that the central decision of the trial had been taken: the odds now favoured the conviction and jailing of the three men on trial. The defence lawyers were disappointed and somewhat surprised. The prosecution responded by asking the court to have the accused men's bail lifted and to have them held in custody for the remainder of the trial. Chief Superintendent John Joy was called to give evidence. He said there was every likelihood the accused would not stand trial in view of the seriousness of the offences and the nature of the evidence and the likelihood of the sentence to be imposed.

Justice Hamilton asked if the evidence was any different then from what had been contained in the book of evidence. The Chief Superintendent said it was not. The prosecution maintained that the statements had now been admitted into evidence which carried a much more serious implication. Judge Clarke noted that the court had not ruled upon the facts within those statements. The judges refused the prosecution application and the three defendants remained on bail.

One of them, at least, was beginning to think of doing what the prosecution feared.

Meanwhile, the atmosphere in court was particularly tetchy after Justice Hamilton had read out the decisions on the statements. Patrick MacEntee, representing Breatnach, asked that a copy of the ruling be made available from the stenographer's shorthand note. The defence should be entitled to see it in order to decide how they should conduct their case from then on, he argued.

The underlying feelings came to the surface when Seamus Sorahan, representing Brian McNally and Nicky Kelly, intervened to support MacEntee. The ruling, he said, "contains reasoning and astounding findings of fact..."

Judge Clarke intervened: I beg your pardon, Mr
Sorahan. What do you mean by that?
Sorahan: Surprise...
Judge Clarke: Are you surprised?
Sorahan: Yes...
Judge Clarke: Then kindly do not make any insinuations
beyond that then.

The three judges considered the request during the lunch
break and then refused it. They also refused to allow the
defence listen to a tape recording of the relevant section of
the trial. Justice Hamilton ruled that it was not necessary
either for the administration of justice or for the defence to
properly conduct their case. He offered to read out any
parts of the judgement required if the defence found itself in
difficulty at any time.

The trial adjourned for the weekend and resumed on
Monday, December 4th 1978. The trial proper was now
being conducted: the previous thirty three days of hearings
had been taken up exclusively with the issue of whether or
not the statements made by the accused in the Bridewell
were made and signed voluntarily. Almost all of the garda
witnesses had given evidence during the trial within the
trial. The prosecution now began to call each of them again,
essentially to ask them one question: was the evidence he
had given already true and correct?

The technique allowed the defence to cross-examine
each witness again. There appeared to be little new information that could be extracted. All of the gardai had already
been cross-examined, some of them at considerable length
and some also at the first trial. They repeated the evidence
they had given already.

Superintendent Ned Ryan was cross-examined at some
length once again. Seamus Sorahan asked him if he ever
noticed that there were discrepancies between the statements of the three men in the dock. They existed in relation
to the journey taken to the scene of the crime and the names
of those said to be present. Superintendent Ryan replied: "I
have never read any statements other than the statement I
took."

Justice Hamilton remarked: "Isn't that a matter for the court. If the discrepancies are there, you can draw the attention of the court to that. You don't have to take up discrepancies with every witness."

Sorahan accepted the direction, noting that that would save an awful lot of time.

Superintendent Ryan again denied the accounts of events given by Brian McNally and Nicky Kelly, denying that he had seen any indications that they were beaten up and repeating the admissions that he said Kelly had made in his presence.

He denied to Patrick MacEntee that he had made out a time-table of which guards had interviewed which prisoner at what time. He said he had had nothing to do with Osgur Breatnach other than to send in two detectives to interview him and to arrest him after his High Court appearance. He told MacEntee that he had interviewed prisoners in the tunnel under the Bridewell himself on several occasions. He could not name any prisoner right then and there but promised to try later.

The relationship between the defence lawyers and the gardai was illustrated by another exchange between the two which showed that the policemen were not prepared to concede anything to the defence in the witness box.

MacEntee: Would you agree that at a certain stage in time that questioning might become oppressive?
Ryan: Interviewing of prisoners, it is never the intention to use oppressive measures.
MacEntee: No, but it could become oppressive?
Ryan: No, I won't agree with that.
MacEntee: There are no circumstances under which interviewing a prisoner could become oppressive?
Ryan: No, my lords.

Superintendent John Courtney and Inspector Michael Canavan were questioned about their interview with Brian McNally after 5.00 am on Wednesday, April 7th 1976. Their evidence – the main evidence against McNally – said that he had given them a verbal account of the robbery during which he described the route from Swords to Sallins via Saint Margarets and Dunboyne, named the people on the robbery and what each of them did.

Superintendent Courtney said he had taken some notes on a torn sheet of paper after McNally had finished his account about 6.50 am. He jotted down a few facts and names that were unfamiliar to him. The two detectives stayed on while McNally signed a written statement and, about 9.30 am, they went to the garda technical bureau where they sat down and wrote out notes of what McNally had said to them initially. They used the notes in giving their evidence to the court.

The prosecution case against Brian McNally was largely dealt with in one day.

The main attention of the court then turned to Osgur Breatnach's case, with the principal witnesses against him repeating for the prosecution that they had nothing further to add to what they had already told the court. Patrick MacEntee asked several of them if they had checked the contents of Breatnach's statement against the known facts of the case.

Garda Thomas Fitzgerald, one of the detectives who interrogated Breatnach, said he had not checked how long it would take someone to get from Burgh Quay or the 7A bus terminus to the scene of the robbery at Hazelhatch. Garda Thomas Ibar Dunne agreed that he had made no effort to check the statement. He accepted that he knew the facts of the robbery, as he had been to the scene and had interviewed the train crew and some of the post office workers. "I didn't check the statement," he told MacEntee. "This statement was made by the accused free and voluntarily and it was signed by him and it was his statement."

MacEntee asked if it was not unlikely that it would take an hour to get from the 7A bus terminus to the robbery scene. "That didn't come into my investigation my lord," Garda Dunne replied. "I made no inquiries in that respect." He added that the first time he had thought about that issue was when he was asked that question in court.

Inspector John Murphy, another of Breatnach's

questioners, admitted that he had not taken any steps to verify the statement either. Asked if he was sceptical about the contents of the statement, he said he had not thought about it at the time. MacEntee suggested to him that Breatnach was left in the room in which he was interviewed after the statement was taken and questioned again because the gardai were not satisfied with the reliability of his statement. Inspector Murphy said that was not correct. Why was Breatnach not charged or sent back to his cell then? "That wasn't my doing," Inspector Murphy replied. "I wasn't in charge of the case."

Two of the gardai who stayed with Breatnach after he had signed a statement were cross-examined in detail about their evidence that Breatnach had gone on to give them an account of the robbery. Garda Gerard O'Carroll and Garda James Butler admitted to MacEntee that they had not told any of their superiors about the interview for some time afterwards. Garda Butler said he had written his notes of the interview later that morning in Dublin Castle and independently of the other detectives who were present.

MacEntee expressed scepticism that all their accounts should be virtually identical in phraseology and thought sequence, especially as part of the interview was conducted in Irish. "I put it in my notes exactly what the accused said," Garda Butler said.

MacEntee: You are able to recall the whole hour's session identical with your comrades, without reference to them, virtually identical?
Butler: I put in my notes exactly what the accused had said, as far as I could remember.
MacEntee: How is your Irish? ·
Butler: It would be only fair to middling.
MacEntee: And yet portions of this revelation from Mr Breatnach were in Irish?
Butler: I can understand Irish but I would be fairly weak to speak it at that stage.
MacEntee: But capable of producing an agreed translation?
Butler: I could understand what the accused was saying.

MacEntee: And translate from one to the other in virtually the same words and phrases and thought sequence as your companions?
Butler: I cannot say what my companions...
MacEntee: A thing I think the holy spirit didn't achieve in the gospels.
Butler: As I said my lords, I put down what I remembered.

The defence asked that Garda Brian McGauran be called as a witness. He had actually given evidence already in the trial but neither Breatnach's lawyers nor some of the judges appeared to realise it. His evidence had been mainly technical, dealing with the serving of an extension order to Nicky Kelly about his detention.

Garda McGauran told the court that he had been on duty in the Bridewell as a jailer on March 31st 1976 and April 5th and 6th 1976 and he remembered Osgur Breatnach being brought into the prison on both occasions. The second time, he commented to Breatnach: "arais aris, Osgur" (back again, Osgur). Any time they spoke it was in Irish: Garda McGauran remembered Breatnach mentioning the word "dlidoir" (solicitor). MacEntee asked in what context. Garda McGauran replied: "I presume that it was that he wished to see a solicitor."

Justice Hamilton: Did he say to you that he wanted to see a solicitor?
Garda McGauran: He did, my lords, but I am unable to say on which date. He mentioned the word "dlidoir" to me alright.
Justice Hamilton: Was it on the occasion of his second detention?
Garda McGauran: My lords, I can't remember whether it was on the 31st or the 5th.

Patrick MacEntee suggested that the garda had indicated to the first trial that the "dlidoir" conversation had taken place after the second arrest. Garda McGauran said it was possible that it was during the second detention. He felt sure that he had had discussions with Breatnach in his cell during that time.

Justice Hamilton asked what the garda had done when Breatnach asked for a solicitor. Garda McGauran said he could not remember but he presumed that he had told the station sergeant. The prosecution counsel, Noel McDonald, asked who the station sergeant was on April 5th. Garda McGauran said it was Sergeant Martin Purtill who, the prosecution noted, had not given evidence. "Certainly, we'll call him now," Noel McDonald remarked. Sergeant William Ryan was station sergeant on the other two dates.

Justice Hamilton said he thought they had heard evidence from every uniformed member of the police who was in the Bridewell during the relevant period. "The case was put to us on that basis and it now turns out that that is not so," he added. McDonald said he would have to investigate this further. It was the first he had heard of Sergeant Purtill.

The prosecution announced later the same day that it intended to introduce three new witnesses, including Sergeant Purtill. MacEntee objected: to what extent could the prosecution run "a darning bee" during the trial, he asked, introducing new evidence every time the defence elicited something in cross-examination. It was not in the interests of justice to patch up their case, he argued, and to try and contradict the evidence of their own witness, Garda McGauran. Noel McDonald denied that that was the purpose of the evidence. The court decided to hear the extra witnesses.

Sergeant Purtill's appearance in the witness box caused further confusion, however. He confirmed for the prosecution that he was the station sergeant between 6.00 am and 2.00 pm on Monday, April 5th 1976. During that time he had not received any request on behalf of Osgur Breatnach for a solicitor.

The confusion began when he was cross-examined by Patrick MacEntee and told him that Breatnach was admitted to the Bridewell at 1.50 pm on that day by Sergeant Carey.

MacEntee: By?

Purtill: Sergeant Carey.

MacEntee: Who is he?

Purtill: Sergeant Michael Carey who has given evidence here.

MacEntee: In relation to Breatnach?

Purtill: Yes.

MacEntee: Sorry, that takes me completely by surprise. When do you say this evidence was given?

Justice Hamilton: The name?

Purtill: Sergeant Michael Carey, my lords.

MacEntee: When do you say this evidence was given?

Purtill: I don't know. He did give evidence.

Justice Hamilton: Where is Sergeant Michael Carey stationed?

Purtill: In the Bridewell. He took up duty at two o'clock on that date, 1.45.

Justice Hamilton: On the 5th of April?

Purtill: Yes, my lord.

Justice Hamilton: You are quite sure about that?

Purtill: I am certain. For some reason I was absent from the office at 1.50, Sergeant Carey was present.

MacEntee: How do you know that?

Purtill: He brought it to my notice at two o'clock.

Justice Hamilton: We have to hear Sergeant Carey. We did not even know of his existence.

MacEntee: Nor did I after a hundred and four days....

Another sergeant, William Ryan, was called to give evidence about his tour of duty as station sergeant on March 31st and April 6th 1976. He explained that the Bridewell system provided for a prison sergeant to be in charge of the prison section between 9.15 am and 5.15 pm each day. Outside those hours, the station sergeant was responsible for the prison as well as the garda station. Asked by MacEntee who the prison sergeant was on March 31st, Sergeant Ryan said it had been a Sergeant Fennessy who was now retired. He confirmed it from the station allocation book, a daily diary of duties allocated to each garda attached to the station. Sergeant Fennessy was identified in it by his number – 19 – rather than by name.

Sergeant Ryan said the allocation book did not record who was prison sergeant on April 5th nor April 6th nor on April 7th. Justice Hamilton asked about April 8th. There was no record, the sergeant replied. The 9th? the judge asked. Missing, Sergeant Ryan said. 10th? Missing. What about the fourth of April, Mr Justice Hamilton inquired. The page was there but the allocation was not entered, Sergeant Ryan said. Neither was it entered for April 3rd. On April 2nd, it was filled in and showed Sergeant Fennessy to be on duty.

The allocation of prison sergeants was blank between April 2nd and April 10th. The regular prison sergeant at the time was Sergeant Fennessy, the witness remarked. MacEntee asked for time to think about Sergeant Ryan's evidence before cross-examining him: the court put it off until the following morning.

Meanwhile, the prosecution produced Sergeant Michael Carey to give evidence. Noel McDonald explained that the sergeant had appeared during the previous trial which explained the references to him giving evidence. Justice Hamilton pointed out that the court had been asked to deal with the admissibility of statements on the basis that all the gardai present in the station at the time had given evidence. It now appeared that three gardai who had dealings with Breatnach had not been called.

The judge complained particularly that Sergeant Fennessy was the officer in charge of the prison in April 5th, 6th, and 7th and was not called to give evidence. The court wanted a satisfactory reason why he and Sergeant Carey were not called at the appropriate time. McDonald said the prosecution were not aware that they were relevant. "All people present were relevant on the basis you presented it in regard to the admissibility of the statement," Justice Hamilton retorted.

The next morning, December 7th 1978, MacEntee resumed his cross-examination of Sergeant Ryan, asking him to read out details from the station allocation book. It showed that the prison sergeant was not always identified in the book. The entry for the 6.00 am to 2.00 pm shift on

Tuesday, April 6th appeared to have been erased and written over. Sergeant Ryan agreed that he was in charge at the time and he appeared to have rubbed out a number relating to the prison section. He said he could not recollect why he had done that but he could remember who was on duty with him at the time – Garda McGauran and Garda Peter Canavan.

When he came to the entry for Wednesday, April 7th 1976, Sergeant Ryan said that it was missing, it did not follow the entry for April 6th. The page for April 8th was a bit torn but showed entries for that morning. Several minutes later, he found the page for April 7th at the back of the book and read out the details. The pages for April 9th and 10th were missing.

While the sergeant looked unsuccessfully through the book for them, Justice Hamilton asked MacEntee what the relevance of the entries was. MacEntee said that the police enquiry had continued after the three accused were interrogated and there might be good reasons why the pages were missing.

Cross-examined by Seamus Sorahan, Sergeant Ryan agreed that a mistaken entry in the allocation book was usually crossed out and the correct entry made beside it. Could he say why? "I can't give any specific reason," Sergeant Ryan replied.

Sergeant William Fennessy, the retired prison officer, was called to give evidence and he said he had been on duty on April 5th, 6th and 7th 1976. He did not remember receiving any request for a solicitor from any prisoner. He said he did not receive any request for a solicitor from Osgur Breatnach or from anyone on his behalf.

Sergeant Michael Carey, whose identity had caused such confusion on the previous day, was also called to give evidence about the arrival of Breatnach in the Bridewell on April 5th 1976. After his brief appearance in the witness box, a succession of gardai who had acted as jailers were called. Most had already given evidence in the trial and their re-appearance was merely to confirm that they had told the truth and had nothing to add to their earlier evidence. With that, the prosecution case closed.

On the previous day, as the court heard evidence from some of the gardai who had witnessed Nicky Kelly's statement, it was realised that the statement had never been read out in court. One of the prosecution barristers, Robert Barr then read it out.

The statement said that Kelly and McNally had left McNally's house in Swords around 1.40 am on the morning of March 31st 1976 to go to Celbridge to hold up a train. They left McNally's car in a laneway about a hundred yards from the railway line and walked towards the railway line where they met two men who pointed out a house two hundred yards away that had been taken over by three others. At the track, he was given a revolver and saw a light-coloured Volkswagen van which, the statement said, was in the field between a fairly big ditch and the railway line. The train was stopped by the detonators and reversed back.

Six of them, including Kelly, loaded the mail bags into the van. They had to throw them over a high ditch to where the van was in the field. When it was loaded, the van was driven away towards Ballymore Eustace to a farmhouse as planned before the raid. Kelly and McNally went back to Swords in McNally's car and got there about 4.30 or 4.45 am. The Volkswagen van was to be left somewhere in Finglas after the mail bags were unloaded in Ballymore Eustace. The statement concluded: "I will now show you the route we took from Dublin to the scene of the robbery last Wednesday morning, 31/3/76."

Seamus Sorahan cross-examined Sergeant Patrick Cleary, one of the detectives who signed the statement as a witness, about the names that Kelly was supposed to have mentioned in verbal statements to the gardai and in the written statement. Sergeant Cleary agreed that the name of Joe Heaney had not been mentioned in the verbal statement. He denied that he had ever seen the list of suspects to be arrested which was used at the garda conference in Dublin Castle on Sunday, April 4th.

The hearing then became immersed in the question of Osgur Breatnach's request for a solicitor and who was on duty at the Bridewell at what times. On the following day,

December 7th 1978 the prosecution completed its case against the three remaining defendants. It was the thirty ninth day of the second trial.

The defence opened its case with submissions to the court. Seamus Sorahan argued that his two clients, Brian McNally and Nicky Kelly, had been in unlawful custody from the moment they were arrested in April 1976. According to the evidence before the court, he said neither of the gardai who arrested them had shown that they had the suspicion necessary to arrest them. Section 30 of the Offences Against the State Act allowed gardai to arrest someone whom they suspected of having committed one of the offences listed in the schedule to that act.

Justice Hamilton asked if Sorahan should not have made that point when the court was considering the admissibility of the statements made by the accused. Sorahan replied that it had not occurred to him then.

It was a vital piece of evidence that should have been proved, he went on. "There is this small tiny gap that you would want some kind of forensic magnifier to show up but, in my submission, it is a vital lacuna in the proofs of the prosecution and, accordingly, my submission is that the original arrest had not been proved to be lawful."

Patrick MacEntee said he adopted Sorahan's submission insofar as it was relevant to Osgur Breatnach's case. Justice Hamilton interjected: "It is not relevant to Mr Breatnach at all because we have held that his arrest is unlawful."

MacEntee had another submission, however. As a result of Garda McGauran's evidence that Breatnach had asked for a solicitor, MacEntee asked the court to reconsider its decision to allow the statement signed by Breatnach into evidence. Breatnach had contended that he had asked persistently for a solicitor and had said that he asked for one at the particular time covered by Garda McGauran's evidence. The garda now agreed that that may be so.

In those circumstances, MacEntee argued, the state could not be said to have discharged the onus on it to prove that Breatnach had not requested a solicitor. He added that the evidence indicated that there was no one around for Garda McGauran to pass on the request to: the prison sergeant was at lunch and the station sergeant was away temporarily.

He also raised the point that the prosecution had run its case on the basis that all the available witnesses had been produced. The court had been invited to disbelieve Breatnach's account of events on the basis that everyone in the Bridewell at the time of his incarceration had given evidence. That had now emerged to be not the case.

"The evidence against Mr Breatnach at this stage is totally unsatisfactory – it has very substantial gaps in it. That being so, your lordships at this stage should hold that Mr Breatnach had no case to meet," he said.

Noel McDonald countered for the prosecution that it was abundantly clear at all times that the accused were arrested on suspicion of involvement in the train robbery. That was the suspicion that was in the minds of the detectives who had arrested McNally and Kelly. "As my friend said, I don't think the particular microscope has yet been invented that would find out the finesse of the point he is making."

In relation to Breatnach's case, he maintained that Garda McGauran's evidence clearly referred to Breatnach's first arrest when efforts were made to get him a solicitor.

If the request was made during the second detention, he said the court would have to decide whether there was a breach of Breatnach's constitutional rights and whether, as a result of that, he had made a statement.

Legal arguments revolved around whether or not the absence of a solicitor had to be the dominating factor in the making of a statement or whether the refusal to meet a request made the whole detention unlawful. Should the gardai have to offer names of solicitors if a suspect did not mention any?

Another point raised was whether or not the denial of the constitutional right to a solicitor was conscious and deliberate. Several legal precedents had laid down that such a denial could only be overlooked if there were extraordinary excusing circumstances. In reply to queries from Justice Hamilton, the defence argued that inadvertence did mean there was a conscious and deliberate violation. Otherwise, a garda could arrest somebody, go out for a few drinks, forget all about him and claim it was an oversight.

Noel McDonald argued that Breatnach claimed he made a statement as a result of garda brutality and not because he was denied a solicitor. "It is quite clear that the presence or absence of a solicitor in no way induced him in the making of his statement," said McDonald.

The court spent most of the day teasing out fine points of law and arguing back and forth about the significance of both the issues, the arrests of McNally and Kelly and the request for a lawyer by Breatnach. Next morning, the three judges announced their decisions. The court said it was satisfied that the prosecution had proved that the detectives arresting McNally and Kelly held the suspicion required. In Kelly's case, they pointed out, the garda had told him specifically that he was being arrested on suspicion of "armed robbery of a mail train at Hazelhatch". Both applications were refused.

The ruling on Breatnach's case took slightly longer. The judges said they had carefully considered the evidence of Garda McGauran and had asked the court stenographer for a transcript of his evidence. Garda McGauran could not remember whether Breatnach mentioned the word "dlidoir" (solicitor) during his first detention on March 31st or his second on April 5th. The accused was entitled to the benefit of that doubt, the court said.

In other words, the court had to assume that the request was made during the second detention. The judges said they were satisfied from the evidence of three sergeants that no request for a solicitor was made to them. A person in detention had a constitutional right to legal assistance if he required it. The failure to take reasonable steps to obtain such assistance upon request was a failure by the Garda Siochana to vindicate such constitutional rights.

The judges went on: "Taking the construction of Guard McGauran's evidence most favourably to the accused, it would appear that a request was made to him and that he failed to take any steps on foot thereof and thus such failure was failure to vindicate the accused's constitutional rights.

"The court is satisfied, however, that such failure, if any, by Guard McGauran was not a conscious or deliberate act or omission on his part but was due to an oversight. The court, consequently, affirms its original ruling on the admissibility of the statement."

In effect, the court had decided again that Breatnach's constitutional rights were infringed but because it decided that the infringement was not deliberate his trial would go on.

Behind the scenes there had been a major row between the three accused and their lawyers about the calling of witnesses in their defence. Osgur Breatnach in particular wanted to call around ten people. They included his wife, a man he said he was with on the night of the robbery and some members of the IRSP whom he hoped would help prove his innocence. MacEntee insisted that none of them were called: he was already thinking of an appeal. He did not want all of Breatnach's options completely shot down in the Special Criminal Court, thus making it more difficult to win an appeal. Witnesses were also targets for the prosecution and could detract from the central issues at stake. Breatnach eventually agreed reluctantly to go along with MacEntee. No witnesses were called – not even Breatnach himself. Seamus Sorahan decided to call both Brian McNally and Nicky Kelly in their own defence.

McNally told the court that he had come to work in Dublin in February 1974 from the North, joined the IRSP about July 1975 and was briefly its treasurer for the Dublin area. In October 1975, he had left the party because he had joined a dance band, playing three to five nights a week. He did not have time to go to party meetings and he was told he would have to resign. He did.

McNally said that he had known John Fitzpatrick from the North: their parents knew each other and he and Fitzpatrick played football together. He had met Michael Barrett through Fitzpatrick and had got to know Nicky Kelly, possibly after he, McNally, had left the IRSP.

On the night of March 30th 1976, he said he had gone to a film called "Date a Lonely Girl" in the Green cinema with a female friend. Afterwards he had driven her back to her home in Ringsend and had a cup of tea. He had arranged to pick up Brian Donnelly (the boyfriend of

307

McNally's friend's sister) at Shelbourne Park greyhound stadium and give him a lift to Ballymun.

McNally dropped him off near the Ballymun roundabout and drove home to Swords, he told the court. He arrived home about 12.45 am on March 31st and drove his white Renault van into the garage attached to the house. Nicky Kelly and his wife, Kathleen, were in the house: McNally said he asked him what he was doing in those parts. Kelly said he was out visiting one of the boys. McNally took that to mean either John Fitzpatrick or Michael Barrett.

They chatted about one of McNally's children who had fallen through barbed wire and had deep cuts in her hands. "We were talking about everything in general, ceilis and the way people have changed, television has done away with the way people used to ceili. Then we started talking about football and Kathleen brought in the tea and, to my surprise, I found that Nicky Kelly had at one time been a very good hurler. We had a lot of interest in sport. I have a lot of interest in sport."

Kelly asked if he could stay the night and McNally told him he could use the third bedroom or boxroom in which the couple's six year old son was asleep. He continued with his direct evidence: "When we were going to bed, my wife was winding up the clock and she said to me 'what time is it' and I says, 'it's ten to three' and she made the remark, 'we might as well have been at a dance', and we went up the stairs. I showed Nicky where the box room was and I looked in at the kids and we went to our room."

He told Sorahan he did not leave the house again that night. Around 6.00 am two detectives called and asked who was in the house. One went up to see Kelly and McNally said that he himself had to empty Nicky out of the bed to wake him. McNally asked what was wrong and one said to him: "Something happened up the road". "What?" McNally replied. "Listen to the news," the garda said, "and you will hear it."

McNally said he heard about the robbery on the radio and later read details of it in the *Irish Independent* or the *Evening Herald* which were delivered to his house by a local newsagent. He said he followed the case with interest because his house had been searched that morning: he read about so many men being involved, about a house being taken over and about a Volkswagen van being hijacked. He said he remembered distinctly the reference to a Volkswagen van being either hi-jacked or dumped.

McNally repeated his account of what happened to him after he was arrested on April 5th 1976. He mentioned during conversation with Garda Grehan that a Volkswagen van was used. The detective asked how he knew that and McNally said he told him he read it in either the *Irish Independent* or some other paper. He said he had never asked for an officer in charge, had asked only for a solicitor, and had never seen Inspector Ned Ryan until Wednesday, April 7th. He denied that he had ever been a "paid agent" or informer.

McNally told the court that he had made no admissions, verbal or otherwise, while in custody. He said his evidence earlier about being beaten black and blue was correct. When he had signed his name to a statement, the atmosphere changed. He was given tea and his tablets.

After their first court appearance, he was put back in a cell in the Bridewell with John Fitzpatrick. As to accusations that they had beaten each other up, McNally remarked: "We wouldn't have been fit to beat each other up." He denied that Fitzpatrick had beaten him or he Fitzpatrick, or that either had beat themselves or run into objects or in any way inflicted injuries or marks on themselves.

In conclusion of his direct evidence, McNally said he had neither foreknowledge nor any hand, act or part in any train robbery.

In cross-examination by the prosecution, McNally denied that he had any prior arrangement to meet Kelly that night. Kelly's visit to the house had been a surprise to him. There was no plan to meet for the train robbery. McNally said he had only seen Nicky Kelly two or three times, with John Fitzpatrick or Michael Barrett.

The next witness called by the defence was John Healy, the news editor of the *Irish Independent* who produced photocopies of reports in the newspaper on April 1st and

April 2nd 1976. Both mentioned a Volkswagen van being used in the robbery. The first said: "The Peugeot and Renault cars belonging to the O'Toole family were later found abandoned in County Dublin but last night the search was still on for the Volkswagen van used to carry the money from the scene." The second report included a sentence referring to the van: "This could provide vital clues to forensic experts who have already examined the Volkswagen van and Peugeot found abandoned after the raid."

Kathleen McNally gave evidence about Kelly calling to her house between 7.30 and 8.00 pm on March 30th 1976. Kelly had called several times before and, as on this occasion, played with the children. He went off for a bus and came back later, asking if he could stay the night. She told him she supposed he could but he should wait and see Brian. About 10.00 pm Kelly went out to make a phone call and returned shortly afterwards. As they waited for Brian, they watched television, drank tea and Kelly put out the bin for the morning refuse collection.

After her husband's return, they all had tea and talked and went to bed about ten to three. She and her husband slept in the same bed: he did not leave it until they were woken up in the morning by the gardai. Nicky Kelly did not leave the house either.

She said she had been a member of the IRSP for a short time but had only attended one meeting. When her husband left, she left as well because she had no way of getting to meetings. She went on to repeat the evidence that she had given earlier in the trial about seeing McNally in the Bridewell on Wednesday, April 7th.

Cross-examined by Robert Barr for the prosecution she said she took it that Kelly had called to the house to see how her daughter was after cutting her hand and being in hospital. When she put the younger children to bed, she knew Kelly was staying because she put her six year old son in the box room in such a position that he would not have to be disturbed when Kelly slept there. She could not say when she put the child to bed but she presumed it must have been after Kelly went for a bus and returned to the house.

Nicky Kelly gave evidence, partly on behalf of McNally and on his own behalf. He described going to McNally's house and waiting there until McNally arrived home. He could not say what time they all went to bed but he never left the box room until two detectives called in the morning. He made some remark to one of the guards about Rip Van Winkle. After the gardai had left, Kelly told McNally he should not have let them into the house unless they produced a search warrant.

Kelly went on to give evidence again about his own arrest in Arklow the following Monday, April 5th, repeating and confirming what he had already told the court earlier in the trial. "Nothing ever happened to me from my first hour in Fitzgibbon Street until I signed the statement only continuous beatings by the heavy gang," he said. Asked by his counsel if he had dictated the statement he signed, he replied: "The special branch through their multiple informers know quite well we did not commit the robbery. It would have been impossible, because I was not involved in the robbery to commit it."

Seamus Sorahan asked if he had or had not dictated that statement as the garda evidence alleged. "It would have been impossible for me," Kelly replied. Sorahan asked: "What is the answer?" Kelly replied: "No." Asked if he had anything to add to the evidence he had already given, he answered: "It doesn't seem that it is worth while adding on to one way or the other."

He denied with a straightforward "no" that he had any hand, act or part in, connection with, or foreknowledge of the train robbery on March 31st 1976. He also denied that he and Michael Plunkett, with whom he was put in a cell after his first court appearance, had injured each other or themselves. "We had enough basic fear and apprehension to occupy ourselves with without inflicting any more injuries upon each other," he said.

He finished his direct evidence five minutes before the court was due to rise for the weekend. Justice Hamilton asked Robert Barr if he would be finished his cross-examination in five minutes. Barr said he would not.

311

Seamus Sorahan said he wanted to have a consultation with Nicky Kelly about the future conduct and progress of the trial. He felt it would not be appropriate for him to do so if the cross-examination had begun.

Patrick MacEntee repeated his request for a copy of the court's ruling on the admissibility of the statement. The defence lawyers had tried to reconstruct it from their notes but felt there were gaps. The court refused again to allow them a copy of the stenographer's transcript. Justice Hamilton suggested that the judges would read the defence version and correct it where necessary.

It was, by then, just after 4.00 pm on Friday, December 8th 1978. The court adjourned until 11.15 am the following Monday morning when the cross-examination of Kelly was due to begin. But the court would not see him again for two and a half years.

Nicky Kelly was deeply depressed about the way events were going. The court's decision to admit all the statements into evidence was a clear signal to the remaining three defendants that they were likely to be convicted. There was some talk among them, their friends and supporters about jumping bail: some arrangements were made to help them if they decided. To everyone else involved, Kelly appeared the most likely to jump: he had no formal family commitments and he seemed to colleagues to be highly nervous and under considerable stress.

On Saturday, December 9th, Kelly decided to disappear. He moved into a house on the north side of Dublin, staying with a man he knew and lay low.

When the court resumed on Monday, Seamus Sorahan said that Kelly had not turned up for a consultation with his lawyers at 10.30 that morning and was not in court. He was at a loss to know why. The prosecution asked that a bench warrant be issued for his arrest. The court agreed but also decided to adjourn for twenty minutes. Later, it adjourned until the afternoon to see what transpired.

Justice Hamilton asked if the accused had been under surveillance. Noel McDonald said they had not. The judge suggested that would have been an elementary precaution if there had been any substance in the garda evidence ten days earlier seeking to have them put into custody. He added that the court would welcome submissions from both sides about its powers to go ahead with the trial.

Noel McDonald remarked that there was no power to proceed against Kelly in his absence. Justice Hamilton replied that there were certain circumstances where it was permissible to proceed with the trial of an accused in his absence. They must be exceptional circumstances, McDonald added. The judge adjourned the hearing until the following day. McDonald asked if the two remaining defendants could remain on bail. The court saw no reason why they should not, Justice Hamilton replied.

Next morning, Chief Superintendent John Joy gave evidence of the garda attempts to trace Nicky Kelly. They had checked with several people, including his parents, in Arklow. The gardai did not have an address for him in Dublin but contacted him through his solicitor whose only address for Kelly was at the IRSP office. All hospitals in the Republic had been checked and no one answering to his description had been admitted. He told Seamus Sorahan that a frontier watch had not been kept on air and sea ports and border crossings into Northern Ireland.

Noel McDonald formally submitted to the court that the trial should not proceed in his absence. The only time a court had ever proceeded without the presence of an accused person was when that person created such a disturbance that the trial could not proceed. He was satisfied that it was only in such circumstances that a trial could proceed without the presence of the accused. Justice Hamilton inquired if there was a difference in principle between that case and an accused deliberately absconding in order to make the trial impossible.

McDonald maintained that the difference was that the court did not know what had happened to Kelly. He might have been assassinated like Seamus Costello, kidnapped, or be suffering from mental or physical illness in hospital. There was no positive evidence that he had absconded.

Seamus Sorahan suggested that it would be hazardous for the court to proceed with the case. The court could not take a jump in the dark by deciding, beyond a reasonable doubt, that Kelly had deliberately and consciously absconded. The court decided to go ahead with the trial and promised to give its reasons after a short adjournment.

Justice Hamilton then said that the court was satisfied that it would have been informed if there were any legitimate excuse to explain Kelly's absence. The court had to presume that his failure to attend was due to a voluntary and deliberate decision on his part. According to legal precedents, trials must be conducted in the presence of the accused unless the conduct of the accused intended to make it impossible. The court was satisfied that Kelly had absented himself deliberately and it directed that the trial against him proceed.

The defence lawyers then began their summing-up and closing addresses to the court. Seamus Sorahan was in a quandary as one of his clients had disappeared: pending a request to the bar council for advice, he went ahead with his address on Brian McNally's case.

He pointed out that he was addressing the members of the court both as judges and as the jury. He did not propose to deal with the verbal statements which the court had already admitted into evidence but to concentrate on areas where doubt might be cast on the veracity of any of the police evidence. Such an area, he suggested, was in relation to the mentions of the Volkswagen van.

Garda James Grehan had said that McNally referred to a Volkswagen van while they were having a general discussion about the robbery. The detective asked how he knew it was a Volkswagen van: he himself had referred to it as a Transit van. Garda Grehan claimed in evidence that McNally had not replied. Then McNally asked to see the officer in charge. In his evidence, however, McNally said he had told Garda Grehan that he read about the Volkswagen van in the newspaper.

Sorahan pointed out that the *Irish Independent* had mentioned the van two days running. He submitted that the probability was that McNally would have said to the garda that he read it in the papers. This was possible where the garda case, if it was partially a fabrication, went off the rails.

"I may have missed a lot of things in the trial and God knows I have tried my best not to do so but this, to my mind, was a point which stood out: it reared as a kind of very high Mount Everest among foothills of the various facts in the case."

It was the kind of point that might make a jury of twelve Dubliners say that there was real doubt about the evidence of the gardai, he suggested. He also proposed that the difference in evidence between Garda Grehan and Inspector Ned Ryan over McNally saying he was "a paid agent" was another issue the court should examine. Garda Grehan was in the room when it was supposed to have been said and would surely have heard it if the atmosphere was as friendly as the guards maintained.

Apart from those instances, there was a direct conflict of testimony. McNally said he made no admissions. The court, Sorahan proposed, must have regard to the fact that the police were capable of lying. The question then arose as to whether there was any strength in numbers, whether the evidence of thirty guards outweighed the evidence of McNally and his wife. Why, he wondered, did Kathleen McNally try to contact a doctor in Swords – as she said in evidence – after visiting her husband in the Bridewell, if she had not noticed something for a doctor to see?

He concluded by quoting the Latin maxim over the Bridewell as "Let right be done though the sky fall". He called on the court, by its collective integrity, honesty and fearlessness, to hold that the statements in this case should not be given sufficient weight to enable the finding of guilt.

Noel McDonald contended that the statements of all three accused were full confessions of guilt. Justice Hamilton asked if the prosecution did not have to prove beyond all reasonable doubt that the content of the statements was true. McDonald said he did not have to prove that the content was true because there may be many things in statements. "I have got to satisfy the court that what is in the statement is an admission of guilt and that part of the statement is true," he suggested. He said he had done that by proving that the statements were made voluntarily and they should be seen as confessions of guilt –

the highest form of proof.

Justice Hamilton noted that the court had sworn testimony from McNally that he was not involved in the crime. Was the court to attach any weight to sworn testimony as against unsworn statements to the guards? McDonald said the court had to look at all the evidence and to be satisfied that the content of the statement was true.

All the statements made by the three accused were admissions of guilt and should be treated accordingly. The incredible thing in all of their evidence was the allegations of brutality, he said.

In his final address, Patrick MacEntee asked that the court reconsider its decision in relation to its ruling about Osgur Breatnach's arrest and his request for a solicitor. He cited a judgement by the Court of Criminal Appeal on the previous day which indicated that the obligation lay on the state to safeguard rights and that a criminal investigation was not a reason to suspend constitutional rights. Indeed, it was the occasion when all the organs of the state were required to be particularly vigilant of constitutional rights.

MacEntee said that the court must continue to presume right up until the end of the trial that Breatnach was innocent. He suggested that the issue of guilt had been decided already. There was a conflict of evidence as to how Breatnach came by the injuries which he undoubtedly had. There was the evidence of Dr Burke from Portlaoise Prison that Breatnach's injuries could not have been self-inflicted. There was the garda evidence that he was seen in his cell during the period after his interrogation and before he met solicitor Dudley Potter: he was seen lying peacefully on his bed and showing no signs of any irregularity of conduct.

Any mental process which said that Breatnach could not be believed and that the evidence of Dr Burke and the garda jailers dispensed with, must be incorrect because it prematurely displaced the presumption of innocence, he said.

He urged the court to look again at the admissibility of Breatnach's statement because the evidence now before it was different from when it made its initial ruling. The prosecution had mounted its case on the basis that the court had heard evidence from every police officer on duty in the Bridewell at the relevant times. They had since heard Garda McGauran and they had also been told that a Garda McGuinness was on duty.

"Who, in heaven's name, after forty four days of this trial is Garda McGuinness? Nobody knows."

The state had also based its case on information from the station allocation book in the Bridewell. They now knew that the book was doctored and a portion of it was inexplicably missing. The court was being asked to allow the prosecution to open its case on one basis and that there was no need to explain if the evidence turned out to be totally different.

Breatnach's statement, he went on, was the barest possible description, a curious document in very bad Irish, although the person supposed to have written it down was a native Irish speaker. There was no single fact in it that was not generally known or verified independently. Indeed, one fact in it – the location of the number of the 7A bus terminus – was demonstrably wrong.

He concluded by asking what he termed "the hard core question" in this case. If a solicitor got to a prisoner, found him injured, got a doctor who has him dispatched to hospital; if the injuries were consistent with allegations of beatings and there was no evidence that they were self-inflicted; if access to a solicitor was refused to the prisoner; if all these things arose from the prosecution case, what more must a prisoner have to give rise to a reasonable doubt?

"Must we wait for a corpse before a reasonable doubt emanates because that seems to be the logic of the situation in which we find ourselves. Is the situation that in Ireland in 1978 we have to solemnly sit around and wait for a dead body in the police station before a reasonable doubt is raised?"

Earlier, Seamus Sorahan had announced that he would not be making any submissions or calling any evidence on behalf of Nicky Kelly. Because he was absent and could not give instructions, Sorahan said he felt he could not take any steps. He had reached his decision after consulting an

317

emergency meeting of the bar council.

After MacEntee's final submission on behalf of Breatnach, the court adjourned to consider its verdict. It was 11.45 am on December 13th 1978, the forty third day of the trial. Justice Hamilton said they would not give their verdict before 2.00 pm.

The courtroom, including the public gallery, was full as the judges prepared to take their places on the bench just after lunch. Justice Hamilton, occupying the centre position, read out the verdicts.

The court had considered in detail all the prosecution evidence in the light of the heavy onus on the prosecution to establish the guilt of each accused beyond all reasonable doubt, he began. With regard to McNally, the only evidence proffered by the prosecution were two verbal statements he made, the first to Superintendent Ned Ryan and Garda James Grehan, the second and more detailed to Superintendent John Courtney and Inspector Michael Canavan. They clearly established his active participation in the robbery and the court was satisfied that the statements were true. The court found him guilty of the two charges against him.

Justice Hamilton said that the court was satisfied beyond all reasonable doubt that all but one of the verbal statements and the written statement made by Nicky Kelly were true and clearly established his guilt. The court rejected his evidence that he spent the night of the robbery at McNally's home and found him guilty of both charges.

The judge said that the court found no reason to change its earlier decision in relation to statements made by Breatnach. If the contents of the statement were true, they clearly established his active participation in the crimes. The court was satisfied beyond all reasonable doubt that these statements were true, and found Breatnach guilty of both charges.

With its verdicts announced, the court then went on to consider its sentences. Superintendent Patrick Casey gave evidence about the two men in the dock.

McNally had not come to the notice of the gardai previously. Breatnach had one previous conviction under the Forcible Entry Act over the occupation of Frascati House in Blackrock, County Dublin in January 1972. Justice Hamilton had declared that they would not deal with Nicky Kelly's sentence for two days.

Tony Sammon, the junior barrister representing McNally, then addressed the court. His instructions were to address the court on the basis that his client was innocent, he said. Justice Hamilton said he could not do that as the court had reached a verdict of guilty. McNally's life had been seriously disrupted since his arrest and his family life had suffered, Sammon said. He asked the court to take this and McNally's involvement in sporting and community organisations into account in deciding the sentence.

Patrick MacEntee told the court he had nothing to say.

The three judges retired again at 2.20 pm. Thirty five minutes later they returned to the bench to announce their sentences. MacEntee and Sorahan then asked the court to postpone sentences until after Christmas. The judges rejected the request.

Justice Hamilton said that the court had taken into account the seriousness of the offences and the fact that the accused had had to undergo the distressful and stressful experience of two long trials. The court accepted that McNally, in accordance with his statement, had not known what was going on until he got to the scene. However, he actively participated in the joint enterprise of stopping the train and stealing the mail. The court had also taken into account his previous record, community involvement and family circumstances. It sentenced him to nine years penal servitude on each charge, both sentences to run concurrently.

No such considerations applied to Osgur Breatnach, the court declared. No plea had been made on his behalf. The court considered the appropriate sentence was twelve years penal servitude on each charge, both sentences to run concurrently.

Standing in the dock, Breatnach fingered some paper in his pocket. It was a rough draft of the speech he hoped to make to the court after sentence was passed on him, his speech from the dock. He realised, however, that he would not be allowed time to give his address and, in the heat of the moment, joined in the general melee of shouting which greeted the announcement of the sentences.

"The state has spent a million pounds framing me. I am innocent," he roared.

Behind and above him in the public gallery there were shouts of "hear, hear" and bursts of applause. Prison warders began to take Breatnach and McNally from the dock, down the steps to the cells below the building.

Justice Hamilton told them to bring back the two men until they were told to remove them and he ordered that the court be cleared of the public. Some thirty gardai moved into the public gallery. There was pushing and shoving as people resisted the police. Several were carried out of the gallery to the street. Outside the cordon around the building, members of the IRSP began a picket complaining about police brutality and calling for the abolition of the court.

* * *

Inside the court, the lawyers were already into the next stage of the judicial process. Seamus Sorahan asked that they be allowed to apply for appeal certificates on the following Friday when the court was due to consider Nicky Kelly's sentence. The court suggested that it would accept their application now and hear their grounds two days later.

On Friday, December 15th 1978 the court resumed and quickly sentenced Nicky Kelly to twelve years penal servitude on both charges. The sentences were to run concurrently. Then, Brian McNally and Osgur Breatnach's lawyers applied for permission to appeal against their conviction and their sentences. MacEntee put forward fourteen grounds on which the trial was unsatisfactory in factual or legal matters. Sorahan put forward twelve reasons why McNally's conviction and sentence should not stand. Pat McCartan, Kelly's solicitor, put forward the same reasons as grounds for an appeal by Kelly. The court adjourned briefly and rejected the applications.

Thus, the trial ended on its forty fourth day. The special criminal court, under two separate sets of judges, had spent 108 days hearing evidence, submissions and arguments. It was two years and nine months since the Cork to Dublin mail train was held up and robbed.

Brian McNally and Osgur Breatnach were taken back to Portlaoise Prison under the usual heavy escort. Nicky Kelly was at liberty of sorts, a wanted man living underground in Dublin.

Part Three

Findings and Facts

14

Imprisoned

Nicky Kelly stayed indoors during the day and avoided his usual haunts in Dublin. He lived with some friends, moving between a couple of houses where he knew he was safe. He did not go near the IRSP offices because they were almost certainly watched by the Special Branch. The gardai carried out a few searches in the days immediately after his disappearance but the feeling among his former political associates was that their efforts were somewhat perfunctory. By the time that Osgur Breatnach and Brian McNally were settling into the routine of life inside Portlaoise Prison, Kelly was making moves to the west of Ireland where he spent Christmas with friends. He wondered what he should do next.

His decision to jump bail was not taken quite on the spur of the moment but neither was there any masterplan. The three had discussed the possibility of running away if their statements were admitted in evidence against them but nothing definite was decided. On Friday evening, December 8th 1978, Kelly went for a drink with some friends who were urging him to run away. They said it was crazy that he should go to prison for a crime he did not commit. Kelly agreed. Now that his statements had been admitted in evidence, he realised a period in prison had become a very real possibility.

The trial had continued and was clearly going to end soon. That afternoon, Kelly had entered the witness box and given evidence in his own defence. At four minutes to four, Robert Barr was about to begin what promised to be a lengthy and intense cross-examination when the court decided to rise until Monday morning. It gave Kelly the weekend to think about the future.

He stayed in Connacht for a few weeks into the new year and then returned to Dublin. He let his hair grow long so that it curled and resembled an Afro-style. He had also shaved off his moustache. He moved about the city with greater ease than before Christmas but always on his guard in case he was stopped. One evening he walked into a pub and almost bumped into a detective he knew. Luckily for Kelly, the detective did not see him. He had another brush with the gardai which could have resulted in his arrest had he been discovered.

He was staying with some friends on the north side of the city when a garda called socially. Kelly was in the back garden, saw the man in uniform enter the house and ran for all he was worth. The following morning, he turned up at the home of another friend in a southern suburb of the city. He asked him for breakfast and a lift back to his first friend's house on the north side. The man was working as a house painter and, after feeding Kelly, he got him to help push start his elderly car. He offered Kelly some work assisting with the painting. Kelly agreed but insisted that he call him "John" – every time that his friend forgot and called him Nicky, Kelly would furiously remind him to call him "John". Kelly stayed painting until the evening before making his way back to his friends.

It was clear that he could not go on living in Dublin without being detected one day and dispatched to Portlaoise to join Breatnach and McNally. He decided to go to America but he needed a passport to get there, however. His own had been surrendered to the gardai after he had been granted bail. Friends of a friend arranged to get one for him: all he had to do was supply two small photographs of himself. A couple of weeks later he had a new passport with his own photograph but a false name. He decided to leave the country through Shannon Airport rather than Dublin to avoid any stopovers on his way to the United States. Kelly was driven to the airport from Dublin on the day of the flight. He wore a three piece blue suit with matching blue shirt and tie. He looked perfectly normal, apart from his slightly incongruous hair style. He stepped on the plane, unnoticed by the usual plainclothes gardai who hung around the departure hall and, with a few hundred dollars in his pocket, took off with a one way ticket to New York. He arrived there in time for St Patrick's Day.

His first few nights in America were spent with people in New York whose address he had been given. Then he went to Philadelphia in Pennsylvania, on to Chicago and back to Philadelphia where he got a job as a warehouse checker for a firm which distributed general merchandise using a fleet of trucks. Kelly was furnished by friends with someone else's driving licence and a false social security number and after a while with the company, he got a job as a truck driver. He delivered goods around Philadelphia and, sometimes, to places as far away as Newark in New Jersey. The majority of his workmates were black, some of whom had been in Vietnam and appeared to Kelly to have been damaged by their experiences there. He was paid around 240 dollars a week but could earn more with overtime. It wasn't a fortune but enough on which to live.

Kelly's initial contacts in the United States were well aware of his status as an illegal immigrant and the reasons why he had left Ireland. In some circles, however, he used the name "Barry Ryan" after a friend introduced him by that name at a party. Gradually, as time passed he became more confident and he let people know who he was. Through his initial Irish-American contacts he also came in touch with some Irish-American lawyers groups which were interested in his case.

There was a growing interest in the fate of Breatnach and McNally and their situation back in Ireland where preparations were going ahead for their appeal hearings. Officials of the Court of Criminal Appeal had become bogged down by the huge task of assembling the mass of paperwork necessary for the appeal hearing. It was almost a year after the conclusion of the Special Criminal Court trial before a full transcript of proceedings was ready. It ran to over 2,500 typed pages and was in more than eighty sections: each one representing a morning or afternoon of the trial. The difficulty compiling the transcript was caused, apart from the sheer size of the job, by the fact that so many stenographers had been used in the trial. Each one had to have his or her notes typed up and then checked against the original notes. Once the transcript was ready, however, copies were made for the three judges who would hear the appeal, the lawyers involved and their clients in Portlaoise Prison.

Portlaoise was the Republic's main high security jail. It stood just outside Portlaoise town on the road to Dublin, some fifty miles away. The prison had high walls made of rough cut blocks of limestone and two towers stood on either side of the large main entrance gates. From the outside, Portlaoise looked every inch a Victorian penal institution until the early and mid 1970s when it took on an appearance more familiar to prisons and police stations in Northern Ireland. As the troubles in the North grew, so too did their inevitable consequences in the Republic and a growing number of people, most of them young men, became involved in subversive activity and politically motivated crimes. Portlaoise was where they served their sentences and the prison became shrouded in barbed wire, all the paraphernalia of modern security and constant patrols by prison officers, gardai and soldiers carrying rifles. Some of the inmates called the soldiers "Brits" – they did not differentiate between Irish soldiers and British troops in Northern Ireland.

When Breatnach and McNally arrived in the prison there were around 140 men held in E wing, the security block reserved for subversive prisoners. The block was rectangular in shape and four stories high. On the inside, each of the floors was little more than a landing, a walkway in front of the cell doors. The floors were connected by a central well which ran from the bottom floor to the top of the block. This meant that a prison officer could stand on the walkway of an upper floor and, looking down diagonally across the block, observe what was going on below.

At either end of the block on each floor there were toilets, workshops, laundry rooms and recreation rooms. Along the side walls were the cells, one prisoner to each. Every cell had a metal frame bed with a foam mattress plus a small press for personal possessions, There was a wash basin, soap, toothbrush and towel. Meals were eaten in cells and so each contained plastic cutlery and a plastic jug. On the wall was a board for pinning up pictures: prisoners were forbidden to hang anything directly on their cell walls. The

328

cell doors were made of wood – covered with metal sheeting. Each had a small observation hole known as the "Judas Hole". The switch for the light was outside the cell door, on the landing.

The top two floors of the block were reserved for members of the Provisional IRA and Sinn Fein. There were seventy two at the beginning of 1979. The first two floors were inhabited by an extraordinary variety of prisoners who fell into a number of groups, illustrating the various splits that had afflicted the republican movement over the years. There were seven members of the Official IRA plus five others who supported the Official IRA but were not members of it. There were six former members of the Provisionals and a further sixteen whom the prison authorities regarded as Provisional IRA rejects. There were thirty one members of what the prison authorities called the Socialist Republican Alliance which was made up at the time of members of the IRSP and the INLA and some other apparently non-aligned people like Eddie Gallagher, convicted of the kidnapping of Dr Tiede Herrema, the Dutch industrialist. On top of all these, there was a category for "other" prisoners whose particular allegiances (or lack of them) made it impossible for the authorities to pigeon hole them into one or other group. There were five "other" prisoners.

The political motivation of most of the prisoners in E wing created special problems for the prison authorities. In 1975, some prisoners staged a hunger strike in support of their demand for a say in which sort of prisoners were allowed in the prison. As far as the coalition government was concerned, this was an attempt by the Provisional IRA to exercise a veto over every other type of prisoner being lodged in Portlaoise. This, the government believed, would turn the place into a sort of prisoner of war camp for the Provisionals.

There were endless small rows between the prisoners and the prison authorities but, for the most part, both sides tried to live with each other and compromises were reached. The subversive prisoners were allowed a degree of freedom of movement within their respective groups once the cells

329

were opened each morning: the Provisionals on the top two landings had free association among themselves and the rest could circulate freely on the lower two landings. None of the prisoners was forced to wear prison clothing and each group elected a spokesperson who dealt with senior prison officers on their behalf. The groups also elected a "quartermaster" whose job it was to request the prison authorities for items like soap.

Each evening when the prisoners had to get back into their cells for the night, they stood to attention outside until their "commanding officer" shouted an order in Irish for them to fall out. It was a touch of paramilitary behaviour which the authorities were prepared to tolerate because it bought peace in the block.

Breatnach and McNally lived in the bottom two floors and both belonged to the Socialist Republican Alliance (SRA). For all the posturing and apparent freedom in the block, life in prison was pretty much a repetitive routine. Cell doors were opened each morning at around 8.30 and prisoners were able to walk along their landing to a trolly to help themselves to cereal, bread and jam, and tea. After breakfast, prisoners were allowed to shower several mornings a week. For the rest of the morning, there was a choice of pastimes: films in the recreation room, a video of something on TV the previous night perhaps, books from the library, a walk in the exercise yard or a visit to the workshop. Many prisoners worked there, producing gifts for their families or wooden harps and celtic style crosses which would be sold, often in America, to raise money for the cause. Breatnach made an elaborate jewellery box for his wife and leather wallets and belts for the IRSP.

At around 12.30 pm, dinner was served. Again, prisoners collected their meal, dessert and tea from a trolley on their landing and then ate their food either in their own cell or that of a friend. The same routine applied throughout the afternoon until tea was served and again until 8.30 pm when prisoners were locked up in their cells for the night.

The block became relatively quiet at night. Prisoners lay in their beds reading or listening to their radios. There were cheers whenever news was broadcast of another British casualty in Northern Ireland. Sometimes, a prisoner would tell a joke out loud and laughter would ripple through the block. Occasionally, a prisoner might have an instrument and music would break the late evening silence. Brian McNally applied to the prison authorities for permission to have an accordion. Breatnach registered for a communications course with the Open University and ordered a range of books on propaganda.

Life in the prison wasn't all routine however. Just over a month after Breatnach and McNally arrived, there was an attempted break-out which cost Breatnach two months loss of privileges. It happened on January 28th 1979 and was said at the time to have involved about a dozen prisoners. A number of them were spotted on the roof of a boiler house which adjoined the main block and was under a window of one of the laundry rooms. When the alarm was raised and a search was carried out, seven folding ladders were found, twelve batons made from broom handles, ten mock prison officer caps made of cardboard, a leather jacket, a partly used tin of black emulsion paint and one false beard which had been made meticulously from a real beard.

Breatnach and a number of others were punished by loss of privileges which meant that for two months they got no letters, visits or evening recreation. Breatnach maintained he was not involved in the escape. He tried to tell the prison authorities that he was sitting in the recreation room when the others tried to stage their escape via the next door laundry room. He insisted that he had no part in the attempted break-out.

There was some further trouble in the prison in May when some prisoners briefly protested about the removal of a workshop door which they said made it impossible to watch TV in the recreation room in peace and quiet. They emphasised their concern by smearing excrement on some cell walls and, in the mornings, throwing their overnight toilet slops over the balconies.

Neither Breatnach nor McNally ever really settled into prison life. Breatnach found it particularly difficult: the loss of freedom left him feeling degraded and vulnerable. Both thought a lot about their impending appeal hearing. They studied the transcript of their trial and discussed the case with their solicitor, Pat McCartan, whenever he came to see them. Any time either of them had a visitor, they always asked earnestly if people had forgotten them, if there was a strong campaign being mounted to help secure their freedom. Breatnach's brother Caoilte was deeply involved in efforts to highlight their plight and there was an established international interest in the case. Amnesty International in London had kept abreast of developments in Ireland and planned to send an observer to the appeal hearing. Observers were also expected from other organisations like the Irish Council for Civil Liberties and the Ponpe Institute of Criminology Study of Holland.

McNally's barrister, Seamus Sorahan, had decided to fight his appeal case on nine grounds, each one of which maintained that in some way the Special Criminal Court had been wrong to convict him. The first ground suggested there had been one trial that finished in circumstances over which he had no control. Ground two said that the Special Criminal Court had made a legal mistake in deciding that the gardai were empowered to question McNally on April 5th, 6th, and 7th 1976. The third ground said the trial was unsatisfactory because the defence lawyers were unable to call every garda witness who had been in the Bridewell while McNally was there. This was because the station allocation book which recorded who was on duty had been altered.

The fourth ground suggested that the Special Criminal Court had been wrong and perverse by finding in the absence of evidence that McNally's injuries were self inflicted. Ground five said that the Special Criminal Court was legally wrong to hold that McNally's admissions were voluntary and ground six said that such a finding was against the weight of evidence. Ground seven said that by admitting McNally's statements in evidence it had exercised its discretion according to wrong principles. Ground eight said the finding that these statements were not obtained as a result of oppression was against the weight of evidence and perverse. The final ground said the Special Criminal Court erred in law and in fact by holding that

McNally's rights were not infringed in relation to his request for a solicitor.

Patrick MacEntee identified fourteen grounds on which Breatnach would appeal his conviction. Most were the same as McNally's but it was also suggested that the Special Criminal Court had been wrong to decide that Breatnach's rights were not consciously and deliberately violated by his illegal arrest and detention on April 5th 1976 and that his rights were not similarly violated when Garda Brian McGauran failed to get a solicitor having been requested to do so.

The grounds of appeal were stated to the Special Criminal Court on the last day of the trial when both barristers applied for leave to appeal. That permission was refused, as happened in almost every case where leave to appeal was sought. As far as the judiciary was concerned, if the Special Criminal Court granted leave to appeal, the three judges were saying, in effect, that they had a slight doubt about their own decision to convict and would be happy to see their decision tested in the appeal court. Clearly there could be few cases in which the three Special Criminal Court judges would make a decision and immediately afterwards tacitly admit by allowing an appeal that they had a residual doubt about what they had just done. In the case of Breatnach and McNally, the Special Criminal Court had no doubt at all that its decision to convict was correct in every respect.

Because people convicted by the Special Criminal Court were almost always refused leave to appeal, they had to apply to the Court of Criminal Appeal against that refusal. The Court of Criminal Appeal then turned the whole business into something of a legal subterfuge by treating applications for leave to appeal as actual appeals. There was ample opportunity for the administration of the law to become lost in semantics.

The Court of Criminal Appeal was established first in 1924 by the Courts of Justice Act. It had to be set up because the High Court and the Supreme Court were both civil courts but persons convicted in the Central Criminal Court had to have a court to which they could appeal. The

Court of Criminal Appeal operated according to the directions of the Chief Justice. It had to sit with a minimum of three judges: the Chief Justice or his nominee from the Supreme Court and two judges from the High Court nominated by the president of the High Court. The president could sit on the court himself if he wanted. The court was bound to sit only in Dublin unless the Chief Justice directed otherwise, decisions had to be announced by the senior judge presiding and none of the other judges was allowed to give a separate judgement.

Decisions of the Court of Criminal Appeal were intended to be final and there was no automatic right of further appeal to the Supreme Court. A further appeal could take place however if the Court of Criminal Appeal decided that its judgement involved a point of law of exceptional public importance. In such circumstances, the court could allow an appeal to the Supreme Court. The only other way that a decision of the Court of Criminal Appeal could be appealed was if the Attorney General certified that a point of law of exceptional public importance was involved. This power of the Attorney General was a rare example of how a political appointee, a member of the executive, could become directly involved in the workings of the judiciary.

The registrar of the Court of Criminal Appeal usually waited for a build up of cases before approaching the Chief Justice with a request that a sitting of the court be arranged. The judges who sat with the court were generally selected from a rota: the judges of the Supreme Court passed the task among themselves while the president of the High Court usually nominated two of his colleagues to the court at the beginning of each legal term. When it came time to hear the appeal of Breatnach and McNally, the judges of the court were Judge Tom Finlay, president of the High Court, Judge Seamus Henchy of the Supreme Court and Judge Donal Barrington of the High Court. Judge Finlay was the presiding judge because, in the pecking order of the judiciary, he was second only to the Chief Justice.

Late in April 1980, sixteen days before they sat to hear the arguments for and against the convictions of Breatnach and McNally, an event occurred to which the defendants and their supporters attached great significance. The Provisional IRA issued a statement claiming responsibility for the mail train robbery. The statement was issued in the name of P. O'Neill through the "Irish Republican Publicity Bureau" in Dublin: both had been used frequently in the past when the Provisionals wanted to identify themselves. Similarly, statements from the INLA were always signed "Clancy" in honour of Seamus Costello.

"The Irish Republican Army now claims responsibility for the Sallins train robbery in March 1976 for which a number of completely innocent people have been convicted and jailed," said the statement. It went on to say that the admission was being made "to formalise what has been common knowledge throughout the country for years...." It said that Breatnach, McNally and Nicky Kelly were "completely innocent victims".

For many of those involved in the case from the arrest of the IRSP suspects, their interrogation, the two trials and eventual conviction of Breatnach, McNally and Kelly, the issues were clear: either you stood with the gardai and the institutions of the state in the Republic or you stood with the subversives, the people who wanted to destroy the state. You believed the gardai and had faith in the integrity of the legal and judicial system rather than the Provisional IRA. As far as Patrick Cooney, the former Minister for Justice, was concerned, the statement was to be treated with a pinch of salt. He saw no reason to believe the Provisionals, whom he regarded as master propagandists for whom the truth was simply another weapon to be twisted, bent and in any way distorted if it helped achieve their ultimate goal. In any event, he was satisfied he knew of at least one instance when the Provisionals told straight lies: the murder of his friend Billy Fox was denied by them but members of the Provisonal IRA were ultimately convicted of his killing.

The statement could have no effect on the hearing of Breatnach and McNally's appeal by the Court of Criminal Appeal. But it bolstered their hopes now that someone else had admitted that they did the robbery: perhaps now they would be released and justice done, as they saw it.

The hearing opened in Dublin on May 12th 1980 in a

crowded room of the Four Courts. It was clear from the number of international observers that every detail of the court proceedings would be scrutinised and opinions relayed to many countries outside Ireland. In a sense, the Irish judicial system was itself on trial.

Seamus Sorahan argued on behalf of McNally that his constitutional rights were breached when Chief Superintendent John Fleming signed an order authorising his detention for a second period of twenty four hours. He said it should be examined whether or not McNally should have had an opportunity to make representations about this order and whether or not the Chief Superintendent was, in effect, a judge in his own cause.

He said that the prosecution's case against McNally rested on three alleged admissions he made during relentless questioning but, argued Sorahan, there was no provision under Section 30 of the Offences Against the State Act which gave the gardai the power to interrogate a suspect after their arrest. McNally had been questioned for twelve hours and the method of garda questioning amounted to oppression, said Sorahan.

He argued that the Special Criminal Court was wrong when it ruled that McNally's treatment in custody was not oppressive: he said the weight of evidence, uncontested evidence, showed the contrary. He said the gardai had exceeded their powers by holding McNally over the forty eight hour limit and had broken the Judges Rules. He concluded his pleadings on behalf of McNally by quoting extensively from US court decisions in relation to the 14th Amendment of the Constitution which dealt with oppression.

Successive questioning by gardai to the extent that a suspect's will became so overborne his statement was not that of a free and rational being, was a grave abuse of power, he said.

Patrick MacEntee began his submission on behalf of Breatnach by referring to the Bridewell's altered allocation book. He said it was only when Garda Brian McGauran was "flushed out" that it became clear Breatnach had indeed asked for a solicitor while in custody but he had not been given access to one.

MacEntee said that Breatnach's arrest on Monday, April 5th 1976, was his second under Section 30 and was an illegal act by the gardai, irrespective of whether they were aware or not that they were breaching his constitutional rights. The fact that the gardai had no system to prevent multiple arrests under Section 30 indicated that the State had failed to vindicate his constitutional rights, he said.

The finding by the Special Criminal Court that Breatnach's injuries were self inflicted was at best speculation unsupported by evidence and was perverse. The finding that his statements were not made as a result of ill treatment was also perverse, he suggested. The questioning which took place in the tunnel under the Bridewell was done to intimidate.

Noel McDonald replied on behalf of the Director of Public Prosecutions to the arguments made by both barristers. He said all relevant witnesses had been made available to the defence and there had been no deliberate or conscious violation of Breatnach's rights when he was arrested on April 5th. Garda McGauran's failure to get Breatnach's solicitor was also not a deliberate or conscious violation of his rights. Mere carelessness or inadvertence did not amount to deliberate, conscious violation of a right, he said. There was also "ample evidence" to satisfy the appeal court that the two had not been ill treated while in garda custody.

The constitution applied to us all, said McDonald. We had constitutional rights and we had to care for ourselves so that we did not make the apprehension of criminals really impossible.

The hearing lasted six days and at the end of it, Judge Finlay said that judgement would be reserved. Breatnach and McNally were taken back to prison where they had an anxious wait for two days until, on May 22nd, they returned to the court to hear the verdict of their appeal.

"Having carefully considered the grounds of appeal on behalf of each of the applicants," Judge Finlay told a crowded and tense courtroom, "the court is satisfied that the statements made by the applicants were not legally

337

admissible...and sets aside the conviction and sentence in each one."

There was immediate wild cheering in the court and, in the dock, McNally threw his arms around Breatnach and hugged him. Breatnach, embarrassed, tried to maintain an awkward dignity: he was already thinking of the press conference where he would call for the abolition of the Special Criminal Court.

Judge Finlay said that the court would give its reasons later for quashing both convictions and everyone left the courtroom unaware, for the time being, of precisely why Breatnach and McNally had been set free. Indeed, at this time, the three judges did not themselves have all the reasons for their decision.

It would be over nine months before they explained themselves. Their written judgement, delivered by Judge Finlay, referred to a number of crimes far removed from the robbery of a train in County Kildare in 1976. One concerned how a Czech immigrant in Britain sold Royal Air Force radar secrets to an agent from Prague, another related to a sex attack and murder of a twelve year old girl in a Kent wood and a third was about the brutal rape and murder of a young County Mayo woman by a man called John Shaw. The extraordinary thing about the Shaw case was that while Judge Finlay cited it in the written judgement of the Court of Criminal Appeal, it did not exist at the time of the court's decision to release Breatnach and McNally. The appeal hearing and release happened in May 1980, the Shaw case was dealt with by the Supreme Court in December 1980 and the explanation of the appeal court decision was published in February 1981. The Shaw case was thus used to help give retrospective justification to a decision which had already been taken.

Each of these other cases was examined by the Court of Criminal Appeal because they were related to the treatment of suspects in custody. This issue was at the centre of Breatnach's appeal. In the case of McNally, his appeal turned on a breach of the Judges Rules. The judgement in his case summarised what it said were the facts proven by the prosecution in the Special Criminal Court. These

338

concerned McNally's arrest, his detention in Fitzgibbon Street garda station and transfer to the Bridewell where questioning recommenced at 10 am on Tuesday, April 6th 1976. The questioning had continued, with two breaks of two and a half hours each, beyond midnight into the small hours of Wednesday. At his trial, the prosecution claimed McNally had made three separate admissions: the first was to Garda James Grehan and Inspector Ned Ryan to the effect that he was "on the job", the second was a more detailed verbal account of the robbery to Inspector John Courtney and Sergeant Michael Canavan and the third was his written statement taken by Inspector Courtney and Garda Grehan. This written statement was partly taken after the forty eight hour legal limit and so was not submitted as evidence at the trial.

McNally was convicted on the basis of the two verbal statements he made, first to Garda Grehan and Inspector Ryan, and then to Inspector Courtney and Sergeant Canavan. The Court of Criminal Appeal, however, made no reference in its judgement to either Inspector Courtney or Sergeant Canavan. Garda Grehan and Inspector Ryan were linked to verbal admissions plural and an uninformed reader of the judgement would not be aware that other gardai were involved with the second statement.

"Neither Garda Grehan nor Inspector Ryan, on the evidence, made any note at the time of the alleged verbal admissions made to them or in their presence," said the judgement, "nor did they, of course, afford the applicant any opportunity to read any such note or have it read over to him or to correct or amend it."

In recounting what had happened at the trial, the appeal court judges appeared to have made an error. No explanation was offered as to why they referred to alleged verbal admissions being made to Garda Grehan and Inspector Ryan when in fact only one statement was alleged to have been made to them and yet a far more important (and damaging from McNally's point of view) statement was made to Inspector Courtney and Sergeant Canavan.

With regard to McNally's allegations of ill treatment by the gardai, the appeal court said it was bound by the

339

Madden case. That case had been dealt with in the Supreme Court and Chief Justice Tom O'Higgins established the practice whereby appeal courts did not question matters which were determined to be facts by a trial court. Chief Justice O'Higgins said it was the function of the appeal court "to determine whether or not the trial was satisfactory in the sense of being conducted in a constitutional manner with fairness, to review so far as may be required any rulings on matters of law, to review so far as may be necessary the application of the rules of evidence as applied in the trial, and to consider whether any inference of fact drawn by the court of trial can properly be supported by the evidence; but otherwise to adopt all findings of fact, subject to the admonitions in the passage cited above."

The appeal court said it was also bound by the Farrell case which was decided by the Court of Criminal Appeal in July 1977. The case concerned the arrest in Donegal in September 1973 of George Farrell, a native of Enniskillen in County Fermanagh. Farrell was questioned by the gardai about a bomb explosion at Mill Street in Pettigo. Alleged verbal and written admissions by him were later produced by the gardai during his trial in the Special Criminal Court. He was convicted and sentenced to fifteen years penal servitude. His appeal was made on several grounds and he was eventually released because the order permitting his detention for a second period of twenty four hours was signed by a garda Superintendent and not a Chief Superintendent, as the law required.

However, other grounds of appeal in the Farrell case related to the Judges Rules and it was a comment on these grounds by Chief Justice O'Higgins that the Court of Criminal Appeal adopted for McNally's case. Chief Justice O'Higgins said that while the Judges Rules were not rules of law, they would be departed from at peril. Only in very exceptional circumstances should a statement taken in breach of the rules be admitted in evidence.

"Where, however, there is a breach of the Judges Rules, such as the failure to make a written record of the alleged confession or a failure to invite the accused to accept or

340

reject the statements, each of such breaches calls for an adequate explanation," said the Chief Justice.

McNally's allegations of ill-treatment had been rejected by the Special Criminal Court and Judge Finlay said that according to the principles laid down by the Madden case, this had been quite correct. But he said that the Special Criminal Court had been wrong in law to allow the alleged statements to be admitted in evidence against McNally because of the unexplained breach of the Judges Rules.

"No explanation other than a previous course of conduct was tendered to the trial court for the failure of the two garda witnesses directly concerned to make a note of the alleged verbal admissions made by the applicant and to afford him an opportunity for correcting, amending or rejecting them," said Judge Finlay. This was a clear breach of Rule 9 and, because the alleged admissions occurred in the small hours of the morning after McNally had been detained and questioned for over forty four hours (interrupted by one night's sleep only), the appeal court was not satisfied that the Special Criminal Court was justified in exercising its discretion to allow the statements to stand.

Because there was no other evidence against McNally, Judge Finlay said the Court of Criminal Appeal was satisfied that the conviction should be set aside and McNally released. The judgement was in effect a rebuke of the Special Criminal Court but any criticism that was implied was far more magnified in the appeal judgement on the Breatnach case. The three appeal judges decided in effect that Breatnach had been oppressed by the gardai and that the Special Criminal Court had been perverse in not accepting this was so on the weight of evidence.

As with the judgement on the McNally case, the appeal court judgement on Breatnach recapped the history of his arrest, detention and alleged oral and written admissions of involvement in the train robbery. The summary correctly outlined where and when Breatnach had been questioned and by whom. It said that he was taken at 5.20 am on Wednesday, April 7th 1976, to "an underground staircase" (the description tunnel was not used) where for about twenty minutes he was questioned by Inspector John

Murphy and Garda Thomas Fitzgerald. It said that he was then brought to "an interview room" (not the sergeants locker room) where he made a written statement in Irish to Inspector Murphy, Garda Fitzgerald and Garda Thomas Ibar Dunne. After this, Breatnach had spoken in the same room to Garda William Meagher and Garda Gerard O'Carroll (Garda James Butler was not mentioned) where he made further admissions, said the summary.

The Special Criminal Court ruled that there had been no deliberate and conscious violation of Breatnach's constitutional rights by the failure of the gardai to get a solicitor for him and that his statements were made voluntarily by him.

The Madden case had the same effect on Breatnach's appeal as on McNally's: what the Special Criminal Court established as fact could not be changed. The appeal court "cannot and should not interfere with the decision of the court of trial" in relation to Breatnach's detailed and serious allegation of physical cruelty by the gardai. The Special Criminal Court had ruled that these allegations were untrue and the Court of Criminal Appeal felt there was nothing more to that issue as far as they were concerned, but the appeal court then went on to re-examine what appeared to be facts established in the Special Criminal Court.

"On the admitted and accepted evidence concerning these statements however," said the appeal judgement, "the position would appear to be that this applicant (Breatnach) was a person fully and amply aware of his rights and had on a previous occasion in connection with an arrest on suspicion of the same crime adamantly refused to be interviewed or discuss the crime with any member of the Garda Siochana until his solicitor arrived. On this occasion, having maintained the same attitude for a period of approximately forty hours, suddenly, at 5.20 in the morning, he decided to make a full confession of his participation in this serious crime."

The judgement then began an exploration of what constituted oppressive questioning and turned first to an unusual case in Britain in 1972 involving a Czech who had become a naturalised British subject.

Nicholas Anthony Prager was born in Czechoslovakia in 1928 and lived there with his parents until 1948 when he came with them to settle in Britain. The following year, he married a Czech woman who had also moved to Britain and he joined the Royal Air Force. He was promoted to sergeant and, because of his skills as an engineer, he came to be involved in some highly secret work at a base near Doncaster. The work was on a project called Blue Diver and it concerned ways of interfering with radar.

In 1956 Mrs Prager was left part ownership of a house in Prague when an aunt there died. The Pragers wanted to sell the house and have the money sent to them in England. They went to the Czechoslovak Embassy in London to sort out exchange control problems and met a man called Malek. He posed as a consul but in reality, Malek was an agent with Czechoslovak intelligence. Malek used the Pragers' eagerness to get the money from the sale of the house to turn Nicholas Prager into a spy. For a brief period in June and July 1961, Prager played at being a spy: he bought a Polaroid camera with a special attachment for taking close-up pictures. He photographed several documents at the RAF base and gave them to Malek.

Not long afterwards, Prager and his wife were in Czechoslovakia and were met in Jevaney by two Czech agents who gave them between £200 and £300. Prager regarded the payment as "an advance against the sale of my house".

Prager left the RAF and nobody was aware of his treachery for ten years until somebody gave information to the police. In January 1971, the police arrived at Prager's home and brought him to a police station to answer some questions. He was questioned during three separate periods: from 9.15 am to 12.30 pm; from 5.40 pm to 7.40 pm; and from 7.40 to 11.30 pm. During the first period, Prager said he never photographed any secret documents and, according to the police, was at one stage taken for a walk in the precincts of the police station. During the second period, Prager continued to deny that he had done anything wrong. However, when he was asked by one policeman if he had regarded himself as a Czech agent, he replied: "It did not happen like that. Anything I have done was done unwittingly but you must know my family are out of this."

The police said at Prager's trial under the Official Secrets Act that they immediately cautioned him and the questioning went into a third, and final, phase during which he made a full confession. The problem for the police was that two months later, while in prison awaiting his trial, Prager swore a statement renouncing his confession. "I was induced to make that statement and I was in a state of fear," he maintained. During his trial in 1971, Prager said that he had wanted to leave the police station, had asked for a solicitor and not been given one and that by 7.30, his mind was blank – he tried to tell the police what he thought from their questions they wanted to hear.

Most of the trial was *in camera* but Britain's Lord Chief Justice, Lord Widgery, decided that it was necessary to examine Prager's claims about the nature of the police questioning and whether or not it was oppressive. He searched for a definition of oppressive questioning and came up with some remarks made by another Judge, Lord McDermott, when he spoke at the Bentham Club in 1968. Lord McDermott said that oppressive questioning was "questioning which by its nature, duration or other attendant circumstances (including the fact of custody) excites hopes (such as the hope of release) or fears, or so affects the mind of the subject that his will crumbles and he speaks when otherwise he would have stayed silent." Lord Widgery said he accepted this definition, ruled there was no continuous "third degree grilling" of Prager by the police and confirmed his two sentences of twelve years in prison.

In September 1965, Martin Priestly met twelve year old Margaret Barrett and took her to a wood in Kent where he sexually assaulted her, strangled her and left her body to be found later the same day. Priestly was the last person seen with the girl when she was alive and he was brought in for questioning. A Chief Inspector urged him to own up. "If something came over you in the woods, you should tell us," said the Chief Inspector. "All your lies will not help you if there is a simple explanation. Did something happen which you could not help? I feel you want to tell the truth but are ashamed of what occurred.''

Priestly then confessed to entering the woods with the girl. He insisted however that she had encouraged him to have sex with her. He said that he "tried to talk sense into her" and to emphasise his point, he held her throat. Her face turned blue and she slumped backwards, her body covered with the marks of his sex attack. Priestly was convicted of her murder despite an argument by his lawyer that his confession was not a voluntary statement.

It was suggested that the comment by the policeman – "All your lies will not help you if there is a simple explanation" – amounted to an inducement and was therefore oppressive as defined in the preamble to the (British) Judges Rules. The Judge dismissed the suggestion (and his view was subsequently confirmed by an appeal court) when he said he would not go into a detailed analysis of oppression but "to my mind, this word in the context of the principles under consideration imports something which tends to sap, and has sapped, that free will which must exist before a confession is voluntary." The Judge was content that this had not been the case with Priestly.

At the time of Priestly's appeal, this was the only reported judicial consideration of oppression by a British court. Judge Finlay said that the Court of Criminal Appeal adopted this definition along with that given in the Prager case. The three Irish appeal court judges may have considered Priestly and Prager before they decided to release Breatnach but they certainly did not consider the Supreme Court decision in the Shaw case because it was not given until seven months later.

John Shaw and Geoffrey Evans were two Englishmen suspected by gardai of involvement in the rape and murder of a woman called Elizabeth who disappeared near Brittas Bay in County Wicklow in August 1976. The following month, gardai in Galway who had been circulated with a description of the two men stopped a stolen car which was believed to have been linked with the disappearance of Elizabeth. At the time, the gardai in Galway had another problem on their hands: a woman called Mary had been abducted near Castlebar in County Mayo and there was a strong suspicion that the two men in the car knew something of her whereabouts. The two men were Shaw and Evans and they were arrested at 11.30 on a Sunday night on suspicion of being in possession of a stolen car.

The senior officer leading the investigation into the abduction of Elizabeth was Superintendent Hubert Reynolds of the technical bureau. He was called to Galway and interviewed Shaw. Over the course of Monday and Tuesday, Shaw confessed to the abduction, rape and murder of Mary who was held captive for five days during which she was abused and then killed. He also accompanied gardai around Connemara and showed them the various places where Mary had been killed and her clothes burned or hidden.

Shaw was tried before a jury in the Central Criminal Court and convicted of the murder. There was a problem about his period in garda custody, however. He was not arrested under the Offences Against the State Act and the gardai therefore had no right in law to hold him for a specified period. Had the gardai reason to believe (and evidence to back up that belief) that Shaw was involved in the alleged crime for which he was arrested, the theft of the car, he should have been brought before a court at the earliest available opportunity and charged. That first opportunity was around 10.30 on the Monday morning after his arrest. By holding Shaw throughout Monday and Tuesday, the gardai had violated his constitutional rights to liberty. If an appeal court accepted this line of argument, then Shaw's confession could not be admitted in evidence against him because it would have been obtained as a result of an illegal detention by the police.

The case went through the Court of Criminal Appeal and on to the Supreme Court which gave judgement in December 1980. Up to the time that Shaw confessed he had killed Mary, the gardai were not sure she was in fact dead but they feared for her safety. One of the issues facing the Supreme Court was a conflict of two opposing rights: Superintendent Reynolds was trying to vindicate Mary's

346

right to life but in so doing, he was denying Shaw's right to liberty. The Supreme Court decided that the gardai had been correct in choosing to protect the more important of the two conflicting rights. The Supreme Court also quoted from another case when giving their judgement on Shaw.

This was the O'Brien case, the kernel of which was the public interest: something which had exercised the minds of the judges of the Special Criminal Court when considering Breatnach's alleged confessions. On that occasion, Justice Hamilton ruled that it was in the "public interest" that his statements be admitted in evidence notwithstanding the fact that the gardai acted illegally. But the wheel was about to come full circle, so to speak, with the endorsement by the Court of Criminal Appeal of the Supreme Court's use of the O'Brien case in relation to Shaw.

The O'Brien case (mentioned by the prosecution during submissions about Osgur Breatnach) concerned two brothers, Gerald and Patrick, who lived at 118 Captain's Road in Crumlin. In October 1960, Gerald was convicted of larceny and Patrick of receiving stolen property. The stolen property was found when gardai raided their home. However it transpired afterwards that the address on the search warrant (the document which gave legal power to the garda action) was 118 Cashel Road, Crumlin. The gardai had in fact raided the correct house but not according to the legal documentation. The search was therefore technically illegal and the conviction of the O'Brien brothers questionable.

Once again, the Supreme Court was called upon to decide between what appeared to be two opposing rights: the right of the O'Brien brothers not to have their home invaded, willy nilly, by the police and the right of the State to bring criminals to justice. Judge Theodore Kingsmill Moore said the wrong address on the search warrant was pure oversight, an unintentional and accidental illegality. The courts had discretion to excuse such a mistake. Judge Brian Walsh said that evidence should be excluded by the courts where there had been a "deliberate and conscious violation of constitutional rights by the state or its agents...." Evidence should be admitted in such circumstances only where there was an extraordinary excuse for the violation of rights. Judge Kingsmill Moore said also that a trial judge had a discretion to exclude evidence "where it appears to him that public policy, based on a balancing of public interests, requires such exclusion."

When considering the Shaw case in December 1980, the Supreme Court made a detailed examination of the Prager, Priestly and O'Brien cases. The judgement delivered by Judge Frank Griffin contained what was, in effect, a definition of what Irish courts would in future regard as oppression by the police. Statements obtained as a result of oppression were not voluntary and could not be used in evidence against an accused person.

Judge Griffin said "a statement will be excluded as being voluntary if it was wrung from its maker by physical or psychological pressures, by threats or promises made by persons in authority, by the use of drugs, hypnosis, intoxicating drink, by prolonged interrogation or excessive questioning, or by any one of a diversity of methods which have in common the result or the risk that what is tendered as a voluntary statement is not the natural emanation of a rational intellect and a free will..." He added that a judge at a trial "should be astute to see that, although a statement may be technically voluntary, it should nevertheless be excluded if, by reason of the manner or of the circumstances in which it was obtained, it falls below the required standard of fairness."

Judge Griffin's comments were of course related to Shaw where the Supreme Court decided he had not been treated unfairly by the gardai but now the Court of Criminal Appeal adopted his remarks and applied them to the Breatnach case.

"If this judgement (Shaw) had been delivered when the present case (Breatnach) was tried," said Judge Finlay, "the above test of admissibility is the one that would have been used by the Special Criminal Court. Now that it has been delivered, it is the one that must be applied by this court."

He continued: "Working on the basis that all the primary findings of fact made by the court of trial are correct or beyond the reach of correction in this court, we are not satisfied beyond reasonable doubt, nor do we think that the court of trial was entitled to be satisfied beyond reasonable doubt, under either head of the test laid down by the Supreme Court in Shaw's case, that the statements made by this applicant (Breatnach) were voluntarily made or that the manner in which they were made satisfied the basic requirements of fairness."

The judge's comments included some curious use of language. There was no explanation of what difference, if any, there was between a finding of fact and a primary finding of fact. Judge Finlay appeared to suggest that the Special Criminal Court had been wrong in its acceptance of some things as facts. The comment that the primary findings of facts were correct "or beyond the correction of this court" implied that were it possible, the Court of Criminal Appeal would like to have been able to overturn some of the things which the Special Criminal Court decided were "facts".

"It is not necessary to rehearse again the circumstances in which the statements were made," Judge Finlay went on, "such as the previous forty hours in custody during which this applicant (Breatnach) obdurately refused to make a statement, the strange fact that the statement was made after questioning not in an interview room but in an underground passage in the early hours of the morning, after the applicant had suffered an untimely awakening from what must have been a much needed sleep, the unsatisfactory explanation for the disturbance of his sleep and of his being brought to what may have been the menacing environment of an underground passage in the Bridewell Garda Station, and the unexcused and seemingly inexcusable fact that, since the previous day, he had been denied the access to his solicitor which he had clearly asked for."

Judge Finlay's comments were clearly a rebuke for the conduct of the gardai and the treatment meted out to Breatnach. He then delivered what amounted to a rebuke of the Special Criminal Court.

"The combination of these and other factors is such that,

in the opinion of this court, it would not be open to the court of trial to conclude, beyond a reasonable doubt, that the statements were voluntary in the legally accepted meaning of that word, or even if they were, that the circumstantial context in which they were made passes the test of the basic fairness. The statements therefore should not have been admitted in evidence."

He said that, without the statement, there was "not enough evidence" to link Breatnach to the robbery. In point of fact, there was no evidence to connect him with it. Because of this, Judge Finlay said the Court of Criminal Appeal had quashed Breatnach's conviction and sentence and ordered his release. The court found in effect that the conduct of the gardai had been oppressive.

Breatnach and McNally were, in the eyes of the law, restored to their status as citizens who were presumed to be innocent. They were not former train robbers: they never had been train robbers as far as the official record was concerned. To the extent that they were free, the system had ultimately worked for them. Justice could be said to have been done.

Nicky Kelly would not be so lucky.

15

Appeals

Nicky Kelly boarded an Aer Lingus jumbo jet at John F Kennedy airport in New York for the overnight flight to Shannon and Dublin. It was June 3rd 1980, twelve days after his co-accused had been set free by the Court of Criminal Appeal in Dublin. He had decided to return, ignoring the warnings of lawyers and friends. The lawyers had pointed out that the court had not yet published its reasons for releasing the other two: they could not say with certainty that it would take the same view of his case. But Kelly had made up his mind. He saw no need to run any longer.

He had given up his truck driving job in the Philadelphia area at the end of the previous April, partly because he was due to go into hospital for tests. He was suffering severe headaches, sleeplessness, a lack of concentration and occasionally felt that the left side of his face had gone numb. His lack of concentration caused him on one occasion to back his truck into a veranda because he forgot to look in the rear view mirror. His departure from the job was marked with a party after his workmates eventually found a pub which allowed blacks and whites to socialise together.

Kelly had asked around for advice about his medical problems and had been directed towards Dr Rona Fields, a psychiatrist who specialised in examining the results of political conflict in Belfast and Beirut. Between February and April 1980 he had weekly sessions with her at her offices in Alexandria, Virginia. She concluded that he was suffering from anxiety and connected psychosomatic disorders including insomnia, headaches, gastric distur- bances and what were termed psycho-motor inadequacies. She recommended a complete neurological examination to see if his problems were caused by anomalies in the brain or the central nervous system.

On May 19th – the day that the submissions concluded in the appeal court in Dublin – Kelly was admitted to New York's Bellevue Hospital for a series of tests. Over the next four days, he had a brain scan, his spinal fluid was analysed and a host of other examinations were carried out. He was aware of the appeal in Ireland and of all developments. As well as receiving letters from friends in Ireland he got Irish newspapers and was informed about developments like the IRA claim to have carried out the robbery. He telephoned Paul O'Dwyer, one of the leading Irish-American lawyers, from the hospital to find out what was happening but O'Dwyer had heard nothing about the end of the appeal.

On May 23rd, the day after his colleagues were released from Portlaoise, Kelly discharged himself from hospital. He could not get a definite answer from doctors about what was happening and they were talking vaguely about keeping him in for a further five days. He found some of the tests painful and he felt worse than he had before he went in. Around teatime, while the hospital was quiet, he found the locker containing his clothes, dressed himself and simply walked out of the building. He went off to The Bronx to stay with some friends and learned next day from O'Dwyer that Osgur Breatnach and Brian McNally had been freed.

Kelly made up his mind to return to Ireland. He talked by telephone to Pat McCartan, his solicitor in Dublin, who pointed out to him that the appeal court had not given its reasons for releasing the other two. McCartan agreed to be at the airport to meet him on his return. Paul O'Dwyer warned him that his belief that the case was now over might be premature. Other friends urged him to think carefully about it. But Kelly had made up his mind. On June 2nd 1980 the *Daily News* in Philadelphia reported that he would be returning voluntarily to Ireland. His lawyer there, John Corcoran, said he was returning to clear his name.

Kelly had been befriended by a *News* columnist, Jack McKinney, and they set off together to the Irish consulate in New York on June 3rd to arrange his return. Kelly had no passport and needed a temporary one. The procedures had already been explained to them by phone and he was carrying two photographs of himself. But the consulate staff did not appear enthusiastic about his return to Ireland. They maintained that they knew nothing about his case, had no arrangements for receiving fugitives and were concerned that he had no way of proving his identity for a temporary passport.

Eventually they agreed to give him the single page document, valid only for one journey to Ireland. It bore the name Edward Noel Kelly, his picture, date and place of birth and his mother's maiden name. He and McKinney left the consulate and went straight to the airport. McKinney kept asking him if he was sure he was doing the right thing. Kelly was sure. He boarded flight EI 104 shortly before 8.00 pm.

Kelly's plans had already preceded him. News of his return was picked up by Sean Cronin, the *Irish Times* correspondent in Washington, and published in the newspaper on June 3rd. Kelly read the story, headlined "Mail train man to return?" on board the plane. He was recognised by several passengers and one of the stewardesses asked him to sign a £5 note for her. He did.

Four detectives were waiting in the terminal building when the plane landed at Shannon early the next morning, June 4th 1980. One of them, Garda Frank Madden, had been involved in the mail train inquiry, interviewing Michael Plunkett and John Fitzpatrick. Kelly did not know the others. He, Kelly, was taken to the Special Criminal Court in Dublin on the warrant that had been issued by the court for his arrest in December 1978.

Kelly and the four detectives set off for Dublin by car. There were lots of smart remarks from the detectives but they seemed to suggest that Kelly would be in prison only for a couple of weeks. One guard told him to make sure he got the case dealt with before the recess. Kelly did not know what he meant: he believed that his release would more or less be a formality once an appeal was heard. Meanwhile, he was being driven to Green Street courthouse when the garda car broke down on the main road to Dublin. They had to wait until someone could bring them petrol.

The Special Criminal Court dealt swiftly with Kelly's return. At a brief hearing, it ordered that he be taken to

353

serve the remainder of his twelve year sentence. His period on the run and in the United States counted as part of the sentence because he was sentenced to penal servitude. The concept of penal servitude had its origins in the sending of convicts to penal colonies abroad and, as such, they were supposed to be out of the country for the period specified in the sentence. For that reason, it dated from the time of sentence rather than from the time at which imprisonment began.

As Kelly settled into Portlaoise he faced, theoretically, a term of imprisonment that would run until December 1990. In the normal course of events, he could expect to receive remission of a third of his sentence for good behaviour which would bring his release forward to 1986. But Kelly was totally confident that none of these possibilities would apply to him. Like many other people, he believed that his release was just a formality after the appeal court decisions on McNally and Breatnach. He expected to be free in a matter of weeks.

The main legal problem was to get the appeal court to hear his case. Appeals had to be lodged normally within seven days of the original trial but the appeal court could vary that requirement. Kelly's lawyers – the same team who had defended him in the Special Criminal Court trials – set about applying to the court to extend the time allowed.

The lawyers put together several affidavits in preparation for lodging the appeal at the end of July. Professor Robert Daly, a psychiatrist from University College Cork who had acted in Ireland's torture case against Britain at the European Court of Human Rights, was asked by McCartan to examine Kelly and saw him on June 12th. He concluded that Kelly appeared to have "a traumatic neurosis resulting from his experience during interrogation four years ago." He added that Kelly had a continuing disability, with neurological as well as psychological symptoms.

Kelly himself swore an affidavit in which he said he had absconded because he had suffered greatly from psychological and physical trauma which resulted from beatings and pressurisation during his interrogation in April 1976. His anxieties were compounded by the protracted

354

nature of the prosecution case against him. Before the first trial began in the Special Criminal Court he had attended a psychiatrist, Dr Noel Browne, who recommended a course of treatment in St Loman's hospital. Kelly said he did not act on that advice because he did not want to cause any further delays in meeting the charges laid against him.

He said he was very distressed mentally when he absconded and felt unable to deal any longer with his predicament. His condition worsened in the US and he suffered greatly from headaches, insomnia, nightmares and difficulties with his eyesight. He was treated by Dr Fields to a course of psychotherapy but his condition continued to deteriorate.

Kelly added that at all times since he absconded he had desired to return to the state in order to vindicate his good name and to clear himself of the conviction. His decision was regardless of the outcome of the appeals of McNally and Breatnach.

Pat McCartan, his solicitor, swore an affidavit saying that he had applied to the Special Criminal Court on December 15th 1978 for leave to appeal on Kelly's behalf. That had been refused. He first heard of Kelly's intention to return on May 29th 1980. McCartan added a list of fourteen grounds on which Kelly wished to appeal against his conviction by the Special Criminal Court. Eight of them were the same as McNally's grounds of appeal, including alterations in the station allocation book for the Bridewell, and the argument that there was not sufficient evidence for the trial court to decide that his injuries were self-inflicted or mutually inflicted. Other grounds contested the legality of Kelly's arrest under common law in the early hours of April 7th 1976 and the legality of his subsequent detention.

Kelly's hopes for an early release were undermined by the fact that he did not manage to have his request heard by the appeal court before the summer recess. It was finally heard on November 11th. Kelly adjusted his expectations in line with the delay in getting into court. He now expected to be released by Christmas 1980.

At the hearing, Seamus Sorahan presented the affidavits to the three judges and argued that a grave injustice might be done if Kelly were denied an extension of the time in which to appeal. Patrick MacEntee pointed out that Kelly was at a grave disadvantage because the judgement of the Court of Criminal Appeal in the case of McNally and Breatnach had not yet been produced. He set out for the court the grounds on which Kelly intended to appeal.

Noel McDonald replied for the Director of Public Prosecutions that Kelly's counsel had glossed over the reasons for the delay in appealing. Kelly was the author of his own misfortune by absconding. He also disputed the contention that Kelly was suffering mentally at the time of the trial. Kelly had spent seven days in the witness box between the two trials in the Special Criminal Court and had not shown any sign of his alleged anxiety neurosis, he said.

McDonald added that at both trials, the Special Criminal Court had utterly rejected the allegations against the gardai. (In fact, the first trial was still in the process of ruling on the admissibility of statements when it was aborted by Judge O'Connor's death.)

The three members of the Court of Criminal Appeal said they would give their decision later. The court consisted of Mr Justice Weldon C. Parke of the Supreme Court, Mr Justice John M. Gannon and Miss Justice Mella Carroll of the High Court. It was Miss Justice Carroll's first time to sit on the appeal court: she had been appointed a High Court judge some five weeks earlier. The three judges gave their decisions more than a month later, on December 18th.

They announced that Kelly would not be allowed extra time in which he could appeal. Their judgement had nothing to do with the merits of his case but arose from, on the one hand, an extremely narrow view of the evidence before it and, on the other hand, a failure by Kelly's lawyers to treat the application like it was a hearing of the actual appeal. His lawyers had approached the court on the basis that they were simply looking for an extension of time. The court was critical of them for not presenting it with all the evidence about his actual appeal. Between the court and the lawyers, Kelly came to the realisation that he was going to be in prison for another while. He was not going to be released by

Christmas.

The court's decision, delivered by Justice Gannon, said the application had been examined on two grounds: did Kelly have a genuine intention of appealing against the Special Criminal Court decision and, if he did, would he have had reasonable grounds for expecting that his conviction would be set aside? The court had to decide these questions on the basis of the evidence put before it. The court could not speculate and must assume that affidavits were true. As Kelly was represented by counsel and solicitor of great experience and highest standing, the court inferred that no material facts had been omitted by inadvertence.

Having said that, the court went on to point out that there was no evidence before it to show the connection between Kelly's beatings and pressurisation and the trial in the Special Criminal Court. The court had been told that the fourteen grounds of appeal corresponded with those lodged on behalf of McNally. But there was no evidence offered to show the pertinence or relevance of any of these to Kelly's case.

Amazingly, the court maintained that there was no evidence before it to connect the beatings to the interrogations nor was there any evidence before it to connect the interrogations with the voluntariness of Kelly's statements. There was nothing before the court to support in any way the grounds of appeal or to indicate that they could reasonably be raised in this case. There was no explanation as to why the same grounds of appeal were used for Kelly as for McNally.

It had been suggested, the court said, that there might be a miscarriage of justice if Kelly was not allowed to appeal along the same grounds on which McNally's appeal succeeded. This line of reasoning seemed entirely contrary to the concept of justice in criminal trials involving more than one person. Each individual should be treated separately: it would be manifestly unjust if one person was convicted just because his co-accused was convicted. Likewise, the court declared, it would be contrary to justice to acquit somebody because a co-accused was acquitted.

357

The court then turned its attention to whether or not Kelly's intentions in appealing were genuine and *bona fide* when the trial was still fresh and whether there was a *prima facie* case to be made that the trial was unfair or unsatisfactory. Kelly made no complaint to the court about the nature of the trial, the way it was conducted or showed any indication of challenging the Special Criminal Court's verdict, the judgement proclaimed. For the purpose of this point, the three judges were obviously ignoring Kelly's grounds of appeal and concentrating solely and exclusively on Kelly's affidavit.

The court complained that Kelly's affidavit gave no information about the period between December 1978 to February 1980 when he attended Dr Fields. Neither did it provide any evidence which showed that he approved of the grounds of appeal chosen by his solicitor. Neither the trial transcript nor any part of it was provided to the court.

The judgement repeated again that the court could only act on the evidence before it and that Kelly was represented by very experienced counsel and solicitor who knew that. It was in the interests of everybody that an appeal against a trial court was brought to the appeal court as early as possible. It did not appear to be in the interests of justice nor fair that the decision of a court of trial should be challenged on legal grounds after a very long interval, particularly if that had not been genuinely contemplated immediately after the trial. From the facts put before the court, it seemed that an appeal was not contemplated until after Kelly's co-accused had been released.

The grounds of other appeals were not relevant to this case because of the principle that each accused person must be dealt with separately from those who were tried with him. Kelly had to show the appeal court that his appeal should be allowed on the basis of facts and circumstances particular to his case.

The court concluded that there was, in the public interest, a presumption that Kelly's trial was conducted regularly, fairly and in accordance with law and the principles of justice. "The onus lies upon him as a convicted person to rebut this presumption. On this application he has failed to adduce evidence of facts or circumstances to which his inaction can be attributed. Even if his inaction could be attributed to his anxiety neurosis.... he has failed to show even the contemplation of dissatisfaction with his trial or the intention to challenge the verdict of the court at any time prior to the 29th of May 1980.

"In the view of this court he has not dispelled that doubt nor discharged that onus nor submitted facts from which an arguable ground of appeal may reasonably be inferred. His application for enlargement of time must be refused."

It was an extraordinary judgement. Kelly was to be made pay the price for what the court clearly considered to be the failings of his lawyers. It was clear to anyone who had followed the case that most of the facts that the court said were absent could have been supplied very easily if the court had asked for them and if the lawyers had thought it necessary to provide them. No one could have doubted that Kelly linked his medical condition to his interrogation and his interrogation to his confessions and his confessions to his conviction by the Special Criminal Court. His dissatisfaction with his trial was never a secret and was among the reasons why he jumped bail. The court's narrow and pedantic view of the evidence before it effectively sentenced Kelly to another year in prison.

Kelly was obviously disappointed but he still believed that all that was needed to secure his release was a hearing of his actual appeal. The legal avenues open to him had been reduced by the court decision but they had not yet been shut off completely. It was possible to appeal the court's decision to the Supreme Court but only on a point of law of exceptional public importance. To take the matter to the Supreme Court, however, required the agreement of the Court of Criminal Appeal or the Attorney General. Preparations began to persuade the Appeal Court to give its sanction to take the matter to the higher court.

Public interest in Nicky Kelly's plight was low. The issue of the mail train robbery case and what had happened in 1976 was closed in many people's minds with the release of McNally and Breatnach. Kelly was just a little piece of unfinished business: most of those who would have been concerned with his fate – civil libertarians, left-wingers and republicans – assumed that his release would be more or less a formality. After the shock of the first appeal court hearing, a committee was formed to try and re-activate interest in the case. Its task was difficult and constantly hampered by the fact that further legal battles were pending. Dwindling interest and the rules of *sub judice* combined to isolate Kelly.

Early in 1981 Kelly contemplated taking action himself by going on hunger strike to highlight his case. Hunger strikes were in the news after one by republican paramilitaries in Northern Ireland had ended in December 1980. In February 1981, Kelly was dissuaded from beginning a fast by the IRSP because another hunger strike of IRA and INLA prisoners was due to start in the North in March. The IRSP did not want any action in the South to detract from the strike in the North. As the Northern hunger strike – which eventually left ten republicans dead – began to attract public attention Kelly noted to a visitor that he could have been the first on strike and leading the rest. Kelly tried again to start a hunger strike in early June, during the general election campaign in the Republic, but was again dissuaded.

In March 1981, Kelly's lawyers were back in the Court of Criminal Appeal, seeking permission to take the case to the Supreme Court on a point of exceptional public importance. The point was the criterion used by the appeal court for deciding not to extend the seven-day deadline on lodging an application for an appeal. The case for and against allowing the issue to be put to the Supreme Court was heard by the Court of Criminal Appeal over two days. Two months later, on May 29th, the court announced that it was giving permission.

Meanwhile, Kelly had been contemplating some other actions of his own. He wanted to switch barristers. He still believed that he would win his release as soon as he got a full appeal hearing and he wanted a new set of barristers to argue his case for him. Seamus Sorahan was told of his views and was none too pleased that Kelly was unhappy with his performance. Several other lawyers were

360

approached about taking on the case. Kelly decided that he would argue his case in the Supreme Court himself but that plan was shattered by court officials. On the eve of the Supreme Court hearing in July 1981, Kelly was given a message by the assistant governor of Portlaoise. Court officials had been on the phone to say he could not argue his own case before the court: he was represented by solicitors and barristers, he was told.

A week after that hearing, the Supreme Court decided to allow him extensions of time in which to appeal. It took until the following January before its reasons were produced and Chief Justice Tom O'Higgins indicated that Kelly need not have applied for a time extension at all. He could have submitted his appeal in the normal way, as of right, and it would have been up to the court of appeal to direct otherwise. The criteria applied to Kelly's application by the court were inappropriate in a criminal case, he said. The court must be flexible and should be guided by what appeared to be just and equitable.

Chief Justice O'Higgins rejected the argument put to him on behalf of the Director of Public Prosecutions that Kelly should not be entitled to a time extension because he had absconded. But he thought the appeal court had taken "a slightly blinkered view" of Kelly's case. The grounds of appeal before the court and the submissions of counsel were sufficient to infer that Kelly questioned his conviction on the grounds of beatings and pressurisation. Justice required that Kelly's case be considered and investigated, he concluded.

Another of the five Supreme Court judges who decided the issue, Mr Justice Seamus Henchy, said that the deciding factor for him was the fact that Kelly, McNally and Breatnach had been convicted after confessions made in the same place and at the same time and as a result of methods which had certain common features. Because of the apparently close connection between them, there was a suspicion that Kelly might be able to show that the evidence against him should have been excluded. "In that state of undissipated suspicion...I would consider that the risk of a miscarriage of justice is so real that the prescribed time should be enlarged to enable the applicant to apply for leave to appeal," he said. Mr Justice John Kenny agreed with him.

Kelly was now in the position that he thought he had been in more than a year earlier when he returned from the United States. The unexpected legal hurdles had been cleared from his path and he was free to pursue his appeal against the Special Criminal Court conviction. Kelly was to spend his second Christmas in Portlaoise Prison before the appeal came to hearing on February 15th 1982.

Nearly four years after they had last argued over the circumstances of Nicky Kelly's alleged confessions, Seamus Sorahan and Robert Barr repeated many of the same points again before the three judges of the Court of Criminal Appeal. The judges were, by design, the same three who had adjudicated on the McNally and Breatnach appeals some twenty one months earlier: the president of the High Court, Mr Justice Thomas Finlay, Mr Justice Seamus Henchy from the Supreme Court and Mr Justice Donal Barrington from the High Court.

Kelly's lawyers went into the court to argue fourteen different reasons why his conviction should be overturned. Two more reasons were added during the four-day hearing while several of the existing ones were merged together or dropped. All of them effectively maintained that the Special Criminal Court was wrong to admit the alleged confessions into evidence for both legal and factual reasons. They were later divided into two categories by the appeal court: claims that the Special Criminal Court was wrong to find that the confessions were not caused by violence or unfair methods, including breaches of the Judges Rules and, secondly, that Kelly's detention was unlawful at different times during which confessions were made.

Seamus Sorahan opened the case by pointing out that the only evidence against Kelly was the alleged confessions. He argued that the police did not have power under the Offences Against the State Act to interrogate a person: they merely had power to require someone to give an account of their movements. Kelly, he submitted, had been illegally interrogated and the resulting material should not have been accepted as evidence.

He maintained that the failure of the prosecution to supply as witnesses all the gardai who were present in both garda stations during Kelly's detention indicated that the prosecution had failed to prove that his admissions were satisfactory. They also rendered the trial unsatisfactory.

He said that there was no doubt that Kelly was injured when he was seen by doctors in Mountjoy prison. The medical evidence was more consistent with the inference that they must have been inflicted by the gardai rather than the inference that they were self-inflicted or inflicted in collaboration with other people. The Special Criminal Court's acceptance of the garda evidence in full was a failure of justice.

Sorahan argued that the verbal admissions allegedly made by Kelly in the early hours of Wednesday, April 7th 1976 had breached the Judges Rules because some were not written down at the time while Kelly was not invited to sign others. The failure to bring Kelly to court until 10.30 pm that Wednesday was in breach of the common law requirement that he be brought before a court as soon as practicable.

The two new grounds of appeal suggested that it was illegal for the guards to move Kelly from Arklow to Fitzgibbon Street to the Bridewell. Since he was brought first to Arklow garda station he should have been held there for the duration of his detention, he argued, because the Offences Against the State Act required that a suspect be held in a garda station, a prison or some other convenient place.

The second new ground of appeal maintained that the extension order signed by Chief Superintendent John Fleming – which allowed the detention of Kelly to be extended for twenty four hours to forty eight hours – was invalid. It referred to Kelly as being detained in the Bridewell although it was signed around 6.00 pm on Monday, April 5th 1976 when Kelly was still in detention in Fitzgibbon Street garda station.

Kelly had given evidence to the effect that he had sought a solicitor on several occasions during his detention. He had previously been arrested under the Offences Against the State Act on several occasions and knew his rights.

On the third day of the hearing, Robert Barr replied for the Director of Public Prosecutions. He claimed that there was a concerted plan by the IRSP to allege brutality by the gardai against their members arrested in April 1976. It was reasonable to infer that if there was any truth in the IRSP protests about brutality, they would have had doctors readily available to examine their men. That was not done and the Special Criminal Court was entitled to reach the conclusion that there was no oppression or brutality. The injuries were only demonstrated after they had been put in cells in pairs. The Special Criminal Court was correct to find that the injuries were self-inflicted or mutually inflicted.

The appeal court was being asked to punish the police for failing to comply strictly with the letter of the Judges Rules on the verbal admissions. There was no evidence to show that any such technical transgression of the rules might have caused Kelly to make his ultimate written statement. Kelly had to show that the breach of the rules caused him to make an admission that he would not have made otherwise, he submitted.

Kelly had given a very detailed account of his participation in a sophisticated robbery which involved a high degree of planning. He had been given time to consider his situation early on Wednesday morning and, immediately afterwards, he had started to make a full verbal admission of his part in the crime without any prodding or interrogation from the gardai.

The hearing ended on the fourth day, February 18th 1982, and the judges went away to consider their decision. Kelly was hopeful that his release was at hand. As the days dragged by, however, he began to lose his optimism. If the court was going to release him, it would do so sooner rather than later: it could free him as it had freed McNally and Breatnach and wait to give its full reasons at leisure. In the days and weeks after the hearing there was no sign of the court returning to a public hearing or of his release. After several weeks and before any formal announcement, Kelly knew the worst.

The decision eventually came forty three days after the hearing, on April 2nd 1982. The Court of Criminal Appeal confirmed the conviction by the Special Criminal Court and the sentence that it had imposed on Nicky Kelly. The judgement ran to thirty four pages and was read by the presiding judge, Mr Justice Finlay. It made no mention of the cases of McNally and Breatnach other than to note that the facts of the crime were contained in the judgements of their appeals. It also dismissed the arguments that it could go beyond the Madden case – which restricted appeal courts to accepting the facts decided upon by the trial court in most cases.

In accepting the facts, the appeal court said it had carefully considered the evidence on which they were based and was satisfied, bearing in mind the onus of proof on the prosecution, that the Special Criminal Court was entitled to make those findings. The appeal court said it could not interfere with those findings. It then set out the facts determined by the Special Criminal Court which, in almost all aspects, corresponded with the garda evidence against Kelly. On the basis of those facts, the court said, the Special Criminal Court was entitled to convict Kelly and reach its conclusion beyond reasonable doubt.

The judgement went on: "And on a review of the whole of the evidence this court cannot say that those conclusions were perverse or insupportable. The pattern emerging from this evidence was of a person who whilst in detention eventually decided for one reason or another to co-operate with the members of the Garda Siochana and to confess his participation in this crime."

The court then cited a number of factors which, it said, amply supported the conclusion of the Special Criminal Court that Kelly's statements were truly voluntary and had not been obtained by any unfair method. These were the number of times Kelly confessed; his willingness to point out areas associated with the crime and to find the guns used in it; his refusal to rest before the journey; a complete absence of any complaint about ill treatment by him to any garda; the implausibilities in his complaints of ill treatment;

365

a lack of congruity between his allegations of duress and his admitted friendliness and co-operation with gardai after he had made a written statement.

The court went on to consider the grounds of appeal which challenged the propriety of individual statements that Kelly was said to have made. His first two detailed verbal admissions breached the Judges Rules, the court decided, because the first was not written down at the time and the second was not offered to Kelly to sign. But the court decided that the Special Criminal Court had been correct in ignoring these breaches because the contents of the verbal admissions were in substance identical to the facts contained in the written statement.

Submissions about the journey to Ballymore Eustace and the alleged admissions in Harcourt Terrace had been based on two legal points: that Kelly was not properly released under the Offences Against the State Act just after he had signed the written statement and before the journey and, secondly, that he should have been brought to court immediately because of his re-arrest under common law.

The court accepted that Inspector Ned Ryan was not an "officer" of the Garda Siochana and that the Offences Against the State Act required that a suspect be charged or released by direction of an officer. ("Officer" is defined as anyone of superintendent rank or higher: anyone of lower rank is a "member" of the Garda Siochana.) But the court decided it would be an anomaly and would be wrong to restrict the release of a person exclusively to an officer.

On the second argument, the court said that the failure to bring Kelly to court on the morning of Wednesday, April 7th 1976, was explained by the desirability of allowing Kelly to rest after the journey to Ballymore Eustace and Bray. The failure to do so later in the afternoon was explained by the necessity to correlate documents and files in a major investigation that was being carried out from Naas and Dublin, to put the information before the Director of Public Prosecutions, to obtain his decision and to arrange a special sitting of the court.

The court noted that the only evidence covered by this point was the alleged admissions made in Harcourt Terrace garda station. They were of minimal probative value compared to the full and detailed written statement. Therefore the court did not think it necessary to express an opinion on this point. Even if it was conceded to Kelly, there could be no question of an injustice occurring because of the statements made in Harcourt Terrace, the court decided.

Thus, the appeal court had decided that the first two full verbal admissions were taken in breach of the Judges Rules – the same point on which Brian McNally was released – and that the final admissions made in Harcourt Terrace as well were taken in possibly dubious circumstances. That left the written statement, on which the court put great store, and the admissions that were implicit or explicit during the journey to the scene of the crime and Ballymore Eustace. Nevertheless, the court had declared the whole pattern to be of a person eventually deciding to co-operate with the gardai – a phrase that was to be echoed by the Supreme Court when it came to look at the case again.

The Appeal Court rejected the legal argument that Kelly should not have been moved from Arklow garda station, the first place to which he was taken after his arrest under the Offences Against the State Act. It said: "On the facts of this case, there are no grounds for holding that any lawyer was at any material time made unaware of the place where the applicant was being detained, or that any attempt to render assistance or have access to the applicant by any person was frustrated by his removal in the first instance from Arklow garda station to Fitzgibbon Street garda station and in the second instance from Fitzgibbon Street to the Bridewell garda station.

"On the evidence, the only person who apparently took an interest in and was concerned with the position of the applicant during the period of his detention was his girlfriend and she was made aware of the fact that he was detained in Fitzgibbon Street garda station from noon on the 5th of April and of the fact that he was subsequently from the 6th of April in the Bridewell garda station. In fact she visited him in the latter garda station."

In reality, the court's statement was not altogether

accurate. Kelly's girlfriend, Nuala Dillon, was with the gardai in Dublin Castle until Kelly's arrest in Arklow on the morning of Monday, April 5th. She then went to the offices of Kelly's solicitor, Pat McCartan, told him Kelly was in Arklow garda station and asked him to act for him.

Nuala Dillon did not know Kelly was in Fitzgibbon Street until she herself was met by gardai that night and taken to the station. She was left home again around midnight. Next day she left a message for McCartan to phone her: she intended telling him that Kelly was in Fitzgibbon Street because he had been unable to find Kelly on Monday. McCartan did not contact her. That night, two gardai called on her again and took her to the Bridewell where she saw Kelly.

The next night, Wednesday, April 7th 1976, Kelly phoned her after his appearance in the district court to ask her to get a solicitor. She called McCartan, who agreed to go to the district court the following morning for the remand hearing. She told the Special Criminal Court all of this under oath the morning of the thirty first day of the trial, November 23rd 1978.

McCartan had tried to find Kelly after Dillon's visit to him on the Monday. He phoned Arklow garda station about noon and was told Kelly was not there. Kelly, in fact, was at Fitzgibbon Street station by then. McCartan tried the Bridewell but Kelly was not there either.

The Appeal Court noted, however, that if a person was moved from one garda station to another in order to harass him or isolate him from assistance or access to which he would be entitled, then that fact of itself would make his detention unlawful.

The court went on to dismiss the second new ground of appeal put before it: that the order extending his detention from twenty four hours to forty eight hours was inaccurate. The court decided that it complied with the terms of the law because the person to whom it was relevant at the time of the extension was the station sergeant in the Bridewell. The document had described Kelly as being in custody in the Bridewell at a time when he was in Fitzgibbon Street.

The thirty four page judgement of the court ended with

the sentence: "The court is therefore satisfied that this application for leave to appeal must be dismissed and the convictions and sentences affirmed." Twenty two months after his return from the United States, Kelly found that what had been unimaginable had turned out to be true. His conviction and his sentence still stood. Three years, three months and some two weeks of his sentence had passed: now he had to serve the remainder. His faith in the judicial system was at an end.

There was one more domestic legal remedy open to him: he could appeal to the Supreme Court. That would have to be, as it was previously, on the basis of seeking clarification on a point of law of exceptional public importance. The Appeal Court, on the day of its judgement, had agreed to allow recourse to the Supreme Court to have the issue of moving people between garda stations determined. Kelly was not anxious for the case to go to the Supreme Court again. He believed it would only give the court an opportunity to copperfasten the Appeal Court decision and make it all the more difficult for him to prove his innocence. His faith in the Supreme Court had not been strong since the Judge O'Connor affair during the aborted first trial in the Special Criminal Court.

His lawyers were more optimistic about going to the Supreme Court, however. They persuaded Kelly to try it and a hearing began on July 13th 1982. It turned out to be a lengthy process, lasting six days which were taken up with legal submissions. Kelly was not present: the court decided that there was no need for him to be there. The brunt of Kelly's lawyers' arguments were similar to the points already made in the High Court. They contended that the Offences Against the State Act had to be interpreted strictly and that this meant that a suspect could not be moved from a garda station once he had been brought there under Section 30. But the Supreme Court took a wider view of the case and allowed arguments to be raised about the other issues which had been decided by the Court of Criminal Appeal.

It did not deliver its judgement until after the summer recess. On October 29th 1982, five judges – Chief Justice

O'Higgins, Brian Walsh, Frank Griffin, Anthony Hederman and High Court Judge Herbert McWilliam – pronounced their decision. They rejected the application but went further to declare that the Court of Criminal Appeal decision was correct.

They noted, in the judgement delivered by the Chief Justice, that Kelly had been given every opportunity to establish that he should not have been convicted. "It is seldom that the appellate jurisdiction of our courts has been so fully exercised but it is proper that it should have been so in order to satisfy the requirements of justice," they declared.

Having disposed of the point at issue – the movement between garda stations – the court turned its attentions to the questions of whether or not Kelly's confessions were voluntary or brought about by violence or unfair methods and whether or not he was in lawful custody at the time he made them. Kelly had named twenty gardai whom, he alleged, had beaten him: six of them had sworn that they had no dealings whatsoever with Kelly. Medical evidence established that on Thursday, April 8th 1976 Kelly had bruising on various parts of his body which, except in one particular (the chair on the hands allegation), were consistent with the violence to which he said he had been subjected. No marks or bruises had been found on his hands in spite of his description of the chair incident. Had this happened, the medical evidence indicated that there would have been excruciating pain, external signs of injury and possibly broken bones. At a later medical examination in Portlaoise prison his body still had bruises but he had also sustained abrasions without being in garda custody.

All the gardai implicated by Kelly had denied his allegations and asserted that no violence of any kind was done to him. The prosecution had also relied on the fact that Kelly had made no complaint of ill-treatment to Nuala Dillon in the Bridewell or to any garda although he admitted to friendliness and co-operation with a number with whom he had contact. Nor did he make any complaint when charged in the district court "on the morning of the 7th April". (This is a factual error in the judgement: Kelly

370

was in the district court on the night of April 7th and again on the morning of April 8th. It is not clear to which appearance the Supreme Court was referring but the context suggests the late night special hearing.)

The Supreme Court noted that the prosecution had relied on the fact that Kelly had an opportunity of inflicting injuries on himself or having someone do it for him between the district court hearing and the medical examination in Mountjoy prison. The Special Criminal Court had heard all the witnesses, saw them being examined and having their credibility tested and it did not believe Kelly's evidence. The Court of Criminal Appeal had been asked to say that the Special Criminal Court was wrong, that its decision was not supported by the evidence and was perverse.

The Supreme Court had now been asked to say that the Court of Criminal Appeal should have decided from reading the trial transcript that the gardai named by Kelly had committed perjury and that Kelly's evidence was true in substance and in fact. "This drastic conclusion... would be arrived at by a court which neither saw nor heard any of the witnesses involved but which nevertheless was to feel itself at liberty to brand as untruthful those witnesses who by their manner, demeanour and evidence had satisfied experienced judges at the trial that they were telling the truth. If such were truly within the powers of a court of appeal in our jurisprudence, one wonders what would be the function of a court of trial."

It had been urged that the Court of Criminal Appeal should have had exclusive regard to the undisputed fact that Kelly's body bore marks of bruising consistent with the administration of blows. From this, it was urged that the Court of Criminal Appeal should have concluded that the garda evidence was a tissue of lies and that Kelly had been beaten and assaulted in the manner described. Kelly's lawyers had argued that an English precedent existed for an appeal court to set aside a conviction because there was a lurking doubt, produced by the general feel of the case, that an injustice had been done.

Chief Justice O'Higgins said that this case had frequently been cited in support of arguments for a wider interpretation of the appeal court's precedures than those laid down in the Madden case. Such arguments had been rejected by the appeal court and, in his opinion, the court was right to reject them.

He went on: "I have come to the conclusion that the submission made that the Court of Criminal Appeal should have interfered with or disregarded the findings of fact made by the court of trial is fallacious and should be rejected. The issue of fact in this case was clear and unambiguous. It was not whether at the time of his remand to Mountjoy Jail the appellant's body was bruised. This was an undisputed fact. The issue was whether that bruising was caused as a result of blows and violence administered to the appellant (Kelly) by various gardai during the course of his interrogation. On that issue there was a clear conflict of evidence which admitted of no compromise and no possibility of error and which could only be resolved by the court deciding where the truth lay. It is abundantly clear from the transcript of the trial that the court approached that task in a painstaking and patient manner, hearing the evidence of all the witnesses in detail over many days and weeks and eventually giving a considered and clear decision. In these circumstances I am quite satisfied that... the Court of Criminal Appeal was correct in regarding the decision of the court of trial on the issue of facts surrounding the making of various statements as one which should not be disturbed. In my view, the Court of Criminal Appeal was correct in accepting the court of trial's findings of fact indicating an absence of oppression in relation to the making of these statements and in concluding that that court's ruling in this respect should not be interfered with."

The Supreme Court re-affirmed the decision of the appeal court about two verbal statements which had been taken in breach of the Judges Rules. It rejected legal arguments that the gardai were not entitled to ask suspects any questions under the Offences Against the State Act other than to require an account of movements. Kelly's lawyers had argued that all answers or statements made by people in custody in reply to police questioning were, for that reason alone, involuntary. That objection was not sustainable, the Supreme Court ruled. It also upheld the appeal court's decision that Kelly had not been released unlawfully because he was released by a garda inspector and the other legal issues concerning the delay in taking him to court and the incorrect information on the extension order to hold him for another twenty four hours.

All the grounds of appeal failed and the judgement of the Court of Criminal Appeal was correct and should be upheld, the Supreme Court declared. Appeal dismissed.

There were shouts of "shame, shame" from the body of the court. Gardai and court officials looked about to see from where the disturbances were coming. O'Higgins ordered one of the protesters to be arrested and brought before him. The Chief Justice let the demonstrator off with a reprimand.

Kelly's protracted legal battle was now over. Since his appearance in the district court at the late night special sitting on April 7th 1976 he had travelled through every legal avenue to the Supreme Court. Two years and four months after returning to Ireland in the expectation of an early release, he was still in prison, facing at least another four years in jail.

His only hope now was his own resources and the efforts of his friends outside.

16

Release

The Supreme Court's decision not to quash Kelly's conviction had at least one positive effect as far as his supporters were concerned: they were now free to mount a full scale campaign on his behalf aimed at securing his release.

Prior to the judgement being delivered in October 1982, his friends had found it difficult to muster the widespread support which they wanted for him because many people were concerned that the case was still *sub judice*. In April, Kelly initiated a civil action against Ireland, the Attorney General and eighteen gardai whom he claimed were involved in his alleged ill-treatment while in custody. The gardai named in the action were Adrian O'Hara, Thomas Ibar Dunne, Michael Finn, James McPartlan, Kieran Lawlor, Thomas Boland, William Meagher, Thomas King, Patrick Rafferty, Joseph Egan, John Jordan, Felix McKenna, Patrick Culhane, Patrick Cleary, John McGroarty, Edward Ryan, Richard Murphy and Michael Mullen. The action was essentially the same one Seamus Costello had in mind in April 1976.

Kelly's friends were also anxious that nothing should be done by them between the hearing of the case and the delivery of the judgement which might damage his chances. Nonetheless, there was a slow, steady build up of interest during 1982 which was helped in no small part by the role of Tony Gregory, the independent socialist TD for Dublin Central. In March, Gregory had extracted a multi million pound deal for the city centre from the Fianna Fail leader, Charles Haughey, in return for supporting Haughey's nomination as Taoiseach. Haughey took power that month with the help of Gregory (and three Workers Party TDs). In return, more workers were hired by the city corporation and some city centre housing developments were also speeded up.

But Haughey's minority administration needed Gregory's almost constant support in parliament if it was to avoid defeat on a major economic issue. Gregory was therefore seen to occupy a position of considerable and continuing influence with the government. The socialist TD needed no persuading with regard to this case: he was convinced of Kelly's innocence. Like Kelly, Gregory was also a disciple of Seamus Costello who had been assassinated while sitting in his car in a Dublin side street in October 1977.

Gregory made a number of approaches to Haughey's Justice Minister, Sean Doherty, and pointed out to him that he had power to order Kelly's release. Doherty, according to Gregory, expressed concern at Kelly's continued imprisonment when Breatnach and McNally had been released. Doherty was unable to do anything however: he was kept busy with other matters. In August, Gregory became the first (and only) TD to visit Kelly in Portlaoise Prison. Permission for the visit was granted by the Department of Justice and Gregory said afterwards Kelly told him he would not serve twelve years in prison. The TD said he told Kelly he would go back to Doherty and press him further. He also said that he would approach Haughey.

The Release Nicky Kelly Committee was meanwhile organising small protests such as pickets on the Department of Justice or the Dail, but it was becoming increasingly anxious over the delay with the Supreme Court giving its judgement. Three days before the judgement was finally delivered in October, Amnesty International again expressed its concern that Kelly should be imprisoned solely on the basis of a confession extracted after a long period in police custody and that he should remain in prison when two others convicted with him were released on appeal.

Immediately after the Supreme Court published its judgement, Amnesty indicated continuing concern by announcing that it would be writing to the Irish government. The Irish Council for Civil Liberties publicly called for Kelly's release. The RTE morning radio programme, *Day By Day,* produced a powerful dramatisation of Kelly's trial by reading excerpts from the trial transcript. The broadcast provoked a protest from the Knights of Columbanus, the ultra conservative Catholic lay organisation, which complained that it helped "undermine and belittle the institutions of the state". RTE rejected the allegation.

Haughey's beleaguered government was under increasing strain that autumn and Gregory pressed Doherty once more. Early in December, shortly before leaving office after their general election defeat, the Kelly case was mentioned at a cabinet meeting by Doherty. With only days to go before the government went out of office, Doherty was told to report back with further information. As far as the Kelly Committee was concerned, this was in effect a refusal to release him. Gregory was not pleased: he had spoken to the Taoiseach and Haughey "gave the impression that Kelly should be released".

Kelly spent his third Christmas in Portlaoise.

Over the winter of 1982/1983, the committee began to seriously examine tactics for what looked like being a long drawn out campaign. There were no signs that the new government was about to act on the Kelly case: they had enough problems unravelling the previous administration's improper telephone tapping and preparing a budget acceptable to both parties in coalition. The committee decided that it would have to broaden its base of support and somehow counter the public perception of it as an IRSP front.

The committee decided that it would have to be independent of any other organisation and those who became involved would have to act as individuals. The campaign would be centered around Kelly and the belief in his innocence.

By spring 1983, they were able to claim the support of a number of individuals whose involvement significantly broadened the appeal of the campaign. They included priests, trade unionists, political activists and journalists. Among them were union representatives Des Bonass, Matt Merrigan, Michael Brennan, Phil Flynn, Noreen Green, Kevin McConnell and John Mitchell; Father Denis Faul, Father Desmond Wilson, Father Raymond Murray and

Father Piaras O Duill; journalists Desmond Fennell, Eamonn McCann, John Mulcahy, Con Houlihan and Vincent Browne; plus Kadar Asmal, the Trinity College law lecturer and anti-apartheid campaigner; Professor Ivor Browne, the psychiatrist; Robert Ballagh, the artist; Ulick O'Connor, the author; Christy Moore the folk singer; and Tony Gregory.

The committee aimed to get support from senior church figures, trades councils and local authorities around the country. A special "information package" was produced which included copies of press cuttings on the case, a chronology of events since the robbery in 1976, a letter from Des McGuinness seeking support, another from Caoilte Breatnach seeking sponsorship and two sample letters, one addressed to the new Justice Minister Michael Noonan, the other to the media, seeking Kelly's release and publicity for his cause. There was also an excerpt from the trial transcript quoting Kelly's allegations of assault by the gardai.

The lobbying for support soon began to show results. Trades councils and urban district councils passed motions expressing concern and calling for Kelly's release. The committee was loaned some space in offices used by the People's Democracy organisation in Dublin and, with the help of a borrowed typewriter, began to pump out letters, press releases and timetables of events organised to highlight Kelly's case. They also complained of undue attention by members of the Special Branch.

In Portlaoise Prison however, Nicky Kelly was becoming impatient and despairing of conventional lobbying ever showing results. The possibility of a hunger strike had been raised frequently since his return from the United States in June 1980 – so often in fact that many people not involved in the campaign for his release did not take the threat seriously. A fast had been mentioned most recently by his sister, Breda. She said immediately after the Supreme Court announced its decision in October 1982 she believed that if Kelly went on hunger strike, he would not come off it this time until he was released. It was not until Easter Monday, April 4th 1983, that he took the irrevocable step:

378

he announced through the committee that from May 1st he would refuse all food in support of his claim of innocence and demand to be released.

The Department of Justice doubted his resolve to stay on hunger strike to the bitter end. Officials feared, however, that he could back himself into a corner with no other way out. Their initial assessment was that Kelly didn't have the necessary determination to slowly kill himself in the manner of the republican prisoners in Northern Ireland two years previously. In the event, they were surprised he lasted so long.

By the time he began his fast, his cause had won support from trade and local councils in Wicklow, Roscommon, Longford, Tipperary and Clare. There were support groups in many parts of the country and others were highlighting his case in Australia, Canada, the US, France, England, Belgium, Holland and West Germany. In Ireland, however, there was little attention paid to the beginning of the hunger strike – the *Irish Times,* for instance, noted it with a one inch report on its front page. After ten days on hunger strike, Kelly's link with the campaign committee outside the prison was cut when the authorities refused to allow Caoilte Breatnach to visit him. Breatnach was PRO on the Kelly committee and had never previously been refused permission to see him. Kelly's other main visitors were members of his family and, as the fast progressed, he and they found visits distressing.

Breatnach got around the problem by visiting Father Vincent Forde who occupied a cell on the same landing as Kelly in E Wing. In March 1981, Forde was sentenced to twelve years for his part in a five man armed robbery of a bank in County Mayo. Forde was born in County Sligo and ordained a priest in 1968, after which he went to Albany in New York. He briefly returned to Ireland in 1971 and became emotionally caught up in the troubles in Northern Ireland. He was committed to the aims of the INLA and after his arrival in Portlaoise he joined the Socialist Republican Alliance. Later that year, the group split into two factions – SRA 1 and SRA 2 – the first of which was eventually led by Father Forde. SRA 2 was led by Harry

379

Flynn, the INLA man who nearly lost his life when a would-be assassin peppered him with a machine gun in a crowded pub one Saturday night. At the time of the hunger strike, Kelly was a member of the SRA 2 which the Department of Justice regarded as the more moderate of the two factions.

Breatnach was able to communicate effectively with Kelly through Father Forde but, as the hunger strike and campaign progressed, the committee's activities became more difficult. There were never enough volunteers to distribute posters around Dublin, not to mention distributing them around the country. People were also needed to write press statements, have them duplicated and sent around to the papers. And there was the need to have public meetings, and to organise pickets on certain government buildings.

At an earlier stage, some of Kelly's supporters had disfigured many prominent walls with "Free Nicky Kelly" slogans painted in white. They had to stop, however, when someone began adding underneath in neat letters "with every packet of Cornflakes". The slogans changed to "Release Nicky Kelly".

Politicians were not allowed to forget that Kelly was in prison, on hunger strike and protesting his innocence. On Sunday May 22nd, the Taoiseach, Garret FitzGerald, was in his Dublin constituency to open Sandymount community week. As he spoke to local people in Sandymount Green, Breatnach and others heckled him. Three of them were arrested and fined £2 each the following day and bound over to keep the peace for a year. But the campaign was having an effect. A few days later, sixty two solicitors from the Dublin area signed a petition asking Noonan to intervene and release Kelly. The solicitors said they were not criticising the courts but justice had not been seen to have been done in the Kelly case. The day after the solicitors' statement, Noonan made his first major comment on the case since the hunger strike began.

He spoke to political correspondents in Leinster House and said that seven of the most senior and distingushed judges in the country had examined Kelly's case. He said that he was not about to adjudicate on Kelly's guilt or innocence; he would not set himself up as a court. However, he indicated that his mind was not completely closed. He said that if anyone came forward with new evidence on the case, matters could be reconsidered in a new light. Noonan's basic position was that if he released Kelly now, it could only be interpreted as a snub on the courts. He said that Kelly was taking salt and drinking Perrier water; his health would not be damaged if he ended his fast now.

The committee reacted by accusing Noonan of continuing "to ignore the facts surrounding the original arrest and detention" of Kelly in 1976. They said that Noonan was responsible for seeing that justice was done and accused the government of "sentencing Nicky Kelly to death".

Behind the scenes, however, there were other moves to try to bring the fast to an end. The Irish Commission for Justice and Peace attempted to act as mediators between Kelly and the Department of Justice. The ICJP was set up by the Catholic Church and had become deeply involved in attempts to settle the Maze Prison hunger strike in Northern Ireland two years previously. The commission's efforts were unsuccessful on that occasion but members could at least bring some experience to bear on the Kelly case. The president of the ICJP was Bishop Dermot O'Mahony.

The Department of Justice refused to concede any status to the Kelly committee because some people involved with it were also associated with subversives. The ICJP on the other hand was able to talk to both sides. On June 1st (Kelly's thirty second day without food), the commission issued a lengthy statement suggesting that Kelly take his case to Europe and that Noonan re-examine his own position, bearing in mind the situation which existed in the country at the time of Kelly's arrest and interrogation by the gardai.

The statement said that the European Commission and Court of Human Rights could "play a benign and positive part in securing a friendly solution acceptable to both parties". Applicants to the European Court had to initiate proceedings within six months of domestic legal remedies having been exhausted. In Kelly's case this meant the Supreme Court judgement of October 1982: an application to the European Commission would have had to be made by April 29th 1983. The ICJP statement said, however, that an application could be made "at any time if a continuing disability is complained of."

The possibility of referring the case to the European Commission of Human Rights was further explored in talks between committttee members and the ICJP leaders. They indicated that the government would not oppose an application on the grounds that it was several months late. The Kelly committee consulted lawyers about the mechanics of applying and the length of time, nine months, that it could take for a preliminary decision. The ICJP also pointed out in these discussions that the human rights commission had a procedure for a "friendly settlement" of disputes and might be able to provide an umbrella for such a resolution of Nicky Kelly's case.

The ICJP was playing a pivotal role, talking to department officials and to the committee. What was the committee's basic demand? the ICJP men inquired at one meeting. Kelly's release, the committee members replied. The ICJP men returned to the committee after meeting the department officials: Kelly's release was not possible, they reported.

The meetings and indirect negotiations were eventually brought to a peremptory end by the Department of Justice. Previous experience in the Republic and what Southern officials viewed as the disastrous handling of the H Blocks hunger strikes in Northern Ireland had left the Department with strong views on how to deal with hunger strikes. Firstly, there would be no concessions while a hunger strike was in progress. Secondly, the person on hunger strike needed to be told clearly that there was no prospect of his action ending in immediate success.

The officials believed that intermediaries only served to cloud this second point. Mediators kept alive hopes of an agreement and served to prolong rather than resolve the fast, they thought. For these reasons they decided to cut off all indirect communications.

The protests at home over Kelly's plight were mirrored by protests abroad. In the United States and Canada, pickets were placed on offices of Irish agencies. In Denmark, two members of parliament presented President Patrick Hillery with a letter calling for Kelly's release. The protest, on behalf of two small left-wing parties, was given a frosty reception by Peter Barry, the Minister for Foreign Affairs who was accompanying the President on his official visit. Barry complained that the Danish groups were interfering in internal Irish affairs.

On June 3rd, the deputy secretary general of Amnesty International, José Zalaquett, wrote a detailed letter to Michael Noonan about the case, after the Minister had refused to meet its representatives. It said that doubts about Kelly's conviction remained on two grounds: first, in relation to Kelly's allegations of ill-treatment and, second, in relation to the standard of law by which his confession was accepted as the sole basis for convicting him, even though it had been made after prolonged and exhausting questioning. Uncontested medical evidence was consistent with Kelly's allegations of ill-treatment. The question of lack of injuries from the chair incident – which the courts saw as an inconsistency in Kelly's account – was not conclusive.

Three other inmates of the jail heard screams at the relevant time. His girlfriend also testified to hearing screams. There were widespread allegations of ill-treatment relating to the period of his arrest and involving some of the same police officers. Amnesty said that the lack of access to a solicitor or other witnesses was an obstacle to verification of allegations of ill-treatment. The superior courts had not addressed themselves to the issue of the remand by the district court to the Bridewell which, to say the least, was not conducive to subsequent determination of the truth. Serious doubt remained about Kelly's treatment, the letter said.

It went on to question the legal definition of "oppressive" interrogation. The Court of Criminal Appeal did not address the question of the length of Kelly's interrogation, did not apply the standard laid down in the Shaw case. The Supreme Court did not comment on the issue. Neither did the Minister for Justice in his central statement during the hunger strike.

Amnesty said that it was in the light of these elements of doubt that it had written to Noonan on December 16th 1982 to express concern about the standards applied for accepting confessions as evidence. In the light of the same elements of doubt, it now urged Noonan to take "remedial action".

On May 27th, Kelly was moved from Portlaoise prison to the hospital in the Curragh military camp where, as a government announcement put it, medical care could be provided more easily if and when the need arose. He was surviving on Perrier water and salt but was weakening considerably. Kelly's sister, Breda, visited him but was only allowed to see him through a security grill. Complaints were made to Noonan about this subsequently and it was removed for future visits.

In early June, a priest from Limerick telephoned Caoilte Breatnach and told him that Michael Noonan wanted to speak to him about the hunger strike. The priest gave him a telephone number which turned out to be a direct line to the Minister's office. Breatnach told the person who answered of his reason for calling and that he would only meet the Minister with another committee member present. The official called him back later and told Breatnach that Kelly wanted to see him: would he go down to the Curragh? Breatnach said he would but that he was not going to ask Kelly to come off the hunger strike. He would tell Kelly what the situation was as the committee saw it.

On June 4th, he set off to meet Kelly. Garret Sheehan, a solicitor and one of Dublin's most prominent criminal lawyers, was due to see Kelly with him and they arranged to meet at the hospital in the Curragh. On the way, Breatnach's car broke down on the Naas dual carriageway: he left it there and hitch-hiked. He got a lift from a man with a dog who also picked up another hitch-hiker who turned out to be a soldier returning to the Curragh. The man dropped both of them at the back gate to the military camp and Breatnach just walked in.

Inside the gate, however, two military policemen stopped him and asked him where he was going. There was some pandemonium when he said he was going to see Kelly. He was held in a room for about forty minutes until a jeep came to collect him and bring him to the hospital. He and Garret Sheehan were searched and then brought to see Kelly. They passed through a doorway that had a steel grill, walked past armed soldiers and sandbagged positions and through another doorway with both steel bars and wire grill.

Inside, the room was very hot. It was furnished with a bed, a table and a chair. Nicky Kelly was sitting at the table, propped up with pillows. To Caoilte Breatnach, who had not seen him since the tenth day of his fast, he looked terrible. His body had shrunk, his bones appeared to be sticking out and his face was thin and very grey. By this stage, Kelly was having occasional black-outs and was spending all his time either in bed or in a wheelchair. His body seemed, almost paradoxically, to become heavier as he lost more weight and his legs felt unable to support him.

He had found that visits from his family were the most difficult part of the protest. They were upset by his gradually deteriorating condition and he, in turn, was upset by their distress. But he firmly believed that something would give as a result of the hunger strike, that it would act as a moral pressure either on the government or on some member of the Garda Siochana who would come forward and substantiate Kelly's account of his interrogation. There was no sign that such a development was imminent.

Caoilte Breatnach and Garret Sheehan set out the situation as they saw it. They talked in detail about an application to the European Commission of Human Rights, explaining to Kelly the prospects and procedures involved. Kelly said he wanted to think about it. Breatnach and Sheehan visited him again the following day and Kelly told Sheehan to initiate an application with the commission. He told them that he would continue with his hunger strike, however: the case could continue posthumously if needs be.

The problem seemed to have reached an impasse. All

communications with would-be mediators, concerned groups and individuals had been cut off by the Department of Justice. Kelly had looked at the legal advice surrounding an appeal to the human rights commission and decided to lodge an application. But he had also decided to continue his fast.

Breatnach travelled down to the Curragh again. It was the thirty eighth day of his hunger strike and McCartan wanted him to sign his will. Kelly was still lucid and alert and the three of them had what turned out to be a lengthy discussion. Breatnach told Kelly it was his impression that the government was going to let him die. Time was not on the side of Kelly or his supporters: he felt that much more public support could be produced if they had more time. People close to the government maintained that nothing could be done while the hunger strike lasted. Breatnach and McCartan insisted that more could be done if he stayed alive. If he died, the human rights commission case would die with him and there was a greater chance that his name would never be cleared.

Kelly played the devil's advocate, propped up with cushions, sipping Perrier water and licking salt from his finger. About 9.30 pm he reached his decision.

"It's over," he said. They all broke down in tears.

McCartan told an army doctor of Kelly's decision and Breatnach rang the committee's temporary office to tell his colleagues that the hunger strike was finished. They had some news for him as well. The government had also issued a statement that legal avenues in the form of a civil action were still open to Kelly. No obstacle had been put in Kelly's way by the prison authorities to his taking such an action, the statement said. If such an action was successful it would be relevant, even if only indirectly, to his imprisonment, the statement added.

Kelly knew nothing about this government statement until he heard it on radio the following morning. Next day both Caoilte Breatnach and Michael Noonan denied that there had been any deals behind Kelly's decision. But a view persisted among some campaign supporters that an agreement had been reached. That would present some problems for the committee in coming months as they tried to maintain interest in Kelly's case.

The case was back again in legal hands. The immediate upshot of his hunger strike was that Nicky Kelly ended up with two new sets of lawyers to pursue his two new legal battles. Greg O'Neill, a former Labour Party activist who switched allegiance to Fianna Fail and specialised in his legal practice in what he liked to term "ball breaker" cases, was the solicitor in charge of the civil action. With him was Tony Sammon, the barrister who had been involved in the mail train case since the second court appearance of Nicky Kelly and three others in Dublin District Court on Thursday, April 8th 1976. The solicitor in the European case was Garret Sheehan. He was backed up by two barristers with particular academic credentials: Mary Robinson, a Labour Party member of the Senate and constitutional expert who had specialised in taking cases to Europe, and Kevin Boyle, a professor of law at University College, Galway and a barrister who had been deeply involved in the initial civil rights movement in Northern Ireland in the late 1960s.

Both cases proceeded quickly at first. A successful application to the High Court allowed Kelly to save time by serving documents on the state during the long summer vacation. Since April 1982, summonses had been issued against Ireland, the Attorney General and eighteen named members of the Garda Siochana. On July 27th 1983, however, the names of the gardai were dropped from the summonses: the case was to proceed against Ireland and the Attorney General.

Greg O'Neill also decided to look into the possibility of sending a petition to the Minister for Justice appealing for clemency. He wrote to Michael Noonan to ask if he would be willing to receive such a plea. Noonan's secretary replied that it was open to any convicted person to petition the Minister at any time: if Kelly petitioned him, it would be considered in the normal way.

Kelly was not wildly enthusiastic about petitioning the Minister only on medical grounds – what O'Neill had in mind – because he did not want to be released for those reasons alone. His primary aim was to clear his name and win recognition for his contention that he had been ill-treated, forced to sign a confession and wrongly convicted and jailed. Kelly insisted on some changes in the approach but preparations for a petition went ahead.

The initial progress in the civil case soon faltered. The state failed to meet the deadline in October for its reply to Kelly's case. A strange haggle then began over attempts by Kelly's lawyers to have him examined by an ear specialist in order to build up evidence for his court case. O'Neill informed the Department of Justice that an appointment had been made for Kelly at the Royal Victoria Eye and Ear Hospital in Dublin on November 11th. No reply was received from the Department and the appointment had to be cancelled. Days later, however, a reply came from the Department dated November 1st but with its envelope postmarked November 15th. It said that Kelly would be taken to the hospital if the Department was given an undertaking that the costs of the transport and security detail would be paid by him within fourteen days of being presented with a bill.

O'Neill protested strenuously in a further letter. He argued that this examination was required for legal purposes and was clearly associated with Kelly's right of access to the courts under the constitution. The demand for payment amounted to an obstruction of his rights of access to the courts. The Department replied in due course that it did not accept any responsibility for the delay in the delivery of its previous letter. It said that it only accepted costs for such medical examinations where they were required by the prison medical staff. The cost of taking Kelly to the Eye and Ear Hospital would range between £800 and £1,200, depending on the amount of security required at the time. The money need not be repaid until after the civil case was heard, the Department now said. By the end of January 1984, however, the official view changed and the medical appointment was arranged without any further demands for money.

That dispute had delayed the preparations of Kelly's case but it eventually got into the High Court for a hearing on a preliminary issue in May 1984. The state argued before Mr Justice Liam Hamilton – the presiding judge at the Special Criminal Court trial almost six years earlier – that the civil action should not go ahead. The state case was simply that the issues involved – including the alleged ill-treatment of Kelly – had already been decided in the criminal trial before the Special Criminal Court. The point at issue was the higher standard of proof required in criminal cases than in civil cases: a criminal court had to decide something *beyond reasonable doubt* while a civil court had to make its judgement on *the balance of probabilities*. If a trial court had decided, therefore, that something was beyond reasonable doubt then a civil action could not try the issue again.

Kelly's lawyers countered that the state should not be allowed to argue this case because of the government statement issued at the end of the hunger strike which invited Kelly to litigate these issues. In addition, the state had failed in July 1983 to raise any objection to the summonses, leaving Kelly to believe that there would be no objections to having the case proceed. Justice Hamilton ordered that arrangements be made for the High Court to decide this issue without a jury.

As the civil action slowed into these legal issues in May 1984, Kelly also learned that his appeal to the European Commission of Human Rights had failed as well. It had been ruled out of order because it was not lodged within six months of the Supreme Court hearing in Ireland in October 1982. The Irish government had told the commission that it would not oppose a hearing but the commission declared that it was not up to the government to waive this rule. It decided that Kelly had not substantiated his claim that his mental state rendered him incapable of lodging a complaint within six months.

It added: "In reaching this conclusion it observes that the applicant in fact lodged his application on the 38th day of a hunger strike when it might be expected, if his account was to be accepted, that his mood and depressive state would be even less conducive, as compared to previous months, to contemplating legal proceedings... Accordingly an examination of the case does not disclose the existence of any special circumstances which might have interrupted or suspended the running of the six month period."

The court never considered the case put to the commission by both sides. Kelly's lawyers had argued that his rights under Articles 3 and 6 of the European Convention on Human Rights had been violated, that there had been a miscarriage of justice and that Kelly was entitled to adequate compensation.

Kelly's lawyers submitted that Article 6 had been broken because the conditions required for a fair trial were not present and because the Article was breached at all stages of his prosecution, conviction and appeal. The police investigation was designed to extract a confession; Kelly's ordinary rights as an accused person were reduced by emergency powers; he was compelled by the law to incriminate himself; he was held incommunicado without access to lawyers or doctors or independent advice for three days; he was denied adequate rest and food.

They also argued that the Special Criminal Court was not an independent and impartial tribunal established by law because it was created by the Offences Against the State Act. Members of the court did not have to be judges and, in Kelly's case, one was a retired judge. He no longer had judicial status nor was he subject to the judicial oath, Kelly's lawyers argued: he was in fact a government employee appointed to the court. (The lawyers were wrong on this point if the person they had in mind was Justice Cathal O Floinn: he continued to serve on the Special Criminal Court after he retired but he had not retired at the time of Kelly's trial.)

They added that the court had offended the principle of equality and the presumption of innocence by holding that his injuries were self-inflicted or inflicted by his co-accused. The court decided this without any evidence to support it from the prosecution.

The government responded that the constitution allowed the establishment of special courts and that the decisions of the Special Criminal Court could be appealed in the same way as those of the Central Criminal Court. The ordinary rules of evidence applied.

The government also claimed that there were radical differences between the cases of McNally and Breatnach on the one hand and Kelly on the other. The state, in one of those quirks of legal argument, found itself stoutly pointing up the flaws uncovered in the McNally and Breatnach cases. In McNally's case, no written statement was tendered in evidence and, in Breatnach's case, written and verbal statements followed questioning in the menacing atmosphere of an underground passage and were inconsistent with his previous conduct during detention. In Kelly's case, however, the state argued, the pattern was of a person who eventually decided to co-operate with the gardai with whom he admitted friendliness. He had not availed of the opportunity to complain of his treatment to his girlfriend or to the district court.

Kelly's lawyers compared in detail the similarities between his case and Breatnach's in particular and maintained that the cases were identical. They said that the rules and precedents about the admissibility of evidence were applied differently in Kelly's case. The appeal court in Breatnach's case had mentioned the Madden case in saying that it had to accept the findings of the trial court. Yet, it had decided that there was oppression in Breatnach's case. In Kelly's case, the appeal court appeared to decide that the issue of oppression formed part of the facts of the case and therefore could not be examined because of the Madden precedent. In Breatnach's case, the appeal court had applied the test of voluntariness set out in the Shaw case: that case was not even considered in relation to Kelly.

Four factors had been found in Breatnach's case to amount to oppression. There were his unexplained change of attitude after forty hours in custody; the questioning in the underground passageway; the time (5.20 am) and the disturbance of his much needed sleep; the failure to follow up his request for a solicitor.

In Kelly's case, his lawyers maintained, there were four comparable elements. Kelly's change of attitude was equally dramatic after a similar period; he was interrogated in a sergeants' locker room; his statement was made in the small hours of the morning and he had not had any rest at all; Kelly, unlike Breatnach, had been unable to prove that he had asked for a solicitor.

They maintained that fairness required the Court of Criminal Appeal and the Supreme Court to consider Kelly's case in the light of the other two. The Supreme Court, in allowing Kelly a late appeal, had noted the similarities in the cases. But his case was then treated in isolation when the appeal was heard. The appeal court should have reasoned its decision by reference to the differences between the cases as there was a presumption that the same factors applied to Kelly. Its failure to justify the different decision amounted to arbitrariness, they argued.

Kelly's case that his treatment breached Article 3 was based on the contention that an unfair trial constituted inhuman treatment when the effects on his personality were considered. Compelling someone to incriminate himself by giving an account of movements under Section 52 of the Offences Against the State Act and to convict someone on the basis of statements made after that also amounted to inhuman or degrading treatment. Kelly's case under this article revolved around the issue of a fair trial, his lawyers stressed.

All their arguments were not formally considered. When the commission decided that there was no reason to extend the time limit to hear the case, it put an end to it. One of Kelly's new legal avenues had been closed off.

The ending of the hunger strike and the opening up of two new legal avenues for Kelly to explore had posed problems for the Release Nicky Kelly Committee. Nicky Kelly ceased again to be a major news story and some of his supporters believed that a deal had been done and that his release was agreed. The committee members had to work hard to maintain the high level of interest that the fast had concentrated into several weeks. They succeeded quite well.

Letters continued to be written, pickets were mounted on Portlaoise prison, the Department of Justice and on the homes of the Taoiseach, Garret FitzGerald, and the

392

Minister for Justice, Michael Noonan. Tony Gregory explained Kelly's plight to interested political and human rights groups during a twelve day visit to the United States in the autumn of 1983. Local councils in several parts of Ireland passed motions calling for his release.

At the end of October 1983 they produced what they thought was a significant card. John Fitzpatrick, the fifth man who had been charged with the robbery back in 1976, came out of hiding to give his story. Like Kelly, he had also signed a statement confessing to the robbery; he was also named in the statement signed by Kelly as one of the main participants in the crime. Fitzpatrick told a press conference in Dublin on October 31st that he had signed the statement only because of the beatings and ill-treatment: "It got to the stage where I just couldn't take it anymore," he said.

The significance of Fitzpatrick's experience did not lie in the similarity of his accounts of brutality with Kelly's. It lay in the fact that he had one of the strongest alibis. He and Michael Barrett (the sixth man originally charged with the robbery) had driven to Limerick on March 30th 1976, the day before the robbery. They had stayed that night in the home of a friend, Tom Hayes, in Castleconnell and returned to Dublin the following day. Hayes, his wife Betty and his brother John all swore affidavits to the effect that Fitzpatrick and Barrett had stayed in their house that night and had been there for breakfast in the morning.

No one at the press conference, however, was aware of the full significance of Fitzpatrick's case. In the winter of 1976, when he was considering whether or not to proceed with the charges against the six men accused of the robbery, the Director of Public Prosecutions had given a great deal of consideration to Fitzpatrick's alibi. The gardai maintained that Fitzpatrick would have had time to appear to go to bed in Limerick, get up, drive to County Kildare, rob the train and return to the Hayes house before breakfast. If Fitzpatrick's alibi was true then he could not have robbed the train: furthermore, if Fitzpatrick could not have robbed the train how did Nicky Kelly and Brian McNally come to name him in their statements?

In deciding what to do, the DPP's office thought it best to leave this conflict to be resolved in court. It was decided not to proceed with the charge against Barrett as the only evidence against him appeared to be that he was with Fitzpatrick: he had not confessed to anything. The gardai were instructed to charge all the others: Fitzpatrick, Kelly, McNally, Breatnach and Michael Plunkett in the Special Criminal Court.

But Fitzpatrick had gone underground before that could be done. He decided to disappear as soon as the district court dropped all the charges on December 9th 1976. When the others were re-arrested on December 17th Fitzpatrick was not to be found. Thus, a central consideration in deciding to bring the case back to court was never adjudicated on by the Special Criminal Court. Fitzpatrick's alibi could not be put before the court because he himself was not on trial.

Fitzpatrick spent most of his time in Dublin, going abroad for brief periods with the help of a false passport. For most of his first year on the run he remained indoors but emerged gradually to do casual work and make some money. As a wanted man, he could not sign on the dole and had no source of income. He grew a beard and kept away from his previous haunts. He had several near escapes but succeeded in evading capture.

On one occasion, he was walking along a Dublin suburban road when he became aware of several detectives in an unmarked car watching him. The car slowed down to a walking pace as they took a good look at him. He turned away towards some shops and walked into the nearest building, a bank. One of the detectives followed him in. Fitzpatrick stood at a desk and filled out a money lodgement form while the detective hovered nearby. Fitzpatrick wrote down a false name that he made up on the spur of the moment. The detective read it over his shoulder and left the bank. Fitzpatrick continued on his own way.

His re-appearance and the renewed interest in the case because of the application to the European Commission of Human Rights caused questions to be asked in official circles. The senior gardai involved in the investigation who were still in the force were brought to a meeting with the DPP, Eamonn Barnes, to explain why the 1976 instruction to charge Fitzpatrick had not been compiled with. Decisions had to be made on whether or not the directive should be implemented now.

Superintendent Ned Ryan led the group of gardai into the DPP's office for a re-run of the consultation they had had almost exactly seven years before. Chief Superintendent John Joy who had led them previously had since retired and died. Superintendent Patrick Casey was still attached to the Central Detective Unit but he was not present at the meeting.

Discussion ranged over the whole case again, concentrating on Fitzpatrick's alibi. The garda view had not changed in relation to Fitzpatrick: in spite of everything that had happened since 1976 they wanted Fitzpatrick charged now. They were quite happy to go through another trial with Fitzpatrick in the dock. No decision was taken at the meeting. Afterwards, Eamonn Barnes reviewed the entire file on the case, including the appeal court judgement in the cases of Brian McNally and Osgur Breatnach. He decided eventually that John Fitzpatrick should not be brought to trial in the light of all the circumstances.

The decision, as is normal practice, was not announced.

Meanwhile, the supporters of Nicky Kelly pinned their hopes for his release on John Fitzpatrick's public statements at his press conference. They maintained that this constituted the "new evidence" that Michael Noonan had deemed to be necessary before he could review the case. Tony Gregory tabled a special notice question in the Dail asking the Minister if he considered this development to be the required new evidence. The question was disallowed on the grounds that it was not an urgent matter and it took its turn on the normal list of questions to Ministers. Noonan eventually rejected Fitzpatrick's disclosures as being new: he said that the lawyers involved in the trial would have known all about the Fitzpatrick story.

By then, Greg O'Neill had finalised his plans for a petition to the Minister from Kelly appealing for clemency.

The formal document was sworn in Portlaoise prison on October 29th in the presence of O'Neill and Tony Sammon. It set out the details of his conviction and said that Kelly "does pray that the sentence of twelve years of penal servitude... be commuted or remitted as to the balance thereof remaining due to be served". It said that the petition was based on several things, including O'Neill's previous letters to Noonan and "the nature and circumstances of the case and the reasons to be offered".

The petition was submitted to Noonan on November 1st along with a report from O'Neill and details from medical reports supplied by two doctors, Dr Sean O'Cleirigh and a psychiatrist, Professor Robert Daly. O'Neill noted in his report that some details were of a forensic nature to be used in Kelly's civil action and might be contentious. These had been omitted from the reports. He also noted that appointments were being made for Kelly with an eye specialist and an ear specialist (the appointment which was about to cause a flurry of angry letters).

The extracts from Dr O'Cleirigh's report said that Kelly complained of soreness in both eyes and blurred vision and he recommended that a specialist examine him. He found limits on Kelly's ability to move his head, his hips and his knees which indicated that he would probably suffer from arthritis in later life. A tenderness in one of the chest muscles had persisted for some time and was likely to lead to some disability in later life. Kelly's left ear was painful and he complained of numbness in the ear and on the left side of his face and dizziness or vertigo.

Dr O'Cleirigh said that Kelly complained of nervousness, lack of self confidence, anxiety, lack of energy, insomnia and headaches which the doctor thought included features of stress. All these factors affecting Kelly's health related to his imprisonment and were perpetuated and intensified by the continuing and unique circumstances of his present imprisonment, Dr O'Cleirigh said.

Dr Daly said Kelly had been suffering from post traumatic stress disorder since he had first seen him in June 1980. In June 1983 he had found that this condition resulted from the imposition of severe emotional stress.

Among its effects were a depressed mood, feeling hopeless and pessimistic. It particularly altered his perception and judgement, not least because of Kelly's experience of the legal process. He had little interest in caring for himself and in his general welfare which ultimately resulted in his embarking on a serious hunger strike.

The arrival of Kelly's formal petition was not accompanied by any sudden change of heart in the Department of Justice.

The Release Nicky Kelly Committee managed to return to a high level of activity by the end of the year. They celebrated the arrival of 1984 by taking advantage of a special postal offer to mark the changeover of responsibility for the post office from a government department to a semi-state body. They posted 750 letters about the Kelly case at a penny each, saving themselves £187.50 on the normal postage.

Committee members concentrated their lobbying efforts on the Catholic Church, trade unions and two political parties, Fianna Fail and the Labour Party. In January, they wrote to every Catholic bishop, seeking support on the basis of the previous year's statement from the church body, the Irish Commission for Justice and Peace. Either as a result of their efforts or otherwise, only one bishop expressed his concern publicly about the case. Bishop James Kavanagh, the auxiliary bishop of Dublin, suggested that investigation and questioning procedures in 1976 would have been different had the recommendations proposed by Judge Barra O Briain's committee been in force.

Cardinal Tomas O Fiaich also maintained his interest in the case in private. He wrote to the Minister in June suggesting that the time was ripe to release Kelly.

The committee and Kelly himself tried hard to point up parallels between his situation and that of an Irish missionary priest, Father Niall O'Brien, who was awaiting trial on a murder charge in the Philippines. The Irish government and church had been deeply involved in a campaign for his release along with his co-accused, an Australian priest, Father Brian Gore, and six local people.

397

In a letter to the media, Kelly said that he, like Father O'Brien, had been framed and subjected to lengthy delays before coming to trial for offences which had been claimed by organisations of which they were not members. He accused the Irish government of hypocrisy for criticising the Philippines government while using the same excuses. The Irish government had also refused to meet representatives of Amnesty International and told foreigners who protested that it was an internal matter.

Father O'Brien was eventually released by the authorities in the Philippines and returned to Ireland to a warm welcome from both the state and the Catholic church in mid-July. It was obvious, the committee noted, that political pressure had secured his release and part of that pressure had been applied by the Irish government.

The Labour Party also proved sympathetic to Kelly's plight. Its annual conference in April passed a motion calling for his release. The resolution, drafted with the help of the Kelly committee, noted the considerable public disquiet about the case, the accepted fact that suspects were ill-treated at the time and maintained that the "new evidence" required by the Minister had been made available.

Committee members were also active at the Fianna Fail ard fheis during which the secretary, Siobhan Troddyn, saw and took an opportunity to make their point on television. In the midst of the presidential speech to the conference by the party leader Charles Haughey, she got onto the platform and walked towards him calling for Kelly's release. She was halfway across the platform before security men halted her and took her away.

Tony Gregory later arranged a meeting for committee members with Haughey who questioned them about the case. His personal contacts within the Garda Siochana had told him Kelly was guilty, he said: the courts had also gone through the case. He wanted to be convinced before Fianna Fail would change its attitude. A second meeting was arranged and held just before the Dail broke up for its summer recess.

Meanwhile, Michael Noonan had changed his mind. He

was giving serious consideration to the Kelly case and sounding out opinion discreetly.

A copy of Kelly's petition received the previous November had been sent to the medical officer in Portlaoise prison for his comments. The Department had also had an eye specialist examine Kelly in October 1983: he reported that there was no damage to the optic nerve and he recommended a course of vitamin treatment. Officials also asked Kelly if he would see a psychiatrist nominated by them. He referred them to Greg O'Neill. They did not put the request to O'Neill: they did not want either Kelly or his lawyers to know that they were looking into his petition.

Kelly's petition was not shown to the gardai and neither was the judiciary asked for its opinion. Discussions within the Department of Justice progressed at a leisurely pace throughout the early year and spring. Michael Noonan had been discreetly sounding out opinion and was impressed at the number of people whose views on other matters he respected who were expressing serious reservations about Kelly's imprisonment. These people were not necessarily saying to Noonan that Kelly was innocent but they impressed upon him that they had serious doubts about the whole case. Noonan had also become concerned at the number of young people of moderate views who, out of genuine concern, had become involved in the Kelly campaign. He feared that this involvement was bringing them into contact with other people who had connections with subversive groups.

By early summer, he had decided that he would order Kelly's release: it was now in the public interest to do so. The only question that remained was when to do it. He was determined to avoid a situation where Kelly's release could be interpreted as a response to any pressure at that particular moment. Thus it could not be done if there was a hunger strike, a peak in the campaign or pressure in the Dail.

On Wednesday, July 11th, he again discussed the problem with his departmental secretary, Andy Ward, and several other officials including Dermot Cole of the prisons section and Ken O'Leary, his private secretary. Between the three of them, they had discussed the case on and off for several weeks. Noonan told them he was going to let Kelly out: the time was right. Once having made the decision, he felt that he had to inform the cabinet. The next meeting was in six days time on Tuesday, July 17th, and the release would have to be delayed until then.

On the morning of the cabinet meeting, he told Garret FitzGerald that he was going to order Kelly's release. The Taoiseach agreed with the move. Just before the meeting, he approached Tanaiste Dick Spring in an ante room off the cabinet room. Could Spring deliver Labour's four votes in favour of Kelly's release? Noonan asked. Spring said he could. When the time came, the subject was not on the agenda for the cabinet meeting. As Noonan brought it up, some of his colleagues seemed taken aback. He made it clear that, in the final analysis, the decision was his but he still wanted to get the views of other Ministers. The discussion lasted well over an hour.

Feelings were far from unanimous. Initially, there appeared to be a clear majority in favour of release. Few speakers declared outright opposition but a significant number expressed doubts and unease. The man recognised by everyone as the main opponent of such a move, Defence Minister Patrick Cooney, was not there. Indeed, his absence itself became an issue. Some of his supporters on the Kelly question suspected that Noonan had timed his move in the knowledge that Cooney was inspecting troops in the west of Ireland. They felt that any decision should be put off until Cooney was present. Foreign Minister Peter Barry and Agriculture Minister Austin Deasy were also absent.

Three main points of view were expressed. There were those who supported Noonan and agreed that Kelly should be released now. There were the opponents of such action and there were others who wanted the decision deferred for further discussion.

Those in favour of release were FitzGerald, Spring and the Labour Party ministers, Ruairi Quinn, Liam Kavanagh and Barry Desmond (although Desmond *spoke* against release), Gemma Hussey and Noonan. Spring who was a barrister by profession had taken a close interest in the whole mail train case. He had asked a couple of his legal friends to analyse Kelly's case and give him some advice. Spring had come to the view many months earlier that Kelly should be out of prison.

Among those against releasing Kelly was the Attorney General Peter Sutherland. He feared that Kelly's release would be interpreted as a criticism of the courts and would undermine the rule of law. He had recently been confronted in an unexpected context with the Kelly issue. He had been in Harvard University speaking on the subject of Ireland's legal responses to terrorism. In a question and answer session afterwards, he was taken to task about Kelly's case by several of the audience. As the government's legal advisor, Sutherland's opinion would be expected to carry weight. Also opposed to release were Finance Minister Alan Dukes, Trade Minister John Bruton, and Public Service Minister John Boland.

In essence, the arguments in favour of release were practical. The time was right, there was no particular pressure on the government, thus providing an opportunity to dispose of the Kelly problem before it resurfaced. For Noonan and those who believed Kelly should be released, it was an ideal opportunity.

The opponents of release rested their case on the fear that it would damage the judicial system. They pointed out that umpteen judges had considered his case and it was not for the government to dispute their conclusions. Two ministers were unable to make up their minds: former Justice Minister Jim Mitchell and Gaeltacht Minister Paddy O'Toole.

Some of those who appeared undecided were willing to accept Kelly's release if it was on the grounds of ill-health. But Noonan made it clear that Kelly was not eligible for this consideration – in fact it was known that Kelly went jogging in the prison exercise yard every day.

The discussion was brought to a conclusion when Noonan made it clear that he had made his decision. Any postponement could lead to renewed pressure if word got out that release was being considered. There was no formal vote but a straw poll indicated a majority in favour. Noonan left the meeting and got word to his officials to set the release in motion.

A letter was sent by hand to Kelly's solicitor, Greg O'Neill, telling him that immediate release had been authorised in response to the petition. The letter noted that the application for clemency had been made without any reference to the validity, correctness or propriety in law of Kelly's conviction. A press statement made up of four sentences was prepared to confirm Kelly's release on "humanitarian grounds" following a petition. Arrangements were also made for someone to drive from Shelton Abbey, an open prison, to Kelly's home town of Arklow nearby to tell his mother that he would be coming home shortly.

Nicky Kelly himself had been locked up in his cell in Portlaoise Prison for the night. He was taken out again and told that he was being transferred to Shelton Abbey. He knew it was an open prison: his father once worked on its estate for the Department of Forestries. Handcuffed to a prison officer in the back seat of a taxi, he left Portlaoise not knowing exactly what was happening. On the way, he heard a news bulletin in Irish on the car radio saying that he had been released. He asked the driver to stop and let him out but the prison officer said he had to go on to Shelton Abbey to be released formally from there.

Meanwhile, on his way back from the west of Ireland, Patrick Cooney was listening to the same radio news bulletin. He couldn't believe his ears and made straight for the nearest telephone to contact his colleagues who were still at their cabinet meeting in Dublin. When his call came through, someone was dispatched to explain to the Defence Minister why the decision was taken. Cooney left them in no doubt of his views. Afterwards, he and others who opposed the release maintained the decision would have been different had all Ministers been present. But no one attempted to raise the matter at cabinet again.

By the time Cooney's view was relayed to his colleagues, Kelly had arrived in Shelton Abbey where he was asked to prove his identity before he was finally set free.

For the first time in five and a half years, Kelly returned openly to his parents' home. It was four years and six weeks since he had returned from the United States to Portlaoise Prison.

He left prison as he had entered it, protesting his innocence and determined to clear his name.

17

Findings

Nicky Kelly was free but he was still a convicted train robber.The campaign for his release had succeeded but he had failed in his attempt to clear his name. He had appealed in every possible way through every available court. All but one of the Supreme Court's six judges and more than half of the High Court's fifteen judges had considered his case in some form or other by the time of his release. All of them had confirmed the original conviction and sentence by the Special Criminal Court.

Kelly appeared to have fallen into the legal equivalent of a black hole in space, an area from which nothing can escape. He seemed to be trapped by court procedures, legal practices, inconsistencies and judicial findings of fact. Even in the final appeal body open to him, the European Commission of Human Rights, he was thwarted by a procedural point: his application had not been lodged within the normal time limit.

Kelly had fallen foul of the same approach with the Court of Criminal Appeal on his return to Ireland from the United States. The Supreme Court overturned the appeal court's decision to prevent him from appealing, partly on the grounds that Kelly's co-accused had been cleared by the same court. Yet in the final appeals Kelly's case had to stand on its own: the experiences of his co-accused were irrelevant in the eyes of the courts.

Similarly, the final appeal court – made up of the same three judges who had heard the Breatnach and McNally appeals – did not apply the same criteria to Kelly as they did to Breatnach. They made no mention in their judgement of the Shaw case which set out the tests to determine whether a statement signed in police custody was voluntary or not. They had found that those criteria were breached in Breatnach's case.

The courts were also inconsistent in their application of

the Judges Rules. McNally allegedly made four "confessions" to the gardai, including a written statement. The first was an admission that he was "on the job". It was followed some time later by an admission that he was involved in the robbery but was unaware of the plan until he got to the scene. The third, immediately afterwards, was a detailed account of the robbery allegedly told to Inspector John Courtney and Sergeant Michael Canavan. They made notes several hours later. The fourth, the written statement, was not submitted in evidence by the prosecution because McNally was unlawfully detained when he signed it: his forty eight hours in custody had expired.

McNally's conviction rested on the three verbal statements. The Special Criminal Court accepted that the gardai had breached the Judges Rules in taking them. The particular rules broken were those dealing with the cautioning of suspects and the obligation on gardai to write down statements, show them to the person who made them and allow him or her to make corrections before they signed. These requirements were not carried out by the gardai in relation to McNally. But the Special Criminal Court decided to tolerate these breaches.

Justice Hamilton said the first statement which was taken without caution was allowed because Rule 6 provided that the absence of a caution did not necessarily render a statement inadmissible so long as the person was cautioned as soon as possible. The second and third statements were admitted into evidence because they were voluntary and would have been written down had Inspector Courtney and Sergeant Canavan not known that McNally was about to make a full written statement – the one not produced in evidence.

The Court of Criminal Appeal took a different view. It said the Special Criminal Court had been wrong to exercise its discretion in this way. The statements were ruled out and, with no other evidence against him, McNally was cleared and released.

Nicky Kelly was alleged to have made several verbal statements to the gardai before he dictated a detailed written statement. The Special Criminal Court decided that

406

the way in which Kelly was questioned was not in breach of the Judges Rules. His answers were voluntary and there was nothing unfair in the questioning.

The Court of Criminal Appeal found that the gardai had breached Rule 9, requiring that the statements be written down and offered to him for correction and signature. But it decided that the Special Criminal Court had been correct to exercise its discretion and allow these statements into evidence. They were admissible because their contents were similar to the contents of the written statement signed by Kelly, the appeal judges declared.

Their attitude was totally at variance with the judgement they had given in McNally's case. In that case they had decided that the breach of Rule 9 was too serious to allow the statements to stand.

McNally's alleged admission that he was "on the job" could have stood against him because Garda Grehan, on his evidence, did caution him just after he said it, as allowed by Rule 6. This was pointed out by the Special Criminal Court. Nonetheless the Court of Criminal Appeal decided to rule it out.

In Kelly's case, the appeal court appeared to take a rigid and narrow view of the Judges Rules. The cumulative effect of allowing most of Kelly's alleged statements to stand against him led on to the situation where the Supreme Court could decide that Kelly appeared to be someone who had decided to co-operate with the gardai at a particular stage during his questioning.

The final judgements of the Court of Criminal Appeal and the Supreme Court revealed other weaknesses in the handling of Kelly's case. In one instance, these led the courts to reach a conclusion which was not based on reality. This concerned the question of whether Kelly had been denied access to his solicitor by being moved between police stations after his arrest. This point was put to the Court of Criminal Appeal and it was the issue on which the case was finally considered by the Supreme Court.

The appeal court dismissed this argument on the basis that there were no reasons to believe that any lawyer was at any material time made unaware of where Kelly was detained or that any attempt to help him was frustrated by his removal from Arklow garda station to Fitzgibbon Street and later from there to the Bridewell. It added that Nuala Dillon was made aware of his presence in Fitzgibbon Street from noon on Monday, April 5th 1976 – an error of fact by the court as she did not know he was there until she was taken to the station by detectives later that night. The Supreme Court said there was nothing to indicate that Kelly was moved between garda stations to harass or isolate him.

It was true, as both courts said, that they had nothing before them to suggest other than what they had indicated. But the reality was quite different. Pat McCartan had tried to find Kelly in Arklow garda station on the day of his arrest and was told he was not there. He also tried to find him in the Bridewell but Kelly was not there either. At that stage, however, McCartan was not certain that Kelly had been arrested at all and he gave up the search after trying the two most likely places where Kelly would be detained if arrested.

This had arisen as a possible issue during the course of the trial in the Special Criminal Court. In their deliberations at that time, the defence lawyers had given some thought as to whether or not McCartan should give evidence about his unsuccessful efforts to locate Kelly after his arrest. They decided he should not go into the witness box. Their decision was based primarily on tactical considerations. It seemed that there was little to be gained at that stage by putting McCartan into the witness box. The defence was conducting its case with an appeal in mind but it was trying to win the case in the Special Criminal Court as well.

The issue was only one of many points of secondary importance at the time of the trial. Five years later, however, it was the main issue before the judges of the Supreme Court. But it was too late by then to introduce new evidence which might have altered the judges' perceptions. The defence had known these facts during the trial, and court rules and practices meant, therefore, that they could not introduce them now. The lawyers were restricted to

408

fighting the case on the ground set out years earlier. Equally, the courts were restricted by their own procedures from looking beyond the existing record.

The structures imposed by the legal system operated to Kelly's disadvantage in other respects as well. The defence made little attempt to challenge the veracity of the details in the statements signed by each of the accused – except for Osgur Breatnach's statement, where details and the language used were put under rigorous examination by Patrick MacEntee. As the Special Criminal Court trial progressed, desultory preparations were made to challenge details in the statements.

A firm of architects was commissioned to drive along the routes described in the statements, measure the distance and time the journeys. (Architects were employed so they could give weighty evidence as professional people.) But there was little serious consideration given to challenging the veracity of the statements. The lawyers believed the courts were not impressed by minor – or even major – inconsistencies. Once the court decided that the statements were made voluntarily they tended to view them simply as admissions of guilt.

This attitude of the courts served to bolster and encourage the heavy reliance by the police on confessions. By 1976 the gardai were relying to a great extent on confessions to prove guilt against members of subversive organisations. Next to catching someone red handed, confessions were the most conclusive proof that policemen could get. They faced the extra difficulties of finding proof of guilt against a well organised paramilitary group whose operations were partly designed to avoid capture.

The spin-off effect of the problems in Northern Ireland was never so great in the Republic as to force the gardai to reassess fundamentally their approach to dealing with paramilitary organisations. The largely traditional methods of policing a small, tightly knit community were applied to tracking down terrorists. But these methods did not work and caused great frustration within the gardai. As a result, many gardai began to rely heavily on confessions obtained during long periods of interrogation. This method of "solving" crime was increasingly applied across the broad spectrum of criminal investigations, not just to crime with political overtones.

As the task of policing became more complex, governments and garda management responded with a series of crisis measures which failed to tackle the fundamental problem. The structure and management of the Garda Siochana remained largely the same as when the force was established in the 1920s.

The garda evidence during the train robbery trial, if accepted at face value, demonstrated an extraordinary level of incompetence in the force. During the interrogations in the Bridewell, detectives were, according to their own evidence, seemingly wandering around at random, uninformed, undirected and so disorganised that several went home for a few hours sleep before telling superiors of major developments. On top of that, many detectives demonstrated a lack of knowledge of the Judges Rules. At a time when confessions figured so prominently in the garda approach to solving crime, many gardai were ignorant of the only guidelines governing interrogations. Even gardai who admitted to being aware of the rules blithely flouted them and offered the court no explanations.

In the train robbery case, the only constant in the "confessions" was the basic details of what happened. The train was stopped by detonators, robbed by armed and masked men who used a hijacked Volkswagen van and took over a nearby house. The remaining information in the confessions which allegedly explained how the robbery was carried out was full of contradictions. The written statements contradicted each other in several respects. There were also contradictions between the verbal and written statements made by particular individuals, especially Nicky Kelly.

There was a major conflict between Brian McNally and Nicky Kelly in their statements describing their route to the scene of the robbery. Both said they travelled in McNally's Renault van (which Kelly called a car). McNally, who interestingly in his written statement called his wife Catherine instead of Kathleen, said he and Kelly drove from Swords to St Margarets, Mulhuddart, Dunboyne, Maynooth, Celbridge and to Sallins. Kelly said they drove to Celbridge but also described, according to the gardai, a totally different route when he travelled with the detectives to the scene. That route took them through Lucan to Celbridge and from there direct to the scene of the robbery. McNally said they drove to Celbridge, then to Sallins and then to the scene of the robbery – a very roundabout route.

Further conflicts were also evident in the written statements. Kelly said that Seamus Costello and Osgur Breatnach boarded the train. McNally said that Breatnach and Fitzpatrick boarded the train. Kelly said that when the mail bags were being unloaded, Thomas McCartan stood guard on the far side of the track. McNally said that McCartan was throwing mail bags over the hedge to himself and Kelly.

Indeed, Kelly maintained in his statement that both he and McNally were on the other side of the hedge, beside the train. McNally's written statement also said that Breatnach had a gun. Kelly's statement said that Breatnach was one of the few men who were unarmed. When the robbery was over, McNally said that Michael Barrett drove away the Volkswagen van; Kelly said it was driven by Gerry Roche.

In Kelly's verbal statements he said, according to Inspector Ned Ryan, that he threw mail bags *up* on to the field. Similarly, McNally referred to a hedge as *overlooking* the railway line. They seemed to agree that the railway was lower than the field. In reality it was some feet above the field.

Kelly's lawyers did not analyse Kelly's statements critically before the court. There were numerous discrepancies between his verbal statements and his written statement. There were also points which could have challenged the veracity of his written statement. It would have been impossible, for instance, for the hijacked Volkswagen van to take the money from the train to Ballymore Eustace and then to go to Finglas within half an hour of the raid. Yet, the evidence available to the gardai and the defence said that the van was abandoned at the itinerant site at Finglas at 3.45 am just over half an hour after the gang left the Hazelhatch area.

One of the verbal statements made by Kelly, to Garda Michael Finn, was not accepted by the Special Criminal Court. Many of the details in that alleged confession were at odds with his other statements. The Special Criminal Court gave no reason for its refusal to accept this statement.

The defence was hampered in that it was unable to point up the discrepancies between the statements signed by McNally and by Kelly concerning their joint activities. This could not be done because McNally's statement was not introduced into evidence by the prosecution. That clearly benefited McNally's defence but its absence may have damaged Kelly's case. The defence could not introduce it because it might be used by the prosecution.

A similar problem surrounded the question of John Fitzpatrick and his alibi that he was in Limerick on the night of the robbery. The gardai appeared to accept that he was in Limerick up to 11.00 pm that night but argued behind the scenes that he could have still carried out the robbery and returned to Limerick in time for breakfast. The statement signed by Fitzpatrick said, however, that he had left Dublin after midnight to go to the scene of the robbery. Kelly, in his verbal confession to Garda Finn, said Fitzpatrick had stolen a Cortina with a black vinyl roof and driven to the scene of the robbery with two others. Kelly's written statement described Fitzpatrick driving a stolen car with a vinyl roof.

When Fitzpatrick resurfaced in 1983, Justice Minister Michael Noonan rejected the depiction of his account of events as "new evidence." He said that the details of Fitzpatrick's alibi were known to the defence lawyers at the time of the trial. He was correct: all the evidence against Fitzpatrick was contained in the book of evidence against the four on trial.

But it was not possible for the defence to use any of that knowledge at the time. Fitzpatrick was not before the court because the gardai had not arrested him. In order to bring his alibi into the reckoning, the defence would have had to produce him as a witness. Clearly, they could not do that.

Fitzpatrick's absence also meant that the trial was

conducted without reference to the central issue on which the case had been brought before the court in the first place. In considering whether to press charges in 1976, the Director of Public Prosecutions, Eamonn Barnes, had given a lot of consideration to Fitzpatrick's alibi. If it stood up, then the case against the others also collapsed. But the gardai were insistent that Fitzpatrick's presence in Limerick was not a watertight alibi. Barnes had decided that the issue was one to be resolved by the courts and he sanctioned the prosecutions.

That issue was never resolved in court because Fitzpatrick was not arrested along with the others.

The Court of Criminal Appeal and the Supreme Court also demonstrated selectivity in their dismissal of Kelly's final applications. The Supreme Court noted – and apparently accepted – the prosecution point that Kelly had not complained of ill-treatment to his girlfriend, Nuala Dillon,when she saw him in the Bridewell around midnight on April 6th/7th. She was the only civilian to see him while he was in custody and she had told the trial that Kelly had not complained of ill-treatment to her. She had also told the Special Criminal Court that he appeared to be distressed: he was sweating and his hand was shaking. The Supreme Court made no mention of her description of how he looked.

The Court of Criminal Appeal placed considerable emphasis on the fact that Kelly had admitted being friendly with the gardai after he signed his written statement. This was one of the factors which, it said, amply supported the conclusion of the Special Criminal Court that his statements had been made voluntarily.

This interpretation distorted Kelly's evidence. He made it clear at all times that he was not on friendly terms with the gardai. He told the trial that the atmosphere had changed after he signed the written statement, in the sense that the beatings stopped. He had also agreed that several gardai had been friendly towards him during his period in detention. But he emphasised that he did not trust any of them: in his view they were all members of the same force which had ill-treated him.

All of these things were known to lawyers or judges who were involved in the mail train case. It now seems that suspects were ill-treated in the Bridewell on Tuesday and Wednesday, April 6th and 7th 1976. Several gardai who were involved in the case have admitted to people in private that a number of those interrogated were assaulted while in custody. None of them is prepared to say so publicly. They appear to want strongly to leave the entire episode in the past.

One of the strongest elements in the case against Nicky Kelly was the journey he undertook to the scene of the robbery with three detectives. In their evidence, the detectives said that none of them had any prior knowledge of the area. They had not visited the scene of the crime during the investigation and, they said, that Kelly gave them directions to get there. Kelly said he did not know where the robbery had taken place and insisted during his trial that it was the detectives who brought him to the scene.

The Special Criminal Court was never told, however, how the detectives knew that the house they maintained Kelly pointed out to them was actually the correct house – the O'Tooles' house which was taken over by the robbers. The detectives were never asked in court how they knew it was the right house.

Inspector Ned Ryan, the senior officer present on the journey with Kelly, volunteered the information that he "subsequently learned there and then" that it was the O'Tooles' house. But he was not asked how he learned that. In court he pointed out O'Toole's house on a map.

Sergeant John McGroarty was asked to explain a phrase in the statement he made "a few days" after the journey which said: "...we came to a bungalow on the right occupied by Conal O'Toole and which *I was aware* was the bungalow entered by the gang of men who had robbed the Cork/Dublin mail train on 31st March." How was he aware? He explained: "I was aware it was the last house in a row of houses was the house taken over by the men who held up the train."

That description could not have been correct. In April 1976, at the time of the journey, O'Toole's house was not

414

the last in a row. It stood alone. Beside it there was an overgrown site consisting of trees, bushes and undergrowth and with a hedge of bushes along the road. The garda map prepared immediately after the robbery and used as evidence in the trials clearly showed the O'Tooles' house standing alone (see page 10). The house that now stands beside it was not built until the autumn of 1977. The third house that stands there now was built in 1981. The O'Tooles' house could not have been the last house in a row in April 1976: there was no row.

The only explanation given to the court of trial as to how the gardai knew that Kelly pointed out the correct house at the scene of the crime they said he committed could not have been accurate.

The mail train case did not establish any great legal precedents. But it will endure as a milestone because of its extraordinary length, because it encapsulated many of the political tensions of its period and because it tested and found wanting the police and judicial systems in Ireland.

Information contained in Nicky Kelly's petition was not obtained from any of his advisors.

Epilogue
1984

Nicky Kelly is a personality, making news with his public appearances. He turns up at the Fine Gael ard fheis, invited in from outside by some young members of the party. He appears on television's main chat show, The Late Late Show, giving most people an opportunity to see the person behind the well known name. He is polite, hesitant. He speaks slowly, volunteers little and pauses before he answers questions. He looks older than his 33 years.

He is adjusting to his freedom and to being, to an extent, a celebrity. He is unemployed and suffers from the psychological after-effects of his experiences. He is still concerned with court cases. His civil action for damages against Ireland remains to be resolved. His life is dominated by the events of 1976.

Other people's lives also remain under the influence of those events. Osgur Breatnach has not been able to find a steady job since his release and acquittal in 1980. His marriage has been in difficulty and he has suffered two nervous breakdowns, one in 1977 and one in 1982. He finds it difficult to cope with stress, to rebuild his self-confidence and he suffers nightmares about interrogations. He, too, is awaiting a civil action in court over his treatment in garda custody in 1976.

Brian McNally has had a series of jobs since his release and acquittal in 1980. One fell through when his employers found out that he had been in prison. He has retained his interest in sports and still coaches youngsters in gaelic games. He is still in financial difficulties. He achieved brief notoriety once again when he was "exposed" in the *Sunday World* as a "bogus doctor". At the time he was running a "Medical & Physical Rehabilitation Clinic" providing physiotherapy for injured sportsmen as "Doctor P.B. McNally".

Michael Plunkett lives in Paris where he has become

something of a *cause celèbre* and is seeking formal status as a political refugee. Several months after his acquittal of the mail train robbery, he was arrested in a house in Dublin and charged with explosives offences. He jumped bail and fled to Paris where he lived unobtrusively until what became known in France as *L'Affaire des Irlandais de Vincennes*. On August 28th 1982, he was arrested in his flat in Vincennes, a suburb of Paris, along with Mary Reid, his girlfriend, and one of their friends, Stephen King. Also arrested was Reid's nine year old child, Cathal Goulding, grandson of the the former chief of staff of the Official IRA.

They were arrested by the GIGN, a brand new anti-terrorist police squad set up by President Francois Mitterand to deal with a wave of anti-semitic bombings in the French capital. The arrests were hailed in a personal announcement by Mitterand as a major breakthrough against international terrorism. It was not long, however, before a huge political and security scandal began to unfold. The new police squad was accused of planting evidence against the three and attempting to suborn witnesses. Internal rivalries within the French security system soon provoked some police officers to give damning evidence against their colleagues. It became obvious that the squad publicly praised by Mitterand had not captured three high grade international terrorists.

The three, however, remained in prison until May 1983. Plunkett was allowed remain in France on short term permits while he pursued his application for political asylum. The mail train case was one of the points he put foward in support of his contention that he was a political refugee.

The man in charge of the police investigation into the mail train robbery, Chief Superintendent John Joy, retired from the Garda Siochana in 1979. He became a security consultant with a banking group and died in 1982. His deputy in 1976, Superintendent Patrick Casey, still works with the Central Detective Unit, now based at Harcourt Square in Dublin. Inspector Ned Ryan, the dominant policeman at the trial, is now a Superintendent in charge of

417

detectives working in the Crumlin area of Dublin. One of the men who works with him is Inspector Michael Canavan, a sergeant in the "Murder Squad" in 1976.

His former associate, Inspector John Courtney, is now the Superintendent in charge of the squad, officially known as the investigation section of the technical bureau at Garda Headquarters. Some of the detectives involved in the train robbery case, like Garda Thomas Ibar Dunne, have remained with the squad. Others, like Garda Gerard O'Carroll, have since joined it.

Sergeant John McGroarty has long since left Finglas garda station. He is now an Inspector. He spent some time with a special drugs intelligence unit based at Garda Headquarters before moving to the main Drug Squad of which he is now head.

There has never been another case like the mail train robbery trial. There have been some changes in the Garda Siochana since 1976: some real, most cosmetic. Many of the gardai involved have pursued their careers, slowly rising up the ladder of promotion. Others are still doing much the same as they were in 1976.

Almost all of the judges who presided at the trial and subsequent appeals are still on the bench.

Appendix I

The Events

1976

March 31st: Armed men hold up the Cork to Dublin mail train near Hazelhatch in County Kildare just after 3.00 am.

Detectives raid houses of suspects including the home of Brian McNally in Swords, County Dublin where Nicky Kelly is staying.

Osgur Breatnach is arrested near the IRSP offices at about 3.00 pm and is held for forty eight hours.

April 4th: Gardai prepare at a conference in Dublin Castle to arrest seventeen named IRSP members.

April 5th: IRSP activists arrested in Dublin, Wicklow, Monaghan and Carlow.

McNally and Kelly taken to Fitzgibbon Street garda station in Dublin. Breatnach and John Fitzpatrick taken to the Bridewell.

April 6th: McNally and Kelly moved to the Bridewell at about 1.00 am.

Michael Plunkett arrested at lunchtime and taken to Harcourt Terrace garda station.

April 7th: Between midnight and 9.00 am, four men confess to the robbery.

At 5.30 am Kelly travels with gardai to the scene of the crime and two other places.

Breatnach is seen by a solicitor who initiates *habeas corpus* proceedings in the High Court.

He is taken to the Richmond Hospital afterwards.

Kelly is taken in the afternoon to confront Plunkett with his confessions.

Kelly, Plunkett, McNally and Fitzpatrick are charged with the robbery at a special sitting of Dublin District Court at 10.30 pm. They are remanded into custody in the Bridewell until the next morning.

April 8th: The four are remanded in custody to Mountjoy Prison where they are examined by prison doctors and two doctors acting for them. All four are suffering from bruises and similar injuries.

Breatnach is discharged from the Richmond Hospital, taken back to the High Court and re-arrested. He is taken before a late sitting of the District Court, charged with the robbery and taken on remand to Mountjoy.

April 11th: Michael Barrett is charged, the sixth man accused of the robbery.

December 9th: The District Court throws out the charges against all six because of the prosecution's failure since April to produce the evidence against them.

December 17th: McNally, Breatnach, Kelly and Plunkett are re-arrested and charged in the Special Criminal Court with the robbery.

420

1977

The trial is delayed because all four are on bail. Their lawyers prepare their defence once the prosecution evidence is provided.

1978

January 19th: The trial opens in the Special Criminal Court.

February 3rd: *Hibernia Weekly Review* reports that one of the three trial judges, John Willie O'Connor, appears to be asleep during the hearing.

February 6th: Dublin architect and Fine Gael member Martin Reynolds visits court and notices Judge O'Connor apparently asleep.

April 26th: The three judges refuse an application from the defence for the trial to be abandoned because Judge O'Connor appears to be asleep. Presiding Judge, James McMahon, says that his colleague is capable of discharging his duties.

April 28th: President of the High Court, Thomas Finlay, refuses defence application to stop the Special Criminal Court trial.

May 3rd: Supreme Court also rejects defence pleas.

May 4th: Michael Plunkett shouts in court that Judge O'Connor is again asleep.

May 11th: *Hibernia* reports that Judge O'Connor appears again to be asleep.

June 6th: Judge O'Connor found dead at home.

Trial abandoned after sixty five days of hearings: the longest trial ever in the state.

October 10th: New trial opens in the Special Criminal Court before three other judges.

October 11th: Court dismisses charges against Michael Plunkett and he is released.

December 1st: The court rejects accounts of ill-treatment by McNally, Breatnach and Kelly and decides that their confessions are admissible as evidence against them.

December 11th: Kelly fails to appear in court after a weekend adjournment.

December 13th: McNally, Breatnach and Kelly are found guilty. McNally is sentenced to nine years, Breatnach to twelve years.

December 15th: Kelly is sentenced in his absence to twelve years penal servitude.

1979
Spring: Kelly flees to the United States of America and eventually settles in the Philadelphia area.
   McNally and Breatnach appeal their convictions and sentences.

1980
April 27th: Provisional IRA says it carried out the train robbery and the three men convicted are innocent.

May 12th: Court of Criminal Appeal begins hearing McNally and Breatnach cases.

May 19th:	Hearings end and the court reserves its decision.
May 22nd:	Court of Criminal Appeal releases McNally and Breatnach. Detailed reasons are to be stated later.
June 4th:	Kelly returns to Ireland voluntarily and is arrested at Shannon Airport. Special Criminal Court orders that he be taken to prison to serve his sentence.
December 18th:	Court of Criminal Appeal refuses Kelly request for extension of time to lodge appeal against conviction.

1981

February 16th:	Appeal court gives reasons for releasing McNally and Breatnach.
March 16th:	Kelly's lawyers ask appeal court for permission to contest its decision to Supreme Court.
May 29th:	Appeal court gives permission for Supreme Court action.
July 29th:	Supreme Court overturns appeal court refusal of time extension for Kelly. Decision leaves way open for full appeal hearing. Supreme Court to give reasons later.

1982

January 11th:	Supreme Court gives reasons for its July decision.
February 15th:	Court of Criminal Appeal hearing opens in Kelly's case.

February 18th:	Hearings end and court reserves its judgement.
April 2nd:	Court announces that the appeal has failed. Kelly's conviction and sentence is to stand.
July 13th:	Supreme Court begins hearings on the appeal court decision.
July 20th:	Hearings completed and judgement reserved.
October 29th:	Supreme Court declares that appeal court decision was correct. Kelly to remain in prison.

1983

May 1st:	Kelly begins hunger strike in Portlaoise Prison.
May 25th:	Justice Minister Michael Noonan says Kelly cannot be released unless there is new evidence about the case.
May 27th:	Kelly is moved from prison to a military hospital at the Curragh.
June 1st:	Irish Commission for Justice and Peace, a Catholic Church body trying to mediate, urges appeal to the European Commission of Human Rights.
June 3rd:	Amnesty International writes to Noonan expressing its concern.
June 6th:	Kelly's lawyers initiate appeal to European Commission.
June 7th:	Kelly decides to end hunger strike after

talks with a supporter and a solicitor.

Government says that he is free to take civil court action on ill-treatment claim.

1984

May 17th: European Commission of Human Rights rejects Kelly's application because it was lodged more than six months after the final Supreme Court judgement in October 1982.

July 17th: Michael Noonan tells divided Cabinet that he is going to release Kelly for "humanitarian reasons". Kelly is taken to Shelton Abbey open prison near Arklow in Co Wicklow and released.

Appendix II

The People

Barrett, Michael:
Native of Abbeyfeale, County Limerick, and IRSP member who was sixth man charged with the mail train robbery. Charges dropped by district court and not resuscitated by the Director of Public Prosecutions.

Breatnach, Osgur:
Born in Dun Laoghaire 1950 and editor of the IRSP newspaper *The Starry Plough.* Convicted of the mail train robbery and jailed for twelve years in December 1978. Conviction and sentence overturned by Court of Criminal Appeal, May 1980.

Fitzpatrick, John:
Born in Dublin and brought up in Armagh. Went underground when charges dropped by the district court and avoided being re-charged. Re-surfaced in 1983.

Kelly, Edward Noel:
Generally known as Nicky. Born in 1951 and brought up in Arklow. Absconded in December 1978 just before he was convicted and sentenced to twelve years for the mail train robbery. Returned to Ireland from United States in 1980 but series of court decisions upheld his conviction and sentence. Released by Justice Minister July 1984.

McNally, Bernard:
Known as Brian. Born in 1942 in County Tyrone. Moved to Dublin in 1974. Sports enthusiast and drummer in showband. Convicted of mail train robbery and jailed for nine years in December 1978. Conviction and sentence overturned by Court of Criminal Appeal, May 1980.

Plunkett, Michael:
Born in Dun Laoghaire in 1951. General secretary of the IRSP. Acquitted of mail train robbery, October 1978.

Butler, James. Detective garda in SDU.
Byrne, Patrick. Detective garda in SDU.

Campbell, Francis. Detective sergeant in Pearse Street garda station, Dublin.
Canavan, Michael J. Detective sergeant in investigations section of Garda technical bureau.
Casey, Patrick J. Detective Superintendent and second in command of Central Detective Unit (CDU) and of train robbery investigation.
Cleary, Patrick F. Detective sergeant in CDU.
Collins, Joseph. Detective sergeant in Ballymun station, Dublin.
Courtney, John. Detective inspector in investigations section of Garda technical bureau.
Culhane, Patrick A. Detective sergeant in SDU.
Cullen, Bernard. Detective garda in SDU.

Drew, Michael J. Detective garda in CDU.
Dunne, Fintan. Detective garda in CDU.
Dunne, Thomas Ibar. Detective garda in investigations section of Garda technical bureau.

Egan, Joseph. Detective garda in SDU.
Egan, Michael J. Detective sergeant in SDU.

Finn, Michael. Detective garda in Store Street station, Dublin.
Fitzgerald, Thomas P. Detective garda in CDU.
Fitzsimons, Owen. Detective garda in SDU.
Fleming, John. Chief Superintendent in charge of SDU.

Grehan, James. Detective garda in SDU.

Hawkshaw, Myles. Detective inspector in SDU.
Hegarty, John. Detective garda in SDU.
Holland, Joseph. Detective garda in Ballyfermot station, Dublin.

Jordan, John. Detective garda in SDU.
Joy, John J. Chief Superintendent, head of Central Detective Unit (CDU) and in charge of train robbery investigation.

King, Thomas. Detective sergeant in SDU.

Lawlor, Kieran. Detective garda in SDU.

McGauran, Brian. Garda in Bridewell, acted as jailer.
McGrath, Vincent. Detective inspector in SDU.
McGroarty, John J. Detective sergeant in Finglas station, Dublin.
McKenna, Felix. Detective garda in CDU.
McPartlan, James, Detective sergeant in SDU.
Meagher, William. Detective garda in CDU.
Mullen, Michael C. Detective garda in SDU.
Murphy, John. Detective inspector in Kevin Street station, Dublin.
Murphy, Richard A. Detective sergeant in Rathmines station, Dublin.

Noonan, Michael. Garda in Hollywood, County Wicklow.

O'Carroll, Gerard P. Detective garda in CDU.
O'Hara, Adrian. Detective garda in SDU.

Raftery, Patrick J. Detective garda in SDU.
Reynolds, Hubert. Detective inspector in investigations section of Garda technical bureau.
Ryan, Ned. Detective inspector in CDU.

Waters, Patrick. Detective garda in SDU.

Barr, Robert. Senior counsel for the prosecution.
Browne, Aidan. Senior counsel who appeared for authorities against Osgur Breatnach in High Court action but gave evidence on his behalf at trial.

Cronin, Maureen. Barrister representing Nicky Kelly.

Giblin, Martin. Barrister representing Osgur Breatnach.

Haugh, Kevin. Barrister for the prosecution.
Heron, James. Barrister representing Michael Plunkett.

McCartan, Pat. Solicitor acting for all accused in mail train trial.
McDonald, Noel. Senior counsel for the prosecution.
MacEntee, Patrick. Senior counsel for Osgur Breatnach and Michael Plunkett.

O'Neill, Greg. Solicitor representing Nicky Kelly in civil action for damages.

Sammon, Anthony. Barrister representing Brian McNally during trial and other accused at different times.
Sorahan, Seamus. Senior counsel representing Brian McNally and Nicky Kelly.

THE JUDGES

Barrington, Donal:
High Court judge who sat on Court of Criminal Appeal that decided McNally, Breatnach and Kelly cases.

Carroll, Mella:
High Court judge who sat on Court of Criminal Appeal which refused Kelly extra time to appeal after he returned from US.

Clarke, Gerard:
Circuit Court judge who was member of Special Criminal Court for the second train robbery trial.

Finlay, Thomas:
President of the High Court. Refused defence application on "sleeping judge" issue during first Special Criminal Court trial. Member of Court of Criminal Appeal that decided McNally, Breatnach and Kelly cases.

Gannon, John M:
High Court judge who sat on Court of Criminal Appeal which refused Kelly extra time to appeal after he returned from US.

Garavan, John:
District court judge who sat on the Special Criminal Court during first trial.

Griffin, Frank:
Supreme Court judge. One of five who upheld the Court of Criminal Appeal's decision to let Kelly's conviction stand.

Hamilton, Liam:
High Court judge. Heard Osgur Breatnach *habeas corpus* action in 1976. Presided at second Special Criminal Court trial. Dealt with preliminary phase of Kelly's civil action.

Hederman, Anthony J:
Supreme Court judge who was member of both Supreme Courts which adjudicated on Kelly's appeals.

Henchy, Seamus:
Supreme Court judge. Member of Court of Criminal Appeal which decided McNally, Breatnach and Kelly cases. Member of Supreme Court which granted Kelly extra time to appeal.

Kenny, John:
Supreme Court judge and member of courts which allowed Kelly extra time to appeal and rejected his final appeal.

McMahon, James:
High Court judge who presided over first Special Criminal Court trial.

McWilliam, Herbert:
High Court judge drafted onto Supreme Court which rejected Kelly's final appeal.

O'Connor, John William:
Circuit court judge who was member of the first Special Criminal Court. Accused of sleeping during trial, his death caused it to be abandoned.

O Floinn, Cathal:
President of the district court who was member of the Special Criminal Court during second trial.

O'Higgins, Thomas J.:
Chief Justice. Rejected application to dismiss Special Criminal Court over "sleeping judge" accusations. Allowed Kelly extra time to appeal and rejected his final appeal.

O hUadaigh, Riobard:
District justice who presided over special hearings at which most of the accused were charged initially. Later threw out charges against them all.

Parke, Weldon C.:
Supreme Court judge who sat on Court of Criminal Appeal which refused Kelly extra time in which to appeal.

Walsh, Brian:
Supreme Court judge and member of courts which allowed Kelly extra time and rejected his final appeal.

Appendix III

The "Confessions"

John Fitzpatrick

Statement of John Fitzpatrick 24 years Builder of 6 Castle Avenue, Swords, Co.Dublin made at 12.30 a.m. 7.4.1976.

On Monday 29th March I went with Mick Barrett to Brian McNally's house at 6 Castle Avenue, Swords. Brian McNally was not in he was away playing somehwre with a group. His wife Kathleen was in the house and his four children were in bed. We had a cup of tea and we went to bed. Mick Barrett and myself slept in the box room. We set the alarm clock for about 5.30 a.m. We got up when the alarm went off at 5.30 a.m. approx. Mick Barrett and myself drove off in my car a green VW beetle regd. no. 447 RRI. We stopped at the all night petrol station on the Swords Road on the right hand side as you go to the city between the Airport and the city. We drove from there down to Abbeyfeale Co Limerick. We arrived there at 10 a.m. approx. We went to Barrett's house on the Kerry side of Abbeyfeale. When we got there we met his two brothers Matt and the younger brother. We had a bit of a chat and Matt made the breakfast. We sat about the house talking for a couple of hours. We drove around Kerry for a while and visited the valley of Knocklanure a few miles from Barrett's house. We drove around Abbeyfeale until about 4 p.m. Then we drove to Castleconnell to Tom Hayes' house arriving there at 5 p.m. approx. He and his wife were in the house. We had a cup of tea there and then we went with Tom Hayes in my car into Limerick City. As we drove into limerick we were stuck in a line of traffic and one of the local Special Branch Gardai walked across the road to a car with one occupant parked on the opposite side. We drove on and drove into the car park near the river on the right hand side as you drive towards Kerry. I parked on the street

432

outside the car park. Tom Hayes got out of the car went into a shop. As Hayes was getting back into the car a special branch Garda or an ordinary plain clothes man passed by and stood at the entrance to the car park about 15 yards away from us. We drove off to a house outside Limerick. He stayed in the house for 5 minutes and then we returned to a Chinese Restaurant in Limerick called "The New Star". It was about 10 p.m. as we went in. We left the restaurant at 10.45 p.m. approx. and went to Hayes' house in Castleconnell. In the house was his wife and her sister. We went to bed shortly afterwards. The two of us slept in the same room. We got up the next morning at approx. 11.30 a.m. After breakfast we drove back to Dublin. We arrived in Dublin at approx. 2.30 p.m. As we drove up the quays I bought an evening papaer from a newsboy on the Quays near Merchant's Quay. We then drove to the offices at Essex Gate. There was nobody there so we went to the new offices in Gardiner Street. We went in for about five minutes. We left and went to a cafe in Dorset Street and had a meal. We left the cafe at 5 p.m. approx. I had a pint in the Royal Dublin Hotel with Barrett and then we went to the pictures namely Russian Roulette in Savoy 3, O'Connell Street. After the pictures we went out to McNally's and stayed Wednesday night at McNally's. This statement has been read over to me and it is correct.

Signed:
Witness: Michael J Drew D/Garda
        Patrick A. Culhane D/Sergt.

John Fitzpatrick

Statement of evidence of John Fitzpatrick of 6, Castle Avenue Swords taken by me D/G John Jordan at Bridewell Station after being cautioned as follows You are not obliged to say anything unless you wish to do so but anything you do say will be taken down in writing and maybe JJ JF given in evidence.

After midnight on Wednesday morning the 31/3/76 I left Dublin in a car with another man we had arranged to meet others in a van on a road off the dual carriageway I was picked up in this van and drove to O Tooles house near the railway bridge. When I got there I saw other men futhering with 2 cars parked near O Tooles house I had arranged to meet these people there. I was in the van and wee drove into the field through the gate which was already open. The other two vehicles followed us. I was in the van with 2 others. In this van wee had a clather of guns. Wee drove down and parked the van in the field near a hedge paralell with the track. The three of us jumped out of the van and the people in the other cars jumped out as well. Those then who had been designated guns took JF JJ them out of the JF JJ the van and took up their positions. Several men took up positions JF JJ with JF JJ near me on the side of the track where wee had the transport parked. Some of the men went up the line and put detonators on the track and one fellow dressed in a donkey jacket with yellow shoulders and a red lamp JF took up a postion further down the track to stop the train. Wee were in position well over an hour before the train arrived. The detonators went off the man with the the red lamp stopped the train. The train stopped. It reversed back the line a good distance to where I was xx JJ JF Somebody got hold of the train driver. They took him off the train. Some of the fellows with me then opened the door I and two others jumped on into the mail carriage. The two men with me had guns I had not. The sorters were held at gunpoint and told to stand still. All three started to throw mail bags which were passed from one to the other JJ JF One of the men knew which bags to take. The bags were thrown out on to the ground and some men on the ground threw them over the hedge to where the transport was parked. There was two or three men on the other side of the hedge where the transport was parked. They packed them into the van. Everybody got into the transport and drove off, I was in the back of the van so I did not notice what direction wee went in. The guns were all thrown in to the back of the van. In driving off wee went out through the field the same way weecame in. Wee drove for some distance

434

along a twirly road. The van stopped and two of us got out of the van. This left one man in the van with the bags and guns. At this point a dark coloured car was waiting for JJ JF us. There was one man in this car I do not know the location as it was very dark and not too familiar with the area. We got into this car the two of us and drove to Dublin. I was dropped off at a friend's house in north city Dublin whose name I do not want to mention. The car drove off with the remaining men JJ JF. I do not know where they went. I knew the van used as transport was hijacked. After leaving the van and getting into the car that drove us to Dublin the van drove off. This statement has been read over to me and is correct. JJ JF

John Fitzpatrick
John Jordan
Francis Madden
7/4/76

Time 8.15 am.

Brian McNally

Statement of Bernard McNally, d.o.b. 3.12.42, musician, 6 Castle Avenue, Sword Co. Dublin made to D/Garda James Grehan and D/Inspector John Courtney at the Bridewell Garda Station on the 7th April 1976 at 7am.

I have been cautioned that I am not obliged to say anything unless I wish to do so but anything I do say will be taken down in writing and may be given in evidence. BMc I arrived home at 12.25 a.m. on 31st March 1976. I entered my home at 6 Castle Avenue, Swords and Nicky Kelly from Arklow was in my house. My wife Catherine was also there sitting at the fire. We had a cup of tea and then Nicky said "We have to go and see some friends. We got in my car a Renault 4L reg. no. YAI – 622 and headed for Swords. In S Swords he said, " Take the shortest way to

Sallins" I drove from Swords to St Margarets, Mulhuddart, Dunboyne, Maynooth, Celbridge, Sallins. On the journey Nicky Kelly told me we had some "job" to do. He told me that we were going to give a hand to unload mailbags from a train which I presumed was a train holdup. We arrived in Sallins around 2 o'clock. As I don't the country there, Kelly directed me where togo. We went through Sallins for a bit, til we came to a laneway where he told me to pull-up. He got out of the car and said "Follow me". I locked the van and followed him up a small lane. We could see the lights of what looked like a house to me on my right. We kept on travelling through the fields went through a hole in the hedge. I saw what I thought to be two or three cars parked in the field, one looked like a vauxhall, one was a volkswagon van and I couldn't be sure of the third one. We approached the cars. Michael Barrett from Abbeyfeale was standing at thevan. I went over to the hedge overlooking the railway and Seamus Costello, Chairman I.R.S.P from Bray told me to stand where I was. I looked to my right and saw a man further down the railway line whom I recognised as Tom McCartan from Belfast but living in Dublin McCartan was walking up the line towards me. John Fitzpatrick was moving about from place to place. When a man came over beside me and said "Hello" I recognised him as Oscar Breanach I.R.S.P. There was another chap lying on the dyke to my right, it was Gerard Murphy from Belfast. At this point Michael Plunkett Sec. I.R.S.P. passed me heading on to the railway track. He was wearing a donkey jacket, blackish colour. He face seemed to be darp. Gerry Roache I.R.S.P. was standing over by the van. Nicky Kelly was standing beside me. I saw Gerard Murphy had a long gun like a rifle. I heard the train coming, I heard three cracks and I heard the train starting to slow down or brake. When Michael Plunkett passed me he was carrying a red lamp and what appeared to be a flag. After the train started breaking I thought I saw a red light flashing on the track. Then the train began to come back and stop. Oscar Breanach and John Fitzpatrick approached the train and got into the carriage. Oscar stayed in the carriage and Fitzpatrick got out. Oscar started to throw mailbags out on

the ground to Fitzpatrick and Tom McCartan. They in turn
threw them over the hedge and Nicky Kelly and I threw
them to Michael Barrett. Barrett put them into the van. I
think Gerry Roache was with Barrett. When the mailbags
were being loaded the engineer of the train was lying on the
ground and Seamus Costello was standing over him. He
wore a mask and had a short gun in his hand. When all the
bags were loaded, Barrett closed the van and he drove it
away. He was accompanied by Roache and Fitzpatrick.
Costello told Kelly and I to "Get to hell home". We ran
back to my van and headed for home. The other van driven
by Barrett went the opposite direction from us. I drove
home to Swords and went to bed. Murphy covered the train
with a gun. I saw Fitzpatrick with a shortgun, McCartan
had a short gun. Oscar Breanach had a short gun. I saw no
guns with anybody else and I had no gun. I have read over
this statement and it is the truth. I wish to add that I am not
sure it was Gerard Murphy but I presumed it was.

Signed: B McNally
Witnessed: James Grehan
        John Courtney, Det.Inspector

Osgur Breatnach   Bridewell Gda Station
                                       6 am 7/4/'76

*Statement of Oscar Breathnach, d.o.b. 25 bl. xx 2a
Cearnog Aine, Carraig Dubh, Baile Atha Cliat, after
being cautioned that "I'm not obliged to say anything
unless I wish to do so but anything I do say will be taken
down in writing and may be given inevidence."*

Timpeall haon-deagh a chlog oiche de Mairt Ceadaoin OB
seo caite 30u La de Mharta 1976. Fuair me sibh o fear
eigin, nil aithne agam air. bhuail me leis ag an 7A Bus
Terminus, Burgh Quay. Bhi se ag tiomaint gluaistean dubh,
nil fhios agam an deanamh a bhi ar an ngluaistean. D'imigh
an bheirt againn i dtreo Parnell Sq. Tar eis uair a cloig no

mar sin, do shroiseamar ait eigin in aice Bothar Iarainn sios fein tir. Bhi eolas an tsli ag an tiomanai ni raibh se agamsa. Chuaigh me sios go dti an Iarann Roid. Tar eis tamaill do chonaic me an traen ag teacht agus stop daoine eigin an train. Sul ar thainig an train chuala me cupla torann agus chonaic me an train ag stopadh. Chuaigh an train ag agaidh beagan agus ar chul aris. Chuaigh me isteach san train Bhi beirt fear in aonacht liom. Bhi beirt fhear ann is doigh liom se sin sa chairaiste. Bhi stoca nylon ar m-aghaidh thug an fear a thug an sibh dom e. Duirt duine eigin a bhi in aonacht liomsa "Stand Back" leis an mbeirt fhear a bhi ar a train, agus chait me neart malai amach ar an ngort in aice leis an mbothar iarainn. Thog daoine eile a bhi istigh sa ghort na malai agus thogadar treasna na pairce iad. Do chuir siad na malai isteach i Van a bhi istigh sa phairc. Bhi ceathrar fear istigh sa OB phairc is doigh liom. D'imigh me as an ait anson agus chuaigh me isteach sa gluaistean, se sin an gluaistean mar fuair me sibh air go dti an ait a stopadh an train. Bhi an fear ceanna ag tiomaint ag dul abhaile agus sroisead an teach timpeall a 5 cuig a chlog ar maidin De Ceadaoin 31/3'76. Ni raibh aon ghunna agamsa ach bhi gunnai ag na daoine a bhi in aonacht liom. Do tharla an robail timpeall a tri a chlog maidin De Ceadaoin 31/3/'76. Nil aon rud eile le ra agam, ta gach rud ceart. Ni theastaiom uaim aon eathru a dheanamh, ach nior fuaireas aon airgead agus ni raibh fhios agam ce mheid airgid a bhi ann.

Sinithe: Oscar Breatnach
Finne: Tomas Mac Gearailt Gda.
Finne: Sean O Murchu D/Ce.

6.50 am 7-4-76

Tomas Iomair O Duinn B/Garda

Nicky Kelly

Statement of Edward Noel (Nicky) Kelly d.o.b. 19.1.1951, 3 Tyndalls Lane Arklow made at the Bridewell Garda Station on 7th April 1976. After he was cautioned

438

*that he was not obliged to say anything unless he wished to
do so but anything he said would be taken down in writing
and may be given in evidence.*

On the morning of 31st March 1976 around 1.40 am I left
Brian McNally's house at 6 Castle Avenue Swords with
Brian McNally. We were in Brian's m/car a white Renault.
We had arranged to go to Celbridge to where we were to
hold up a train. We had arranged to meet the following
people at the railway line outside Celbridge where the
Cork/Dublin train was due to pass at 2.50 am. When we
arrived there at about 2.30 am, at Celbridge near the
railway line, we left Brian's car in a laneway about a 100
yards from where we stopped this train. When we walked
towards the railway line we met Michael Barrett from
Kerry and John Fitzpatrick from Armagh who were
standing in a field off the roadway. They told us everything
was O.K. and pointed to a house about 200 yards from the
railway track and said Mick Plunkett Gerard Roche and
Sean Gallagher were in this house. It was arranged that
they would take over this house and wait for the train.
There was a Volkswagen van a light colour parked near the
house, I was with Brian McNally at this time. We all went
down towards the track and I saw Ronald Bunting, Thomas
McCartan, Joe Heaney standing at the side of the track at
the far side from the roadway. I saw Seamus Costello and
Oscar Breathnach standing at the side of the railway line
nearest the road. Around this time Plunkett (Michael) went
onto the railway line, he was wearing a black donkey jacket
with yellow on the back. The yellow on the back of the
jacket looked rough. Gerard Roche drove the Volkswagen
van down beside the railway line in the field. The van was
in the field beside a fairly big ditch and the railway line.
Mick Barrett had given me a .45 revolver at this time.
Ronald Bunting and Joe Heaney had a rifle each.
Everybody else had a revolver each except Gerry Roche
and Oscar Breathnach and Michael Plunkett. Plunkett was
carrying a danger lamp in one hand, it was lighting. There
were detonators placed on the line before we got there.
When the train arrived the denotators exploded and the

train halted, it travelled on for some distance and then reversed back. At this stage Plunkett who was on the line was waving the signal lamp. Seamus Costello and Oscar Breathnac then boarded the train. Costello then went to the driver pointed a gun at him and told him to get out and took him out to another carriage. Ronald Bunting took up a position at the front of the train with a rifle. At this time Sean Gallagher was still in the house near the railway line. Oscar Breathnac and someone else I cannot remember who, unloaded a nummber of mailbags onto the track. Roche, Ml.Barrett Seamus Costello John Fitzpatrick Brian McNally and myself loaded the mail bags into the Volkswagen van. We had to throw the bags over a high ditch to where the van was in a field. At this time Thomas McCartan and Joe Heaney were on the far side of the track keeping guard. We loaded about eleven or twelve mail bags into the van. Some were big about 5′ high large and bulky. Others were small about 2′ and 3′ and bulky. They had labels on the bags, some were grey mauve, yellow bags. It took about eight minutes to load the van. While this job of loading the van was going onI heard Seamus Costello giving commands to all of us. He was telling us to hurry up and load the van. When the van was loaded Gerard Roche drove away with the load of mail bags, and Michael Plunkett. It drove away in the direction of Ballymore Eustace in the opposite direction to Celbridge. I knew they were taking it to a farmhouse in Ballymore Eustace as this was planned before the raid. The name of the man they were going to was John, I dont know his surname he's living with his wife(Phil)NK and father in a farmhouse a bungalow type its about half a mile outside Ballymore Eustace that if you take the Dublin road to Ballymore Eustace turn left in Ballymore Eustace and go out about half a mile. The house is on the right hand side. There is four houses there together all bungalow type. Its the second or third house as you go out. The mail bags were to be left at this house for a few days. John is about 40 years 5 – 8″/ 9″, medium build, Besides this Volkswagen van we had the following cars with us, Brian McNally's Renault and three stolen cars. John Fitzpatrick drove one of these m/cars, a big black one with a vinyl roof with   after the Volkswagen van. Brian McNally and myself went in Brian car back to Swords. Seamus Costello went away in a (brown)NK big brown Vauxhall which is belonging to a friend of his. Barret was driving one of the other stolen cars I think it was a big car, dark colour but I dont know what make. I did not see the rest of them go away. We were back in Swords 4.30 a.m. or 4.45 a.m. This robbery was planned about a couple of weeks ago, I was told this train was carrying a lot of cash. I knew these mail bags were full of cash as Costello knew the bags to put out. Gerry Roche was to leave this Volkswagen van somewhere in Finglas after he unloaded the mailbags in Ballymore Eustace. John Fitzpatrick was to leave the car he was driving on the Canal Bank somewhere near Finglas. The operation was to get funds for the I.R.S.P. I did not get any cash from this robbery. This statement has been read over to me and it is correct. I will now show signed – NK you the route we took from Dublin to the scene of the Robbery on last Wednesday morning 31/3/76

Signed: Eamon N Kelly
Witness: Patrick F Clery D/Sgt.
         John J McGroarty D/Sgt.
         Ed Ryan D/Inspr.
7.4.76

Appendix IV

The Judges Rules

1. When a police officer is endeavouring to discover the author of a crime there is no objection to his putting questions in respect thereof to any person or persons, whether suspected or not, from whom he thinks that useful information may be obtained.

2. Whenever a police officer has made up his mind to charge a person with a crime, he should first caution such person before asking him any questions, or any further questions as the case may be.

3. Persons in custody should not be questioned without the usual caution first administered.

4. If the prisoner wishes to volunteer any statement, the usual caution should be administered. It is desirable that the last two words of such caution should be omitted, and that the caution should end with the words "be given in evidence."

5. The caution to be administered to a prisoner when he is formally charged should therefore be in the following words: "Do you wish to say anything in answer to the charge? You are not obliged to say anything unless you wish to do so, but whatever you say will be taken down in writing and may be given in evidence." Care should be taken to avoid the suggestion that his answers can only be used in evidence against him, as this may prevent an innocent person making a statement which might assist to clear him of the charge.

6. A statement made by a prisoner before there is time to caution him is not rendered inadmissible in evidence merely because no caution has been given, but in such a case he should be cautioned as soon as possible.

7. A prisoner making a voluntary statement must not be cross-examined, and no question should be put to him about it except for the purpose of removing ambiguity in what he has actually said. For instance, if he has mentioned an hour without saying whether it was morning or evening, or has given a day of the week and day of the month which do not agree, or has not made it clear to what individual or what place he intended to refer in some part of his statement, he may be questioned sufficiently to clear up the point.

8. When two or more prisoners are charged with the same offence and their statements are taken separately, the police should not read these statements to the other persons charged, but each such persons should be given by the police a copy of such statements and nothing should be said or done by the police to invite a reply. If the person charged desires to make a statement in reply the usual caution should be administered.

9. Any statement made in accordance with the above rules should, whenever possible, be taken down in writing and signed by the person making it after it has been read to him and he has been invited to make any corrections he may wish.

INDEX OF SELECTED NAMES

Asmal, Kadar 378

Ballagh, Robert 378

Barnes, Eamonn 28, 92, 115-19, 395, 413

Barr, Robert 134, 152-3, 159-60, 166, 179-81, 194, 196, 212, 214, 220-1, 222-4, 231-2, 236, 265, 275-80, 289-90, 303, 311, 325, 362, 364

Barrett, Michael 36, 64, 73, 107-8, 116, 118-19, 245-6, 254, 256-7, 273-4, 275, 282, 307, 393-4, 411

Barrington, Judge Donal 334, 362

Barry, Peter 383, 400

Best, William 48

Bohan, Sgt. Patrick 172, 226-7, 285

Boland, John 401

Boland, Garda Thomas 272, 375

Bonass, Des 377

Bowe, Garda Philip 79, 211, 218-19, 226, 230

Boyle, Prof. Kevin 387

Breatnach, Caoilte 69, 79, 90-1, 332, 378, 379-80, 384-6

Breatnach, Deasun 83

Breatnach, Osgur 47, 54, 67, 97, 118, 168, 245, 255, 257, 263, 318-19, 411, 416; arrests 41-4, 62, 81, 103-4, 119, 127, 194-8, 212-13, 304-5, 316-17; interrogation 64-5, 71, 75-6, 78, 79-86, 90-2, 95, 295; statement 76, 202-4, 296-7, 409, 437; medical examinations 83-5, 99-100, 103, 105-6, 210-12, 227, 230-1; trial 133, 143, 150-1, 193-234, 296-307, 319-20; imprisonment 321, 328, 330-2; appeal 333-50, 362, 365, 391-2, 395, 405

Breen, Brendan 211

Brennan, Michael 377

Bride, Anne 186

Britton, Garda Tom 44

Browne, Aidan 85-6, 92, 100, 103, 104, 224-6

Browne, Prof. Ivor 378

Browne, Dr. Noel 355

Browne, Vincent 378

Bruton, John 401

Bunting, Ronnie 41, 52, 71, 72, 245, 257, 263

Burke, Dr. Richard 106, 181, 211-12, 230, 262, 316

Butler, Garda James 68-9, 209, 218, 297-8, 342

Campbell, Sgt. Francis 35-6, 58-60, 162-3, 172, 237-8, 269

Canavan, Sgt. Michael 76, 87, 88, 89, 153, 160, 162, 167-70, 178, 189-90, 201, 295, 318, 339, 406

Canavan, Garda Peter 198, 302

Carey, Sgt. Edward 68, 86, 107, 111, 114

Carey, Sgt. Michael 299-300, 301-2

Carey, Dr. Patrick 99-100, 213-14, 227, 230

Carroll, Donal V. 109

Carroll, Judge Mella 356

Casey, Supt. Patrick 32, 41, 73, 74-5, 82, 92, 196, 236, 318, 395, 417

Clarke, Judge Gerard 151, 293-4

Cleary, Sgt. Patrick 74, 75, 77, 242, 244-5, 246-7, 256-9, 262, 264, 266-7, 274, 290, 303, 375

Clerkin, Garda Michael 122, 126

Cole, Dermot 399

Collins, Gerry 30

Collins, Det. Sgt. Joseph 45, 64

Connett, Herbert 155

Connolly, Joseph 22, 155

Connolly, Garda Thomas 155

Conroy, Garda Michael 65

Cooney, Patrick 28-9, 30-1, 114-15, 120-1, 124-5, 139, 335, 400, 402

Corcoran, John 352

Cosgrave, Liam 28, 121, 123

Costello, Declan 115

Costello, Maoliossa 41, 107, 215

Costello, Seamus 41, 43, 44, 45-57 *passim*, 67, 71, 93, 107, 109-10, 113, 132, 168, 245-6, 257, 265, 280, 313, 375, 376, 411

Cotter, Joe 23, 155

Coulson, Marjorie 29

Courtney, Insp. John 76, 88, 160-1, 162, 167-9, 178, 189-90, 201, 295-6, 318, 339, 406, 418

Cronin, Sean 353

Culhane, Det. Sgt. Patrick 73, 375

Cullen, Garda Bernard 107, 194, 195

Daly, Prof. Robert 354, 396
Davis, Dr. Samuel 100, 105-6, 181, 185, 210-11, 261-2
Deasy, Austin 400
Deignan, Joseph 261
Dempsey, Noel 155
Desmond, Barry 400
Dillon, Nuala 37-9, 59, 72, 79, 95, 235, 237, 238, 242, 245, 254, 256-7, 269; police-station visit 61, 73, 90, 241, 243, 249, 255, 271, 273-4, 285, 286, 288-9, 367-8, 408; evidence 281-3, 413
Doherty, James 71
Doherty, Sean 376-7
Donegan, Patrick 123
Donnelly, Brian 57, 60, 307-8
Dowling, Sgt. Martin 267-8
Drew, Garda Michael 36-7, 57-9, 73-4, 163, 172-4
Dukes, Alan 401
Dunne, Garda Thomas Ibar 36, 76, 86, 114, 199, 281-2, 301, 342, 375, 418; Kelly interrogation 58-9, 61, 70, 73, 163, 235, 255, 269-76 *passim*, 279; McNally interrogation 172-3; cross-examination 164, 204, 238-42, 285, 288, 296
Dunne, Det. Thomas 45

Egan, Garda Joseph 41, 44, 74, 176, 196-7, 242, 256, 259, 375
Egan, Sgt. Michael 81, 89-90, 194, 195, 196, 212, 219, 226, 229
Evans, Geoffrey 345-7
Ewart-Biggs, Sir Christopher 120-1

Farrell, George 340
Faul, Rev. Denis 377
Fennell, Desmond 378
Fennessy, Sgt. William 82, 92, 301, 302
Ferguson, Hugh 54
Fields, Dr. Rona 351, 355, 358
Finlay, Judge Thomas 126, 143-4, 193-4, 334, 337-8, 341, 348-50, 362, 365
Finn, Garda Michael 89, 238; Kelly interrogation 61, 70, 74, 87, 236, 242-5, 256, 258, 269-74, 278-9, 284, 287-8; McNally interrogation 60, 162, 177, 185, 275, 375, 412; cross-examination 243-4, 262-4

FitzGerald, Garret 42, 138-9, 380, 393, 400
Fitzgerald, Garda Thomas 70, 71, 75-6, 82, 85, 165-6, 174-5, 189, 197-8, 200, 202-4, 216-17, 296, 342
Fitzpatrick, Ann 186
Fitzpatrick, Garda Edward 44
Fitzpatrick, John 36, 97, 116-19, 168, 178, 245-6, 254-7, 262-3, 307, 309, 353, 411; arrest 44-5, 71, 93-5; interrogation 64, 73-4, 76-7, 78, 108, 110-11, 113-14; medical examinations 101, 106; statement 76-7, 111, 432-5; trial 116-117; alibi 64, 73, 116, 393-5, 412-13
Fitzsimons, Garda Owen 43, 194, 228
Fleming, Chief Supt. John 172, 198, 336, 363
Flynn, Phil 377
Forde, Rev. Vincent 379-80
Fox, Senator Billy 29, 121, 241, 335
Fox, Sean 54-5
Freaney, Garda Pierce 155

Gallagher, Eddie 26, 329
Gallagher, Sean 69, 71, 101, 245, 257, 262-3
Gannon, Judge John M. 356-7
Garavan, Judge John 133, 142, 146-7
Garland, Sean 46
Garvey, Edmund 26, 131
Gaughan, Michael 30
Godkin, Garda Christopher 86, 87, 114, 201
Gore, Rev. Brian 397
Goulding, Cathal 49, 55, 56
Green, Michael 221
Green, Noreen 377
Gregory, Tony 375-7, 378, 395, 398
Grehan, Garda James 36, 57-9, 60-1, 74, 76, 155, 159-62, 172-8 *passim*, 190, 194, 195, 314-15, 318, 339, 407
Griffin, Judge Frank 144, 348, 370

Hamilton, Judge Liam 82-6, 92, 99-100, 103-4, 150-3, 158, 182, 187, 190-1, 195, 200, 214, 224,

227-36 *passim*, 260-3, 279, 287, 290, 293-5, 298-9, 302-20 *passim*, 389, 406, 408
Hanlon, Insp. Frank 97, 99
Harrington, Peter 126, 182-4
Haughey, Charles 375-7, 398
Hawkshaw, Insp. Myles 74, 161, 166-7, 175-6
Hayes, Betty 393
Hayes, Richard 114
Hayes, Tom 64, 73, 118, 393
Healy, John 309-10
Heaney, Joseph 257, 303
Hederman, Judge Anthony 370
Heffernan, Garda James 155
Hegarty, Garda John 74, 166, 176-7, 194
Henchy, Judge Seamus 144, 334, 361, 362
Herrema, Dr. Tiede 26
Hillery, Patrick 383
Hoey, Eamonn 126, 192-3
Holland, Joseph 39-40, 61, 235-6
Houlihan, Con 378
Hussey, Gemma 400

Jones, Gerry 56
Jordan, Det. Garda John 72, 76-7, 111, 113-14, 236-7, 238, 249, 254-6, 272-3, 375
Joy, Chief Supt. John 32, 73, 74, 77, 91, 117, 185, 194-5, 236, 244, 293, 313, 395, 417

Kavanagh, Bishop James 397
Kavanagh, Liam 400
Kelly, Breda 378, 384
Kelly, Nicky 31, 47, 52, 56, 57-8, 117, 168, 178, 204, 303, 307-8, 310; arrests 37-40, 119, 306; interrogation 12-15, 59-64, 70-2, 73, 74-5, 77-8, 87, 90-1, 93-5; statement 74-5, 78, 87, 93, 199, 303; trip to Kildare 12, 74, 247, 258-60, 265-7, 275, 414-15; medical examinations 101, 102, 105-6, 260-2, 284-5, 370-1, 396-7, 399; trial 133, 143, 151, 235-68, 269-92, 311-12, 320; escape 312-14, 317, 321; appeal 351-73; hunger-strike 360, 378-86; campaign for release 375-403; since release 405-15, 416
Kenny, Judge John 144, 362

Kerr, Eamon 54-5
Kiely, Niall 135-6, 140-1, 143, 146
Kiely, Det. Tom 45
King, Stephen 417
King, Garda Thomas 375
Kirwan, Henry 155
Korff, Douwe 124

Lanigan, Prof. John Paul 99-100, 103, 213-14
Lawlor, John 32
Lawlor, Garda Kieran 37, 60, 135, 163-5, 173, 272, 375
Lee, Robert 71
Leitch, Dr. James 85, 209, 230
Liddy, Michael 92
Looby, Garda Patrick 39
Loughlin, Paddy 44

McAliskey, Bernadette 53, 55
Mac an Aili, Ciaran 79
McCann, Eamonn 378
McCartan, Pat 40, 43, 79, 98, 101, 131, 132, 139, 143, 145, 180, 194, 283, 320, 352, 354-5, 368, 386, 408
McCartan, Thomas 43, 168, 245, 257, 263, 411
McCarthy, Det. Gabriel 155
McCluskey, Anthony 44
McConnell, Kevin 377
McCourt, Tommy 56
McDermott, Lord 344
McDonald, Noel 134, 142, 147, 156-8, 166, 179, 181-90 *passim*, 195-8, 210, 224-9, 283-7, 299, 305-6, 312-13; appeals 337, 356
MacEntee, Patrick 82-5, 98-9, 103-4, 131-4, 141-6, 151-7 *passim*, 181-2, 193, 196-200, *passim*, 229-32, 287, 293-305 *passim*, 316-20, 409; appeals 333, 336-7, 356
McEvoy, Jimmy, 22
McGauran, Garda Brian 298-9, 302, 304-6, 317, 333, 336-7
McGee, Dr. David 101-2, 180, 285
MacGiolla, Tomas 50, 56
McGrath, Insp. Vincent 39, 40, 41, 103-4, 212-13, 236-7, 238, 244-5
McGroarty, Sgt. John 75, 77, 140, 246-7, 257, 258, 259-60, 375, 414, 418
McGuinness, Garda 317

446

McGuinness, Des 378
McKenna, Garda Felix 70, 71, 165, 174-5, 197, 375
McKinney, Jack 352-3
McMahon, Judge James 133, 136, 140, 142, 146-7
McMillan, Billy 54
McNally, Brian 31, 40, 90, 239, 245-6, 262-3, 303; arrests 35-7, 119, 127, 304, 306; interrogation 57-62, 63, 70-2, 74, 76, 78, 93-5; statement 76, 296, 393, 410-11, 412, 435-7; medical examinations 101-2, 105-7, 179-80, 181, 185; trial 97, 133, 143, 151, 159-91, 307-11, 314-16, 319, 416; imprisonment 321, 328, 330-2; appeal 319-21, 332-50, 357, 362, 365, 391, 395
McNally, Kathleen 31, 35, 36, 180-1, 307, 310, 315
McPartlan, Garda James 375
McVeigh, Dr. Paul 100-1, 185, 191, 260-1
McWilliam, Judge Herbert 370
Madden, Bartholomew 127, 189, 342, 365, 391
Madden, Garda Frank 76-7, 353
Martin, Alan 184-5
Meagher, Garda William 39, 40, 59-61, 70, 164, 173, 204-7, 236, 238, 286, 342, 375
Merrigan, Matt 377
Mitchell, Jim 401
Mitchell, John 377
Moore, Christy 378
Moore, Judge Theodore Kingsmill 347-8
Mulcahy, John 378
Mullen, Garda Michael 264-5, 290, 375
Murphy, Elizabeth 107
Murphy, James 107
Murphy, Insp. John 75-6, 155, 198-202, 296-7, 341-2
Murphy, Insp. Richard 264, 290, 375
Murray, Noel and Marie 137
Murray, Rev. Raymond 377

Ni Cionnaith, Ita 101
Noonan, Michael (Justice Minister) 378, 380-1, 384-7, 393, 395-402, 412

Noonan, Garda Michael 248, 265-7

O'Briain, Judge Barra 125, 397
O'Brien, Conor Cruise 28
O'Brien, Gerald and Patrick 347
O'Brien, Rev. Niall 397-8
O'Carroll, Garda Gerard 76, 205, 207-9, 218, 297, 342, 418
O'Cleirigh, Dr. Sean 101-2, 179-80, 188, 191, 278-9, 284-5, 396
O'Connor, Judge John 133, 135-6, 139-47 passim
O'Connor, Ulick 378
O Dalaigh, Chief Justice Cearbhall 28, 122-3
O Duill, Rev. Piaras 378
O'Dwyer, Paul 352
O Fiaich, Cardinal Tomas 397
O Floinn, Justice Cathal 151, 390
O'Hara, Det. Adrian 37, 39-40, 61, 235, 243, 267, 375
O'Higgins, Chief Justice Tom, 144-6, 340, 361, 370, 371-2
O'Keefe, Andreas 82, 103-5
O'Leary, Ken 399
O'Mahony, Bishop Dermot 381
O'Neill, Greg 387-8, 395-6, 399, 402
O'Rourke, Michael 120
O'Toole, Conal 11, 20-3, 31, 134, 152-4, 414-15; identification 70-1, 87-9, 153-4, 156-8
O'Toole, Marion 11, 20-3, 31, 134-5, 154-5
O'Toole, Paddy 401
O hUadaigh, District Justice Riobard 94-5, 98, 105, 116-17, 171

Parke, Judge Weldon 144, 356
Phelan, Christopher 56
Plunkett, Michael 45, 47-56 passim, 65-8, 79, 168, 178, 242, 245, 253, 255-7, 262-5, 275, 280, 311, 353, 416-17; arrest 65-9, 93-5, 153, 171; identification 87-9, 153-4, 156-8; interrogation 86-90, 93, 111-13, 114; statement 93, 118; medical examinations 101, 106; trial 97, 133, 143, 146, 149, 151, 158
Potter, Dudley 79-82, 84, 91, 97-100, 103-4, 213, 219, 222, 228, 230

447

Prager, Nicholas A. 343-4
Priestly, Martin 344-5
Purtill, Sgt. Martin 299-300

Quigley, Declan 115
Quinn, Ruairi 400

Rafter, Rosaleen 21
Raftery, Garda Patrick 375
Reid, Mary 417
Reidy, Dr. John 210
Reynolds, Supt. Hubert 155, 346
Reynolds, Ray 20, 71, 152, 175
Reynolds, Martin 136-9, 140-1, 143, 145
Reynolds, Garda Michael 137
Robinson, Mary 387
Roche, Gerry 47, 53-4, 69, 88, 93, 101, 168, 245, 257, 262-3, 411
Roche, Tom 22, 24
Royale, George 182-3
Royale, William 182-3, 184
Ryan, Det. Insp. Ned 31-2, 37, 39, 70-7 passim, 89, 94, 98, 103-4, 108, 160, 190, 236-54 passim, 262, 265-7, 272, 274, 281-2, 309, 318, 339, 366, 375, 395, 414, 417; in court 134, 136, 170-2, 213, 244, 285, 286, 294-5, 315
Ryan, Judge Noel 27
Ryan, Sgt. William 172, 299-302

Sammon, Tony 97-8, 116, 170, 189, 319, 387, 396

Shaw, John 338, 345-7, 348-9, 384
Sheehan, Garret 95, 384-5, 387
Sheridan, Judge Diarmuid 147
Smith, Dr. Noel 83-4, 222-4, 227, 230, 232
Smyth, Garda Joseph 37
Sorahan, Seamus 131-2, 135, 141, 144, 147, 161-72 passim, 180, 186, 188-9, 235, 239-43 passim, 248-67 passim, 273-5, 287-9, 293-5, 302-7 passim, 312-20 passim; appeals 332, 336, 355-6, 360, 362-3
Spring, Dick 400-1
Stagg, Frank 30
Surdival, Mary 186
Sutherland, Peter 401

Troddyn, Siobhan 398

Van Hout, Els 69

Walsh, Anthony 109
Walsh, Judge Brian 347, 370
Walsh, Dermot 85, 99, 100
Ward, Andy 399
White, Larry 127
White, Michael 131, 143, 145
Widgery, Lord 344
Wilson, Rev. Desmond 377
Wright, Angela 124

Zalaquett, José 383

Index compiled by Helen Litton